Gender and Cultural Studies in Africa and the Diaspora

Series Editor
Oyeronke Oyewumi
Brooklyn, NY, USA

This book series spotlights the experiences of Africans on the continent and in its multiple and multilayered diasporas. Its objective is to make available publications that focus on people of African descent wherever they are located, targeting innovative research that derives questions, concepts, and theories from historical and contemporary experiences. The broad scope of the series includes gender scholarship as well as studies that engage with culture in all its complexities. From a variety of disciplinary, interdisciplinary, and transdisciplinary orientations, these studies engage current debates, address urgent questions, and open up new perspectives in African knowledge production.

More information about this series at
http://www.springer.com/series/14996

Caroline A. Brown · Johanna X.K. Garvey
Editors

Madness in Black Women's Diasporic Fictions

Aesthetics of Resistance

palgrave
macmillan

Editors
Caroline A. Brown
Department of English
University of Montreal
Montreal, QC, Canada

Johanna X.K. Garvey
Department of English
Fairfield University
Fairfield, CT, USA

Gender and Cultural Studies in Africa and the Diaspora
ISBN 978-3-319-58126-2 ISBN 978-3-319-58127-9 (eBook)
DOI 10.1007/978-3-319-58127-9

Library of Congress Control Number: 2017940219

Printed on acid-free paper

This Palgrave Macmillan imprint is published by Springer Nature
The registered company is Springer International Publishing AG
The registered company address is: Gewerbestrasse 11, 6330 Cham, Switzerland

Acknowledgements

I would like to thank Johanna Garvey, my co-editor, and all of our contributors; this book would not have been possible without your hard work and patience. I would also like to thank Robert Schwartwald, former Chair of the English Department at the University of Montreal, for offering to host the panel, "Re-membering Slavery/Rewriting Its Archives," as a part of the department's Visiting Speakers Series, in April 2014. This event was instrumental in providing the momentum to turn what had been individual panels into a book project. The students of my graduate course, ANG6720, "Women Writing Madness: Art, Aesthetics, Experimentation," were a constant source of delight and insight. Thank you for your interest in the topic and for making it so much fun to work with often emotionally wrenching texts. Thanks also to my family and friends for your support through the conception and completion of this project.

Caroline A. Brown

I thank Caroline Brown for inviting me to co-edit this book with her, and all of our contributors for their faith in the project. I thank my sister Michaela Hayes, my colleagues, and my friends for their support as the project has evolved and come to fruition.

Johanna X.K. Garvey

Contents

Editors and Contributors

About the Editors

Caroline A. Brown is an Associate Professor of English Literature at the University of Montreal. She is the author of *The Black Female Body in American Literature and Art: Performing Identity* (Routledge 2012). Her articles have appeared in *African American Review*, *Comparative Studies of South Asia, Africa, and the Middle East*, *National Women's Studies Association Journal*, *Comparative American Studies*, and several other journals and edited collections.

Johanna X.K. Garvey received her BA (in French) from Pomona College, Claremont, CA, and her MA and Ph.D. (in comparative literature) from the University of California, Berkeley. She is an associate professor of English at Fairfield University, where she was founding co-director of the Women's Studies Program and founding co-director of the Program in Black Studies: Africa and the Diaspora. She is currently director of Black Studies. Her areas of expertise include Caribbean women writers, literature of the African Diaspora, gender and sexuality studies, and global women's literature in a cultural studies framework. She has published articles and book chapters on Ann Petry, Michelle Cliff, Merle Collins, Paule Marshall, Dionne Brand, Shani Mootoo, Patricia Powell, Maryse Condé, and others, in *Callaloo*, *The Journal of Commonwealth and Postcolonial Literature*, *Textual Practice*, *Anthurium*, *Emerging Perspectives on Maryse Condé*, *Black Imagination and the*

Middle Passage, *Black Liberation in the Americas* and elsewhere. She is completing a book manuscript, *The Sides of the Sea: Caribbean Women Writing Diaspora*, has a book-in-progress on Afro-Caribbean author Dionne Brand, and has begun a book-length study of Toni Morrison's "geographies of trauma."

Contributors

Majda R. Atieh is a Fulbright scholar and an associate professor in the English Department of Tishreen University, in Latakia, Syria. She received her MA and Ph.D. from Howard University's Department of English in African American and Arabic Literatures (USA 2002–2007). Atieh's research explores intersections between women's writings (particularly those of black and Middle Eastern diasporas), Sufism and Islamic studies, disability and psychosis scholarship, food pathology, and postwar trauma. Atieh has published on various topics in refereed journals and edited collections, including *MELUS*, *Tishreen University Journal*, *Damascus University Journal*, *The Strangled Cry: the Communication and Experience of Trauma* (Oxford: InterDisciplinary Press, 2013), *Is this a Culture of Trauma?* (Oxford: InterDisciplinary Press, 2013), and *Contemporary African American Fiction: New Critical Essays* (Ohio State University Press, 2009).

Nancy Caronia is a teaching assistant professor with West Virginia University's English Department. She is the co-editor of *Personal Effects: Essays on Memoir, Teaching, and Culture in the Work of Louise DeSalvo* (Fordham University Press, 2015).

Richard Douglass-Chin is an associate professor of American and post-colonial literature at the University of Windsor, Ontario, Canada. His monograph, *Preacher Woman Sings the Blues,* investigates literary connections between contemporary African American female authors and their eighteenth and nineteenth-century predecessors. He has been a featured speaker at Isaac Royall House and Slave Quarters in Medford, MA, presenting his ongoing and groundbreaking research on one of the first extant records of African American women's experience in writing—the 1783 petition of Belinda Royall to the Massachusetts Legislature. His examination of the influence of Asian and African literary and philosophical traditions on American transcendentalism, modernism, and postmodernism have taken him to South Africa, the Caribbean, and the Yale-China Institute of the Chinese University of Hong Kong. His short story "Blood Guitar," about the profound influence of West African art on Picasso's cubism and on modernism in general, appeared in *The African American Review* in 2015.

Raquel D. Kennon is an assistant professor in the Department of Africana Studies at California State University, Northridge, CA. She teaches courses in writing, literature of the African Diaspora, and cultural studies. Her research focuses on literary and cultural legacies of slavery and resistance in the Americas, and African Diasporic literature. She received her Ph.D. from Harvard University in comparative literature, and her scholarly writing has appeared or is forthcoming in *Callaloo*, *Oxford Bibliographies Online*, and the *Cambridge Journal of Postcolonial Literary Inquiry.*

Victoria Papa is an Assistant Professor in the Department of English and Communications at the Massachusetts College of Liberal Arts at Northeastern University, in Boston, MA, where she completed her Ph.D. in English in 2016. Her book project, *The Invention of Survival: Time and the Transformation of Trauma in American Modernist Literature*, examines a temporal link between creativity and survival in American modernist writing concerned with traumas related to race, gender, and sexuality. Additional teaching and research areas include contemporary multiethnic literatures, queer theory, visual culture, and the digital humanities.

E. Kim Stone is an associate professor of Postcolonial Studies in the English and Africana Studies Departments at SUNY Cortland. Her research focuses on representations of single women in postcolonial fiction and film. She has published in a variety of academic journals, including *ARIEL: A Review of International English Literature*, *Camera Obscura*, and *JCWL: The Journal of Commonwealth Literature.*

Seretha D. Williams is a professor in the Department of English and Foreign Languages and an affiliated faculty in the Women's and Gender Studies Program at Augusta University, in Augusta, GA. She is a co-editor of the essay collection *Afterimages of Slavery, and* her current work on Margaret Walker and Langston Hughes discusses the role of trauma in the creative works of African American authors. A past Fulbright-Hays fellow, Williams is interested in African and African Diaspora literatures and transnational contexts.

Introduction: Women, Writing, Madness: Reframing Diaspora Aesthetics

Caroline A. Brown

> ....For Blacks of the diaspora, the tension between memory and the loss of memory has been a defining feature. Forced migration from Africa to the Americas and the persistent negation of Black humanity ensured that the ghosts of the past would haunt the present. Blacks have constantly sought both to hold on to and to retrieve faded memories of the past, to grasp a sense of an at-times illusory Africa and to seize genuine moments of resistance and revolt against White domination. Black and diasporic memory is about revolt.
> But can we genuinely speak of authentic Black or diasporic memory, a coherent experience drawn from disparate histories?
> —David Austin, *Fear of a Black Nation* (28)

All I could see were her hands and arms. They were a dark brown, her palms stained a deep orange. Otherwise, she was wrapped in what looked like rags. Mummified within a shroud of dirty cloth—a nightgown, sheets and blankets, some towels—she would sit silently, passively, on one street corner or another of the urban, residential Los Angeles neighborhood where I was living during my sabbatical year. As I walked my dog in the morning, afternoon, early evening, I would intermittently spot her. For several weeks during the autumn of 2012, as cars whizzed by and I passed a few stray pedestrians, I would identify her by

C.A. Brown (✉)
University of Montreal, Montreal, QC, Canada

C.A. Brown and J.X.K. Garvey (eds.), *Madness in Black Women's Diasporic Fictions*, Gender and Cultural Studies in Africa and the Diaspora, DOI 10.1007/978-3-319-58127-9_1

the mounds of cloth covering her body, the scattered possessions in small piles around her, the torn cardboard boxes she sat on. I was not unused to seeing homeless people, the majority of whom were black men. But when I looked at them, whatever their individual affect, they were clearly engaged with the world around them: setting up a lone encampment for shelter and an evening's rest, or more likely dismantling it; pulling wheeled suitcases, toting knapsacks, or pushing shopping carts; requesting spare change and then walking into the supermarket or returning to panhandle on a busy sidewalk. They were often on the move, unmistakably negotiating their environment. Even speaking frantically to no one in particular or screaming at invisible tormentors, there was a coherence about their interaction with the environment. When my gaze fell on her, it was different. She would appear suddenly, as if from nowhere. She was so still apart from her head bobbing, her face obscured by the cloth in which she was swaddled. With so little of her identity on view, her body became a blank, a negation of itself: she was almost spectral, ghostly.

But equally telling for me was my own response. I felt a deep dread. If possible, I would turn and walk down another street. One cause for my unease was her absolute vulnerability due to, what I assumed, her status as a woman alone and unprotected. Her proximity to physical danger and the elements themselves: sun, dirt, rain, waste, wind, heat, pestilence, disease. But as significantly, I felt a concern when I gazed at her, a worry and anxiety. How had she come to sit on that corner? Who was she? What was her name? What had caused her abjection? But I also felt a shame: the desire to not look, to turn away, to forget. And perhaps as significantly I was affected by my comprehension that I would make no effort to get to know her or alter her circumstances despite our shared racial and gender status as black women. I was aware of the profound psychosocial chasm symbolized in our respective relationships with those streets. I assumed she was mentally ill and was myself terrified of stepping, slipping into the web of her madness. As an associate professor on a paid sabbatical leave, I was enmeshed in a world of privilege few can comprehend and that was impossible for me to deny. Yet as a black woman from a working-class, immigrant family, the world of work—of classroom, departmental meetings, scholarly research, conferences—and social life often felt alien and antagonistic, both in the United States—where I was born, raised, educated, and began my career—and in Canada, where I am currently employed. It is not simply a matter of being in a place or inhabiting a role, it was an existential issue, a question of fit, of belonging. And that could prove a more elusive goal. In the period between the civil unrest of Occupy Wall Street and what would become the Black Lives Matter movement, I sensed a tension in the air, a deep divide between the promise of America and the reality of the socioeconomic dispossession experienced by an ever-increasing percentage of Americans. While this precarity was traditionally the lot of black people and other minority groups, it was now affecting not only the white working class but increasingly the middle classes of all stripes. When I beheld this anonymous woman, I felt my alienation as an almost cosmic force—both as drift and suffocation. As significant, however, was the fact that I had just begun working on an earlier version of *Mad Epiphanies*, a book about mental illness—or its uses—in the fictions of diasporic black women novelists. Looking at this woman both underscored the reality of and threatened to collapse the divide between the world of the page, conference, and classroom, and the world of such radical dispossession. It thus accentuated the contradictions, even the hypocrisy, of researching and writing about mental illness when the object of this study, so seemingly abject and afflicted, was ultimately not its audience, consumer, or beneficiary, which reiterated the marginalization and inequality I saw around me.

I begin with this narrative because it captures the paradox inherent in my experience working on scholarship that is at once intellectually compelling and a source of emotional ambivalence, aesthetically resonant yet socioculturally taboo. Madness works powerfully as a metaphor; mental illness, as a reality, is a minefield that individuals, families, communities, and entire social systems often, at the very best, stumble through. Black creative writers return to psychopathology again and again in their written texts—including fiction, nonfiction, memoir, poetry and plays—mining its pathos, ambiguity, disjunctures, and multiplicity for the rich emotional and symbolic reserves informing their imagined worlds or reproduced realities; the critics who specialize in those works often step gingerly around its chaos. However, in conceptualizing this book, I feel it essential to address the trenchant critique posited by Marta Caminero-Santangelo in her *The Madwoman Can't Speak: Or Why Insanity Is Not Subversive*. According to Caminero-Santangelo, generations of feminist theorists have romanticized the figure of the madwoman, using her as a symbol of gender transgression and political protest in situations that would generally indicate otherwise. Rather than a "rupture with constraining traditions and stale conventions"(17),[1] she stresses that, in twentieth-century narratives by American women creative writers, and in her own estimation, madness is a site of powerlessness and erasure that underscores women's marginalization, not their sociopolitical agency.

If the madwoman cannot function within the discursive tradition of a dominant culture, then she is effectively silenced rather than actively resisting. In nodding to Caminero-Santangelo, I have to acknowledge that a significant facet of my discomfort was realizing that there is danger in the proffering of the madwoman as an embattled heroine and madness as a strategic essentialism. The woman on the street was not a metonym. And the complexity of her life could not be contained within the metaphor of resistance. However, here I want to pause.

Mad Epiphanies focuses on "mad" heroines. Centered on the authors' use of modernistic narrative strategies to disrupt the gridlock of the realistic novel and its received nationalist history, the book incorporates madness as both psychological disturbance and heightened mental state that leads the reader to each novelist's deconstruction/re-writing of that state-sanctioned history. In my enthusiasm for the project, I decided to organize a series of panels to motivate me to work on the monograph. By attending conferences and presenting my ongoing research, I planned to write individual book chapters and thus efficiently complete the monograph within a set period of time. As is often the case, however, my plans stalled. A pall hung over the project, in part because I was tired. I had only recently finished *The Black Female Body in American Literature and Art: Performing Identity*, my first academic monograph. But perhaps more ominously, I found that I could not reconcile myself to the contradiction of the madwoman as I was constructing her. I could not intellectually claim this figure I regarded with such emotional wariness. Nevertheless, although I was not making the progress I intended, the panel experiences permitted me a sense of a larger and more dynamic conversation than I was experiencing writing as a solitary scholar. In participating in the conferences and creating a conversation with other scholars around the diverse uses of madness in black women's diasporic fictions, and specifically the aesthetic experimentation that became so emblematic a feature of this trope, I was allowed an important insight. While there is danger in the reliance on the "madwoman" as a romanticized figure constructed in opposition to the status quo, I also understood that the either/or of this proposition becomes its own fallacy. What became more important to me was the question of *why* so many black female diasporic writers were invested in incorporating mental illness in their fictional works,[2] and what specifically was allowed by "mad" or experimental writing? With that said, I was struck by what these narratives were revealing about the aestheticization of political protest. No less notable was the representation of race and/or gender as these concepts are interwoven with the pursuit of social justice, and of blackness as an enactment of diaspora consciousness. While the scholars I had the opportunity to interact with were developing projects that paralleled or intersected with mine, they were often coming to very different conclusions or adopting distinctive routes to get there, a process exhilarating both to behold and to participate in. As I met these individuals, and read and listened to their words, I felt that I was becoming a part of a community of scholars with complementary yet distinctive experiences and investments in the field; I wanted the experience to continue. I contacted Johanna Garvey, of Fairfield University, a friend and colleague with whom I had organized the 2013 MLA panel, "Madness and Mayhem in Women's Novels of the Black Diaspora," and together we decided to co-edit this essay collection.

In constructing *Madness in Black Women's Diasporic Fictions: Aesthetics of Resistance* as a collection of scholarly essays by a range of literary critics, Johanna and I specifically wanted to produce what a single-authored monograph could not provide: the strength of multiplicity, the intellectual thrill generated by a diverse community of voices analyzing these diasporic novelists and their dynamic fictional works and worlds. This project was rooted in panels hosted by the MLA, NeMLA, and the ALA[3]—and the vibrant conversations that blossomed from there; we felt it was crucial to witness their development as a scholarly text that could be shared beyond those specific moments. This is not a conference procedural but rather the cultivation of conversations that began as individual research, grew into a multifaceted and polyvocal dialogue, and one we want to see continued beyond the scope of this volume. Rather than one specific way to interpret psychopathology in fictional narratives of the black diaspora, it becomes a means of creating a map to better comprehend those cross-cultural networks, intellectual currents, and forms of artistic exposure that have influenced the development of what I only loosely term this tradition. It is finally to underscore the fact that the existence of these works is neither haphazard nor incidental but instead related to the continuing histories of interpersonal engagement, aesthetic exchange, political struggle, and cultural evolution—for generations of creative writers and the scholars who study them.

With this said, there is a broad and increasingly diverse field of studies on female psychopathology in fiction. Classic scholarship often orbits around Anglo-American works, largely novels from the Victorian to the modernist era of the first half of the twentieth century. Foremost among these is Sandra Gilbert's and Susan Gubar's *The Madwoman in the Attic*,[4] with its madwoman as authorial double who inscribes onto the written page feminist rage and anguish Elaine Showalter's *The Female Malady: Women, Madness and English Culture, 1830–1980*[5] provides a social history of the expansion of male-dominated British psychiatry; each chapter presents the female psychiatric patient as a signifier of the laws, customs, literary output, and sexual anxieties of the larger society. *Invalid Women: Figuring Feminine Illness in American Fiction and Culture, 1840–1940*,[6] by Diane Price Herndl, posits the invalid as a site of both the political resistance and marginalization of American women, as well as the representation of cultural transformation, whether literary, medical, or historical. Jane Woods's *Passion and Pathology in Victorian Fiction*[7] explores the interrelationship of medicine and literature in the understanding of the interplay between mind and body and the gendering (both male and female) of this process.

Significantly, much of the work on women of color and madness/mental health can be found as journal articles or individual book chapters in either monographs or larger edited collections. I would argue that what results is that literary "madness" is conflated with whiteness. Scholarship on black women, in particular, is either dominated by work on a few celebrated writers or circumscribed within regional,[8] national, or linguistic boundaries. The two most notable texts on madness in black diasporic literature are Valérie Orlando's *Of Suffocated Hearts and Tortured Souls: Seeking Subjecthood through Madness in Francophone Women's Writing of Africa and the Caribbean*,[9] which examines works by Francophone women of the Caribbean, Sub-Saharan Africa, and the Maghreb, and Kelly Baker Josephs's *Disturbers of the Peace: Representations of Madness in Anglophone Caribbean Literature*,[10] a study that focuses on mid-twentieth-century Anglophone Caribbean literature across the gender divide. Several texts do incorporate women of color into broader investigations of mental illness and theorizations of wellness. Both Monika Kaup's *Mad Intertextuality: Madness in Twentieth-Century Women's Writing*[11] and Marta Caminero-Santangelo's *The Madwoman Can't Speak: Or Why Insanity Is Not Subversive*[12] offer analyses of women of color within their respective works. While not marginal to the greater framework, their discussions are circumscribed. Like the goal of her larger volume, which is to provide a global template of various genres of women writing madness, Kaup's examination of black women's texts is quite abbreviated, limited to a short chapter and scattered references. Caminero-Santangelo focuses on twentieth-century US writers, several of whom are women of color; however, only Toni Morrison is African-American. Three more recent texts specifically examine novels by women of color or minority populations. Gay Wilentz's meticulous *Healing Narratives: Women Writers Curing Cultural Dis-ease*[13] considers five world writers in English (Native American, Maori, Afro-Caribbean, African American, and Jewish American) who use illness as a way to meditate on cultural alienation and offer a path to the retrieval of indigenous and/or hybrid healing traditions that promise greater spiritual equilibrium. Ann Folwell Stanford's *Bodies in a Broken World: Women Novelists of Color and the Politics of Medicine*[14] explores novels by US women writers of color, incorporating sickness and healing into questions of social justice, access to medical care, and bioethics. Hershini Bhana Young's *Haunting Capital: Memory, Text, and the Black Diasporic Body*[15] departs from psychotherapeutic models based on individual injury; instead, she relies on the metaphor of the ghost to capture the haunting and psychic/physical violence of historical and social injustice on the collective black diasporic body.

Madness in Black Women's Fictions and the Practice of Diaspora attempts to complement, contribute to, and further broaden the parameters of the current conversation. The authors of the fiction examined represent an inclusive and nonhierarchical intersection of diasporic literary voices—canonical as well as emerging—from Africa, the Caribbean, Europe, Canada, and the United States. In the process, the volume crosses cultural and national divides, staging overlapping but distinctive critical dialogues regarding the diverse uses of madness in the literary text and the role of aesthetics in its representation. It interrogates the function of madness in works invested in narratives of resistance, particularly as embodied in experimental writing practices. Central to this volume is acknowledging the significance of aesthetics in black women's fictional output. While the figure of the madwoman inevitably appears in *Madness in Black Women's Diasporic Fictions*, perhaps more crucial to this collection is the question of how and why the quest for social justice is mobilized within a specifically aestheticized framework. Thus, not only is "madness" what results from the experience of social and political injustice, here raced and sexed, by individual characters but it is often a narrative strategy that deprives the reader of the certainty allowed and enforced by both the realistic tradition and sanity as an epistemology and ontological construct. While this process has grown out of the radical technical innovations of the twentieth century, including literary modernism and postmodernism, its outcomes are diverse, influenced by intersecting yet distinctive aesthetic traditions and political histories, transnational movement, and cross-cultural pollination. Yet what specifically do these forms reveal about how contemporary black women writers rely on the past to engage the present and (re)claim the future? As significantly, what does this process illuminate about the uses and construction of the black diaspora as an organizing principle?

The majority of the novelists explored in this collection rely on madness to serve as the refraction of the cultural contradictions, psychosocial fissures, and often-buried political tensions of the larger society. Throughout the African diaspora, various forms of cultural incursion have occurred that have adversely affected those of African descent. These have included the African, Atlantic, and Arab slave trades; the colonization of Africa and the Americas by European powers; the establishing of apartheid regimes and neocolonial nation states; and current patterns of global migration based on the often-gendered transfer of human capital from poorer nations to wealthy ones. Blacks have been subjected to social domination, economic exploitation, and political marginalization, both from without and within. The result has been movements of political and cultural resistance as well as persistent, if under-documented, psychic trauma. Within the fictional text, mental illness serves as an especially resonant metaphor for the disruption caused by oppression and by alienation not only from the larger social structure but, most pervasively, from the very self. Thus, the deconstruction and/or transformation of narrative form mirrors deeper psychosocial schisms: of individuals (usually women) on the verge, or in the midst, of psychic collapse; of societies that, constructed on inequality, buckle under the weight of injustice normalized as the status quo. In addition, with its tangled roots in often racist and hypocritical Western scientific discourses and legal history, structures of madness force the ultimate question: Who or what is (more) mad, the individual or the dysfunctional sociopolitical system creating the very classificatory systems? Nevertheless, to reiterate and reframe David Austin's rhetorical query: "[C]an we genuinely speak of authentic Black or diasporic memory, [as] a coherent experience drawn from disparate histories?"[16] In short, are these novelists speaking to each other, forging a dialogue across time and space? And if so—and I would contend that they are—how and why? We believe that the answer is in the affirmative as exhibited in our chapter breakdown, as mapped below.

In Part 1, "Revisiting the Archive, Reinscribing Its Texts: Slavery and Madness as Historical Contestation," *Madness in Black Women's Diasporic Fictions* explores how black women writers recreate and deconstruct the archive as a fundamental component in both reimaging the black presence in history and rethinking the construction of history itself. Specifically, this section actively ponders the slave experience in the creation of black diaspora(s). Who gets to write history? How is it re-membered and subsequently recommitted to the page? The essays in this section examine how black women writers' reliance on experimental literary formats, including aesthetic hybridity, allows them to challenge histories premised on black invisibility by reclaiming and revising the very archival documents that have traditionally permitted and enforced the silencing and erasure of blackness. Madness then becomes not only a metaphor for the dispossession felt by individual characters but a pivotal aesthetic strategy that will force new ways of reading, engaging, and understanding history as both ancient past and active present.

In Chapter One, "The Violence of Displacement in Bernadine Evaristo's *The Emperor's Babe*," Nancy Caronia explores *The Emperor's Babe* (2001), a work that calls into question the purity and privilege of contemporary Britain's whiteness by confronting notions of racial and gender tensions in London, aka Londinium, Britannia, AD 201—a heterogeneous outpost of the Roman Empire. Purposefully anachronistic, Evaristo's poem as novel emulates Ovidian epic form in order to examine violence as both the means and the refusal of individual and collective madness. Madness is represented through the spectacle of the arena as well as through the narrative's refusal to maintain linguistic accuracy. The narrator, Zuleika, the daughter of Sudanese merchant immigrants, switches between Latin and contemporary slang to reveal the ways in which she cannot occupy more than a tentative space in Londinium or in any of her relationships. In this configuration, violence is both sacrifice and self-gratification. Linguistic, cultural, and personal violence becomes the means through which to express or deny the madness of an oppressive and constraining social system.

Violence also marks Chap. 2, "Madness and Translation of the Bones-as-text in Marlene NourbeSe Philip's Experimental *Zong!*" (2011), by Richard Douglass-Chin. For Douglass-Chin, Philip's *Zong!* is ostensibly a long poem. However, the text destabilizes and re-imagines generic boundaries, becoming at times dramatic performance and at other times experimental novel. In doing so, it exposes the madness of a British legal system that, in the 1783 case of the slave ship *Zong*, labeled deliberately drowned Africans as "lost goods" to be insured. Douglass-Chin demonstrates how Philip breaks apart and then reconstitutes as novel/drama/poem the standard English text of the original eighteenth-century document from which *Zong!* derives.

Chapter 3, "Embodied Haunting: Aesthetics and the Archive in Toni Morrison's *Beloved*," returns to the archive as configured by Jacques Derrida. According to Victoria Papa, Derrida's concept of archive fever presumes that to know history is to burn up in the feverish pursuit of the past. The archive thus testifies at once to the violence of forgetting and the desire to know—a desire that is aligned as much with the past as it is with the future. Taking Derrida's concept as a lens through which to examine the archive's disavowal of black female subjectivity, this chapter argues that Toni Morrison's novel *Beloved* (1987) presents a history of slavery in which the erasure of enslaved mothering within the archive is re-imagined as a transformative space to reclaim subjectivity within literature. In *Beloved*, Morrison enters the archive's troubled space of deferred longing through a recuperation of the historical figure of Margaret Garner—an escaped slave who killed her daughter to prevent her daughter's re-enslavement. Through the novel's depiction of the troubled mother/daughter relationship of Sethe and Beloved, the creative reenactment of Garner and her daughter, Morrison transforms the archive's erasure of Garner's story into a literary testimony to trauma.

The second part of the collection, "The Contradictions of Witnessing in Conflict Zones: Trauma and Testimony," focuses on works from areas of regional conflict. Central to each context is the role of gender in the experience of national unrest: these texts serve as a chronicle of black women's experience of political disruption, displacement, and sociocultural marginalization. Madness thus functions not only as a tool of repression but a tactic to survive its physical and psychic assault. However, by juxtaposing the fabrication of the narrative against the materialization of the black female body upon the printed page, reenacting the slipperiness and elusiveness of the process through traumatized retellings, these essays both bear witness and interrogate the adequacy of the text to do so.

In Chap. 4, "Fissured Memory and Mad Tongues: The Aesthetics of *Marronnage* in Haitian Women's Fiction," Johanna Garvey explores manifestations of madness, resistance, and healing experienced by women in texts by two authors, one writing from within Haiti and one from its *dyaspora*.[17] The discussion centers on Evelyne Trouillot's novel *Rosalie L'Infâme* (2003), a fictional evocation of maroons and the enslaved in Haiti leading up to the Revolution, and Roxane Gay's recent novel, *An Untamed State* (2014), which recounts the kidnapping, rape, and abuse suffered by a Haitian American woman in contemporary Port-au-Prince. Each text suggests how to stitch the torn fabric of Haitian history, both individual and collective, revisiting horrific acts in a process of testifying and witnessing. Drawing upon the figure of the maroon, Garvey argues that the female protagonists perform both literal and figurative *marronnage*, expressing themselves from the space created by rupture and *déchirure*. This space serves as a refuge that affords each of them the opportunity to remember, redact, and reflect as they tell their stories of madness and gendered/sexualized violence.

In Chap. 5, "'Dark Swoops': Trauma and Madness in *Half of a Yellow Sun*," Seretha D. Williams proposes that Chimamanda Ngozi Adichie's novel, *Half of a Yellow Sun* (2006), examines the systemic, individual, and gendered traumas of the Nigerian-Biafran War in an attempt to comment on the aftermath of empire. For Adichie, the postcolonial experience of an independent Nigeria is the beginning of a new chapter in the legacy of colonialism. Independence leads to the Nigerian-Biafran War of 1967–1970 and its resultant devastation. Within this framework, Olanna—after discovering the massacred bodies of her family members—loses control of her bodily functions and suffers psychosomatic paralysis of her legs, flashbacks, and paranoia. She attempts to narrate her traumatic experience; however, other characters silence her. She thus begins to experience dark swoops, which she describes as "[a] thick black descend[ing] from above and press[ing] itself over her face, firmly, while she struggled to breathe" (156). The dark swoops, a symbol of Olanna's temporary madness, can also be interpreted as a characterization of Nigeria's experience with colonialism. In this essay, Williams specifically explores the intersection of personal and national traumas and gendered representations of madness.

Chapter 6, Raquel D. Kennon's "'We Know People by Their Stories': Madness, Babies, and Dolls in Edwidge Danticat's *Krik? Krak!*," analyzes emblematic scenes from *Krik? Krak!* (1995), Edwidge Danticat's short story collection, that illustrate the nexus between writing, mothering, and the displacement of the Haitian diaspora through madness. Kennon argues that these matrilineal stories register madness not as a disease or impairment of mental functioning for the central female characters. These narratives can be perceived instead as strategies that map how women mentally distance themselves from the mayhem by which they are surrounded, including the often horrendous quotidian realities of life under dictatorship. Most strikingly, madness emerges in the thorny boundary between those alive and dead, and even the confusion between the corpse of a human baby girl and a baby doll. The inability or refusal to distinguish between the animate and the inanimate allows the women to exert some measure of creative control over the trauma in their environments through the process of (re)fabrication. The slippage between a person and thing problematizes what it means to live in a state of political unrest.

Part 3, "Novel Form, Mythic Space: Syncretic Rituals as Healing Balm," analyzes madness as it emerges from interstitial spaces of trauma and dispossession, of characters out of sync with both the social systems in which they live and their own deepest potential. Instead of a distant past or modern-day arena of sociopolitical conflict, the culturally and stylistically hybridized novels in this section move between them, simultaneously dismantling the concept of linear time; often, they are set within fanciful, frightening, or allegorical fictional landscapes. However, healing is as crucial as madness to the design of the text—healing as creolized ritual that both character and reader must submit to in order to symbolically return to the expunged past and reformulate appropriate responses not only to its depredations but to its cultural wealth. The novels discussed re-envision the initial trauma of slavery and subsequent dispossession, both acknowledging the impact of African and Atlantic slavery on diasporic populations and expanding the discourse beyond its framework. Through madness and healing as sites of psychic return, these novels become contemporary parables that allow the materialization of a symbolic path to cultural renewal and spiritual redemption.

Chapter 7, Majda R. Atieh's "Sharazade's Sisters and the Harem: Reclaiming the Forbidden as a Site of Resistance in Toni Morrison's *Paradise*," offers an Islamic interpretation of Toni Morrison's epic novel. In so doing, Atieh consults the historical records and cultural studies of the institution of the Islamic harem to better comprehend the literary architecture of Morrison's text. Central to this process is her investigation of the construction of speech. For Atieh, the oral narration and competing voices in *Paradise* (1997) can be perceived as being aligned with the rhetoric of Shahrazade. She thus demonstrates how the novel, with its suggestions of the harem and *hijab*, transforms itself into a subversive act of narratological mimicry. As in *Arabian Nights*, Morrison's oral harem relies on an elliptical structure of framing that transforms scenes of madness into women's healing and solidarity.

Chapter 8, "Magic, Madness, and the Ruses of the Trickster: Healing Rituals and Alternative Spiritualities in Gloria Naylor's *Mama Day*, Erna Brodber's *Jane and Louisa Will Soon Come Home*, and Nalo Hopkinson's *Brown Girl in the Ring*," explores the strategic deployment of the trickster/conjurer figure in the work of New World, Afro-diasporic fiction. According to Caroline A. Brown, in each of the works listed above—by the Afro-Jamaican Brodber (1980), the Jamaican-Canadian Hopkinson (1998), and the African-American Naylor (1988)—culturally alienated protagonists are driven to the brink of madness by social circumstances and their own emotional ambivalence; they are then directed onto psycho-spiritual quests by creolized healer figures. Yet these healers are symbolic tricksters, individuals who cannot easily fit within a Western paradigm based on moral precision or ethical clarity. Who, then, guides the reader? How does he or she effectively solve the literary puzzle, the enigma of the text, to attain what Gay Wilentz deems "cultural healing"? According to Brown, the reader—thrown into the increasingly disordered chronicle unwinding as mystery, myth, and ritual—must partake of that journey and, in so doing, actively decipher and define what is madness and what is sanity, in the process untangling the web of the novel as a cultural riddle.

In Chap. 9, "'Recordless Company': Precarious Postmemory in Helen Oyeyemi's *The Icarus Girl*" (2005), E. Kim Stone argues that Oyeyemi, like many third-generation novelists of the Nigerian diaspora, reimagines the coming-of-age tale as a narrative of transnational subject formation. When the novel opens, Jessamy Harrison, an 8-year old with an English father and a Nigerian mother, despondently hides in cupboards and underneath beds in her London home, preferring to spend her time reading and "amending" classic Anglo-American girls' texts—*Little Women*, *A Little Princess*—rather than interacting with girls her own age. Her low spirits rise on a trip to Nigeria, where Jess befriends Titiola, a girl whom only Jess can see. Like Jess's parents who bring her to a psychiatrist back in London, Western readers of *The Icarus Girl* would find it easy to interpret Titiola as an imaginary playmate produced from Jess's mental instability. However, Oyeyemi quickly dismisses psychiatric discourse as too limiting to account for Jess's "madness." This essay argues that the novelist purposefully produces an intertextual entanglement of Yoruba vernacular paradigms with British Gothic aesthetics to implicate both cultures in the African slave trade. Just as Jess has "amended" the classic literary narratives of Western girlhood, she must disentangle Titiola's unfamiliar aspects from this forgotten history of slavery and then interrogate the unsung potency of this re-memory in order to reconcile this fraught past with her burgeoning diasporic identity.

Madness in Black Women's Diasporic Fictions is an important addition to scholarship on black women's literature of madness because it analyzes the works of a range of black diasporic women writers within a multiplicity of contexts, crossing temporal divisions, geographic boundaries, literary genres, and cultural divides. In addition, it incorporates interdisciplinary frameworks that borrow from psychology, history, literary theory, and aesthetics in interrogating the varied uses of madness in the works of diverse black women authors. In doing so, it maps the ways in which aesthetics matter, how they manifest political tensions, cultural change, national obsessions, and diasporic connectedness, thereby engaging race, gender, belonging, and citizenship. As significantly, it allows a greater understanding of the role of the aesthetic in the representation of black literary subjectivity—particularly its tangled roots in slavery and Western imperialism, twentieth-century literary movements, cultural exchange, political uprising, and geographic migration. Fundamental to this larger process is the volume's interrogation of the very existence and organization of a black diaspora, of blackness as an identity that can cross—or transcend—national, regional, cultural, and/or linguistic boundaries. Yet what specifically do these forms reveal about the aestheticization of political protest? About blackness as an enactment of diaspora consciousness? About the representation of race and/or gender as these concepts intersect with the pursuit of social justice? This volume engages these questions within the structure of its diverse essay selection. We hope that this book will serve to enable both the production and elaboration of those conversations that are ongoing and those that have yet to begin.

Notes

1. Marta Caminero-Santangelo, *The Madwoman Can't Speak: Or Why Insanity Is Not Subversive.* (Ithaca: Cornell University Press, 1998), 17.
2. There is a rich, developing tradition of madness as incorporated into diasporic black women's fictional narratives. These include in the United States, Paule Marshall (*The Chosen Place, The Timeless People* and *Praisesong for the Widow*), Toni Morrison (*The Bluest Eye*, *Beloved*, *Jazz*, and *Paradise*), Alice Walker (*The Color Purple* and *Possessing the Secret of Joy*), Toni Cade Bambara (*The Salt Eaters*), Gloria Naylor (*The Women of Brewster Place* and *Linden Hills*), Gayl Jones (*Corregidora*, *Eva's Man*, and *The Healing*), Carolivia Herron (*Thereafter Johnnie*), Edwidge Danticat (*Breath, Eyes, Memory*), and Ayana Mathis (*The Twelve Tribes of Hattie*); in the Caribbean, Sylvia Wynter (*The Hill's of Hebron*), Erna Brodber (*Jane and Louisa Will Soon Come Home, Myal, and Louisiana*), Michelle Cliff (*Abeng*), Elizabeth Nunez (*Blue Hibiscus*), Jamaica Kincaid (*Annie John*), Marie-Elena John (*Unburnable*), Simone Schwarz-Bart

(*Pluie et vent sur Télumée Miracle*), Maryse Condé (*Heremakhanon*), Myriam Warner-Vieyra (*Juletane*), Marie Chauvet (*Amour, Colère, et Folie*), Suzanne Lacascade (*Claire-Solange, âme africaine), Michèle* Lacrosil *(Cajou);* in Canada, Dionne Brand (*In Another Place, Not Here*), Tessa McWatt (Out of My Head), and Esi Edugyan (*The Second Life of Samuel Tyne*); in Africa, Tsitsi Dangarembga (*Nervous Condition* and *The Book of Not*), Bessie Head (*A Question of Power* and *Maru*), Zoë Wicomb (*David's Story*), Chimamanda Ngozi Adichie (*Purple Hibiscus, Half of a Yellow Sun, Americanah*), Calixthe Beyala (*C'est le soleil qui m'a brulée* and *Tu t'appelleras Tanga*), Mariama Bâ (*Un Chant écarlate*) and Ken Bugul (*Le baobab fou*); and, in the United Kingdom, Helen Oyeyemi (*The Icarus Girl*) and Bernardine Evaristo (*The Emperor's Babe*).

3. MLA: Boston, MA; panel: "Madness in Black Women's Diasporic Novels and the Aesthetics of Resistance" (January 2013); NeMLA: Boston, MA; panel: "Madness and Cultural Mourning in Women's Novels of the Black Diaspora" (March 2013); ALA: Washington, DC; panel: "Mad Writing in Black Women's Fictional Narratives: the Caribbean and the United States" (May 2014).
4. Sandra M. Gilbert and Susan Guban, *The Madwoman in the Attic: The Woman Writer and the Nineteenth-Century Literary Imagination* (New Haven, CT: Yale University Press, 1979).
5. Elaine Showalter, *The Female Malady: Women, Madness, and English Culture, 1830–1890* (London: Virago, 1987).
6. Diane Price Herndl, *Invalid Women: Figuring Feminine Illness in American Fiction and Culture, 1840–1940* (Chapel Hill, NC: University of North Carolina Press, 1993).
7. Jane Wood, *Passion and Pathology in Victorian Fiction* (New York: Oxford University Press, 2001).
8. Mary Susan Lederer. *Tsitsi Dangarembga, Bessie Head, and Doris Lessing: The Social Context of Madness* (Los Angeles, CA: University of California Press, 1991).
9. Valérie Orlando, *Of Suffocated Hearts and Tortured Souls: Seeking Subjecthood through Madness in Francophone Women's Writing of Africa and the Caribbean* (New York: Lexington Books, 2003).
10. Kelly Baker Josephs, *Disturbers of the Peace: Representations of Madness in Anglophone Caribbean Literature* (Charlottesville, VA, and London: University of Virginia Press, 2013).
11. Monika Kaup, *Mad Intertextuality: Madness in Twentieth-Century Women's Writing* (Trier, Germany: Wissenschaflicher Verlag, 1993).
12. Caminero-Santangelo, *The Madwoman Can't Speak.*
13. Gay Wilentz, *Healing Narratives: Women Writers Curing Cultural Disease* (New Brunswick, NJ: Rutgers University Press, 2000).

14. Ann Folwell Stanford, *Bodies in a Broken World: Women Novelists of Color and the Politics of Medicine* (Chapel Hill, NC: University of North Carolina Press, 2003).
15. Hershini Bhana Young, *Haunting Capital: Memory, Text, and the Black Diasporic Body* (Hanover, NH: Dartmouth College Press, 2006).
16. David Austin, *Fear of a Black Nation: Race, Sex, and Security in Sixties Montreal* (Toronto, ON: Between the Lines, 2013), 28.
17. The spelling that Haitians give to their specific dyaspora, distinguishing it from the larger African Diaspora, is used here.

Bibliography

Austin, David. *Fear of a Black Nation: Race, Sex, and Security in Sixties Montreal*. Toronto: Between the Lines, 2013.

Caminero-Santangelo, Marta. *The Madwoman Can't Speak: Or Why Insanity Is Not Subversive*. Ithaca: Cornell University Press, 1998.

Gilbert, Sandra M. and Susan Gubar. *The Madwoman in the Attic: The Woman Writer and the Nineteenth-Century Literary Imagination*. New Haven: Yale University Press, 1979.

Herndl, Diane Price. *Invalid Women: Figuring Feminine Illness in American Fiction and Culture, 1840-1940*. Chapel Hill: The University of North Carolina Press, 1993.

Josephs, Kelly Baker. *Disturbers of the Peace: Representations of Madness in Anglophone Caribbean Literature*. Charlottesville and London: University of Virginia Press, 2013.

Kaup, Monika. *Mad Intertextuality: Madness in Twentieth-Century Women's Writing*. Wissenschaflicher Verlag Tier, 1993.

Lederer, May Susan. *Tsitsi Dangarembga, Bessie Head, and Doris Lessing: The Social Context of Madness*. Los Angeles: University of California Press, 1991.

Orlando, Valérie. *Of Suffocated Hearts and Tortured Souls: Seeking Subjecthood through Madness in Francophone Women's Writing of Africa and the Caribbean*. New York: Lexington Books, 2003.

Showalter, Elaine. *The Female Malady: Women, Madness, and English Culture, 1830-1890*. London: Virago, 1987.

Stanford, Ann Folwell. *Bodies in a Broken World: Women Novelists of Color and the Politics of Medicine*. Chapel Hill: University of North Carolina Press, 2003.

Wilentz, Gay. *Healing Narratives: Women Writers Curing Cultural Dis-ease*. New Brunswick, NJ: Rutgers University Press, 2000.

Wood, Jane. *Passion and Pathology in Victorian Fiction*. New York: Oxford University Press, 2001.

Young, Hershini Bhana. *Haunting Capital: Memory, Text, and the Black Diasporic Body*. Hanover, New Hampshire: Dartmouth College Press, 2006.

PART I

Revisiting the Archive, Re-inscribing Its Texts: Slavery and Madness as Historical Contestation

Resisting Displacement in Bernardine Evaristo's *The Emperor's Babe*

Nancy Caronia

ain't no one never gonna write
about your life but you. Once you're dead,
you never existed, baby, so get to it.
Venus to Zuleika in *The Emperor's Babe*[1]

Bernardine Evaristo's *The Emperor's Babe* (2000) is a literal and literary remapping of London. Set in AD 210 in a fictionalized version of Roman Londinium, Evaristo's idea for the novel emerged after she read Peter Fryer's assertion that a "[black] presence … [in England] goes back some 2000 years."[2,3] Noting that the English landscape has "always been … mixed racially and culturally," Evaristo predates her novel more than a millennium before British colonization.[4,5] Londinium's global population is drawn from the Roman Empire, which "stretched … over 9000 kilometers into Africa and Asia," and those who colonize the metropolis enslave Britannia's indigenous people.[6]

Zuleika, the black female protagonist charting this multicultural landscape, immigrates to Londinium as a child with her parents, former slaves to the King of Meroe.[7] Her character is the establishment of

N. Caronia (✉)
English Department, West Virginia University,
Morgantown, WV, USA

C.A. Brown and J.X.K. Garvey (eds.), *Madness in Black Women's Diasporic Fictions*, Gender and Cultural Studies in Africa and the Diaspora, DOI 10.1007/978-3-319-58127-9_2

black life on British soil well before any consanguineous presence to a present-day white English population. Zuleika's mapping of Londinium erases homogeneous depictions of the city, especially the "reign of 'Cool Britannia,' when [newly elected Prime Minister] Tony Blair's New Labor Party rebranded London as the global capital of coolness."[8] The New Labor Party's view reinforced a white nostalgic imaginary of imperialism where coolness was cast as a by-product of colonialist expansionism.

Zuleika's narrative acuity pushes against this construction through an unsentimental brand of linguistic cool. She intersperses Latin and anachronistic references to London at the Millennium to subvert the couplet form of Roman epic and Romantic poetry—genres that elevate the heroic. She ignores the verse ascribed to gods, warriors, or artists in favor of the slang spoken by a merchant-class black female subject. At once a diary, a memoir, and a cultural history, Zuleika's writing includes copious expletives and fashion by Armani, Gucci, and Valentino.[9] She references drinking "Dom Falernum," an allusion that at once recalls the twentieth century's popular champagne Dom Pérignon, a sweet syrup used in cocktails connected to the Caribbean during the height of British expansionism, and the name of a Roman wine popular during the Roman empire.[10,11] Her epoch-smashing verse deflects notions of the black woman as object or mad and unearths the madness of institutions across time and space. Her detail of Londinium's cultural life shifts perspective from those with privilege to those caught on the margins of political and economic power.

In Gayatri Chakravorty Spivak's now-iconic reading of Bhubaneswari Bhaduri's death by suicide, Bhaduri's cultural narrative casts suicide as a political act inherent to avoiding institutionally and culturally constructed erasure. Bhadari asserts agency and control of her life and death within the madness of a postcolonial system that chooses to ignore her humanity, her actions, and her voice. Her death sounds a warning regarding any endemically flawed and illogical system. Listening becomes key, not for what is absent, but to what information, groups, or individuals are pushed aside. Cultural narratives like Bhaduri's signal a warning that moves beyond economic calculations. The cost of repression focuses on how alternative ideas to material wealth become obstructed due to a single-minded focus on economic rather than cultural traditions or gender roles. Like Bhaduri, Zuleika's action, in this case, her written account of her Londinium life, is her resistance to erasure. As James Baldwin suggests, "That victim who is able to articulate the situation of the victim has ceased to be victim: he, or she, has become a threat."[12] Zuleika's writing is the means she uses to shift from an innate victimhood to a dangerous woman. Her anachronisms destabilize the couplet form of heroes and focus on the life of a black female subject who lays bare the madness of those who objectify her and close off any avenue of agency she cultivates. Her words inscribe the black female subject onto Londinium's landscape while destabilizing notions of English purity and sanity in the present day global city.

The Ethos of Madness

Jennifer DeVere Brody notes that male authors as diverse as Daniel Defoe, Lewis Carroll, and Salman Rushdie have each privileged a "muddied, muddled, and meddled with (hence impure)" English history.[13] Brody also notes how "'black' ... women were indispensible to this construction of Englishness as a new form of 'white' male subjectivity."[14] These black females were not considered British subjects, but were subjugated. Their resistance was ignored, erased, or viewed as madness and/or hysteria. Western literature since the nineteenth century reinforces this view, according to Anne McClintock, with the casting of female characters as flawed objects. These women *are* mistakes who bring ruin and failure to privileged white males through what are deemed their "degenerative" and "*behavioural* flaws."[15] They are forced or coerced—especially those who are partly or wholly black—into internalizing personal and institutional abuses. Their "flaws," viewed as "immoral" actions, become an obfuscation legitimizing dehumanization from miscegenation and slavery to unfair immigration policies.[16]

Hershini Bhana Young argues: "Illness must be seen as a logical consequence of the physical, epistemic, discursive, and linguistic violence of the colonial and postcolonial machine."[17] She draws from Fanon's ideas regarding the *epidermalization* of the colonized so that those who are oppressed internalize feelings of inferiority made manifest through the oppressor's language and actions. Their psychic pain is contextualized within the parameters of institutionalized racism and oppression. Contemporary feminist theorists have further "reinterpreted" notions of "hysteria" as "an expression of women's anger [and] oppression," according to Jane Ussher.[18] In this view of hysteria, Lynette Goddard suggests that "women's madness ... [is] a resistance to patriarchy, a refusal to enter into the symbolic world where the laws of the father prevail."[19] In promoting agency, hysteria and madness become choices women make to battle against "cultural racism *and* (hetero-) sexism."[20] These women are responding to cultural norms that view them as objects or ignore them completely. Their behavior is not an obfuscation of but a response to dehumanization and erasure. There is an inherent damage that these women bear, but the damage is recognized as an external force.

In *The Emperor's Babe*, the British Empire does not exist. Zuleika writes her life story to avoid erasure. In carving out that space, she destabilizes the familiar colonial and postcolonial tropes of the black female as blank canvas, muse, or madwoman in the attic.[21] Zuleika is not marked impure or with a *behavioral* flaw. Her anger is not a strategic resistance to her husband's denial of her position. She is not a postcolonial subject stuck in what Homi Bhabha has marked the "in-between" of "the colonialist Self and the colonized Other."[22] Like Proserpine, the goddess snatched from her home by her uncle and taken to live in the underworld against her will, Zuleika is a child-woman who has no say in whom she marries or where she lives. Like Proserpine, she moves between two worlds, but Zuleika is not traveling between her husband's and her mother's homes, she is linguistically traveling between epochs.

Proserpine's story occurs in her silence.[23] In the earliest Greek and Roman texts, her abduction is told through her mother's grief or her uncle's privilege. Proserpine is a silent witness over whom the gods—brothers and sisters—fight. The goddess emerges as a silent archetype for abused women and the road between childhood and womanhood. Zuleika's narrative differs in that her experience and feelings are privileged. Her voice is loud and insistent as she critiques Londinium society. Zuleika's language upends dominant tales of a white British history. In establishing black female British presence in Britannia, Zuleika's narrative is a contrast not only to Charlotte Brontë's Bertha or Jean Rhys's Antoinette, women who embody the madness of the subjugated hybridized other, but also to white English embodied female protagonists like Elizabeth (Lizzie) Bennet.[24]

Zuleika and Lizzie are connected, if not through London, then through their mercantile fathers and upwardly mobile marriages. They possess intellect and stubbornness that bring them strife. They offer incisive critiques of the lives they are forced to live. But in *Pride and Prejudice* (1813), Lizzie's commentary is focused on white English society and is used to find a man worthy of controlling her destiny.

A profitable marriage for the Bennet family is the end game in Lizzie's social critique. Zuleika's reflection begins *after* she is married and becomes aware of the horrors that being a Londinium wife and subject of Rome entails. She may be marginalized like Lizzie, but she is not a map holder waiting to discover where she will wind up. Zuleika is a mapmaker, "rewrite[ing]" Londinium history and etching the ignored and suppressed voice of the black female onto Britain's literary and historical archives.[25] She uses the analogy of Proserpine's marriage to Pluto to clarify her situation, but she rejects silence and suppression. She is the embodiment of Fanon's declaration: "I am not a potentiality of something; I am fully what I am."[26] Her verse illuminates the institutional, not personal, roots of madness and how privilege within this system allows her husband, the Roman senator; her father; and her lover, the Roman emperor, to behave abhorrently and reap benefits.

A Maddening Discourse

Since the *Windrush*'s arrival at London's Tilbury Dock from Jamaica in 1948, lawmakers have worked to disenfranchise the black British population from citizenship rights in England. Kathleen Paul asserts lawmakers have refashioned policies continuously so that "residents of the United Kingdom [are viewed as] … white, Christian, conservative, and true custodians and owners of the title 'British.'"[27] In 1978, Prime Minister Thatcher declared: "[P]eople are really rather afraid that this country might be rather swamped by people with a different culture."[28] Those "rather afraid" were white and Thatcher's swamping metaphor was the precursor for the 1981 British Nationality Act, which kept black British citizens from migrating to England.[29]

If policies like the 1981 British Nationality Act are the legal means to erase black British citizenry from England, London's Millennium celebrations are a cultural displacement of maddening proportions. *The Emperor's Babe* is a challenge, most directly, to the culturally myopic view that emanates from the rebranding effort of the New Labour Party in the 1990s. In *Britain™: Renewing Our Identity*, Mark Leonard calls for a "renewal of identity," recasting the "enormous success" of the British Empire for a twenty-first-century global economic model.[30] Leonard argues for a return to how "our ancestors invented a new identity … free from any sentimental attachment to the traditions they had inherited."[31] This avoidance of sentimentality is attached solely to the violence of

British expansionism. The economic successes of colonialism and globalization are celebrated without any references to slavery or colonial expansionism and include a "'living museum of the future' ... or 'Millennium City' in Greenwich to act as a showcase of the future of health, learning, retailing, and democracy."[32] In contrast to the legal means used to disenfranchise the black British population, the branding of Cool Britannia reduces migrants' heritages to a Disney-like theme park attraction. Multiculturalism and globalization become touchstones upon which to re-inscribe white hegemonic authority, both economically and culturally.

Formed in 1993, London's Millennium Commission was tasked with creating "a national 'festival'" that would recall the Great Exhibition of 1851 and the Festival of Britain in 1951, events that celebrated white British colonization.[33] These preparations were, according to Denis Cosgrove and Luciana Martins, "locally significant in terms of urban regeneration, [but more important to] London's claims to global centrality: once represented through the figure of empire ... [and] exercised today largely through mastery of financial space/time in the City of London."[34] The commission chose site-specific installations along the Thames leading to Greenwich, where the Millennium Dome—now called the O^2 Dome—would serve as the city's centerpiece of the global future. Through Greenwich, which had been made the universal Prime Meridian in 1884, "London ... proclaim[ed] ... its centrality in the measurement of secular time and the representation of global space."[35,36] Blair played upon this notion of space and time when he declared that children who visited the Millennial Dome should have "an experience so powerful and memories so strong that it gives them that abiding sense of purpose and unity that stays with them through the rest of their lives."[37] He pushed this sentimental notion by claiming that the exhibits would serve as a reminder that Britain was not only "a country with a glorious past," but also one "with a powerful future."[38] Blair's *glorious past* normalizes objectification, subjugation, and erasure in the same way that Thatcher's *swamping* does. Blair, embracing this sentimental notion of the past, focused on a homogeneous economic enterprise and ignored those who do not further a global agenda except as public relations or tourist board fodder.

In thinking through slavery and post-slavery discourses of sex, violence, and desire, Christina Sharpe argues "the everyday mundane horrors that aren't acknowledged to be horrors" create a bridge between what is familiar and expected and what is violent and accepted.[39]

She calls these connections "monstrous intimacies" and focuses on the subjugation and subjection of the black female subject from slavery to the present day. Like Sharpe's construction of monstrous intimacies, Young suggests oppression is not a static or linear construction only affecting "the individual psyche in the present."[40] Those in the present have ingrained in their DNA a history of "the hegemonic quotidian violations of people and spirits long embroiled in colonial and postcolonial struggle."[41] Thatcher's rhetoric of a homogeneous England conflates the familiar and violent through a national narrative that normalizes the continued legal scrutiny that is meted out to its black British citizens. Blair's sentimental proclamation of a unified London ignores not only political and economic disenfranchisement but also a cultural displacement of the global city's black citizens and their ancestors.

In meeting new global paradigms for economic wealth, memories of slave trading that occurred on and fueled the economic success of the docks along the north side of the Thames, across from the Millennium Dome, were eliminated from the millennium map. In the eighteenth and nineteenth centuries, these docks had been "funded primarily by the commercial and mercantile classes."[42] In the last 31 years of the trade—from 1776 to 1807, "more than 40 docks investors are identifiable as slave traders, and between them they organized half of the identified slave voyages" from London.[43,44] These docks are also where Sarah Baartman, infamously named the Hottentot Venus, arrived in London in 1810. According to Natasha Gordon-Chipembere, Baartman "has been the object of an external gaze (in body and text) for 200 years."[45] Baartman's body was used as an economic model of success, and, through "scientific objectification," proof of the white race's superiority.[46] As Janell Hobson notes, Baartman's body "was turned over to scientists by her 'animal trainer' in Paris in 1815" so that her "brain" and "genitalia" could be "pickled."[47] Like Spivak's suggestion that Bhaduri's suicide was a political act no one could read, any resistance on Baartman's part was erased by the disavowal of her humanity.[48]

Slavery, whether institutional or insinuated, is the paradigmatic clash between economics and ethics. Thatcher's and Blair's rhetoric suggest that they map Great Britain, and London especially, as sites of what Paul Gilroy names, "natural, inevitable events."[49] Yes, slaveholding was terrible, just as Baartman's *pickled* genitalia are terrible, but that is not the present where one worries about *swamping* or maintaining the illusion of a *glorious past*. During the Millennium celebrations, the Thames was integral to branding London as a space of global innovation and economic growth and "'race' [was pushed] outside of history."[50] The river as a site of degradation and enslavement was ignored to map Cool Britannia onto present day London as another mode of "England for the English."[51,52]

In *The Emperor's Babe*, Zuleika's language is a challenge to Blair's suggestion that British citizens focus on the *glorious past* in order to create a *powerful future*. The *glorious past* Zuleika inhabits has no "English" citizens and those indigenous to the area are slaves fighting to return to the "jungle" of Britannia.[53] Like Proserpine or Walter Benjamin's angel of history, who is witness to eternity's ever-growing "pile of debris," Zuleika cannot turn away from the storm that "irresistibly propels [her] into the future to which [her] back is turned."[54] Zuleika sees the entirety of the past, not as "a chain of events" in a fixed linear story but as "one single catastrophe, which keeps piling wreckage upon wreckage and hurls it in front of [her] feet."[55] This wreckage is a reminder that history repeats itself, but there is more to this repetition than an endless cycle of chaotic destruction. The "pile of debris" is humanity's disavowal of responsibility—humanity creates the wreckage and *is* the wreckage.[56] But unlike both the goddess and the angel of history, Zuleika is not a silent witness. She gives voice to how the debris manifests, and how her body is used to create that debris, and in that naming, she creates an expansive dialogic of the black female subject.

Zuleika is not a warrior like Virgil's Aeneas, who establishes an empire, nor is she a postcolonial subject caught in the *in-between* like Gibreel Farishta and Saladin Chamcha in Rushdie's *The Satanic Verses* (1988). She is a young and inconsequential black female whose self-reflection and observations linguistically transform Londinium. She rejects sentimentality as a mode of discourse or survival and recognizes she must inscribe her place in Londinium. Her resistance is formed by what she can manage to control: her "magna opera of words."[57] Her voice remains flexible and mobile, shifting as her circumstances change. She moves from self-identification as one of the "wild girls of Londinium" to her husband's "*Illa Bella Negreeta,*" her declaration as *The Emperor's Babe*, and her final naming that she is "*Zuleika, / Who in her final summer/ Lived a life fuller than any other.*"[58] Her words reinforce not only her existence but also her agency. Her perspective is an antidote to branding efforts that maintain the status quo.

Zuleika pins herself with the moniker: "Londinium Tour Guide (Unofficial)."[59] She is neither Lizzie Bennet nor Mary Poppins, dressed in a prim outfit, carrying an umbrella, and pointing out the monuments; instead, she roams Cheapside with her "porcelain" skinned friend Alba.[60] These pre-teens "tour the tenements / of Aldersgate," "raid" a local bakery after closing where they find the owner dead "in a cloud of flour," and "go to the [Thames], / sit on the beach, look out towards the marshy islands of Southwark, / and beyond to the jungle that was Britannia."[61] She and Alba are friends with Venus, neé Rufus, a Camulodunum-born transgender who owns "Spank ... / a shop for the lady with a prick and no tits."[62,63] The trio interact with "the fucking Scots, Pict and Saxon Bastards" and the employees of Zuleika's father's shop, who are "Syrian, Tunisian, Jew, Persian, / hopefuls just off the olive barge from Gaul, / ... anyone who'll work for pebbles."[64]

Zuleika's tour offers nothing that is found in Thatcher's or Blair's speeches, or a *Baedekers*. She knows the out-of-the-way restaurants and shops touted in a *Lonely Planet* guide, not as someone who is searching for those places as an exotic experience of the local, but as a local who is claiming ownership of her space. She engages in discriminatory language regarding Britannia's indigenous people, but Zuleika views her neighborhood as an adventure with a rotating cast of zany, but not especially dangerous, characters. She operates as a free agent and privileges an impure torrent of interaction as the foundation of the globalized metropolis. She is neither sentimental nor naïve enough to believe that anyone, except her friends Alba and Venus, are interested in her opinion. Her freedom of movement reveals how people use each other to gain access to goods, jobs, and sex.

Her understanding emanates from the knowledge, learned by "aged three," that her brother, Catullus, would "inherit the key to the Kingdom of Pops."[65] She may be envious of her brother's position as son and successor, but she also likes her unfettered independence since her parents do not pay much attention to her shenanigans. Zuleika's only sense of herself as an object arrives by way of the neighborhood brothel's pimp, "a Gaul with a wet donkey's tail / of a moustache," who tells her he "need[s] a Blackie" to complete "the Woppy, [the] Chinky, [the] Honky, [the] Paki, / [the] Gingery, [and the] Araby" prostitutes he already employs.[66] His list reads like the possibilities on a contemporary overseas sex tour, and Zuleika's presence would round out his exotic product line.

When the Roman patrician Felix "thrice [her] age and thrice [her] girth" spies Zuleika "at the baths of Cheapside," he claims her for a more high-end and legal means of prostitution.[67] Like a slave being looked over for flaws at the docks, Felix examines Zuleika and deems her a perfect specimen. She is a commodity to be sold by her father, who has waited for her to ripen like a prized vegetable. When she returns to her old block as Felix's new bride, the local pimp is dumbfounded by her transformation into a "real uptown chick."[68] Her newly manicured body and the haute couture she wears remove her from his sphere on the cheap brothel circuit. Zuleika becomes the ultimate and untouchable commodity. The 11-year-old bride begins her confrontation with subjugation. Upward mobility comes at a cost to those not in a position to negotiate, and Zuleika pushes against this tide throughout her life. Naming herself a tour guide on the trip of her life gives her a measure of control as to how her story unfolds. She insists she is the explorer, not the object being explored.

Late twentieth-century Cool Britannia rebranding is undone by Zuleika's role as witness and actor and "unsettles" what Gabriele Griffin argues is "the imaginary which nostalgically retains coloniality."[69] Zuleika inserts her black body and voice into the annals of British history. Her writing reveals how the madness of power cannot be hidden by exhibits, laws, or sentimental declarations of the *glorious past*. That madness, whether locally, nationally, or globally controlled, resides not within black women's psyches but is palpably expressed in, on, and about her body and the body of Londinium/London.

Recasting Time and Madness in the Global City

Zuleika's husband Felix views Londinium as a "less than dazzling little colonia," but when he spies the 11-year-old Zuleika at the baths, after years of "enjoy[ing] bachelorhood," he is reminded "of the girls back in Ægyptus, / where [he] spent most of his teenage years" during his father's reign as "governor."[70] He remembers these girls as "mysterious, dark ones" who "oil[ed] his limbs" and "waft[ed] soundlessly around him" as they did their duties.[71] His is an exotic and sentimental rendering of the other. Like Thatcher and Blair, he has a mono-cultural and myopic view of history, connections, and rights. Felix's needs supersede everyone else's humanity.

His possession of his "*Illa Bella Negreeta*" has to do with maintaining an illusion of youth, virility, and desirability.[72] Zuleika names Felix's objectification of her an "awful desire," and unlike Elizabeth Bennet, Zuleika is not destined for a blissful ending.[73] Felix traps her within a "white stucco villa [in] Cheapside" that he inhabits only "three months a year."[74] When he is home, he uses her sexually without thought for her desire or physical limitation. She regularly "pass[es] ... out" during intercourse, but Felix continues to pleasure himself with her body.[75] Zuleika likens the "villa with its very own latrina" to the underworld and Felix is a Pluto who demands his child bride is compliant.[76]

Like Proserpine's mother Ceres, Zuleika's mother has no say in Zuleika's fate. Her father, acting as Jupiter, eagerly accepts Felix's marriage proposal since the suitor is a "hot-shot senator in Rome."[77] This union will elevate the merchant to the position of "father-in-law to Lucius Aurelius Felix, no less."[78] As a merchant and an immigrant, he focuses on selling product and investing wisely. Zuleika's father will allow nothing to stand in his way of becoming a top tier merchant along the Thames. The phrase "no less" tagged onto his son-in-law's title suggests Zuleika's father has been hopeful that his daughter would bring a good price. His exploitation of her is a business transaction to enlarge his mercantile territory. He risks his daughter's well-being for economic stability and status.

Felix's sister Antistia reinforces Zuleika's place as possession with the warning, after 3 years of marriage, that Zuleika is "no longer a novelty."[79] She reminds the now-teenage wife that "[she] will never be one of us" and her position is limited by how long she continues to delight Felix.[80] The phrase "never be one of us" echoes Thatcher's *swamping* metaphor but also recalls more emphatically Enoch Powell's 1968 speech to the London Rotary Club where he ended with his assessment that "the West Indian or Asian does not, by being born in England, become an Englishman. In law, he becomes a United Kingdom Citizen by birth; in fact he is a West Indian or an Asian still."[81] In suggesting Zuleika can never be Roman, Antistia's rhetoric echoes Powell's and Thatcher's sentimental constructions of national identity, ownership, and race.

Antistia and Felix's privilege is an exhibition of "*behavioural* flaws" reserved in nineteenth- and twentieth-century Western discourse for those of Zuleika's station.[82] When Antistia visits, Felix "bolt[s Zuleika's bedroom] door" after dinner.[83] He is not protecting her; he is monopolizing his favorite "*objet d'art*."[84] He wants no one else to possess

Zuleika. When she hears children's "screams" from behind the door, Zuleika empathizes.[85] Like the painful sex she endures with Felix, she recognizes their pain is for others' entertainment.

Zuleika views sex as a duty to be performed and to recover from. She believes she has a choice, even if the children she hears do not. Once she meets the emperor Severus, who wears Armani and shouts "Basta" to his adoring masses, Zuleika recasts her notions of sex and desire.[86] She names *the emperor* as her sexual object in spite of Alba and Venus's admonishments: "He'll be having a different townie tart every night."[87] Though Zuleika's desire objectifies him in the way contemporary culture objectifies and elevates celebrities, the emperor's view of Zuleika is similar to Felix's. She reminds Severus of a "desert girl in Londinium. So beautiful," and he feels a nostalgic connection to home in her presence.[88] He promises Zuleika that he will "take [her] out of the city, many times" to "Greenwich," "Hyde "Park," and "the jungle of Notting Hill," but he can offer her nothing beyond a quick affair, leaving her vulnerable to Felix's jealousy and rage.[89] Zuleika blinds herself to danger even as her verse reveals the emperor's objectification of her. She thinks Severus will make her "world larger," but this expansion is contingent upon her sexual availability.[90] If Felix views her as his personal exotic re-creation of home, the emperor casts Zuleika as a sentimental vision of home. Felix and Severus cannot imagine who Zuleika is in their absence.

When Severus takes her to the opening of the new "Mithras Gladiators Training Academia" in Greenwich, the event is a boring job for him, but to Zuleika the suppression, submission, and sacrifice in the arena is a metaphor for the collective madness in her life.[91] Zuleika's perspective is a reclamation of Greenwich, not as a site of Great Britain's control of global space and time, but as the place where the attempt to control time and space can most blatantly be viewed as depraved and mad. The opening is a chaotic event where the "ecstatic crowds" roar "*Vivat Emperor Sevva!*" to garner attention and feel part of the emperor's visit.[92] Like any good politician, Severus "smil[es] indulgently" and "swish[es] his toga like a toreador" at his constituents.[93] Zuleika, part of "[h]is posse of the great, good and yours truly," lives vicariously through the crowd's adoration of their emperor.[94] Her epoch-hopping slang recalls the chaos that ensues whenever Princess Diana or One Direction makes a public appearance. The horde's uproar elevates everyone's status and concretizes positions of power. Everyone is a supporting character in the emperor's visit—an appearance legitimizing the Roman colony as an important global metropolis.

Zuleika desires to "straddle [the emperor, and] send the masses into a frenzy" in order to concretize her own position.[95] Her choice of the word "frenzy" does not signal the "degenerative" and "*behavioural* flaws" found in women of the British empire, but does suggest that the ability to create a frenzy in others is one way to be noticed.[96] This "frenzy" garners attention if not remembrance. Zuleika imagines her exhibitionism as a declaration of ownership, her "shiny, black, shimmering arse" hanging out for the entire arena to witness.[97] This exposure of her backside, a sly recognition of Baartman, reveals her desire to be seen and the impossibility of that occurring. She craves the power she imagines her husband, her father, and her emperor possess, but she is unable to imagine a powerful female persona beyond sex or commodity.

In casting herself as an "*objet d'art*," she declares her desire to legitimate her connection to the emperor.[98] She wants to "SHOCK [THE] NATION" in order to receive "recognition" and "commitment."[99] She wants to "straddle him" in public in order to see her name "sprawled all over the *Daily Looking Glass*," an anachronistic reference to London's *Daily Mirror*.[100] The gossip and half-truths found in tabloids are a means of safety, even if an infamous act causes her visibility. Her daydream reveals her fear. She is not the emperor's "official consort."[101] Whether visible or invisible, legitimate affair or not, she has been in danger from the moment Severus's "desert eyes ... roam[ed] over / [her] voluptuous corpus."[102] He made her body his temple during his stay in Londinium, which he views as "pigs' ca ca in comparison" to the beauty of his home: the Sahara.[103] He is, like Felix, solipsistic and does not recognize or care about the danger Zuleika faces once he leaves the Roman colony of Londinium.

When the gladiators are "marched / into the arena," Zuleika learns the truth hidden from readers in tabloids, historical accounts, and branding initiatives.[104] The well-oiled "Über-hunks" who were "Guests of Honor at feasts" are absent. Zuleika sees "old slaves, convicts, / Christians, prisoners of war and the poor."[105,106] She is surprised by "the back row [of] female[s]," "beast-fodder, several noticeably pregnant."[107] There is nothing *glorious* about what happens to "beast-fodder."[108] These women's appearances are not a marker of individual "degenerative" and "*behavioural* flaws," but society's collective fear and depravity.[109]

Zuleika has learned to internalize the irrational rationality of the power dynamic. She embraces her ability to dress as she wants and has happily purchased personal slaves—Valeria and Aemilia, "two ginger girls ... captured / up north the freckled sort (typical / of Caledonians)"—who resent her attempts to have them conform.[110] But the women in the arena compromise Zuleika's ability to hide behind the limited privilege of her marriage and her affair.

At the end of the games, "five pacing lions were rolled noisily / across the sand by mules," before the "five naked women," like Proserpine emerging from the underworld, are led out of a trapdoor.[111] They do not speak; they cannot since they are "gagged," "chained at the wrists and ankles ... [and] heavy with child."[112] Unlike the goddess, there will be no return for these women. They are not deity or human but animals led to the slaughter. They cannot compete against the lions; they are not meant to be a challenge. These women are the ultimate construction of devocalization and erasure. Only Zuleika's phrasing, "heavy with child" is a reminder that the women are human.[113] They would give birth to another human being: an infant, not a cub or a calf. Their "wild-eyed" demeanor is the only clue they are terrified.[114] This fear is legitimate. There is no recourse or escape from the hungry lions. The crowd too is trapped—everyone must conform to and accept this equation. Sacrificing these women means survival for another day, especially for those at the margins of power like Zuleika.

The women's annihilation occurs during the hottest portion of the day, when "[t]he amphitheatre was a brazier, / [making] it ... too hot to look up at the sky."[115] The heat of the sun forces the crowd to set their gaze onto center stage. The entire arena, including the musicians, is silent for the first time since the games begin. The lion's lunch could be an engrossing puppet show or temple ritual. No longer locked behind a bedroom door, Zuleika, like the masses, must watch as the lions devour the women. Only the lions chomping on "chunks // for the butcher's block: raw tenderloin/ breast, brain, liver, heart" break this silence.[116] These women may be reduced to beef stew, but under the blazing sun Zuleika names their humanity. She transgresses what is normally hidden behind flowery language like *glorious past* and *swamping*. She details what remains of these women's human features: "breast, brain, liver, and heart."[117] She names those body parts and organs that allow these women to nurture, to think and to feel. The last detail of their living has to do with their hearts, the organ that opens itself to love. Their deaths, a phantasmagoria of horror and human remains, shore up her lover's position and keep those who would climb higher in place.

The pregnant women's sacrifice reveals the vulnerable position in which everyone lives. Their deaths are an acknowledgement of the power constructions that force the crowd to worship the emperor no matter what he does or does not do. No one turns away or raises a voice in horror or consternation—no one attempts to stop the killings. It is a collective madness designed to maintain the status quo. To negate the women's presence as life and life force acknowledges the crowd's position both as decision-makers and the negation of real decision-making. The emperor's presence forces everyone, including Severus, into a submissive posture.

This scene is devoid of Zuleika's joyous anachronistic declarations of a *cool* Londinium. Her couplets throw back the veil on the dehumanization of females in and through global time and space. As the angel of history and kindred spirit of Proserpine, Queen of the Dead, Zuleika's recording of this scene can be piled onto the endless number of slaves who have been erased from the annals of British history. No names, no histories, and in the case of slavery, no final scene or tableau—only the internalization of what has been lost by those who continue to lose.

Brody suggests that "the unspeakable cannot be rendered forever inexpressible; the most persistent mode of forgetting is memory imperfectly deferred."[118] Until the scene in the arena, Zuleika's recollections minimize what has happened to her and what occurs around her. She has placed uncomfortable feelings in her "Pandora's Box."[119] These women's end unleashes Zuleika's suppressed memories. The pregnant women's total debasement and objectification mirrors Zuleika's relationship with her husband—how her father sold her, how her sister-in-law Antistia views her, how Felix and his sister treat their entertainment, and how she treats her personal slaves.

She recognizes in their deaths her fear of erasure. When the orchestra breaks the silence, the crowd, including Zuleika, "stood / and roared."[120] The sassy girl disappears behind "boiling red drops" of tears as she remembers "the girl / who so long ago had been stillborn // inside the woman."[121] Like these women, she has been dehumanized. She has pretended that painful, violent sex is the only price for living in the "villa with its very own latrina."[122] When Felix returns home after each of his trips, she needs "months of recuperation" after the doctor's "sewing is undone" from her husband's tearing of her genitalia.[123]

In the arena, Zuleika understands Felix will never recognize her humanity. As a Roman citizen, he does not need to humanize or empathize with her. Recalling the collective sexual abuse meted out by her husband as one endless string of nights where she "woke up … in the Kingdom of the Dad, Dead, Father," Zuleika cries for the first time since her wedding night.[124] More than the empathetic stance she takes upon hearing the children crying in her home, Zuleika understands how the lions' appetite mirrors those around her. She is everyone's prey.

Through her tears, Zuleika recognizes she cannot escape her husband's depravity any more than those women could have triumphed over the lions. She wants to believe the emperor will protect her and disregards his inability or desire to intervene for the pregnant women. She ignores the emperor's view of her. Theirs is a public affair—they meet at the theater, he invites himself to her home, he takes her to the arena—all of these things amuse him. She amuses him. Sexual intimacy allows him to indulge nostalgically for a place to which he will never return. He is a lion, momentarily sated. She will be forgotten the moment he leaves Londinium.

After the arena, he whisks her from Greenwich to Notting Hill for an overnight. This Notting Hill is not an affluent and upscale neighborhood filled with trendy high-end shops and restaurants but an untamed "jungle" where the surrounding area must be cleared by the emperor's "soldiers [who] … cut … a path with axes."[125] Severus is "Pluto," driving "four furious stallions" "in an open carriage" "down the Strand," "[up] the winding path of Haymarket," "over the sloping grassland of Mayfair," and "across the wheatfields of Hyde Park."[126] This shift in how she views her lover is the only indication of her doubt with regard to his intentions. Like Felix, Severus is god of the underworld. They arrive to a quiet domestic setup of a Bedouin tent with accouterments for a prolonged sexual encounter. There are soldier camps "stationed at every stage // of the journey … // and beyond to Kensington High and way out to Fulham."[127] The implications are clear—wherever the emperor travels, he sets aside time for extracurricular activities and makes sure he is safe and satisfied.

If Zuleika is Severus's return to a nostalgic imaginary of home, she is also a receptacle for his sexual needs. She "squeeze[s]" and "massage[s]" his "tension" away—a tension perhaps created by the arena's games.[128] Her witnessing of the women's deaths shifts her demeanor and she becomes aggressive, tying the emperor's hands. Severus views Zuleika's action as a game of "*slap and tickle.*"[129] His smile pushes his lover to more aggressive actions and she "slap[s]" him, "kick[s him] hard in the ribs," and forces him to crawl on his "tied hands and knees" through the mud.[130] His response to her heightened aggression is to call her a "*silly* girl" and "laugh... / hysterically like a naughty child."[131] He cannot acknowledge Zuleika's anger as hers, but views it as an act to heighten his sexual pleasure. Zuleika's perspective reveals his edge; the emperor becomes hysterical when he is not in control. She forces Severus into a state of feminized disempowerment—the position the women in the arena held, the space Zuleika holds in her marriage. On the margins of the metropolis and in the wilds of Britannia, Zuleika refuses erasure.

If Greenwich is the site of death and destruction on a global scale, Zuleika inscribes Notting Hill as the site where she claims the fullness of her emotional expression. She moves from the margins of power to the central power, although it cannot be maintained. She repeats the question "who's the boss now?" until the emperor stops laughing. Only when he cries, "you are the boss ... // Don't leave me now, come home / with me, // maman, take me home," does she offer him sexual completion.[132] Zuleika, as Proserpine, unleashes her rage. Her fury reveals the god Pluto to be a lost boy searching for home. The emperor, the ultimate symbol of imperial and political power, only maintains control if he is not challenged. Zuleika, the symbol of the marginalized and erased black British female, acts out violently in the manner others have acted upon her. As the couple orgasms, their bodies covered in mud, Zuleika fantasizes a married life with the emperor "on the Palatine Hill" complete with a daughter named "Claudia."[133] Under her aggressive, angry stance is her fantasy, never spoken, of being loved. This feeling is, perhaps, the first emotion hidden in her "Pandora's box."[134] Growing up with parents who did not love each other, witnessing the lack of love in the relationships around her, and being married to man who views her as a possession, Zuleika suppresses any need for love. Her disorientation and confusion in Notting Hill emanates from her knowledge that Severus, like Felix, is a Pluto who would dismiss her vulnerability and desire. Her rage is grounded in the knowledge that she is lovable and deserves to be seen and heard.

Resituating the Word

In *The Emperor's Babe*, Zuleika responds to madness, but that madness is not in and of itself hers. Her insistence on her right to exist and act is not a psychological instability due to "degenerative" or "*behavioural* flaws."[135] She may, for a time, internalize the notions of inferiority pushed upon her, but even before she expresses her rage on the emperor, she has already asserted: "Civis Romana sum"—I am a Roman citizen.[136] This statement is legally untrue, but in mapping her history, she concretizes her place as a female of the Roman Empire and a black woman of British history.

Zuleika's use of the Proserpine myth foregrounds her freedom before marriage and details how a child-woman negotiates the space of marriage when she is subjugated. Zuleika's narrative departs from Proserpine's story not only by privileging the subjugated individual's perspective but also by detailing her relationship with her mother. Ceres is a fertility goddess and sister to Pluto and Jupiter, Proserpine's father. She searches for and fights to rescue her daughter from an untenable situation. She engages with her brothers in a battle, forcing them to return Proserpine to her. In fighting for Proserpine, Ceres expresses her agency. Zuleika's mother is no Ceres. Her grief is a miasma of unending sorrow connected to the loss of her homeland.

In contrast to Toni Morrison's *Beloved* (1987), where Sethe, as a combination of Ceres and Medea, is the main figure searching for understanding and forgiveness, Zuleika's mother is a shadow figure who has no power or influence over her daughter. In *Beloved*, Sethe insists she did not abandon her daughter Beloved or her sons but commits infanticide to save them from the degradation of slavery. Sethe's grief is central to Beloved's visibility. Without Sethe, Beloved cannot and would not have anyone to whom she could return. Once Sethe connects to her community and receives forgiveness for her actions, Beloved literally combusts. Beloved is the articulation of her mother's need for forgiveness from her community. She is a ghost who haunts everyone's freedom. In *The Emperor's Babe*, Zuleika's mother has no community to help her navigate her grief and isolation. She becomes a shadow figure in Zuleika's narrative.

If Ceres weeps until her daughter returns to her, Zuleika's mother gives her a "loving embrace" at her wedding.[137] Zuleika calls this last show of affection "a performance."[138] If her mother is distraught, Zuleika will never know. Her mother is caught in the underworld, married to her brother, both children to one of King Meroe's concubines. They are "a human chain, belonging to King Meroe, / with no breakages for generations."[139] Zuleika cannot unwind if her mother is "*[her] aunt*," if she is her mother's "***daughter and niece***," or "*[her] own* *cousin*."[140] The mother/daughter relationship has been tainted by the imperial construction of Meroe, but her mother is grief-stricken at the loss of that lineage. She is psychically damaged, which causes her to dismiss the needs and the safety of her daughter.

As a child, Zuleika watches as her father uses her mother's "sweet cakes" to set up his first "kerb[-side]" business.[141] Like Ceres, her mother is analogous to nurturance. In addition to mothering two children, she feeds the people through her cakes. She receives no credit for her work and recognizes she cannot care about Zuleika since her daughter is a commodity to be sold by her husband. The only time Zuleika's mother relaxes or shows affection is when "she rocked [her son] Catullus / to sleep."[142] Zuleika cannot turn to this damaged woman, a victim who has internalized the inferiority of a maddened system, any more than her mother can reach out to her daughter.

Zuleika is left alone to negotiate how to survive the lion's den of Londinium, but this solitude forces her to claim her place in the metropolis. Zuleika, at 11 years of age, cannot comprehend the psychic devastation from which she and her mother suffer. Her mother is married to her brother in a loveless marriage, far from anything or anyone who is familiar. She hides behind "voluminous / black robes over her head, slumped / into a corner, still as a sack of potatoes."[143] She is caught in the *in-between* and "yearn[s]" ceaselessly "for the city of Meroe, and safety."[144] She cannot comprehend how Meroe is not a safe space any more than Zuleika is able to ask for help. Only her father—who states: "When you're a slave you dream of either / owning slaves or freeing them"—is glad for his ability to create his own destiny after "a famine, plague or flood," killed the king and allowed him and his wife/sister to migrate with Zuleika.[145] As a freed male, that is her father's birthright, but Zuleika and her mother's choices are narrower.

Zuleika maintains a practicality regarding her marriage. She views it as a business transaction for her husband's pleasure and her father's economic gain. This male privilege highlights how those with institutional power are cognizant only of their "desire," whether carnal, materialistic or political.[146] The women become minor voices in the weaving of the dominant script. Like Proserpine, her arranged marriage forces her to mature quickly. The upward mobility of which she and Alba dreamed turns out to be far from fact. They imagined that they "were gonna steal from the rich, // give to the poor ... // live in one of them mansions // with a thousand slaves feeding us cakes."[147] Instead,

Zuleika's married life clamps down on her freedom. She cannot spend money, take a walk, or visit with friends without Felix's permission. She doesn't have a thousand slaves who wait on her lovingly. She wants her personal slaves, Valeria and Aemilia, to be her "devotees," but instead Valeria insists that her "Mammy an Faither were chieftens."[148] Zuleika dismisses her claims with a "where had I heard *that* before," but worries that "these wretched girls will play [her] / like a lyre."[149] After she denies their request for "manumission," she feels "pure odium oozing out of every freckled pore / in their bodies."[150] They view her as "Public Enemy Numerus Primus" and they turn on her once her lover, the emperor, is dead (*The Emperor's Babe* 209). In exchanging information with Felix about her affair with Severus, these women gain their freedom and flee Londinium. They refuse to play by Zuleika's rules and reject her view that "life began for the girls when we met."[151] If Zuleika embraces her role as their master out of some sense of wanting to control someone's life, they refuse to accept her colonization of them. Zuleika uses these females to give herself a sense of privilege, but she forgets that her position is a temporary one gained, ostensibly, through her body, like theirs, being sold to the highest bidder. For her slaves, Zuleika's affair becomes information to be traded for freedom.

Felix's discovery of her affair unleashes a misogynistic and classist rant. He believes that he "created a lady / out of a sewer rat" and her affair has made him a "laughing stock."[152] His outrage echoes Enoch Powell's "Rivers of Blood" speech where Powell suggests that in order to avoid a "preventable evil"—"a black man [having] the whip hand over the white man"—it would be best if Commonwealth Black citizens did not migrate to England since allowing them any legal sanctions was akin to giving them the upper hand.[153] Gilroy argues, "[Powell's] horror was at the prospect of blacks being afforded limited legal protection and it was this debasement of the legal sanctions which appalled him rather than the issues of mass migration itself."[154] Similarly, Felix rethinks his placement of Zuleika in a high position within *his* household. His idea of trust, like Powell's desire to control the movements of the Black Commonwealth citizen, is to lock Zuleika away and allow her in public only when he deems necessary. He is "*utterly* humiliated" when he realizes his cage has not held her.[155] He has no understanding of how she was able to gain closer access to the emperor than he ever did. Zuleika has learned what it means to be a "victim," she refuses the trope and now she is a "threat" to Felix's manhood and privilege.[156]

Antistia has made Zuleika feel subordinate since the Roman siblings "had dined with the emperor's children, [while Zuleika's] father spoke pidgin-Latin, / [and they] ate off [their] laps in the doorway," but this couplet belies the fact that Felix has never met the emperor.[157] Felix recognizes too late that the Libyan born emperor Severus has played him a fool and sent him "to lead a trading / expedition to India" in order to fuck his "*Illa Bella Negreeta*."[158] His rage is directed not at the affair proper, but at his lack of control over her person and his awareness of misreading his wife's character. Despite his "selfish[ness]," emanating from the fear he has married beneath him, he feels he has been bested.[159] If he had set up their meeting and orchestrated the emperor sleeping with Zuleika for profit, he would not be angry. It is not about the sex. Felix has not recognized that his "knock-out *objet d'art*" has a power and intellect separate from him.[160] She has been able to reach further, without the proper pedigree, than he ever could.

He reasserts the only control he has ever had over her—the power of life and death. He forces his servant Tranio to poison Zuleika with "arsenicum hidden in spicy sauces."[161] Like Proserpine, Zuleika unwittingly eats food that will send her to the land of the dead. Felix's privilege allows him to run away and clothe himself in the falsity that he is the one who has been wronged. He leaves before the poison takes full effect, rendering him innocent of Zuleika's murder and travels to Severus's funeral in Rome. Felix must act as if he is ignorant to the emperor's cuckolding of him, but he is not the victim as Mr. Darcy is constructed. Felix's behavioral flaws of pride, selfishness, and depravity are presented as a counter to Zuleika's integrity. She refuses to ask her friends Alba or Venus for assistance in escaping since she knows: "Felix would hunt [her] down and make them pay."[162] She cannot "be angry with [Tranio]. ... Because he had not spilled the beans, / as he should have" (*The Emperor's Babe* 243). She refuses to escape her "fate" and views "the actual act of dying [as] mere procedure."[163] She suggests, "Felix isn't a bad man .... He's the person he was brought up to be," which is, ironically, a bad man and a mad man.[164] Her ability to place her friends' and servants needs over her own and to have compassion for her husband, negates Felix's passive aggressive reassertion of his power over her. His right has nothing to do with Zuleika's humanity. When he sees that she is not mere ornamentation, and that he could have a real relationship with her as his partner, the lifeblood of Londinium, he instead views her agency and self-definition as an insult to his position. He chooses to destroy her.

Zuleika avoids the "crisis of genesis narratives" where contamination is connected to "the race that strays too far from its proper place."[165] She has not strayed from imperial constructions of power; her husband has not seen her humanity—he is the one who is mad. She has not strayed, but accepts her place as a trophy wife and mistress to the emperor; her husband has ignored her humanity—he is the one who is mad. He cannot fathom how high she has flown within the imperial construction of power. Her residence in the "villa, grander than any [she] and Alba / imagined" is a place of outward beauty, but inward degeneration.[166] Greenwich and the arena are the eye of the storm, but what occurs on the block with the "white stucco villas" is marked on Zuleika's map of Londinium as the dark side of town. The heart of Londinium is not where the expensive houses and pampered people reside; it is located where people, in all their permutations commingle. Her remapping of the city forces Felix to recognize her humanity or destroy her. Like Proserpine, Zuleika's "metamorphosis," initiated by her abductor and acted out with her lover, acknowledges the madness of desire—her husband's, the emperor's, and, by proxy, the Roman empire's.[167]

In *The Emperor's Babe*, Zuleika cannot avoid the psychic devastation of ongoing abuse and marginalization. Once she "articulates" her position within her husband's household and becomes cognizant of her rage and need for love, she succumbs to some of the pleasures her position enables, but this agency compromises her husband's sense of control.[168]

Zuleika's negotiation of the power dynamics within her household reveals the depravity and double-dealing necessary to maintain hierarchal models of success. At the same time, her epoch-skipping verse upends notions of present-day homogenization and purity in London. As Londinium's mapmaker, Zuleika decimates the false strength of those in power in Rome, but as the angel of history, she smashes notions of Cool Britannia and London's role in the continued oppression of the Commonwealth's black citizens. Her narrative is a transgressive and radical act of self-formation pushing against erasure and marginalization. Her life is an indictment of those, like Thatcher and Blair, who view history through a monochromatic, sentimental lens of lies and obfuscation. She upends Millennium celebrations that whitewash British expansionism and writes herself into the annals of British history. She maps her life—a life that may not change legal policy but serves as the lifeblood of the global metropolis.

Notes

1. Bernardine Evaristo, *The Emperor's Babe* (New York: Viking Penguin, 2002), 45.
2. Peter Fryer, *Black People in the British Empire: An Introduction* (London: Pluto Press, 1988), xiv.
3. Evaristo was also "inspired by" Ivan Van Sertima's *African Presence in Early Europe*, J. A. Rogers's *Sex and Race*, and Florence Dupont's *Daily Life in Ancient Rome*. Bernardine Evaristo, "Alastair Niven in Conversation" *Wasafiri* 16, no. 34 (2001): 15.
4. Evaristo, "Alastair Niven in Conversation," 19.
5. The Anglo-Saxon migration did not begin until the fifth century AD, and the Normans' win at the Battle of Hastings occurred on October 14, 1066 AD. Queen Elizabeth II is a direct descendent of William II of Normandy.
6. Bernardine Evaristo, "On the Road: Bernardine Evaristo Interviewed by Karen Hooper." *The Journal of Commonwealth Literature* 41, no. 3 (2006): 6.
7. Meroe is present day Sudan.
8. Ken Urban, "Cruel Britannia," in *Cool Britannia? British Political Drama in the 1990s*, ed. Rebecca D'Monté and Graham Saunders (New York: Palgrave Macmillan, 2008), 39.
9. For Evaristo's use of "Romanness" as "a clever stand-in for 'Englishness'" see Pilar Cuder-Domínguez, "Ethnic Cartographies of London in Bernardine Evaristo and Zadie Smith" *European Journal of English Studies* 8, no. 2 (2004): 178.
10. Evaristo, *The Emperor's Babe*, 170.
11. According to Andrew Dalby, "In Roman literature of the late Republic and early Empire, Falernian is the almost ubiquitous symbol of fine wine and convivial pleasures." Andrew Dalby, *Food in the Ancient World from A to Z* (London: Routledge, 2003), 138.
12. James Baldwin, *The Devil Finds Work* (New York: Random House, 2000), 115.
13. Jennifer DeVere Brody, *Impossible Purities: Blackness, Femininity, and Victorian Culture* (Durham, NC: Duke University Press, 1998), 6.
14. Brody, *Impossible Purities*, 7.
15. Anne McClintock, *Double Crossings: Madness, Sexuality, and Imperialism* (Vancouver, Canada: Ronsdale, 2001), 10.
16. McClintock, *Double Crossings*, 11.
17. Hershini Bhana Young, *Haunting Capital: Memory, Text, and the Black Diasporic Body* (Hanover, NH: Dartmouth College Press, 2006), 28.
18. Jane Ussher, *Women's Madness: Misogyny or Mental Illness* (London: Harvester Wheatsheaf, 1991), 75.

18. Lynette Goddard, "Middle-Class Aspirations and Black Women's Mental (Ill) Health in Zindika's *Leonora's Dance*, and Bonnie Greer's *Munda Negra* and *Dancing on Blackwater*," in *Cool Britannia? British Political Drama in the 1990s*, ed. Rebecca D'Monté and Graham Saunders (New York: Palgrave Macmillan, 2008), 99.
20. Goddard, "Middle-Class Aspirations," 99.
21. See Sandra M. Gilbert and Susan Gubar, *The Madwoman in the Attic: The Woman Writer and the Nineteenth-Century Literary Imagination* (New Haven, CT: Yale University Press, 2000); Susan Gubar, "'The Blank Page' and the Issues of Female Creativity," *Critical Inquiry* 8, no. 2 (1981): 243–263; Ussher, *Women's Madness*; and Goddard, "Middle-Class Aspirations," 96–113.
22. Homi Bhabha, *The Location of Culture* (London and New York: Routledge, 2010), 64.
23. On Prosperine, known as Persephone in Greek mythology, see Timothy Gantz, *Early Greek Myth: A Guide to Literary and Artistic Sources*, Vol. 1 (Baltimore, MD: The Johns Hopkins University Press, 1993); and Kathie Carlson, *Life's Daughter/Death's Bride: Inner Transformation through the Goddess Demeter/Persephone* (Boston: Shambala, 1997).
24. In *Jane Eyre* (1847), Charlotte Brontë uses the trope of the madwoman in the attic to throw a chink in the romance between a rich and arrogant Mr. Rochester, and a poor, but honorable Jane Eyre. In *Wide Sargasso Sea* (1966), Jean Rhys reimagines Brontë's minor character, Bertha Mason, as the protagonist Antoinette, a Caribbean creole whose mental state deteriorates after her marriage to an Englishman. Charlotte Brontë, *Jane Eyre* (1897, Project Gutenberg, 2013), https://www.gutenberg.org/files/1260/1260-h/1260-h.htm; and Jean Rhys, *Wide Sargasso Sea*, ed. Judith L. Raskin (New York: Norton Critical Editions, 1998).
25. Evaristo, *The Emperor's Babe*, vii.
26. Frantz Fanon, *Black Skin, White Masks* (New York: Grove Weidenfeld, 1967), 114.
27. Kathleen Paul, *Whitewashing Britain: Race and Citizenship in the Postwar Era* (Ithaca, NY: Cornell University Press, 1997), 22.
28. Margaret Thatcher, "Interview by Gordon Burns," *World in Action*, aired January 27, 1968 (Granada TV).
29. The 1981 British Nationality Act ostensibly divided the British Commonwealth into three tiers of nationality: "British citizenship, British Dependent Territories citizenship, and British Overseas citizenship. … All three categories of citizen created by the 1981 act may travel on a British passport; all three may seek British consular protection; yet only the first enjoys the right to live in the United Kingdom." Paul, *Whitewashing Britain*, 182–183.

30. Mark Leonard, *British^{TM}: Renewing Our Identity* (London: Demos, 1997), 5.
31. Ibid., 1; 5.
32. Ibid., 5.
33. Clive Gray, "The Millennium Dome: 'Falling From Grace,'" *Parliamentary Affairs* 56 (2003): 442.
34. Denis Cosgrove and Luciana L. Martins, "Millennial Geographics," *Annals of the Association of American Geographers* 90, no. 1 (2000): 102–103.
35. Ibid., 99.
36. The Millennium Dome cost the government both in resources and reputation. According to Clive Gray, "By the time [the Dome] closed for business, it had cost £628 million in grants from the government, the Millennium Commission and the National Lottery." Cosgrove and Martins state other structures built for the celebrations included the Millennial Bridge, "the city's first new river crossing in a century, [which] connect[ed] the financial heart of London … to a new Tate Gallery of Modern Art at Bankside." Gray, "The Millennium Dome", 441–442; and Cosgrove and Martins, "Millennial Geographics," 102.
37. Quoted in Cosgrove and Martins, "Millennial Geographics, 102.
38. Quoted in *The Economist*, "All Mod Cons," September 27, 1997, 61, http://search.proquest.com/docview/224108165?accountid+28991.
39. Christina Sharpe, *Monstrous Intimacies: Making Post-Slavery Subjects* (Durham, NC, and London: Duke University Press, 2010), 3.
40. Young, *Haunting Capital*, 28.
41. Ibid., 28.
42. N. Draper, "The City of London and Slavery: Evidence from the First Dock Companies, 1795–1800, *Economic History Review* 61, no. 2 (2008): 437.
43. Draper, "The City of London," 442.
44. According to James A. Rawley, by the time the slave trade ended in 1807, "more than 2500 ships [had] cleared the port of London for Africa." James A. Rawley, *London: Metropolis of Slave Trade*. (Columbia, Missouri: University of Missouri Press, 2003), 19.
45. Natasha Gordon-Chipembere, "Introduction: Claiming Sarah Baartman, a Legacy to Grasp," in *Representation and Black Womanhood: The Legacy of Sarah Baartman*, ed. Natasha Gordon-Chipembere (New York: Palgrave Macmillan, 2011), 12.
46. Janell Hobson, *Body as Evidence: Mediating Race, Globalizing Gender* (Albany, NY: SUNY Press, 2012), 67.

47. Ibid., 67.
48. For ways in which Baartman's resistance is read today, see Natasha Gordon-Chipembere, ed., *Representation and Black Womanhood: The Legacy of Sarah Baartman* (New York: Palgrave Macmillan, 2011).
49. Paul Gilroy, *'There Ain't No Black in the Union Jack': The Cultural Politics of Race and Nation* (Chicago: The University of Chicago Press, 1991), 11.
50. Ibid., 11.
51. David Morrissey, "The National Front Disco," *Your Arsenal*, Warner Off Roster ASIN B000002LUL, 1992, compact disc.
52. Morrissey insisted "The National Front Disco" was not racist. In an interview for *Q*, he did admit: "[B]lack people and white people will never really get on." In 2007, he reiterated his stance: "Although I don't have anything against people from other countries, the higher the influx into England the more the British identity disappears." Deevoy, Adrian. "Morrissey: Taking Up Your Arsenal/Ooh I say!," The *Q* Interview, *Q: The Modern Guide to Music and More*, September 1992, http://motorcycleaupairboy.com/interviews/1992/isay.htm; and Oliver Duff, "Morrissey Blames Immigration for 'Disappearance' of British Identity," *The Independent*, November 29, 2007, http://www.independent.co.uk/news/uk/home-news/morrissey-blames-immigration-for-disappearance-of-british-identity-760825.html.
53. Evaristo, *The Emperor's Babe*, 12.
54. Walter Benjamin, *Illuminations*, ed. Hannah Arendt, trans. Harry Zohn (New York: Harcourt, Brace & World, 1968), 260.
55. Ibid., 259.
56. Ibid., 260.
57. Evaristo, *The Emperor's Babe*, 159.
58. Ibid., 9; 3; 249.
59. Ibid., 9.
60. Ibid., 93.
61. Ibid., 12.
62. Ibid., 48.
63. Camulodunum is the Roman name for the Celtic settlement known today as Colchester.
64. Ibid., 42; 4.
65. Ibid., 20.
66. Ibid., 45.
67. Ibid., 4.
68. Ibid., 46.
69. Gabrielle Griffin, *Contemporary Black and Asian Women Playwrights in Britain* (Cambridge: Cambridge University Press, 2003), 7.

70. Evaristo, *The Emperor's Babe*, 15.
71. Ibid., 15.
72. Ibid., 3.
73. Ibid., 19.
74. Ibid., 17; 156.
75. Ibid., 29.
76. Ibid., 27.
77. Ibid., 3.
78. Ibid., 4.
79. Ibid., 53.
80. Ibid., 53.
81. Enoch Powell, "Speech to London Rotary Club, Eastbourne." *Enoch Powell: Life and Views.*, November 16, 1968, http://www.enochpowell.net/fr-83.html.
82. McClintock, *Double Crossings*, 10.
83. Evaristo, *The Emperor's Babe*, 52.
84. Ibid., 75.
85. Ibid., 53.
86. Ibid., 171.
87. Ibid., 118.
88. Ibid., 220.
89. Ibid., 158.
90. Ibid., 220.
91. Ibid., 169.
92. Ibid., 171.
93. Ibid., 171.
94. Ibid., 171.
95. Ibid., 174.
96. McClintock, *Double Crossings*, 10.
97. Evaristo, *The Emperor's Babe*, 174.
98. Ibid., 75.
99. Ibid., 174; 175.
100. Ibid., 174.
101. Ibid., 174.
102. Ibid., 114.
103. Ibid., 221.
104. Ibid., 175.
105. Ibid., 175; 176.
106. There have been numerous iterations of the noble gladiator, including Howard Fast's 1951 historical fiction *Spartacus*, upon which the 1960 film starring Kirk Douglas and Laurence Olivier was based. The New Zealand-based popular Starz television series *Spartacus* (2010–2013) is

a purposefully anachronistic tale where gladiators are eye candy. Ridley Scott's *Gladiator* (2000) focuses on the warrior mentality found in and out of the arena, but the titled character is a proper Roman citizen who has been unfairly enslaved. *Gladiator*, released in the same year when *The Emperor's Babe* was published, makes no room in the arena for women, especially women of color, and only white women appear as spectators. The one series to examine other cultural narratives besides the ruling or gladiator classes is the HBO series *Rome*, but in this construction, there are few people of color and females play subordinate roles to male dominance. They are victims who can be saved only if they are pure and then only by their loving men. These series follow most British renderings of the Roman Empire—those in charge sound and act like the ruling members of the British Empire.

107. Ibid., 176.
108. Ibid., 176.
109. McClintock, *Double Crossings*, 10.
110. Evaristo, *The Emperor's Babe*, 55.
111. Ibid., 178.
112. Ibid., 178.
113. Ibid., 178.
114. Ibid., 178.
115. Ibid., 178.
116. Ibid., 178–179.
117. Ibid., 179.
118. Brody, *Impossible Purities*, 7.
119. Evaristo, *The Emperor's Babe*, 180.
120. Ibid., 179.
121. Ibid., 179–180.
122. Ibid., 27.
123. Ibid., 33.
124. Ibid., 179.
125. Ibid., 218.
126. Ibid., 217–218.
127. Ibid., 219.
128. Ibid., 222.
129. Ibid., 224.
130. Ibid., 225.
131. Ibid., 225.
132. Ibid., 227.
133. Ibid., 229.
134. Ibid., 180.
135. McClintock, *Double Crossings*, 10.
136. Evaristo, *The Emperor's Babe*, 54.

137. Ibid., 29.
138. Ibid., 29.
139. Ibid., 24.
140. Ibid., 24.
141. Ibid., 4.
142. Ibid., 20.
143. Ibid., 19.
144. Ibid., 27; 25.
145. Ibid., 25.
146. Ibid., 22.
147. Ibid., 9–10.
148. Ibid., 56; 57.
149. Ibid., 57; 108.
150. Ibid., 206; 208.
151. Ibid., 207.
152. Ibid., 241.
153. Enoch Powell, "'Rivers of Blood' Birmingham speech," Midland Hotel, April 20, 1968, *The Telegraph*, November 6, 2007, http://www.telegraph.co.uk/comment/3643823/Enoch-Powells-Rivers-of-Blood-speech.html.
154. Gilroy, *'There Ain't No Black in the Union Jack,'* (86).
155. Evaristo, *The Emperor's Babe*, 241.
156. Baldwin, *The Devil*, 115.
157. Evaristo, *The Emperor's Babe*, 54.
158. Ibid., 238; 3.
159. Ibid., 33.
160. Ibid., 75.
161. Ibid., 243.
162. Ibid., 242.
163. Ibid., 244; 245.
164. Ibid., 247.
165. McClintock, *Double Crossings*, 9; 12.
166. Evaristo, *The Emperor's Babe*, 33.
167. Ibid., 33.
168. Baldwin, *The Devil*, 115.

Bibliography

Austen, Jane. *Pride and Prejudice*. 1813. Reprinted, with an introduction by William Dean Howells. New York: Charles Scribner's Sons, 1918.

Baldwin, James. *The Devil Finds Work*. New York: Random House, 2000. First published in 1976 by Bantem Doubleday Dell Publishing Group, Inc.

Benjamin, Walter. *Illuminations.* Edited by Hannah Arendt. Translated by Harry Zohn. New York: Harcourt, Brace & World, 1968.

Bhabha, Homi. *The Location of Culture.* London and New York: Routledge, 2010. First published in 1994 by Routledge.

Brody, Jennifer DeVere. *Impossible Purities: Blackness, Femininity, and Victorian Culture.* Durham, NC: Duke University Press, 1998.

Brontë, Charlotte. *Jane Eyre.* Illustrated by F. H. Townsend. Reprint of the 1897 London edition, *The Project Gutenberg*, 2013. https://www.gutenberg.org/files/1260/1260-h/1260-h.htm.

Carlson, Kathie. *Life's Daughter/Death's Bride: Inner Transformation through the Goddess Demeter/Persphone.* Boston: Shambala, 1997.

Cosgrove, Denis and Luciana L. Martins. "Millennial Geographics." *Annals of the Association of American Geographers* 90, no. 1 (2000): 97–113.

Cuder-Domínguez, Pilar. "Ethnic Cartographies of London in Bernardine Evaristo and Zadie Smith." *European Journal of English Studies* 8, no. 2 (2004): 173–188.

Dalby, Andrew. *Food in the Ancient World from A to Z.* London: Routledge, 2003.

Draper, N. "The City of London and Slavery: Evidence from the First Dock Companies, 1795–1800. *Economic History Review* 61, no. 2 (2008): 432–466.

Deevoy, Adrian. "Morrissey: Taking Up Your Arsenal/Ooh I say!," The *Q* Interview. *Q: The Modern Guide to Music and More.* September 1992. 60–66. http://motorcycleaupairboy.com/interviews/1992/isay.htm.

Duff, Oliver. "Morrissey Blames Immigration for 'Disappearance' of British Identity." *The Independent*, November 29, 2007. http://www.independent.co.uk/news/uk/home-news/morrissey-blames-immigration-for-disappearance-of-british-identity-760825.html.

Dupont, Florence. *Daily Life in Ancient Rome.* Translated by Christopher Woodall. Oxford: Blackwell, 1992. First published as *La vie quotidienne du citoyen romain sous la République* in 1989 by Hachette, France.

Evaristo, Bernardine. "Alastair Niven in Conversation with Bernardine Evaristo." *Wasafiri* 16, no. 34 (2001): 15–20.

———. "On the Road: Bernardine Evaristo Interviewed by Karen Hooper." *The Journal of Commonwealth Literature* 41, no. 3 (2006): 3–16.

———. *The Emperor's Babe.* New York: Viking Penguin, 2002. First published in 2001 by Penguin Books Ltd.

Fanon, Frantz. *Black Skin, White Masks.* New York: Grove Weidenfeld, 1967.

Fast, Howard. *Spartacus.* Armonk, NY: North Castle Books, 1996. First published in 1951 by M. E. Sharpe.

Fryer, Peter. *Black People in the British Empire: An Introduction.* London: Pluto Press, 1988.

Gladiator. Film. Directed by Ridley Scott. California: DreamWorks Pictures, 2000.

Gantz, Timothy. *Early Greek Myth: A Guide to Literary and Artistic Sources*, Vol. 1. Baltimore, MD: The John Hopkins Press, 1993.

Gilbert, Sandra M. and Susan Gubar. *The Madwoman in the Attic: The Woman Writer and the Nineteenth-Century Literary Imagination*. New Haven, CT: Yale University Press, 2000. First published in 1979 by Yale University.

Gilroy, Paul. *'There Ain't No Black in the Union Jack': The Cultural Politics of Race and Nation*. Chicago: The University of Chicago Press, 1991. First published in 1987 by The University of Chicago.

Goddard, Lynette. "Middle-Class Aspirations and Black Women's Mental (Ill) Health in Zindika's *Leonora's Dance*, and Bonnie Greer's *Munda Negra* and *Dancing on Blackwater*." In *Cool Britannia? British Political Drama in the 1990s*. Edited by Rebecca D'Monté and Graham Saunders. New York: Palgrave Macmillan, 2008. 96–113.

Gordon-Chipembere, Natasha. "Introduction: Claiming Sarah Baartman, a Legacy to Grasp." In *Representation and Black Womanhood: The Legacy of Sarah Baartman*. Edited by Natasha Gordon-Chipembere. New York: Palgrave Macmillan, 2011.

Gray, Clive. "The Millennium Dome: 'Falling From Grace.'" *Parlimentary Affairs* 56 (2003): 441–455.

Griffin, Gabrielle. *Contemporary Black and Asian Women Playwrights in Britain*. Cambridge: Cambridge University Press, 2003.

Gubar, Susan. "'The Blank Page' and the Issues of Female Creativity." *Critical Inquiry* 8, no. 2 (1981): 243–263.

Hobson, Janell. *Body as Evidence: Mediating Race, Globalizing Gender*. Albany, New York: SUNY Press, 2012.

Leonard, Mark. *British™: Renewing Our Identity*. London: Demos, 1997.

McClintock, Anne. *Double Crossings: Madness, Sexuality, and Imperialism*. Vancouver, Canada: Ronsdale, 2001.

Morrison, Toni. *Beloved*. New York: Penguin Putnam-Plume Book, 1998. First printed in 1987 by Alfred Knopf.

Morrissey, Steven Patrick. "The National Front Disco." *Your Arsenal*. ℗ 1992 by Warner Off Roster. CD ASIN B000002LUL.

Paul, Kathleen. *Whitewashing Britain: Race and Citizenship in the Postwar Era*. Ithaca, NY: Cornell University Press, 1997.

Powell, Enoch. "'Rivers of Blood' Birmingham speech." Midland Hotel. April 20, 1968. *The Telegraph*. November 6, 2007. http://www.telegraph.co.uk/comment/3643823/Enoch-Powells-Rivers-of-Blood-speech.html.

———. "Speech to London Rotary Club, Eastbourne." *Enoch Powell: Life and Views*. November 16, 1968. http://www.enochpowell.net/fr-83.html.

Rawley, James A. *London: Metropolis of Slave Trade*. Columbia, Missouri: University of Missouri Press, 2003.

Rhys, Jean. *Wide Sargasso Sea*. Edited by Judith L. Raskin. New York: Norton Critical Editions, 1998. First published in 1966 by André Deutsch.

Rogers, J.A. *Sex and Race*. Vols. 1–3. New York: Helga Rogers, 1968–1972.

Rome. Television. Directed by Michael Apted, et al. London: BBC, UK and HBO, USA, 2005–2007.

Rushdie, Salman. *The Satanic Verses*. New York: Random, 2008. First printed in 1989 by Viking.

Sharpe, Christina. *Monstrous Intimacies: Making Post-Slavery Subjects*. Durham and London: Duke University Press, 2010.

Spartacus. Television. Created by Steven S. DeKnight. USA: Starz Entertainment and 20th Century Fox Entertainment, 2010–2013.

Thatcher, Margaret. "Interview by Gordon Burns." *World in Action*. Granada TV, January 27, 1968.

The Economist. "All Mod Cons." September 27, 1997, 59–61.

Urban, Ken. "Cruel Britannia." In *Cool Britannia? British Political Drama in the 1990s*. Edited by Rebecca D'Monté and Graham Saunders. New York: Palgrave Macmillan, 2008. 38–55.

Ussher, Jane. *Women's Madness: Misogyny or Mental Illness*. London: Harvester Wheatsheaf, 1991.

Van Sertima, Ivan. *African Presence in Early Europe*. New Brunswick, NJ: Transaction Books, 1985.

Young, Hershini Bhana. *Haunting Capital: Memory, Text, and the Black Diasporic Body*. Hanover, NH: Dartmouth College Press, 2006.

Madness and Translation of the Bones-as-Text in M. NourbeSe Philip's Experimental *Zong!*

Richard Douglass-Chin

We witen that we been translated from death to life.
—John Wyclif, Select English Works, c. 1380, II, 318

Zong! as radically experimental black female long poem employs an aesthetics of madness against the brutal insanity of "rational" eighteenth-century European philosophical, legal, and literary assumptions that denied the humanity of African peoples and that continue to inform the relations between diasporic Africans and the West today.[1] Those assumptions, in the historic 1783 case of the slave ship *Zong*, underpinned the labeling of between 130 and 150 deliberately drowned Africans as lost "cargo" for which an insurance claim was made on the part of the owners of the slave ship.[2] The *Zong* case became a flashpoint in England's abolition debate. As Markus Rediker observes, the case exposed the

R. Douglass-Chin (✉)
Department of English Language Literature and Creative Writing,
Chrysler Hall North University of Windsor, Windsor, ON, Canada

C.A. Brown and J.X.K. Garvey (eds.), *Madness in Black Women's Diasporic Fictions*, Gender and Cultural Studies in Africa and the Diaspora, DOI 10.1007/978-3-319-58127-9_3

extremes of terror and violence routinely enacted by crews upon enslaved Africans.[3] Abolitionist Granville Sharpe argued that criminal charges of negligence be brought against the *Zong*'s captain for his failure to provide water for the Africans and for his subsequent drowning of the dying Africans in order to claim insurance monies; however, Solicitor General Justice John Lee declared: "'What is this claim that human people have been thrown overboard? This is a case of chattels or goods. Blacks are goods and property; it is madness to accuse these well-serving honourable men of murder… The case is the same as if wood had been thrown overboard.'"[4] Madness indeed.

Zong!'s aesthetics of madness is textual violence—a disruption of narrative certainty, a detonation of the word, a derailing of the sentence. *Zong!* is mad, black female augury—a seeing that subverts "the Westernized paradigm of madness as metaphoric lack, and acknowledge[s] the trauma, the psychic violence that necessarily accompanies colonization and subjugation, that is its source."[5] While such mad aesthetics have their roots in literary modernism,[6] *Zong!* examines the ways in which modernity and literary modernism are themselves *born out of madness*[7]: the madness of the triangular trade in African people beginning in the period of the 1500s—a peculiar trade underpinning a system of brutal slavery that walked hand in hand with genteel empire and "fostered the rise and consolidation of capitalism" as we know it[8]; the madness of Europe's grand theft of West African artifacts during Europe's "scramble for Africa"—artifacts that showed the cubist-to-be and father of modernism Picasso what art really was: "'a form of magic that interposes itself between us and the hostile universe, a means of seizing power by imposing a form on our terrors as well as on our desires. The day I understood that, I had found my path.'"[9] *Zong!*'s aesthetics of madness, then, is a return and a returning. It is a return to the initial monstrous herding of millions of Africans aboard the slave ships—and a recognition that this act that Europe and the white Americas called "sane" was inherently insane. It is also a returning of Africa, her stolen goods, epistemologies, ontologies, and peoples—absented from genteel, amnesiac white history—to a place of recognition in the collective global consciousness. We begin to understand that "Europe" and "Africa" as white ideas—aestheticized under the Enlightenment, modernity, and modernism—served to *anesthetize* white consciousness concerning Europe's and white America's deep complicity in the monstrous realities of imperial domination.[10] As Toni Morrison observes, "[W]e should not be surprised that the Enlightenment could accommodate slavery; we should be surprised if it had not.... Nothing highlighted freedom—if it did not in fact create it—like slavery"; we see that monstrous hypocrisy sublimated in the tropes of "reined-in, bound, suppressed and repressed darkness" that infuse American literature from its very beginnings.[11] *Zong!*'s aesthetics of madness challenges the anesthetizing aesthetics of Euro- and Euro-American Empire. *Zong!* suggests that our contemporary twenty-first-century world, with its "overlapping territories [and] intertwined histories—was already prefigured and inscribed in the coincidences and convergences among geography, culture, and history" of our collective pasts,[12] and that—like *Zong!*'s nameless white seaman—it is only in our understanding of our interbeing[13] that we are able (1) "to make the connection between the prolonged and sordid cruelty of practices such as slavery, colonialist and racial oppression, and imperial subjection on the one hand, and the poetry, fiction, philosophy of the society that engages in these practices on the other"[14]—and (2) to make the necessary connections between the cultures of imperialism and the cultures from which imperialism "borrowed."

Philip breaks apart and then reconstitutes the standard English text of the original eighteenth-century legal document of the *Zong* case. Her reconstitution of this document as disruptive, mad, black female augury involves five strategies:

1. The persistence of haunting and fugue-like black women's voices throughout the work;
2. the radical disruption of standard syntax;
3. the use of great gaps and spaces of silence in the text;
4. the blurring of the certainties of Western generic boundaries as the work slides between long poem, epistolary anti-novel, as-told-to African slave narrative, and performance—challenging the social assumptions of first two forms, and valorizing the liberating power of the latter two;
5. the employment of African languages and thought, at the augural climax of the work, to reconstruct and *translate* fatally savaged and silenced African bodies from death on the sea-bottom to life in the written *African* word.

I use the term *translate* to suggest a mediation between different languages, but also in the word's Latinate sense—a "carrying over/

removal of the bones of a dead hero/saint from one place to another."[15] Throughout its trajectory, *Zong!* is translation-as-carrying over: Philip's translation of the original, rational legal eighteenth-century document to exploded, seemingly irrational text; her use of silence as a space of psychic transformation; the epistolary novel-become-mad-letters as challenge to the Eurocentric philosophical assumptions of that eighteenth-century form; the transition from English to African languages and creole used aboard the slave ship.

Through these augural strategies that subvert the insanity of rape and brutality aboard the *Zong*, that fly in the face of the supposedly rational presuppositions of the "insurance" case itself, Philip accomplishes an astounding *transfiguration*. I borrow the term *transfiguration* from Paul Gilroy, who suggests that as a conduit to the slave sublime[16] —that which aims to repeat the unrepeatable, to represent the unrepresentable— "the politics of transfiguration" constitute not only a counter-mainstream discourse but a "counter*culture* [my emphasis] that defiantly reconstructs its own critical, intellectual, and moral genealogy in a partially hidden public sphere of its own."[17] *Zong!*'s transfiguration—literally a changing of shape—suggests a way of African becoming in modernity. African presence in the text resists the ongoing absenting and "disavowal" (to use Sibylle Fischer's term) of Africans and other subjugated peoples from history as formulated by Euro-modern and postmodern hegemonic cultural systems. *Zong!*'s disruptions of standard syntax, its uses of silence, its exploding of generic boundaries, and its rendition of African languages and thought all work to constitute a politics of transfiguration existing contentiously within modernity and postmodernity, affirming a modern and postmodern African presence, and asserting the possibility of a twenty-first century in which the West begins to understand itself as merely one part of a much larger global cultural system.

Such understanding is now more necessary than ever. The work of *Zong!* as an aesthetics of madness, and as linguistic and cultural translation serves to counteract the violent effects not only of invasive, stultifying, and monolingualizing forms of twenty-first-century globalization on the one hand, but also of globalization's resistant, explosive, and chauvinistic nationalisms on the other. A competent reading of the world view of an "other," translation or carrying-over allows us to enter into conversation with that "other" as she articulates her world view through language. Edith Grossman observes: "As the world seems to grow smaller and more interdependent and interconnected while, at the same time, nations and peoples paradoxically become increasingly antagonistic to one another, translation has an important function to fulfill.... The alternative is unthinkable."[18] In the specter of 9/11 and other forms of religious and nationalistic resistance to American hegemony around the world, we have all too recently witnessed the sociopolitical and emotional ramifications of modern globalization, slavery, dehumanization, terror, and empire, and the explosive ways in which we continue to be haunted by the ghosts of imperialism as a postmodern global society. *Zong!*'s mad aesthetics resist the cultural and psychic insanity of that historical trajectory; in its dissolution of established eighteenth-century European laws, its strategies of translation, and its confounding of literary genres, *Zong!* opens up a way to reimagine generic boundaries and reconstruct new voices and moral genealogies in the very spaces and silences of such dissolution.

Black Women's Voices as Fugue

The central consciousness of *Zong!* is that of a nameless white English seaman, but his thoughts and his letters home to his betrothed Ruth betray his mental unraveling as he witnesses and partakes in the moral depravity and violence perpetrated against Africans—especially women—aboard ship: "... cut// her// shape/ tie her// ripe/ toes// round// and firm// the cord/ it is// dead she went/ over &// under she was// wet put// ashes// on her water/s// leak oil/ her and bring// her// to me..."[19] In that mental unraveling, the seaman's voice becomes less and less discernible from other, fugue-like, voices that thread themselves through the work. As Philip explains in *Zong!*'s penultimate chapter "Notanda": "[W]omen's voices surfac[e] in the text.... [S]uddenly [there are] references to menstruation and childbirth and rape—in contrast with the absence of women in the larger Caribbean text as it's articulated at present..."[20]

If there is a gradual surfacing of women's voices throughout the poetic narrative, that surfacing finds power and presence in "Notanda," where Philip—in her own sustained voice—journals her artistic process in her writing of *Zong!* In "Notanda," she explains that she struggled to find the appropriate medium in which to render the unarticulated and unspeakable story of the murdered Africans. She confronted the only extant record—the legal text of the *Zong* case:

> The irony… is that the story is locked within the text of those individuals—members of the judiciary, one of, if not *the* most powerful segment of English society—who were themselves an integral part of a system that engaged in the trade in humans. A system of laws, rules, and regulations that made possible the massacre on board the *Zong*. It is a story that cannot be told; a story that in not telling must tell itself, using the language of the only publicly extant document directly bearing on these events—a legal report that is, at best, only tangentially related to the Africans on board the *Zong*.[21]

Zong!, then, accomplishes an impossibility: it tells the story of the Africans, a story we can never know. It becomes in Philip's words: poem, chant, shout, ululation, moan, mutter, howl, shriek, "pure utterance." *Zong!* is song—"the Song of the untold story".[22] If the legal text—articulated by white males in positions of great power—"uses language as a tool for ordering," Philip writes, "I want poetry to disassemble the ordered to create disorder and mayhem so as to release the story that cannot be told, but which, through not-telling, will tell itself."[23]

These disordered, fugue-like voices privilege a number of women—for example, the mythological witch Circe and the African queen Dido, two characters who, in Western masculinist epic, act as seductive antagonists to the Greek Odysseus and Roman Aeneas, respectively. We may link Circe to other "evil" witches of Western literature such as Hecate of Shakespeare's *Macbeth*, or Cycorax mother of Caliban the indigene-as-monster, in Shakespeare's *Tempest*. But in the cacophony of voices that comprise *Zong!*, Circe and Dido question and ultimately dismiss the Western patriarchal valorization of Rome and Eden as foundational myths: "… *first// act/ third scene//* circe argues with eve// about eden/ on the eve// of murder// rome mourns// her// misfortune// her// *mort//* her// *p/ tit mort/ turns//* from/ ruins// of forts// and/ fortunes// to// found// a// city// on// death// on// murder circe// to eve// there is no// evidence of eden…"[24]

At another moment in the text, the voice of the seaman, in an anguished reverie addressed to Ruth, is directly followed by—and seems to become—the disruptive voice of another, female-identified narrative entity referring to previously represented Dido: "ruth i b/eg you *let// us have a ne/w act a new/s// cene new a/ct new sce// ne* so here/ is dido she//discove/red the save// in africa/ find/s a hid//e found/s a/ city again// st ro// me and the vise// of time…".[25] This voice, completely sympathetic to the outlooks of Circe and Dido, is perhaps the same one that urges us in the early pages of the poem, before we become privy to the epistles of the seaman: "question therefore/the age…"

Philip herself speaks of the original legal text, from which she derives her poem, as a "matrix—a mother document"—out of which she gestates the black "flesh" and "bones" of *Zong!*.[26] In the opening chapter titled "Os"—in Latin: bones, mouth or, significantly, the entrance to the uterus—this putting on of flesh and bones[27] begins in the eerie aphasia of the drowned spirits attempting to articulate the lack of potable water aboard the slave ship:

w w w   w   a   wa
        w   a   w a   t
er   wa   s
    our   wa
te r gg   g   g   go
    o   oo   goo   d
        waa   wa   wa
w w waa
        ter   o   oh
on   o   ne   w   one
        won   d d d
ey   d   a[28]

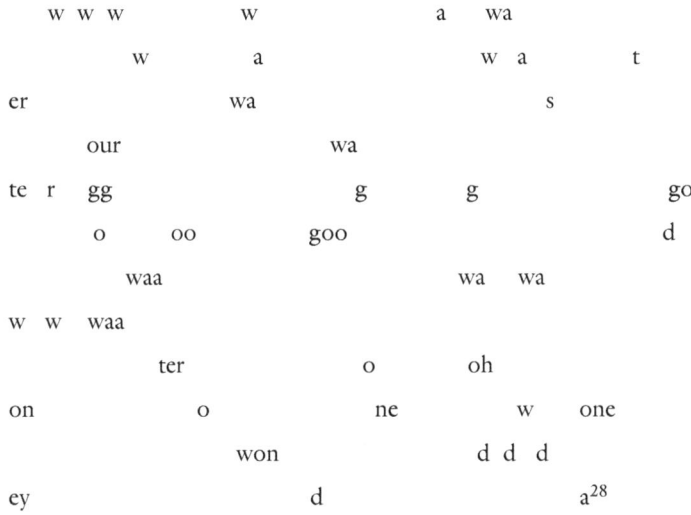

"Water was, water was; our water good; water, o, oh, one day, one day's water, water of want."[29] In this rebirthing, the legal text is transformed, becoming a "hauntology"[30] in which the dead speak, their long-lost voices rusty with disuse and the salt of ocean depths, unaccustomed to verbal articulation. In the movement from trauma to transfiguration, this birthing brings to life African-diasporic women's ways of (re) membering history and myth, of wailing, crying, moaning and shouting[31] the things which have not been told.

Syntactical Disruption as Poetics/Politics of Transfiguration

A poetics of transfiguration refuses the occidental-modern compartmentalization of ethics from aesthetics and considers the world in terms of the possibility of "emancipatory transformation."[32] Indeed, we cannot separate the aesthetics of Philip's *Zong!* from its ethical enterprise. As Philip writes: "[T]here is a mystery here—the mystery of evil."[33]

Her poem is not only an ethical examination of the insanity of that evil but also a way *out* of evil, a realization of the mad, black female augural text as *possibility*, as emancipatory transformation. As such, a poetics/politics of transfiguration departs from the "semiotic, verbal, and textual," and "strives in pursuit of the sublime, struggling to repeat the unrepeatable, to present the unpresentable."[34]

As the "unrepeatable" and "unpresentable," *Zong!*'s sublime encompasses not only the brutal African realities but also the emancipatory possibilities that were denied any valorized textual or performative representation under the dictates of Euro-modernity, slavery, and their attendant institutions. But *Zong!*'s transfigurative sublime must first visit the horrors and madness of the slave ship before arriving at any place of emancipatory transformation. This transfiguration of the madness of the *Zong* and the ensuing *Zong* case is accomplished through textual mutilation. The mutilated text of the poem is derived from the words of the 1783 two-page standard-English legal document of the maritime insurance case of *Gregson vs. Gilbert*. Philip writes: "The legal text parallels a certain kind of entity—a whole, a completeness which like African life is rent and torn. This time though I do the tearing.... I white out and black out words… I murder the text, literally cut it into pieces, castrating verbs, suffocating adjectives, murdering nouns, throwing articles, prepositions, conjunctions overboard…"[35] Hers is a kind of chiasmic reversal of the Euro-modern violence of absenting from modern texts and contexts the experience of entire races and categories of people. While the legal document of *Gregson vs. Gilbert*—figuring Africans in Euro-modern terms as *insurable property*—represents the epitome of Euro-modern rationalism, Philip's chiasmic violence marries ethics to aesthetics in a long poem that examines this evil and the ethical madness of the initial violent erasure and, through a mad, explosive aesthetics of its own, transforms that erasure.

In her mad, disordered, contorted untelling—her violent distortions of English syntax—Philip accomplishes what she calls a textual "*crumping*"—or krumpin(g).[36] Krumpin(g) not only aesthetically and physically articulates, but seeks to exorcise—through its very articulation—the fatal violence that Africans sustained in the trans-Atlantic slave system. Diasporic Africans continue to sustain such violence linguistically in the English language itself,[37] and socially, physically, and environmentally in impoverished neighborhoods all across the diaspora. Krumpin(g) is not merely counter-mainstream discourse, but counter-mainstream *culture*—a mode of hyperkinetic, expressive dance performance originating in the late 1990s, in the black neighborhoods of Los Angeles, as a way to comment on and avoid the insanity of gang warfare and other forms of violence as responses to the ongoing and soul-killing trauma of racism in America[38]; black youth krump instead of kill, contort—not resort—to violent expressions of frustration, aggression, and rage. Krumpin(g) is similar in its intent to the drumming, dancing, and performing rituals that Africans maintained when they arrived in the Americas—those very same rituals that were integral to the development of modern blues and, later, the intricately discordant sounds of bebop and jazz.

Gaps and Silences

Zong!'s "untelling" is marked by great gaps—spaces of silence in the text. The immense silences demand honoring. They accomplish at least two things: first, they allow for the possibility of multiple meanings, multiple voices—like the cacophonous voices aboard the *Zong*—to be heard. For example

won   d d d

ey   d   a

dey   a ah   ay

s   one   day s

wa   wa [39]

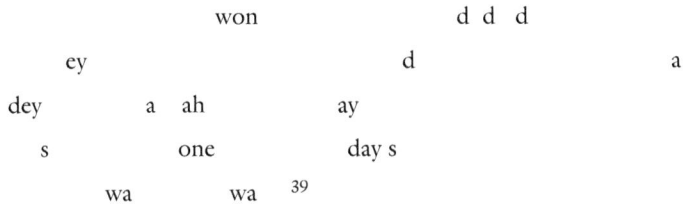

suggests not only "one day's water," but a rhizomatic web of possibilities: the stutter of the aphasic dead in "d d d"; the possibility of "one" as "won" or winning (although who has won what in this zero-sum equation of moral horror is an irony beyond words); the transformation of the standard English word "day" into the creole demotic "dey"—signaling early in the text a strategy of creolization of English that is used throughout; and finally the despair signaled in the fragments "a ah ay."

Second, the silences when honored become transfigurative Silence—the brutal silencing imposed by the enslavers upon the Africans—both aboard the *Zong* and in eighteenth-century philosophical, legal, and literary works where Africans function as *absence*—becomes another kind of Silence in Philip's work—she creates Silence as an African space of necessary mourning, healing, and empowerment.

Philip writes of the gaps in the text, describing her placement of the words in terms of her careful arrangement of space above each word or phrase on a line: "[E]very word or word cluster is seeking a space directly above within which to fit itself and in so doing falls into relation with others either above, below, or laterally."[40] Words and phrases seek open space above them, as the Africans on board the *Zong* would have sought life-giving air, both in the stifling hold of the slaver, and as they sank to the bottom of the sea.

In solo performance, Philip allows long silences to create an initial discomfort in audiences unaccustomed to such sustained cessation of speech: feet shuffle; polite coughs punctuate the absence of words. Even small children sense the necessity to be quiet. In the silence, a strange communal reverence begins. It is the commencement of a ceremony—a rite of consecration in which we honor the souls of the African dead.

Philip's concern with silence is evident in many of her works. For example, *She Tries Her Tongue, Her Silence Softly Breaks* and *Looking for Livingstone: An Odyssey of Silence* both explore monstrous effects of racist European epistemologies upon black peoples' voices, especially women, and the possibility of Silence as transformation before new voices can be generated. This new Silence is perhaps a Door of *Return*—the antithesis of the "Door of No Return" through which manacled Africans passed to board the slaving ships bound for the horrors and obliterations of the Americas. Through the doorway of Philip's Silences, we reenter African *presence*.

Zong!'s Challenging of the Boundaries of Genre

Zong! is ostensibly a long poem, engaging a venerable Western form that originates with the epic works of Homer and Virgil, and continues to operate in the traditions of history-, myth-, and nation-making. As such,

Zong! works to establish a refreshingly ***diasporic African female*** presence vis-à-vis such traditions. But *Zong!*'s status as exploded long poem is complicated by the preponderance of letter-writing throughout, letters that chronicle the unraveling of the psyche of the nameless white seaman whose sanitized[41] sense of self inside his previously unchallenged European systems of thought and existence is irrevocably altered amidst the foul, debased events in which he participates aboard ship. Ultimately, he consigns himself, along with the drowned Africans, to the bottom of the sea. We may say that we witness the seaman's psychic unraveling as *psychic evolution*—he begins to understand the true meaning of the horrors unfolding aboard ship. His letters to his beloved Ruth suggest the possibility of reading the work as epistolary novel, a reading to which I will return.

Zong!'s genre-blurring also engages other forms; its title-page designation "As told to the author by Setaey Adamu Boateng" immediately suggests yet another mode of writing, one that has historically circumvented the "problem" of English illiteracy—that of the slave narrative dictated by an African to an amanuensis. The dictated slave narrative subverts the narrative of letters because the former is *orally* transmitted. We can only imagine that Setaey Adamu Boateng is one of the African souls aboard the *Zong*. The true author of *Zong!*, then, is this African, Boateng, and "M. NourbeSe Philip," is her/his amanuensis. As such, *Zong!* as anti-epistolary is an oral "as told to" tale.

Philip's most recent experimentations with *Zong!* have ventured into the realm of audience-interactive performance. Initially giving author-readings of her work, Philip has begun to engage her audiences in impromptu, communal readings that have taken *Zong!* into another realm entirely. An announcement of Philip's book-length performance of *Zong!* in 2013 reads:

> On November 29th, 2013, there will be the second durational performance of *Zong!* at b current [sic]. We, the participants/readers/watchers/witnesses/translators, will read the book over the course of an evening. This reading will be dynamic, with each section of the work being animated in a different way. Participants are invited to come and go as they please. Please wear white if you are able to.[42]

Communal readings of *Zong!* have produced the sense of reverence and ceremony that Philip has created in single-author engagements, but during the communal readings that I have witnessed, something even more astounding begins to occur; out of the cacophony of voices that sound simultaneously—sometimes from the same page, sometimes from entirely different pages—the chaos of the slave ship seems to be replicated: amidst the voices, an audience participant loudly begins to shout the names of the drowned Africans listed in small font as footnotes under the poems Zong#1 to Zong#26[43] as though he were searching among the manacled for his own beloved; someone chants over and over, "question therefore/ the age"[44]; one participant reads "was the cause was the remedy was the record was the argument was the delay…."[45] and the rest of page 45 continuously. But this cacophony is punctuated by moments of stunning euphony: Amai Kuda, a singer and musician who often accompanies Philip in readings of *Zong!*, begins to sing a haunting African melody; out of a strangely unorchestrated moment of group silence, Philip's lone voice emerges, chanting "Sum sum/ I am/ Sum sum. Sum sum/ I am/ Sum sum…" over and over again.[46] These moments of euphony evoke what George Lamming has called the "Ceremony of Souls" or "Ceremony of the Dead." Philip comments:

> The bones of the undead *can* find a resting place within us. Each time I perform *Zong!*, it manifests as Ceremony. Drawing on the brilliant essay by the Caribbean novelist, George Lamming, on the Ceremony of the Dead he witnessed in Haiti, I would agree with him that there is a sense in which the living and the dead share an interest in the future, albeit in different ways. Within African cosmologies this is not at all unusual, since the Ancestors, albeit no longer alive, are a living force.[47]

Zong! as performance, then, explodes the confines of the text-bound page to become embodiment—*Zong!* as performance begins to inhabit participants of all races, replicating the demographics of the slave ship but also creating a space in which trauma may begin to find healing, a space for what begins as a microcosm of twenty-first-century global reconciliation.

As *Zong!* explodes the confines of the page, unsettles the restrictions of genre, and subverts the rationalistic order of the legal text, it also challenges the order, idealism, and conventional social mores of the eighteenth-century novel—that "narrative form that uniquely expresses the condition of Western culture and consciousness since the emergence of….the modern age."[48] The realist novel of the eighteenth century emerges with Daniel Defoe's *Robinson Crusoe* (1719) and Samuel

Richardson's epistolary novel *Pamela* (1740), and attains its highest level of development in the works of the novelists of the nineteenth century. In such novels, Africans are registered as absence at best, and at worst, representatives of the "heart of darkness"[49] that resides in all Europeans.

The extended narrative action of *Zong!* and its sustained character development suggest a novelistic form. In addition, the action of the texts unfolds in five chapters: Os, Sal, Ventus, Ratio, and Ferrum, in which Os constitutes an exposition; Sal, Ventus, and Ratio a rising action; and Ferrum a climax, falling action, and resolution. However, Philip's anti-epistolary novel violates traditional generic norms and plays against the expectations and presuppositions upon which the realist epistolary novel is predicated. Like Richardson's novel *Pamela*, *Zong!* is also epistolary. But here the similarity ends. In *Zong!*, virtue is not rewarded, and no happy marriage blesses its conclusion. Interestingly in *Pamela*, Mr. B's illegitimate daughter by another woman comes to live under the roof of the newly wedded Mr. B and Pamela, while the slave colony of Jamaica serves as the sanctuary to which the bastard child's mother is conveniently relegated out of sight and out of mind. In Jamaica, this white woman can discard her old identity as spurned mistress and unwed mother, easily adopting a new persona as bereaved widow. In the safe sanctuary of Jamaica, she too is happily married. *Zong!*, however, unfolds around a protracted letter written by the white seaman to his beloved Ruth, amid the "shit,"[50] the "pus," and the "clap"[51] of the slave ship—a ship destined also for Jamaica. But this is not the drawing-room Jamaica of *Pamela*—it is the *other* Jamaica—the Jamaica insanitas of Europe's heart of darkness—and Africa's nightmare.

In *Zong!*, another letter is dictated to the white seaman at the climax of the story by the African Wale, who desires to send a missive to *his* wife, Sade, before the Africans are deliberately drowned. The white seaman's long epistle becomes a record of the psychic disassociation of eighteenth-century English society, torn as that letter is between the seaman's awareness of the social niceties of his married life in England and his involvement in the monstrous events of rape, abuse, and murder aboard the slave ship: "i pen this// to you// when i am/ her// able/ paps her// dugs/ her// teats// leak in necessity/ there// was sin a good/ supply of// ply the negroes/ with// toys lure them// visions of l/ace for a queen// my queen..."[52] *Zong!*, as chronicle of this seaman's gradual psychic unraveling-as-evolution, culminates in his final epistolary encounter with the African Wale before both men jump into the sea.

YORUBA AS THE TRANSFIGURATIVE WRITTEN AFRICAN WORD

The entry into this final moment of crisis and insanity in the text—the deliberate drowning of 150 Africans—is rendered almost entirely in Yoruba:

the ob *a* sobs ag

ain & a gain the *oba* so

bs *oh ye ye* *lantic oh* *oh ye ye oh*

omi omi omi [water] oh *we be aro* *oun* *ebora [spirits]*
omi oh

omi oh *omi ojú [tears]* *ye ye lantic oh* *omi omi omi oh*

eyo [sacred rite] *aro orun* *oh ye ye oh ye ye oh…*[53]

What follows this lamentation continues largely in Yoruba. I examine the passage in detail, since it renders one of the most poignant and powerful laments I have ever read in literature. But before the passage begins, a singular allusion establishes the moment as intensely sacred: "How long had they lain their skin on fire" elides two possible suggestions, two jarringly incompatible scenes—one is a scene of sexual union between Wale and Sade; the other is the ineffable suffering of Africans packed into impossibly cramped shelving compartments in the putrid hold of the slaving ship. The sacredness of the mourning of both these grossly incompatible moments is established in the next conjuration: "Wale and Sade have one go at *agbo*…"[54] To "have a go at" something—in this instance in relation to an *abgo* or, small male goat—suggests the capturing and/or killing of the animal, most ostensibly for the purpose of sacrifice.[55] But if the *agbo* is the sacrificial goat, so also are Wale and Sade sacrifices—as representatives of the millions of Africans sold into slavery in the Americas. Indeed, the seamen aboard the *Zong* repeatedly "have a go at" Sade and other African women, in recurring scenes of rape in the text: "… pin/ her hold her/ legs wide wet/ her…"[56] or "… her scent on/ my fingers my hand// the scent of// africa is with/ me ever/ on// my skin my// lips…"[57] The climactic transformation that comes out of this complicated juxtaposition of scenes—lovemaking, enslavement, sacrifice, and sacred mourning—is signaled in the chant-like lament, sobbed by the oba, that follows: "*oh ye ye lantic oh oh ye ye oh omi omi omi oh we be aroun ebora omi oh omi oh omi oju ye ye lantic oh omi omi omi oh eyo aro orun*..."[58] The gathering of the ebora (elevated spirits, mystic beings) further establishes this moment of mourning, memory, and historical chronicling of traumatic human loss as intensely sacred. This *eyo*—in the West African country of Lagos, a sacred funereal rite to mourn the death of an *oba* (king)—is a libation of tears (omi oju), in which images of water (*omi*) abound: omi mí mó (sacred water); omi ero (tap water); odo (river water); omi nla (vast water); omi omu (breast water—mother's milk); omi ora (all bodily fluids); abu di ni omi okun (what is inexhaustible is the violent Atlantic); omi osa (peaceful Atlantic); omi mi mo (holy water); omi abo wa ba (water you return to meet); orun omi osun (water for Osun—the river god); omi di dun (sweet water).[59]

This Yoruba voice performs a series of broken and oracular utterances that become a catalyst for the fugue which subsequently unfolds in several voices distinguished by specific type-fonts: that of the English seaman to whose tortured thoughts we have been privy throughout the poem (regular Roman font); the inscription of a letter the seaman decides to write to Ruth (hand-scripted font); and the demotic voice of the African Wale, who confronts the Englishman and demands a favor before he (Wale) must leap overboard (italicized font—significantly, also used for the oracular Yoruba voice mentioned above). This moment of convergence, of crisis in the poem, is the ultimate moment of translation in which Philip accomplishes a transfigurative restitution: as English-speaking readers, we are forced to translate the Yoruba of the oracle, and in that act, translate ourselves as Westerners into an African indigenous world system.

The white seaman, writing to his beloved Ruth in this final moment of psychic crisis becomes, himself, strangely transfigured: "they as/k for bread we/ give them se/ a... was that a fair/ trade ruth... ble/ss me *pat/ er* for i have set a snare for *wale & sad/ e*... *w/ale* and *sade* are ti/ red we grow tir/ed... my pen ca/n write no mo/re here on the s/kin of the sea/ how do i ge/t this to you... i hear only the ro/ar of r/aw water t/he seas voi/ce a fis/t to the he/ad if you hap/ pen upon my s/in in the sea gi/ves up it s d/read secret w/ho can bear t/o hear the bo/ nes of g/od lie here."[60] The Englishman's gradual identification with the African Wale is signaled in the line: "Wale and Sade are tired, *we* [my emphasis] grow tired."[61] The seaman now experiences the effect of his own transgressions as he becomes the "we" of Wale and Sade, and asks the sea to speak for him, as it will also speak for the drowned Africans. In the final moments of the poem, the Englishman is confronted in his cabin by Wale who asks the seaman to write for him a goodbye letter to Sade (note the seaman's responses to Wale in Roman font): "*y/ou big man// me I see yo/u to wri// te wri/te a// ll ti// me me wa/le you wr/ite for m// e* such an uncommon man *i s// ay you writ/e on pap/er* i wri// te *de/ar sade you b// e my queen e/ver me I mi/ss you and a// de al/l my lif/e* I a//m do ne…[62] (Who speaks the words "I am done"? Wale? The seaman? Both?)

In what occurs next in this transfigurative moment, the word of the text becomes flesh, entering the body of Wale:

…   he ta   ke s the pa
per e   ats it the   n he fa
ll s on his li   ps *sa*
de fe   *me i*
fa if   *if*   *a* if o
nly *ifa* he fa   lls to the we
ight & wa   it in w
ater i ca   ll his na
me & f
all too t   o my on
ce my no   nce queen…[63]

"Fe me": love me; marry me. "If Ifa, if only ifa": Ifa, the ontology and faith of the Yoruba people. Wale's last words to Sade are a proposal of commitment and love within a West African belief system. He then eats this letter to his beloved—a letter he has just dictated to the white man-as-amanuensis—and jumps into the sea.

What does it mean, to eat the text? To make the word become flesh? The Christian symbolism of such an act is obvious, but in the context of West African encounters with Europeans, how are we to read it? In Western psychology, Wale's eating of paper falls under the categories "abnormal," and "savage." Western psychology deems this act a "disorder"—*pica*.[64] "Savages" eat the seemingly inedible—paper, or dirt. "Savages" also eat the flesh of other people. But this is an act sanctified in its metaphorical form by the Roman Catholic and Anglican Churches—churches to which the seamen aboard the *Zong* would have belonged[65]—in their sacrament of communion. In that sacrament, the *signs*—the bread and the wine—become the sacred things themselves. They are the body and blood of Christ, as we iterate and reiterate the story of Christ's death and resurrection—this narration of the Good News[66] of our communal salvation. Wale's eating of the word, then, transforms *sign* (absence) into *body and blood* (presence); Wale becomes the Christ whose death saves us. The white seaman is complicit with Wale in his writing of the word for Wale to ingest. Both acts—the writing and the eating, become supreme acts of civility in the sense of civility as moral decency: *we are both men, both wanting to contact our wives,* Wale implicitly addresses the white seaman. *Will you write for me a letter to my wife, as you have just written a letter to yours?* In these final moments of the text, Philip asks us to question the marriage the Euro-West has made between the characteristics of moral *goodness,* reason, and the sacred; and characteristics of whiteness and Euro-Western culture. It is as though, in the last minutes of Wale's life, instead of seeking to harm the white seaman (perhaps the most obvious and natural action), the African requests the seaman's help in writing Sade a letter; Wale then eats the word, thus performing a ritual of holy communion that NourbeSe Philip appropriates for her own retelling—an African rebirth, a resurrection of the drowned Africans from the depths of the Atlantic ocean.

But if Heaven is the destination of the resurrected souls of the Christian slave-bartering faithful, the souls of Wale and the seaman might find refuge under a different cosmology. Water as conduit to a blessed afterlife figures prominently in the African American story of the Ibo of the Gullah Sea Islands, whose famous suicide by drowning has become emblematic of Africans' "flying away" home. As African American elder Floyd White, interviewee for the Georgia Writers' Project recalls: "Heahd bout duh Ibo's Landing? Das duh place weah dey bring duh Ibos obuh in a slabe ship an wen dey git yuh, dey ain lik it an so dey all staht singing an dey mahch right down in duh ribbuh tuh mahch back tuh Africa, but dey ain able tuh git deah. Dey gits drown."[67] The communal singing and marching of the Ibo who triumphantly choose suicide over enslavement, suggest not defeat, but victory—and a return to the continent most Africans would not see again in their lifetime. It is a mythical return to the ancestors, figures who loom powerful in African ontology and epistemology as conduits of culture, family, systems of belief and knowing. In the horrific New World, myth becomes of the utmost importance for Africans in their "struggle to maintain a sense of self and to move forward into the future."[68] Across the sea, the drowned Africans—in *Zong!*, a white seaman accompanying them—return home.

The Atlantic functions in the text as the human sea of consciousness. In that sea, African peoples worldwide harbor in their cells (seventy-five percent water), the ancestral memories of the great disaster that came to Africa in the form of the insanity of the European slave trade; similarly, in that same sea of consciousness, white descendants of the European cultures that condoned the monstrous traffic in Africans also bear these memories, most often ignored, repressed, and unexamined. As Wale enters the sea, the nameless white speaker drowns also, in communion with the African. The white man writes, "I call his name and fall too…."[69] In this moment of naming, of transfiguration, self becomes other, white man becomes black; word and flesh become one; and the sea engulfs both men in their baptismal crossing from earthly existence to eternal life, from lover to beloved, from madness to restitution.

Conclusion

Thus does NourbeSe Philip herself become resurrecting medium, mad oracular amanuensis for the drowned Africans, whose message, "posted" to their loved ones in the madness of the *Zong* massacre only now reaches us. Philip has translated the bones home, creating out of the "order" of a Euro-modern legal text-as-matrix a poetic anti-epistolary of translation and transfiguration that effects the breaking open of silences and the exploding of generic boundaries and European philosophical assumptions that have kept modern African presence disavowed. As such, she signals the ways in which modern African presence might become postmodern possibility—the birthing of something torn and new,[70] in a twenty-first century marked by a real understanding of the complex interconnections that define modernity, and by global community, restitution, sanity, and hope.

Notes

1. See, for example, Peter Birkenhead, "Why We Still Can't Talk About Slavery," *Salon*, December 27, 2011, accessed May 18, 2014, http://www.salon.com/2011/12/27; Michelle Alexander, *The New Jim*

Crow: Mass Incarceration in the Age of Colorblindness (New York: The New Press, 2011); Tom Burrell, *Brainwashed: Challenging the Myth of Black Inferiority* (New York: Smiley Books, 2010); Derald Wing Sue, *Microaggressions and Marginality: Manifestation, Dynamics and Impact* (Hoboken, NJ: Wiley, 2010).

2. James Walvin, *Black Ivory* (Oxford: Blackwell Publishers, 2001), 15; Marcus Rediker, *The Slave Ship: A Human History* (New York: Viking, 2007), 240; NourbeSe Philip, “Notes,” *Zong!* (Toronto, ON: Mercury Press, 2008), 208. James Walvin cites 131 Africans killed; Markus Rediker cites 132. Philip cites 150, observing that the number of Africans killed “remains a slippery signifier of what was undoubtedly a massacre.”
3. Rediker, *Slave Ship*, 239–244.
4. “The Zong Massacre,” *BlackPast.org*, accessed August 21, 2014, http://www.blackpast.org/gah/zong-massacre-1781.
5. Brown, Caroline. “A Divine Madness: The Secret Language of Trauma in the Novels of Bessie Head and Calixthe Beyala,” in *Comparative Studies of South Asia, Africa and the Middle East* 28.1 (2008): 95.
6. Louis Sass, *Madness and Modernism: Insanity in the Light of Modern Art, Literature, and Thought* (Boston: Harvard University Press, 1998).
7. Paul Gilroy, *The Black Atlantic: Modernity and Double Consciousness* (Massachusetts: Harvard University Press, 1993); Henry Louis Gates, “Harlem on Our Minds,” in *Critical Inquiry* 24.1 (1997): 1–12; Cornel West, “Race and Modernity” in *The Cornel West Reader* (New York: Basic Civitas Books, 1999); Sibylle Fisher, *Modernity Disavowed* (Durham, NC: Duke University Press, 2004). Paul Gilroy and other theorists such as Henry Louis Gates Jr., Cornel West, and Sibylle Fischer have noted that we cannot examine modernity without also examining the coterminous development of the Atlantic slave trade, European colonialism, and the supposedly rational ideas concerning race that arose to support these enterprises. Like Sibylle Fisher, I contend that modernity as we know it could not have developed without the contestatory and transformative power of the Black Atlantic. The African cultures of the Black Atlantic played an integral role in modernity, their power deriving from the ways in which their traditions, epistemologies, and historic struggles *shaped* modernity, and modern ideas of democracy, freedom and art. Cubism, literary modernism, and jazz, for example, could not have developed without the influence of West African epistemologies.
8. Edward Said, *Culture and Imperialism* (New York: Vintage, 1994), 94, 102.
9. Andrew Meldrum, “Stealing Beauty,” *The Guardian*, March 15, 2006, accessed May 19, 2014, https://www.theguardian.com/artanddesign/2006/mar/15/art. Meldrum writes: “Picasso was visiting Gertrude Stein at her Paris apartment in the spring of 1907 when Henri Matisse

stopped by with an African sculpture he had just purchased. According to Matisse, the two artists were enthralled by its depiction of a human figure. Soon afterwards, Picasso went to the Trocadero Museum of Ethnology (now the Musée de l'Homme) with another artist friend, André Derain. That visit, Picasso later claimed, was pivotal to his art."

10. Said, *Culture and Imperialism*, 130.
11. Toni Morrison, *Playing in the Dark: Whiteness and the Literary Imagination* (Boston: Harvard University Press, 1992), 38.
12. Said, *Culture and Imperialism*, 48.
13. Nhat Hanh, Thich. *Interbeing: Fourteen Guidelines for Engaged Buddhism*. Berkeley, CA: Parallax Press, 1987.
14. Said, *Culture and Imperialism*, xiii–xiv.
15. "Translate." *Oxford English Dictionary* (Oxford: Oxford University Press, 2016), http://www.oed.com/.
16. Paul Gilroy, *The Black Atlantic: Modernity and Double Consciousness* (Boston: Harvard University Press, 1993), 16 and 37–38. Gilroy first mentions the sublime in reference to J.M.W. Turner's 1840 painting "The Slave Ship," a depiction of the *Zong* that Gilroy suggests "aims directly for the sublime in its invocation of racial terror, commerce, and England's ethico-political degeneration." Gilroy later refers to the "slave sublime" as that which "will never be enough to communicate its unsayable claims to truth… struggling to repeat the unrepeatable, to present the unpresentable."
17. Ibid, 37–38.
18. Edith Grossman, *Why Translation Matters* (New Haven: Yale University Press, 2010), xi.
19. Philip, *Zong!*, 71. For purposes of expediency I use a single back-slash to represent spaces within a line and a double back-slash to represent the end of a line. Actual arrangement of text as it appears in *Zong!* may be seen on pages 60, 61, 64, 71 and 74, where I have chosen to replicate Philip's form for the purposes of the argument I present on those pages. On pages 60, 61 and 64: to demonstrate the use of silence and gaps in the text; and on pages 71 and 74: to preserve the intensity of the final moments of Wale and the white seaman aboard ship.
20. Philip, "Notanda," in *Zong!*, 201.
21. Ibid, 199.
22. "Notanda," 207.
23. Ibid.
24. Philip, *Zong!*, 83–84.
25. Philip, *Zong!*, 133.
26. "Notanda," 200.
27. Zora Neale Hurston, *Their Eyes Were Watching God*, (Champaign, IL: University of Illinois Press, 1937), 14. I borrow this idea of the putting

on of flesh and bones from Hurston: "Pheoby's hungry listening helped Janie to tell her story. So she went on thinking back to her young years and explaining them to her friend in soft, easy phrases, while all around the house, the nighttime put on flesh and blackness." Hurston's is a novel about black women's development of their own voices against the social and historical silencing of black women.

28. Philip, *Zong!*, 3–4.
29. Ibid.
30. Philip, "Notanda," in *Zong!*, 201.
31. Philip, "Notanda," in *Zong!*, 203.
32. Gilroy, *Black Atlantic*, 75.
33. Philip,"Notanda," in *Zong!*, 190.
34. Gilroy, *Black Atlantic*, 37–39.
35. Philip, "Notanda," in *Zong!*, 192–3.
36. Ibid, 205.
37. For example, the word "black" or the root word "nig" as in "niggardly" still connote evil, negativity, and smallness of spirit.
38. As the formation of the Black Lives Matter movement in response to the police killing of Trayvon Martin in 2012, as well as several protests and riots such as the November 2014 events in Ferguson, MO, will attest, black rage at the disproportionately high percentage of controversial situations in which black youth are gunned down and killed by white policemen is hardly a phenomenon of the past.
39. Philip, *Zong!*, 3.
40. Philip, "Notanda," in *Zong!*, 203.
41. The Latin "sanus," meaning healthy, is the root of our English words "sanitary," and "sane."
42. NourbeSe Philip, "*Zong!* the story that must be told," *Facebook*, November 17, 2013, accessed May 31, 2014, https://www.facebook.com/events/1430942087118272/.
43. Philip, *Zong!*, 3–45.
44. Ibid, 14.
45. Ibid, 45.
46. Ibid, 117.
47. Paul Watkins, "We Can Never Tell the Entire Story of Slavery: In Conversation with M. NourbeSe Philip," in *Toronto Review of Books*, April 30, 2014, http://www.torontoreviewofbooks.com/2014/04/in-conversation-with-m-nourbese-philip/.
48. John Richetti, *The Columbia History of the British Novel* (New York: Columbia University Press, 1994), xi–xii.
49. Joseph Conrad, "Heart of Darkness," in *Blackwood's Edinburgh Magazine*, February, March and April, 1899. See also Chinua Achebe's

critique of this novel, "An Image of Africa: Racism in Conrad's *Heart of Darkness*," in *Masachusetts Review: A Quarterly of Literature, the Arts, and Public Affairs* 18.4 (1977): 782–794.
50. Philip, *Zong!*, 143.
51. Ibid, 75.
52. Ibid, 65.
53. Ibid, 168.
54. Ibid.
55. See Margaret Drewal, *Yoruba Ritual: Performers, Play, Agency* (Bloomington, IN: Indiana University Press, 1992), 29, 40, 42, 166.
56. Philip, *Zong!*, 108.
57. Ibid, 114.
58. Ibid, 168.
59. Yoruba translations thanks to Dr. Lanre Ikuteyijo, *Department of Sociology and Anthropology, Obafemi Awolowo University, Ile-Ife, Nigeria.*
60. Ibid, 170–172.
61. Ibid, 171.
62. Ibid, 172.
63. Ibid, 172–173.
64. See *Diagnostic and Statistical Manual of Mental Disorders,* (Arlington, VA: American Psychiatric Association Publishing, 2013).
65. NourbeSe Philip, *Zong!* (Toronto, ON: Mercury Press, 2008), 97. A continuous thread of Catholic ejaculations runs through the text. For example, "rise/ say the/ *aves &/ salves* the/ *meas/ &/ culpa s* pray/…"
66. *Holy Bible, Good News Translation,* Catholic Edition (New York: American Bible Society, 1993). See Romans 10:15–16.
67. Quoted in Alan Rice, *Radical Narratives of the Black Atlantic* (Great Britain: MPG Books Ltd., 2003), 94.
68. Alan Rice, *Radical Narratives of the Black Atlantic* (Great Britain: MPG Books Ltd., 2003), 95. Here, Rice quotes bell hooks and Julie Dash.
69. Philip, *Zong!*, 172.
70. I borrow this term from Ngugi wa Thiong'o, *Something Torn and New: An African Renaissance* (Philadelphia: Basic Civitas Books, 2009).

Bibliography

Achebe, Chinua. "An Image of Africa: Racism in Conrad's *Heart of Darkness.*" *Massachusetts Review: A Quarterly of Literature, the Arts, and Public Affairs.* 18.4 (1977): 782–94.

Alexander, Michelle. *The New Jim Crow: Mass Incarceration in the Age of Colorblindness.* New York: The New Press, 2011.

Brown, Caroline. "A Divine Madness: The Secret Language of Trauma in the Novels of Bessie Head and Calixthe Beyala." *Comparative Studies of South Asia, Africa and the Middle East.* 28.1 (2008): 93–108.

Birkenhead, Peter. "Why We Still Can't Talk About Slavery." *Salon.* December 27, 2011. http://www.salon.com/2011/12/27/why_we_still_cant_talk_about_slavery/.

Buck-Morss, Susan. *Hegel, Haiti, and Universal History.* Pittsburgh: University of Pittsburgh Press, 2009.

Burrell, Tom. *Brainwashed: Challenging the Myth of Black Inferiority.* New York: Smiley Books, 2010.

Conrad, Joseph. "Heart of Darkness." *Blackwood's Edinburgh Magazine,* February, March and April, 1899.

Diagnostic and Statistical Manual of Mental Disorders V. Arlington: American Association Psychiatric Publishing, 2013.

Fischer, Sibylle. *Modernity Disavowed.* Durham: Duke University Press, 2004.

Gates, Henry Louis. "Harlem on Our Minds." *Critical Inquiry.* Vol. 24, No. 1. (1997): 1–12.

Gilroy, Paul. *The Black Atlantic: Modernity and Double Consciousness.* Cambridge: Harvard University Press, 1993.

Grossman, Edith. *Why Translation Matters.* New Haven: Yale University Press, 2010.

Holy Bible, Good News Translation. Catholic Edition. New York: American Bible Society, 1993.

Hurston, Zora Neale. *Their Eyes Were Watching God.* Champaign: University of Illinois Press, 1937.

Meldrum, Andrew. "Stealing Beauty." *The Guardian.* March 15, 2006. https://www.theguardian.com/artanddesign/2006/mar/15/art.

"Modernity." *A Dictionary of Geography.* London: Oxford University Press, 2009. https://oxfordreference.com.

Morrison, Toni. *Playing in the Dark: Whiteness and the Literary Imagination.* Cambridge: Harvard University Press, 1992.

Ngugi, wa Thiong'o. *Something Torn and New: an African Renaissance.* Philadelphia: Basic Civitas Books, 2009.

Philip, NourbeSe. *Looking for Livingstone: An Odyssey of Silence.* Toronto: Mercury Press, 2006.

——— "Notanda." In *Zong!* Toronto: The Mercury Press, 2008.

——— *She Tries Her Tongue: Her Silence Softly Breaks.* PEI: Ragweed Press, 1989.

——— *Zong!* Toronto: The Mercury Press, 2008.

———"*Zong!* the story that must be told." *Facebook.* November 17, 2013. Accessed May 31, 2014.

Rediker, Markus. *The Slave Ship: A Human History.* New York: Viking, 2007.

Rice, Allan. *Radical Narratives of the Black Atlantic.* Great Britain: MPG Books Ltd., 2003.

Richetti, John. *The Columbia History of the British Novel.* New York: Columbia University Press, 1994.

Said, Edward. *Orientalism.* USA: Vintage, 1979.

——— *Culture and Imperialism.* New York: Vintage, 1994.

Sass, Louis. *Madness and Modernism: Insanity in the Light of Modern Art, Literature, and Thought.* Boston: Harvard University Press, 1998.

Sue, Derald Wing. *Microaggressions and Marginality: Manifestation, Dynamics and Impact.* New Jersey: Wiley, 2010.

"Translate." *Oxford English Dictionary.* Oxford: Oxford University Press, 2016. http://www.oed.com/.

Walvin, James. *Black Ivory.* Oxford: Blackwell Publishers, 2001.

Watkins, Paul. "We Can Never Tell the Entire Story of Slavery: In Conversation with M. NourbeSe Philip." *Toronto Review of Books.* April 30, 2014. http://www.torontoreviewofbooks.com/2014/04/in-conversation-with-m-nourbese-philip/.

West, Cornel. "Race and Modernity." In *The Cornel West Reader.* New York: Basic Civitas Books, 1999.

Wyclif, John. "Translate." *Oxford English Dictionary.* Oxford: Oxford University Press. http://www.oed.com/.

"The Zong Massacre." *BlackPast.org.* 2007–2015. Accessed August 21, 2014. http://www.blackpast.org/gah/zong-massacre-1781.

Embodied Haunting: Aesthetics and the Archive in Toni Morrison's *Beloved*

Victoria Papa

"*If I hadn't killed her she would have died and that is something I could not bear to happen to her*"—so Sethe, the protagonist of Toni Morrison's *Beloved*, reasons about having murdered her daughter, Beloved, in order to prevent her from being re-enslaved (emphasis mine).[1] Within the paradox of Sethe's reasoning—for her, the only *bearable* alternative to the most certain figurative death of slavery is actual death—the maddening conditions of enslaved mothering come to the fore. In the most literal sense of the word, there is no *viable* option for Sethe when she is faced with an unthinkable scenario of either letting Beloved be returned to slavery or killing her infant daughter herself. Yet, as logic collapses within the chiastic structure of Morrison's line—*if I hadn't killed her she would have died*—a space is cleared for the unspeakable "*that*" which Sethe "*could not bear.*" In other words, Morrison creates a space in which the paradox of Sethe's reasoning testifies to the broader madness of slavery in which her dire situation is contained.

V. Papa (✉)
Department of English, Massachusetts College of Liberal Arts,
North Adams, MA, USA

C.A. Brown and J.X.K. Garvey (eds.), *Madness in Black Women's Diasporic Fictions*, Gender and Cultural Studies in Africa and the Diaspora, DOI 10.1007/978-3-319-58127-9_4

However, it is when Beloved defies all earthly logic and returns from the dead as a ghost of corporeal form that the maddening conditions of enslaved mothering are most readily revealed in the novel. Beloved's *embodied* return illuminates how slavery as an institutionalized form of bodily subjection is predicated upon and producing of a madness, which historical archives, shaped by white patriarchical discourse, perpetually repress. Morrison's great achievement in *Beloved* is to engage the psychic space of this historical repression by taking as an entry point what Jacques Derrida has theorized to be the archive's drives to both record and erase. The novel's enigmatic dictate, "[T]his is not a story to be passed on," speaks to the paradoxes at the heart of the archive.[2] *Beloved* is not a story to be retold and, simultaneously, it is not a story to be passed on, or rather *passed up*—it is a story that cannot be recounted, and yet it cannot be denied. The material consignation of slavery's trauma to the archive alerts us to what is missing in the telling of this history: what is absent speaks as loudly as what is recorded. Similarly, it is when Beloved materializes, as a ghost with bodily needs and wants, that the absence of her life along with the maddening conditions of her death are *felt* by the living: Beloved the ghost asserts as a "real presence" who "demand[s] its due" among the novel's characters—most notably, Sethe.[3] That is, until Beloved's ghostly body cannot survive among the living, finally "erupt[ing] into her separate parts."[4] By the novel's close, all that remains of Beloved is "just weather."[5] Like the weather, Beloved's legacy is an elusive power; everywhere and nowhere at the same time, unable to be remembered or recorded; yet alive and ongoing. As Kevin Quashie writes, "Beloved is an unflappable presence (even as an absence), a palpable flesh to be/held and behold. She is undeniable. But as much as she exhibits memory's precision and irrepressibility, she also enunciates its ambiguity and fluency."[6] The duality of Beloved—as both real and "undeniable" as well as absent and "ambig[uous]—is part of her force." As this essay argues, the novel's close in which Beloved "erupts into separate parts" also motions towards the possibility of transforming a history of trauma and erasure into one of survival and presence, as it is precisely the dissipation of her corporeal form that births a new incarnation of Sethe as the witness to her own survival, as a mother who is able to move towards the reconciliation of her own past as a self-realized survivor of slavery's trauma.

Moreover, Morrison's complicated address of slavery's violent history is also depicted on a metatextual level through the novel's aesthetics that appeal to readerly presence—as to be explained, such aesthetics emerge in Morrison's treatment of Beloved as a "real" ghost that creates a readerly experience of "haunting." As Morrison writes in the Foreword to the 2004 twentieth-anniversary edition of *Beloved*: "I wanted the reader to be kidnapped, thrown ruthlessly into an alien environment as the first step into a shared experience with the book's population—just as the characters were snatched from one place to another, from any place to any other, without preparation or defense."[7] Such readerly "kidnapping" suggests that slavery's story cannot be "passed on" in a discursive manner aligned with an archival attempt to consign meaning to history through facts and evidence. Other, more affective methods of storytelling are needed. For Morrison, such methods involve "invit[ing] her readers [...] into the repellant landscape" of a traumatic past so as to "render enslavement a *personal experience*" (emphasis mine).[8] In turn, the *embodied* haunting which this essay's title announces refers not only to Beloved's assuming corporeal form and Sethe's reclaiming of her own embodied life at the novel's close but also to the presence of the reader: the embodied space in which the "personal experience" unfolds.

By prompting its reader to question what is knowable about history, *Beloved* subverts the archive's erasure of slavery's trauma. Moreover, the novel both embraces and challenges Derrida's concept of *archive fever*—which presumes that the ability to know history burns up in the feverish pursuit of an ultimately unknowable, unclaimed past. Reading *Beloved* alongside Derrida's theory illuminates how Morrison's text creates an alternative ontology of the archive as a site of erasure as well as documentation. For Morrison, mothering is the key platform on which to reveal the archive's disavowal of slavery's systemic erasure of black female subjectivity as a raced and gendered form of "madness"—a disavowal that precisely makes itself known through its resistance to the archive's erasure.

The mother/daughter relationship is an especially important site for considering the historical disavowal of black female subjectivity because, as Quashie argues, the "vexed quality of motherhood" rooted in the African diaspora still persists in contemporary black culture.[9] "Motherhood is an amazingly political and ambivalent site for many Black women [in the United States]," as Quashie explains, since either choosing to have or not to have children is a political act of resistance "[within] a legal system designed to restrict and control Black women's reproduction."[10] However, despite what he calls the "the impossibility [of] Black mothering," Quashie insists that in the specific context of the adult mother/daughter dynamic, and the relationality it entails, "motherhood [for the mother] can be thought of as a consideration of the creative power of one's self, the ability to have made an/other self, the engagement of the failure and successes of this making."[11] Quashie's reading of the potentiality proffered in the adult mother/daughter dynamic—despite the "impossibility" it faces—provides a context for understanding how Sethe's reclaiming of her own embodied life comes by way of Beloved's return. Moreover, his understanding of "the impossibility of Black motherhood" illuminates the prevailing effects of slavery's disavowal of black women and the maddening conditions that it incites.

In this essay, I use the term "madness" in disparate but related registries: firstly, the madness of mothering within slavery's system—a gendered form of violence rooted in the paradoxical demand often placed upon female slaves to bear children without the freedom and rights to *mother*; secondly, the madness of the archive—what Derrida frames as an insatiable desire to consign meaning to history through a documentation process encoded by hegemonic discourse; thirdly, the rendering of madness through the aesthetics of Morrison's novel—which, building upon previous *Beloved* scholarship, I specifically examine as the disorienting effects of a *textual haunting* that "kidnaps" the reader. While many scholars have examined the novel's investment in the archive as well as its treatment of madness, mothering, and the enslaved body—as I will show in the following pages—by putting Morrison in conversation with Derrida, I offer a new reading of *Beloved* that further considers its complicated address to slavery's fraught past. Both Derrida and Morrison display an acute concern with the *corporeality of history*—the living, material presence of the past in the present—which is rendered through bodily allusions of the archive: Derrida's appeal to fever and Morrison's emphasis on the embodied presence of a ghost.

Morrison's aesthetic investment in the body is emblematic of a resistance to be pulled toward either polarity of the archival drive: it reflects the fluid, affective life of memory as opposed to the fixed, singular logic like the documented history of the archive. Recent scholarship on the novel has paid particular attention to Morrison's investment in the body as site of traumatic memory. Kimberly Juanita Brown illuminates how the "repeated bodies" throughout the novel—what she calls the "'three Beloveds' (the baby, "crawling already," the ghost in the home, and the woman who returns to 124 Bluestone Road to take the baby's fleshed-out and grown adult female form)"— reinforce the reverberating and repetitious effects of slavery's transgenerational trauma.[12] Through its "corporeal repetitions," Brown argues that the novel illuminates how "it takes many generations to grasp the horrendous event of slavery."[13] Similarly, Evelyn Jaffe Schreiber writes that, "specifically [in the works of Morrison] the body becomes a placeholder for memory and trauma, accounting for personal and cultural behavior (of both blacks and whites) and explaining why trauma persists, transferred from one generation to another."[14] For Emma Parker, the novel's reliance upon a "corporeal discourse to articulate what is otherwise unspeakable" mirrors the psychic operation of hysteria in which repressed memories often find articulation only through bodily symptoms.[15] In her analysis of *Beloved*, Cynthia Dobbs builds upon Paul Gilroy's work on the expressive cultures of African American history by citing Morrison's emphasis on the body as a staging of both personal and collective memory within a radical black modernist aesthetic. "In Sethe's story," Dobbs writes, "Morrison thus reveals the conditions for a politically and aesthetically radical self-possession, one defined by claiming one's body."[16] Lastly, for Jean Wyatt, it is Morrison's treatment of the maternal body in particular that illustrates an aesthetic resistance to the "normative discourse" of the archive: "[Sethe's] insistence on her own physical presence and connection to her children precludes an easy acceptance of the separation and substitution that govern language."[17] As these scholars' varied examinations of the body in *Beloved* suggest, Morrison's aesthetic depiction of the black female body is a site of traumatic memory able to enact radical forms of testimony unlike those which can be offered by conventional, discursively bound archives.

While Morrison's novel engages in theories of the archive through her representations of the body as a figurative archival space, it also directly engages with the literal archive through its retelling of a historical account of enslaved mothering. As is widely known among Morrison scholars, *Beloved* is inspired by the story of Margaret Garner, whom the author describes in the novel's Foreword as "a young mother who, having escaped slavery, was arrested for killing one of her children (and trying to kill others) rather than let them be returned to the owner's plantation."[18] Morrison's literary evocation of Garner marks her concern with the material consignation, categorization, and cataloguing of history. Yet to tell the story behind the historical Garner, she recognized a need to move beyond the "strictly factual."[19] As Morrison claims, "[there was] too little imaginative space [in the archival materials concerning Garner's case] for my purposes."[20] In recovering the sensational Margaret Garner case, Morrison creates a "heroine [who] would represent the unapologetic acceptance of shame and terror; assume the consequences of choosing infanticide; claim her own freedom."[21] The archival records on Garner did not reconcile a story that dwells in paradox and bears the impact of a traumatic trace that offers no resolve. In and of itself, Morrison's desire to know Garner's experience is symptomatic of archive fever, but it is the writer's insistence upon leaving the archive behind that differentiates her longing from the impulse which Derrida suggests is at the heart of the archival drive.[22] In turn, what Morrison calls for is not an institutional inscription of slavery's traumatic past in an archive but rather that her readers know its absence or, as Nellie Y. McKay writes, to know "what is missing" from history "to remind us to never let this atrocity happen again."[23]

To offer a space for her readers to experience a history of erasure, then, Morrison creates a textual haunting that mimics Beloved's ghostly return within the storyline. Thus, as it is for the novel's characters, Beloved's haunting is dismantling for the readers; we become disoriented within the text's "reality" when the impossible happens and Beloved comes back from the dead. Our confusion about how to read Beloved—as a "real" character within the text, a figment of the other characters' imaginations, a psychological projection of Sethe's traumatic repression, or even as a purely literary "symbol" of loss—captures the difficulty of speaking the truth of an unspeakable past. The novel repeatedly puts its readers to task: how to read Beloved?—a question that gestures towards a broader inquiry about Morrison's literary aesthetics.

Responding to questions regarding her writerly style, Morrison has stated an allegiance to an aesthetic rooted in African American heritage: "[My] effort," she has claimed 'is to be *like* something that has probably only been fully expressed perhaps in music" (Interview with McKay, 427).[24] In his study of the black Atlantic, Paul Gilroy argues that the systematic terror of slavery was predicated upon and producing of a "topos of unsayability," which both generatively and problematically became a site of resistance within the cultural expression of the black diaspora.[25] Importantly, Gilroy clarifies that "though [slavery's traumas] were unspeakable, these terrors were not inexpressible."[26] For Gilroy, "the pre- and anti-discursive constituents of black metacommunication" are most readily identified in music.[27] "Thinking about music," he writes, "[…] raises aspects of embodied subjectivity that are not reducible to the cognitive and the ethical."[28] These "aspects of embodied subjectivity" rely upon affective modes of knowing to communicate that which language resists; they are not only "aspects" of embodiment, but testimonies to the aliveness of a human subject that can *feel*. Like Gilroy,

Morrison pays heed to the rich musical heritage of black culture, recognizing its resonance with elements of African American experience that language seems strained to convey. Morrison's appeal to a musical flourish in her literary aesthetic is evident in her privileging of *feelings* as an alternative mode of communication that is more beholden to bodily experience than linguistic communication, which places emphasis upon cognitive thinking. Morrison values *feelings* as a legitimate form of sense-making in a manner that is overwhelmingly absent from dominant Western ideology and its accompanying archive.[29] For Morrison, "language must get out of the way" so that she may write in a way that situates affective experience as a mode of meaning-making.[30] Through the disorientating effects of Beloved's embodied haunting, Morrison is able to get in touch with her reader's feelings, as it were.[31]

As the site of affective experience, the body is a repository of traumatic memories that are not easily articulated through conventional discursive modes of expression. In her study of the affective force of traumatic histories, Ann Cvetkovich names both Morrison and Derrida's contribution to her analysis of queer archives, which similar to other archives of trauma such as slavery's, "must enable the acknowledgement of a past that can be painful to remember, impossible to forget, and resistant to consciousness."[32] Cvetkovich turns to both Morrison and Derrida because they both place trauma at the center of history, thus forging new ways of thinking of archival space as the representation of resistance on two levels: the resistance of consciousness to trauma but also more active forms of resistance that alternative archives might engender. For example, Cvetkovich suggests that Morrison illustrates this duality of resistance through her focus on the emotional nature of traumatic memory:

> Central to traumatic memory is what Toni Morrison, in the context of remembering slavery, has called emotional memory, those details of experience that are affective, sensory, often highly specific, and personal. Subject to the idiosyncrasies of the psyche and the logic of the unconscious, emotional experience and the memory of it demand and produce an unusual archive, one that frequently resists the coherence of narrative or that is fragmented and ostensibly arbitrary.[33]

Morrison emphasizes emotional memory as embodied feelings—the intuitive knowingness that arises through direct realization and action in a manner that resists the logic of the archive. She constructs an "unusual Archive" in *Beloved*, particularly around the story of enslaved mothering, by stepping outside of a logic bound only to the consultation of history, ultimately suggesting that the truth of experience is accessed in the embodied presence of one's life. At the center of Morrison's narrative is an act beyond logic—a mother taking her child's life, an act that cannot be understood by the conventional modes of knowledge that dictate the archive.

The concept of *archive fever* provides an illuminating theoretical framework for approaching the novel's complicated address of slavery's haunted past because, like Morrison, Derrida is concerned with both the pragmatic function of the material archive as well as the underlying psychological drives and defenses that shape it. These drives and defenses are at play in the novel as Sethe faces the simultaneous impossibility and necessity of constructing a story about her past that she can both literally and figuratively *live with*. Furthermore, they are mimicked in the novel's creation of a "personal experience" that situates its reader in a disorientating space of textual haunting in which the story's "truth" seemingly cannot be located. Such textual haunting aligns itself with the archive's endless mode of seeking. As Derrida argues, the archive is animated by a "question of the future" that "contains a promise and a responsibility for tomorrow."[34] The futurity of the archive—its embodiment of "a promise and a responsibility for tomorrow" that is tied to a messianic promise of salvation—is always couched in a mode of reaching for the past's "truth," which is displaced within the record-keeping and meaning-making processes of the archive. The archive is fixated upon the past so that it may control history in hopes to better secure the future. Pulled in different temporal directions, then, the archive is suspended in a deferred longing for both the past and the future, neither of which it is able to contain. Moreover, as Derrida explains, the archive is prompted and sustained by what "in truth [is] a patriarchic function" to assign, or rather, "consign" meaning to its material, discursive documents or otherwise, by "gathering together signs" with the "aims to coordinate a single corpus, in a system or a synchrony in which all the elements articulate the unity of an ideal configuration."[35] While the body of the archive—its "single corpus"—may be aimed at an "ideal configuration" of a hegemonic order, it is continually meeting a maddening disruption as its paradoxical impulses continually cancel each other out. It is this very repressed madness of the archive that, paradoxically, drives its existence.

In *Beloved*, Morrison enters the archive's troubled space of deferred longing in order to know slavery's history of erasure that seemingly exists beyond the bounds of a knowable history or, rather, beyond what the archive has instituted as knowable. Morrison does not offer resolution to the archive's paradoxes, for ultimately even the "single corpus" of Beloved does not hold at the novel's close: "In the place where long grass opens, the girl who waited to be loved and cry shame erupts into *her separate parts*, to make it easy for the chewing laughter to swallow her all away" (emphasis mine).[36] Rather, as Beloved's return necessarily fails and Sethe mourns a loss the world fails to recognize, Morrison generatively participates in the refusal to name this loss. In turn, Morrison bears witness to the trauma of enslaved mothering—a trauma erased by the archives that have shaped history and what it desires us to know.

The novel's primary plot line centers on an uncanny inversion of the mother-daughter relationship. Beloved's return, and eventual exorcism, births a new incarnation of Sethe, as a mother who is able to claim her freedom and role as heroine, allowing the narrative to culminate in a transformative moment of recognition when Paul D finds Sethe, distraught and disheveled, under the "quilt of merry colors" in Baby Suggs's old room.[37] Here Sethe, on the verge of succumbing to the oblivion of psychic pain that overtook Baby Suggs, laments the loss of Beloved, telling Paul D: "'She left me.' [...] 'She was my best thing.'"[38] After the narrator explains that Paul D "wants to put his story next to hers," Paul D corrects Sethe: "'You your best thing, Sethe. You are'," to which she replies "'Me? Me?'"[39] The interrogative form of Sethe's last line presents a discursive return to herself that is enacted in the reader's silent affirmation of her rhetorical question. This rhetorical maneuver doubly works to return the reader to herself; she must engage in the presentness of her own embodied life to locate this affirmation, which the page does not provide.[40] Just as Paul D "put[s] his story next to hers," as readers, we put our readings of Beloved next to Sethe's in this closing scene as Morrison calls upon us to act as witnesses to this transformative moment. "Language get[s] out the way" as the interrogative form of "'Me? Me?'" leaves the answer to Sethe's inquiry suspended. Thus, Morrison calls upon the reader to know the truth behind this question through an embodied form of sense-making that transcends the logic of the archive.

In her reading of this scene, Wyatt points out that "Sethe answers [Paul D] expressing surprise and disbelief, perhaps, but also recognizing herself in the first person singular" (484).[41] Importantly, as Wyatt argues, Sethe's recognition of herself as subject is accompanied by Paul D's physical touch: "[He] leans over and takes her hand. With the other he touches her face."[42] Thus, embodied touch acts as a necessary prerequisite for communication not only between Paul D and Sethe but also for Sethe's "acceptance of the separate subjectivity required by language systems."[43]

The narrative's close is able to effectively beckon the readers' participation in recognizing Sethe as her "best thing" because throughout the novel we, too, have experienced the disorienting effects of Beloved's haunting as an othering unto ourselves. Morrison has remarked in an interview about *Beloved* that she "started out wanting to write a story about the feeling of Self."[44] Similar to the way that the archive's violence of forgetting paradoxically drives its existence, only through the disorientation from the self—what Morrison describes as "the sense of things being both under control and out of control"—is the reader, like Sethe, able to recognize the Self at the novel's end.[45] The double return to "the feeling of Self" for Sethe and the reader defies the ruling ideologies of the archive by privileging affect over discursively bound logic. The privileging of affect over logic is instrumental in bearing witness to the trauma of Sethe's story and to understanding Morrison's dictate that "language must get out of the way" to aesthetically render the experience of slavery.

What is more, by writing to her reader's own embodied presence and "feeling of Self," Morrison showcases not only how traumatic experience strongly resonates with affective experience but also how trauma *silences* linguistic expression. This silencing—or *unspeakability* of trauma—is a complex and repeated trope throughout African American literature and its criticism, especially as it pertains to the legacy of slavery's trauma. In *Beloved*, despite the *unspeakableness* of her past, Sethe is ultimately able to access the redemptive self-knowingness regarding Beloved's infanticide that appears at the novel's close. This self-knowingness is an affective experience that transcends linguistic representation in a manner that is aligned with what Gilroy terms "the pre- and anti-discursive constituents of black metacommunication." In turn, the reader's own engagement in the text acts as the platform on which the *feeling* of Sethe's struggle and survival takes on a transformative edge.

Thus, it is when Sethe attempts to literally *speak* about Beloved's murder or, what in the novel is known as "the Misery," that she encounters the aporetic force of trauma's unspeakability—a force the archive cannot document. In these moments, Sethe meets an impasse in linguistic communication that is simultaneously the impetus for her to uncover what she intuitively knows: that she is her own "best thing."[46] After Stamp Paid shows Paul D an old newspaper article with Sethe's picture and narrates the details of her conviction of infanticide, a bewildered Paul D questions Sethe about the murder. In response, she struggles to tell her lover about the horrific day when schoolteacher (the slave owner from whom she escaped), his pupils, and the sheriff walked into the yard of 124—her home—to re-enslave herself and her children. Rather than hand herself and her children over to schoolteacher, Sethe performs the ultimate act of resistance, murdering Beloved with the intention to kill all her children as well as her self.

The scene that plays out between the two lovers mimics the operation of *archive fever* as Sethe attempts to tell the story recounted in the newspaper in her own words. Hers, as she recognizes, is not a story that can be consigned to a single narrative. The events of that day simply cannot be catalogued by any record of past experience, even that of Sethe's own telling: "Circling, circling" around the room as she "circles" around the murder, Paul D grows "dizzy" listening to Sethe's disjointed tale.[47] The story, like a "circle," is a non-linear, perpetual loop, unable to be "pinned down" by language: "Sethe knew the circle she was making around the room, him, the subject, would remain one. That she could never close in, pin it down for anybody who had to ask. If they didn't get it right off—she could never explain. Because the truth was simple: not a long-drawn-out record of flowered shifts, tree cages, selfishness, ankle ropes, and wells."[48]

Sethe concludes that the "truth" of this experience exists outside any information that a "long-drawn-out record" of uneasy details might provide. She surmises that "if she thought anything" at the instance when "she saw them coming and recognized schoolteacher's hat [...] it was No. No. Nono. Nonono. Simple."[49]

Understanding trauma as a psychic break that creates an absence along the continuum of lived experience, Cathy Caruth writes that a story of trauma is "always the story of a wound that cries out, that addresses us in an attempt to tell us of a reality or truth that is not otherwise available."[50] While in the discourse of literary trauma studies, madness is generally not discussed as a phenomenon of traumatic experience, I would suggest that within Morrison's depiction of enslaved mothering, trauma often resembles the haptic insistence reminiscent of madness. In the scene at hand, this is evident as Sethe is tasked with giving voice to an "impossibility," to use Quashie's phrase. In turn, her interior dialogue is a discursive manifestation of a traumatic wound that cannot be told through conventional modes of discourse. The "truth" of her trauma signifies as absence or pure negation with a maddening insistence: "No. No. Nono. Nonono." Thus, it is not what Sethe tells Paul D about the event but rather what she refuses to say that testifies to the madness of the impossibility contained within the trauma of that day.

Moreover, I would argue that Morrison offers her reader a latent message that lies in the imperative of *no's* homophone—*know*—that echoes throughout the line. As readers, we are prompted to *know* something by way of Sethe's refusal that the historical archive of Margaret Garner cannot bear witness. In this way, Morrison indirectly offers an uncanny answer to a maddening question at the heart of enslaved mothering. This question is most poignantly rendered in Saidiya Hartman's study of slavery's "blank spaces of historical record" in *Lose Your Mother: A Journey Along the Atlantic Slave Route*, in which she asks: "How does one write a story about an encounter with nothing?"[51] Morrison's aesthetics suggest that to write about "nothing" demands handing the story over to readers so that they may supply a *something* that may be known. Drawing her reader into the presentness of trauma contained in this scene, Morrison prompts her reader to fill in the truth of slavery's violence to which Sethe indirectly refers, reminding us of the rightful simplicity of "no" as an answer to what was once the absurdly complex and troubled debate of slavery. Thus, Morrison offers her reader the position of someone who doesn't "have to ask", who "gets it right off", who *knows.* A "truth that is not otherwise available" emerges within this space of irony: the belated address of Sethe's trauma and the impossibility to which it testifies makes itself known within the text's capacity to allow the desperate and *mad* alternative of infanticide to resonate with the reader.

The competing impulses of the archive—the violence of forgetting and desire to know—emerge most readily when Sethe attempts to relay "the Misery" in a story. Significantly, as Sethe attempts to tell her story in the previous scene, she begins by reminiscing to Paul D about mothering Beloved. Recalling Beloved's memorable ability to crawl as a very young infant, she says:

> One week, or less, and the baby who was sitting up and turning over when I put her on the wagon was crawling already [...] when I got here, she was

> crawling already. No stopping her either. She loved those [stair] steps so much we painted them so she could see her way to the top.[52]

Sethe's recollection of this particular memory of Beloved is striking because of its emphasis on embodied movement—movement that Sethe mimics in the scene's present moment as she "circles," "wheels," "spins," and goes "round and round."[53] There is dynamism to the scene that runs counter to the archive's effort at consigning meaning or, to use Sethe's phrase, "pinning it down": there is "no stopping" the story, just as there is "no stopping" Beloved in her rambunctious crawling, or her haunting for that matter. The scene, like Beloved the ghost, is caught in flux, in the space of a repressed madness that longs to testify to the impossibility of enslaved mothering.

Following the logic of the archive, a violence emerges in Paul D's rejection of not "what Sethe had done" but rather "what she claimed."[54] Paul D seeks explanation where it cannot be found—in a "long-drawn-out record" of what was "done" that tells "nothing" of the maddening conditions that provoked Sethe's unspeakable act. Sethe's "claim" is to a "love" for her children that Paul D dismisses as "too thick."[55] In one of the novel's most famous lines, Sethe counters: "'Love is or it ain't. Thin love ain't love at all.'"[56] In due time, Paul D reconciles Sethe's past in his own love for her that draws him back to 124 at the novel's close; in this moment, he is unable to recognize what Henderson describes as Sethe's "counter-narrative that reconstitutes her humanity and demonstrates the requirements of mother-love."[57] Sethe's fierce "mother-love" is dynamic, embodied, and intuitive—like the narrative movement that animates her story that you either "get right off" or don't.

In contrast to the difficulty Sethe finds in storytelling with Paul D, she experiences a new found delight when talking of the past to Beloved. These exchanges between mother and daughter allow Sethe to claim agency over her past by tracing out slavery's history of erasure in the embodied presence of her storytelling. In Henderson's reading, Sethe is particularly empowered when "privileging specifically female tropes [...] within the context of intergenerational black women's experiences as represented in memory and in narrative."[58] Such is the case when—referring to a pair of earrings that were once given to Sethe years ago by her slave mistress, Mrs. Garner—Beloved asks Sethe to "tell me your diamonds:"

> It became a way to feed her [...] Sethe learned the profound satisfaction Beloved got from storytelling. It amazed Sethe (as much as it pleased

> Beloved) because every mention of her past life hurt. Everything in it was painful or lost. She and Baby Suggs had agreed without saying so that it was *unspeakable* [...] But as she began telling about the earrings, she found herself wanting to, liking it. Perhaps it was Beloved's distance from the events itself, or her thirst for hearing it—in any case it was an unexpected pleasure (emphasis mine).[59]

Significantly, this story about a lost pair of earrings unfolds in a piecemeal fashion during intimate moments of domesticity and maternal care between Sethe, Beloved, and Denver. Eventually, the story leads back to Sethe's recollection of her own mother, whom she barely remembers, as well as to her memory of a one-armed woman named Nan who cared for her as a young child. To herself, Sethe recalls a story told to her by Nan, long ago, about how she inherited her name from her father:

> She threw them all away but you. The one from the crew she threw away on the island. The others from more whites she threw. Without names, she threw them away. You she gave the name of the black man. She put her arms around him. The others she did not put her arms around. Never. Never. Telling you. I am telling you, small girl Sethe.[60]

Contained within Nan's disturbing tale, Ashraf H.A. Rushdy suggests, is "Morrison's most powerful introjection into the Margaret Garner story—the establishing of a context for Sethe's act. Sethe's own mother kills all the children fathered by whites who raped her."[61] Rushdy importantly draws our attention to the transgenerational impact of sexual violence present in Nan's tale. Yet here I wish to highlight the more nuanced ways the passage testifies to trauma in its complex construction of a relationship between mother-love, naming, and (dis)embodiment—a relationship that ultimately returns us to the question of the archive and its "promise of futurity."

Nan's story is a type of interior *mise-en-scène*—or a story within a story—that plays in the background of Sethe's mind as she speaks of her own mother to Denver and Beloved. The past moment of Nan's storytelling to the child-Sethe foreshadows the narrative's present moment in which Sethe, now as maternal figure, takes on the role of storyteller. Here, storytelling becomes aligned with mother-love—it is a manifestation of care and affection that Sethe recalls in her remembrance of "Nan holding her with her one good arm, waving the stump of the other in the air."[62] The image of Nan's arms—the "good arm" and "the stump"—creates a visual imperative in the scene highlighting Nan's storytelling as an embodied act, but one that is curiously paired with the disabled arm. The arresting image of Nan's arms is then uncannily superimposed upon the reference to Sethe's mother's arms: "She put her arms around him. The other she did not put her arms around." In the scene's present moment, the image of the arm repeats itself as Sethe and her daughters fold laundry: "Sethe walked over to a chair, lifted a sheet and stretched it as wide as her arms would go."[63] The repeating arm acts as an archival trace in the scene that links together the mother-figures and connects the act of storytelling to embodied life and the materiality of history. For the women of Sethe's past, their arms and their actions stand in for the unspeakable trauma that haunts their stories: Nan's mutilated arm waves furiously as she speaks of Sethe's mother—who refused to put her arms around the white men who raped her. The "stump" of Nan's arm signifies a story partly told as the sexual violence contained in it is not named but only implied. Yet at the same time, Nan's disfigured arm seems to reach out into the future through its motion that is mirrored in the insistence of her words: "Telling you. I am telling you, small girl Sethe." She pleads with Sethe to recognize what she is *telling* her so that the message contained in the story's unspeakableness might be heard and carried on in Sethe. What Nan is *telling* Sethe is that her name—and in turn, she herself—bears the trace of her mother's radical acts of resistance: her ability to love—"to put her arms around" Sethe's father—in the midst of unspeakable trauma and her choice to murder her children that were conceived because she was repeatedly raped by white men. In the moment of the current scene, the heaviness of this trace stops Sethe in her action: "Holding the damp sheets against her chest, she was picking meaning out of a code she no longer understood."[64]

Nan's story and its message left a young Sethe "unimpressed," but "as grown-up woman Sethe she was angry, but not certain at what."[65] Here, Sethe's anger is arresting: it halts her folding of laundry and her storytelling; she grows silent and still in the midst of Beloved and Denver as she thinks back to Nan. The trace of her name and that of her inherited trauma seems too much to bear. She is stalled in the maddening conditions of her mother's life as a slave, ones which so closely resemble the maddening conditions that give way to her own trauma. In the same manner that Sethe's act of infanticide is not simply emblematic of the agency of mothering but rather the impossibility of claiming such agency within the context of slavery, her own mother's actions are disturbingly irreconcilable. It is Sethe who is given a name that consigns this history; she carries its legacy in her life. Even while the scene's storytelling comes to an abrupt end, its message of resiliency is performed in Sethe's action: she "lifted a sheet and stretched it as wide as her arms would go." Sethe's "sheet" alludes to the *blank page* of slavery's historical record; with her arms, Sethe "stretches" this blankness to her embodied capacity. The "unexpected pleasure" of storytelling that Sethe finds at the beginning of this chapter ends with her "holding [...] the sheets against her chest" in what can be read as hesitancy but also as a symbolic gesture of taking ownership over her personal history as she holds this story as her own. Here, Sethe directs her attention inward, to herself, in the recollection of Nan's tale: it is the pivotal moment in the novel in which she can return to "the message—that was and had been there all along."[66]

Importantly, this scene foreshadows the event of Beloved's murder, which chronologically precedes this moment but has yet to be rendered in the narrative. When we encounter the image of Sethe's arms holding something against her chest again, it is her dead daughter: "...blood-soaked child to her chest with one hand and an infant by the heels in the other."[67] As readers, we are aware of a future in which Sethe will rewrite this traumatic scene in the embodied presence of Beloved and Denver. In the future, the traumatic legacy of Sethe's foremothers, which befalls her as well, is "a code that she no longer underst[ands]." In his analysis of *Beloved*, Roger Luckhurst argues that "a haunting does not initiate a story; it is the sign of a *blockage* of a story, a hurt that has not been honored by a memorializing narrative.[68] The geography of *Beloved*, [Luckhurst continues] is punctured by traumas that have not been bound into a story."[69] While a haunting may signify a "blockage of a story," the materialization of Beloved does, in fact, initiate storytelling for Sethe. It is Beloved's active asking about her mother's history—an asking that is enabled by way of the madness that is contained in Beloved's material presence in the narrative—that prompts Sethe to reshape her understanding of the past and reimagine a "code" of mothering that could include it. In turn, Morrison depicts mother and daughter(s) working together, in tandem, to retrace their maternal lineage and give voice to the unspeakable traumas that haunt their transgenerational history. Thus, while the "blockage" of Sethe's trauma thwarts her storytelling with Paul D, Sethe is moved to a verbal expression with Beloved and Denver, that encourages interior access to past pain: to "[remember] something she had forgotten she knew."[70] Recounting the past becomes a way for Sethe to move through her trauma; she begins to embody a past life marked by loss through a dynamic dialogue now marked by survival.

In her study of haunting as an epistemology, Avery Gordon emphasizes the affective quality of haunting as its distinctive characteristic: "Being haunted draws us affectively, sometimes against our will and always a bit magically, into a structure of feeling of a reality we come to experience, not as cold knowledge, but as transformative recognition."[71] Building upon Raymond Williams's concept of "structures of feeling," Gordon highlights the dynamic quality of haunting as a constitutive element of "transformative recognition." Haunting is a movement both towards and away from "cold knowledge"; in a haunting paradigm, knowing happens within the extension and return of the self to embodied life. The knowing, or "recognition," that happens in haunting feels a bit like "magic," outside the realm of logic. For Morrison, "magic" presents itself in the uncovering of what is already known to you; this return to one's existing knowledge is nothing short of "miraculous." As she writes in *Beloved*: "No gasp at a miracle that is truly miraculous because the magic lies in the fact that you knew it was there for you all along."[72] Morrison conflates "magic" with "fact" by turning the general understanding of a "miracle," as something spontaneously granted to one by an outside force, on its head. In *Beloved*, miracles happen by coming closer to one's self; the "magic" unfolds in finding out what one already knows. Thus, Sethe's "remembering something she had forgotten she knew" sets the stage for the miraculous. For the true miracle of the novel is not simply Beloved's return from the dead but also Sethe's return to life.

The intuitive knowing that Morrison emphasizes in her aesthetics of haunting juxtaposes the material archive's systematic consignation of information that relies upon concealment as a mode of erasure. In Caruth's theorization of Derrida, such concealment is instrumental to the functioning of the "*archives du mal*—archives of evil (or suffering)—because they not only leave an impression but hide their impression."[73] Caruth further explains:

> [*Archives du mal*] involve evil or suffering, that is, precisely because they hide or prohibit their own memory: because they are themselves [as according to Derrida] "hidden or destroyed, prohibited, diverted,

repressed." They consist precisely in hiding themselves; they become events insofar as they are, precisely, hidden.[74]

Morrison's aim to "write a story about the *feeling* of Self" directly challenges the epistemology of *archives du mal*. The task of accessing the "feeling of Self" is in opposition to an archive that refuses to name that which it seeks to tell; this task involves, instead, a radical stripping away of what is "hidden or destroyed, prohibited, diverted, repressed." Morrison's ultimate refusal to name the unspeakable in the novel's final meditation on Beloved's diffusion into "separate parts" distinguishes itself from the archive's repression because her aesthetics have directed the reader back to the *feelings* of such unspeakability throughout the novel.[75] Morrison's text thus involves a movement towards a "simple" truth of coming closer to one's self in order to understand the double meaning in Sethe's repeated *no/know*.

The repression of memory is an integral element of Beloved's return as a ghost made flesh. She becomes a living imperative to eradicate the *archive du mal* of enslaved mothering as it is encapsulated in Margaret Garner's story. Her return illuminates the psychic madness—both inevitable and impossible—contained within the disavowal of black female subjectivity. Her return necessarily fails in the novel in order to reveal the complexity of a traumatic past that can only be "circled" around and never "pinned down." The reaching for a "single corpus" that demands the erasure of competing narratives perpetuates history's inscription of madness. To step outside of history's violent consignation, both Morrison and Derrida suggest that we entertain the "truth" of delusion—the truth that is found in being drawn affectively to the experience of haunting. For Derrida, "a truth of insanity or of hauntedness" is uncovered when we recognize the contained within *archive fever*:

> Freud recognizes [...] there is a truth of delusion, a truth of insanity or of hauntedness
>
> [...] this truth is repressed or suppressed. But it resists and *returns* [...] It *returns*, it belongs, it comes down to spectral truth. Delusion or insanity, hauntedness is not only haunted by this or that ghost [...] but by the specter of the truth which has been repressed. The truth is spectral, and this is its part of truth which is irreducible by explanation.[76]

To bear witness to such "spectral truth" is the task that *Beloved* poses to its readers. It asks us to read Beloved as "real" ghost. We must proceed, perhaps even against our wills, toward a "formidable and pathless [...] terrain," "into [a] repellant landscape" that requires the abandoning of a historical discourse shaped by the white patriarchical forces behind the institution of slavery: from such discourse's signposts, Morrison recognizes, one cannot reach the desired destination.[77] Reaching, like the arms extending through Sethe's maternal lineage, is the state that Morrison leaves us in. The blank sheet beckons, ushering in new possibilities in the transformative witnessing of a "truth which is irreducible by explanation."

Beloved's embodiment is representative of a seeking at the heart of the *archives du mal*—of stories that cannot be retold or passed up. Because the past can only be reexperienced as the present, Beloved's return from the dead, in its attempt to defy an impossibility, cannot be reconciled. It is this struggle of reconciliation with a ghost that paradoxically gives way to Sethe's own return to her "feeling of Self," a self-witnessing that is not only of the past but also of the present—of her embodied survival and the latent possibility that survival affords. Asking, "'Me? Me?,'" Sethe's gaze shifts from the past to a present in which slavery's effacement of her own life is transformed within the affirmation of our reading.

Notes

1. Toni Morrison, *Beloved* (New York: Vintage International, 2004), 235 (emphasis mine).
2. Jacques Derrida, *Archive Fever: A Freudian Impression* (Chicago: University of Chicago Press, 1996), 324.
3. Avery Gordon, *Ghostly Matters: Haunting and the Sociological Imagination* (Minneapolis: University of Minnesota Press, 1997), xvi.
4. Derrida, *Archive Fever*, 324.
5. Ibid.
6. Kevin Everod Quashie, *Black Women, Identity, and Cultural Theory: (un) becoming the Subject* (New Brunswick, NJ: Rutgers University Press, 2004), 102.
7. Morrison, *Beloved*, xvii.
8. Ibid., xix (emphasis mine).
9. Quashie, *Black Women*, 66.
10. Ibid.

11. Ibid., 67.
12. Kimberly Juanita Brown, *The Repeating Body: Slavery's Visual Resonance in The Contemporary* (Durham, NC, and London: Duke University Press, 2015), 6.
13. Ibid., 6.
14. Evelyn Jaffe Schreiber, *Race, Trauma, and Home in the Novels of Toni Morrison* (Baton Rouge, LA: Louisiana State University Press, 2010), 2.
15. Emma Parker, "A New Hystery: History and Hysteria in Toni Morrison's *Beloved*," *Twentieth Century Literature* 47.1 (2001): 1.
16. Cynthia Dobbs, "Toni Morrison's Beloved: Bodies Returned, Modernism Revisited," *African American Review* 32.4 (1998): 577.
17. Jean Wyatt, "Giving Body to the Word: The Maternal Symbolic in Toni Morrison's *Beloved*," *PMLA* 108.3 (1993): 474.
18. Morrison, *Beloved*, xvii.
19. Ibid. Concerning the research for her book *Mothering across Cultures: Postcolonial Representations*, Angelita Reyes writes of the complications of performing archival research on Margaret Garner: "Obviously, nineteenth-century women like Garner did not and could not leave any nicely written narratives or legal briefs about the remarkable events in their lives. Because they were illiterate many of them could not write their own stories into history. Would they have wanted to? Would they have thought of leaving evidence for us, their historical descendants? In slavery, survival and resistance often depended on covering up evidence. Deliberate amnesia was a survival tactic. The people may have needed secrecy in order to gain a measure of stability in their unstable world. Many of their secrets will never be known." *Mothering across Cultures: Postcolonial Representations* (Minneapolis: University of Minnesota Press, 2002), 22. Reyes's claim that for some enslaved persons "deliberate amnesia was a survival tactic" gestures toward a radicalization of Derrida's theory by making its application literal. For enslaved women, Reyes suggests that forgetting was a conscious decision to exercise control over one's memory: within the institutionalized subjection of slavery in which slave owners violently robbed slaves of their bodily freedom, control over one's memory became a platform for resistance.
20. Ibid.
21. Ibid.
22. Morrison reflects upon what drew her to Garner's story in the novel's Foreword: "I think now it was the shock of liberation that drew my thoughts to what 'free' could possibly mean to women […] These thoughts led me to the different history of black women in this country—a history in which marriage was discouraged, impossible, or illegal; in which birthing children was 'required,' but 'having' them, being

responsible for them—being, in other words, their parent—was as out of the question as freedom. Assertions of parenthood under conditions peculiar to the logic of institutional enslavement were criminal." *Beloved*, xvii.

23. Nellie Y. McKay, "Introduction," *Toni Morrison's Beloved: A Case Book*. Ed. William L. Andrews and Nellie Y. McKay (New York: Oxford University, 1999), 3.
24. Nellie Y. McKay, "An Interview with Toni Morrison," *Contemporary Literature*. 24.1 (1983): 426.
25. Paul Gilroy, *The Black Atlantic: Modernity and Double Consciousness* (Cambridge, MA: Harvard University Press, 1993), 74.
26. Ibid., 73.
27. Ibid., 75.
28. Ibid., 76.
29. Indeed, Derrida's concept of *archive fever* in its allusion to bodily sickness suggests a return to the body as a mode of knowing and a site of remembrance.
30. Morrison, *Beloved*, xix.
31. *Feelings* within the context of the black diaspora is a vexed concept as Saidiya Hartman suggests in her book *Scenes of Subjection*. Here, Hartman examines the contentious ground of *shared feelings* in the writings of John Rankin, the abolitionist: "So intent and determined is Rankin to establish that slaves possess the same nature of and feelings as himself, and thereby establish the common humanity of all men on the basis of extended suffering, that he literally narrates an imagined scenario in which he, along with his wife and child, is enslaved [...] By believing himself to be and by phantasmically becoming the enslaved, he creates the scenario for shared feelings." *Lose Your Mother: A Journey along the Atlantic Slave Route* (New York: Farrar, Straus and Giroux, 2007), 17.
32. Ann Cvetkovich, *An Archive of Feelings: Trauma, Sexuality, and Lesbian Public Cultures* (Durham, NC: Duke University Press, 2003), 241.
33. Ibid., 242.
34. Derrida, *Archive Fever*, 36.
35. Ibid., 3.
36. Morrison, *Beloved*, 323 (emphasis mine).
37. Ibid., 319.
38. Ibid., 321.
39. Ibid., 322.
40. In *Lost Bodies: Inhabiting the Borders of Life and Death*, Laura Tanner argues that the critical work on mourning and death in modernity has marginalized the embodied experience of loss. For Tanner, the

displacement of the body in the process of grief speaks to the modern privileging of the mind over the body. She insists that grief be considered in terms which "reinstitute the pressure of materiality on a dialogue shaped by linguistic and cultural forms that privilege the subject over the object." *Lost Bodies: Inhabiting the Borders of Life and Death* (Ithaca, NY: Cornell University Press, 2006), 7. I would argue that Morrison's emphasis on embodiment in the work of mourning participates in a "reinstitut[ion] [...] of materiality." Moreover, I would suggest that what Tanner marks as a modern phenomenon has its origins in slavery's systemic robbing of bodily life, which displaced the subject as an object.

41. Wyatt, "Giving Body," 484.
42. Morrison, *Beloved*, 322.
43. Wyatt, "Giving Body," 484.
44. Reyes, Angelita Dianne. *Mothering across Cultures: Postcolonial Representations.* Minneapolis: University of Minnesota, 2002., 76.
45. Morrison, *Beloved*, xix.
46. The impasse that paradoxically drives Sethe to uncover what she intuitively knows operates as an aporia much like the archival drive itself. In *Aporias*, Derrida establishes death as the original aporia or irresolvable conundrum. Since death cannot possibly be experienced in life, it represents what he describes "as the difficult or the impracticable, here the impossible passage, the refused, denied passage, indeed nonpassage, which can in fact be something else, the event of a coming or of a future advent [...] which no longer has the form of the movement that consists in passing, traversing, or transiting." *Aporias* (Stanford, CA: Stanford University Press, 1993), 8. Death represents the most essential aporia because it beckons a person to consider the opposite of that which is most fundamental: embodied human existence. It not does proffer a problem to be solved but instead presents an irremediable dilemma or "nonpassage." Yet what is uncanny about this aporia is that its impossibility simultaneously contains the potential for a transformative "something else."
47. Morrison, *Beloved*, 189.
48. Ibid., 192.
49. Ibid.
50. Cathy Caruth, *Unclaimed Experience: Trauma, Narrative, and History* (Baltimore, MD: Johns Hopkins University Press, 1996), 4.
51. Saidiya V. Hartman, *Lose Your Mother: A Journey along the Atlantic Slave Route* (New York: Farrar, Straus and Giroux, 2007), 16. In her book, Hartman analyzes the complex relationship between loss and survival in the African diaspora and the archives of erasure that shape its historical record. The saying "lose your mother" refers to the literal loss of an enslaved

person's mother during the Middle Passage and the subsequent loss of collective history and personal past that enslavement makes inevitable.
52. Morrison, *Beloved*, 188.
53. Ibid., 187–189.
54. Ibid., 193.
55. Ibid., 192.
56. Ibid., 194.
57. Mae G. Henderson, "Toni Morrison's *Beloved*, Remembering the Body as Historical Text," in *Toni Morrison's Beloved: A Case Book*, ed. William L. Andrews and Nellie Y. McKay (New York: Oxford University Press, 1999), 98.
58. Ibid.
59. Morrison, *Beloved*, 69 (emphasis mine).
60. Ibid., 74.
61. Ashraf H. A Rushdy, "Daughters Signifyin(g) History: The Example of Toni Morrison's *Beloved*," in *Toni Morrison's Beloved: A Case Book*, ed. William L. Andrews and Nellie Y. McKay (New York: Oxford University Press, 1999), 47.
62. Morrison, *Beloved*, 74.
63. Ibid., 73.
64. Ibid., 74.
65. Ibid.
66. Ibid.
67. Ibid., 175.
68. Roger Luckhurst, *The Trauma Question* (London: Routledge, 2008), 93.
69. Ibid., 93.
70. Morrison, *Beloved*, 73.
71. Gordon, *Ghostly Matters*, 8.
72. Morrison, *Beloved*, 208.
73. Cathy Caruth, *Literature in the Ashes of History* (Baltimore, MD: John Hopkins University Press, 2013), 76. In Caruth's theorization of Derrida, she follows in his footsteps by focusing on the archive as a manifestation of contemporary disasters. She states (and in part quotes Derrida): "The question of the archive is a question of today—of a particular historical period, a question with its own historical place—because it is linked, today, to the 'disasters that mark the end of a millennium'" (76). Moreover, Caruth suggests that concerns of the archive arise with the emergence of a psychoanalytic theory of trauma following World War I. As is implicit in the essay's argument, "the question of the Archive" is particularly relevant to traumatic histories preceding the twentieth- and twenty-first centuries, i.e., slavery. As Paul Gilroy and Hortense Spillers have argued, psychoanalytically minded theories of trauma have, overall,

been negligent in addressing slavery's history of subjection. For a detailed analysis of recovering psychoanalysis with race matters in mind, see Hortense J. Spillers, "'All the Things You Could Be by Now If Sigmund Freud's Wife Was Your Mother': Psychoanalysis and Race," *Critical Inquiry* 22.4 (1996): 710–34.

74. Caruth, *Ashes of History*, 76.
75. Morrison, *Beloved*, 323.
76. Derrida, *Archive Fever*, 87.
77. Morrison, *Beloved*, xii.

References

Brown, Kimberly Juanita. *The Repeating Body: Slavery's Visual Resonance in The Contemporary*. Durham and London: Duke University Press, 2015.

Caruth, Cathy. *Literature in the Ashes of History*. Baltimore: John Hopkins University Press, 2013.

———. *Unclaimed Experience: Trauma, Narrative, and History*. Baltimore: Johns Hopkins University Press, 1996.

Cvetkovich, Ann. *An Archive of Feelings: Trauma, Sexuality, and Lesbian Public Cultures*. Durham: Duke University Press, 2003.

Derrida, Jacques. *Aporias*. Stanford, CA: Stanford UP, 1993.

———. *Archive Fever: A Freudian Impression*. Chicago: University of Chicago, 1996.

Dobbs, Cynthia. "Toni Morrison's Beloved: Bodies Returned, Modernism Revisited." *African American Review* 32.4 (1998): 563–78.

Gilroy, Paul. *The Black Atlantic: Modernity and Double Consciousness*. Cambridge, MA: Harvard University Press, 1993.

Gordon, Avery. *Ghostly Matters: Haunting and the Sociological Imagination*. Minneapolis: University of Minnesota Press, 1997.

Hartman, Saidiya V. *Lose Your Mother: A Journey along the Atlantic Slave Route*. New York: Farrar, Straus and Giroux, 2007.

Henderson, Mae G. "Toni Morrison's *Beloved*, Remembering the Body as Historical Text." In Toni *Morrison's Beloved: A Case Book*, edited by William L. Andrews and Nellie Y. McKay, 79–106. New York: Oxford, 1999.

Luckhurst, Roger. *The Trauma Question*. London: Routledge, 2008.

McKay, Nelli Y. *Contemporary Literature*, 24.4 (Winter, 1983), 413–429.

———. "Introduction." In *Toni Morrison's Beloved: A Case Book*, edited by William L. Andrews and Nellie Y. McKay, 3–20. New York: Oxford, 1999.

Morrison, Toni. *Beloved*. New York: Vintage International, 2004.

Parker, Emma. "A New Hystery: History and Hysteria in Toni Morrison's *Beloved*." *Twentieth Century Literature* 47.1 (2001): 1–19.

Reyes, Angelita Dianne. *Mothering across Cultures: Postcolonial Representations.* Minneapolis: University of Minnesota Press, 2002.

Rushdy, Ashraf H. A. "Daughters Signifyin(g) History: The Example of Toni Morrison's *Beloved.*" In *Toni Morrison's Beloved: A Case Book*, edited by William L. Andrews and Nellie Y. McKay, 37–66. New York: Oxford University Press, 1999.

Quashie, Kevin Everod. *Black Women, Identity, and Cultural Theory: (un)becoming the Subject.* New Brunswick: Rutgers University Press, 2004.

Schreiber, Evelyn Jaffe. *Race, Trauma, and Home in the Novels of Toni Morrison.* Baton Rouge: Louisiana State University Press, 2010.

Spillers, Hortense J. "'All the Things You Could Be by Now If Sigmund Freud's Wife Was Your Mother': Psychoanalysis and Race." *Critical Inquiry* 22.4 (1996): 710–34.

Tanner, Laura. *Lost Bodies: Inhabiting the Borders of Life and Death.* Ithaca, NY: Cornell University Press, 2006.

Wyatt, Jean. "Giving Body to the Word: The Maternal Symbolic in Toni Morrison's *Beloved.*" *PMLA* 108.3 (1993): 474–88.

PART II

The Contradictions of Witnessing in Conflict Zones: Trauma and Testimony

Fissured Memory and Mad Tongues: The Aesthetics of *Marronnage* in Haitian Women's Fiction

Johanna X.K. Garvey

I

The African Diaspora begins in a kind of madness, as Édouard Glissant reminds us: "Off the coast of Senegal, Gorée, the island before the open sea, the first step towards madness."[1] What does it mean to inhabit the disaster areas, to live in and as the *crises* of madness, silent yet mutely screaming to be recognized and heard?[2] For those who inherited the insanity and who are haunted by the fragmented memories of the barracoons, the slave castle, the ships, and the passage, history is fissured, and resistance entails constructing new genealogies. At the center of the disaster area of the Diaspora lies the island known variously as Quisqueya, Saint-Domingue, Hispaniola, its western third the country of Haiti since independence in 1804. The first and only successful revolution of the enslaved in the Western hemisphere created a Black nation in the heart of the colonized world, an oxymoron, a site of freedom that has been violently resisted by much of the Atlantic world from the Revolution to the present day. If the "Western" mind encountering the "New World" saw insanity in its other—the indigenous peoples, the enslaved Africans and

J.X.K. Garvey (✉)
Fairfield University, Fairfield, CT, USA

C.A. Brown and J.X.K. Garvey (eds.), *Madness in Black Women's Diasporic Fictions*, Gender and Cultural Studies in Africa and the Diaspora, DOI 10.1007/978-3-319-58127-9_5

their descendants—that ideology further solidified when the colonized site revolted and denied imperial powers the right to own, to name, to control, to enslave, claiming the plantation as its own and attempting to eject or erase the colonizers. Concomitantly, however, the seduction of power, the poison of the inherited binaries, perpetuated the dichotomies and left women in Haiti silenced and oppressed, condemned to a version of internment and insanity.[3]

This essay explores manifestations of madness, resistance, and healing in the face of trauma experienced by Haitian women in texts by two contemporary authors, one writing from within Haiti and one from the *dyaspora*. The discussion centers on Evelyne Trouillot's novel *Rosalie L'Infâme* (2003), a fictional evocation of maroons and the enslaved in Haiti leading up to the Revolution, and Roxane Gay's recent novel *An Untamed State* (2014), which recounts the kidnapping, rape, and abuse suffered by a Haitian American woman in contemporary Port-au-Prince. Each text suggests how to stitch the torn fabric of Haitian history, both individual and collective, revisiting horrific acts in a process of testifying and witnessing. Drawing upon the figure of the maroon, I argue that the female protagonists perform a contemporary *marronnage*, writing from the space created by rupture and *déchirure*, a refuge that affords each of them the opportunity to remember, redact, and reflect, as they tell their stories of madness and violence in what one critic has termed a "rape culture of silence."[4] These narratives employ what I term "mad marooning" as an aesthetics to subvert a political order that oppresses and abuses the disempowered, from the violations of enslavement to the post-Duvalier era, striking at those sources of pain and fragmentation as if setting fire to modern incarnations of the plantation, igniting a blaze that might purify, cleanse, and heal shattered female psyches.[5]

If, as Tonya Haynes posits, Sylvia Wynter's thought offers the "possibility to effect an epistemic shift" in Caribbean feminist theorizing, Haiti provides "demonic grounds" on which to test those theories.[6] The two texts at hand, one set in the 1750s, one in the twenty-first century, span the country's history from pre-Revolution decades to the present post-Duvalier era. While Haynes focuses on Caribbean feminist approaches, I would expand that application of Wynter to the African Diaspora, Haiti occupying a central place in that geography. Haynes offers a succinct explication of a core component of Wynter's analysis of "race" and "gender":

> For Wynter, there is no liberation in Woman's access to the world of bourgeois Man (the public sphere of the world of work under capitalism), as it does nothing to challenge the inequities which constitute that world. Wynter is not denying gendered power relations; she is essentially arguing that 'gender' is part and parcel of Western bio-logic which naturalized both the human/savage binary and the male/female binary. Challenges to gendered power relations must be made from a vantage point outside of the episteme, not from within it.[7]

To those two sets of binaries, I would add those of "rational/irrational" and "sanity/madness," as does Wynter in several of her landmark essays.[8] Thus, the concept of "mad marooning" serves as that site outside of the Western episteme that solidified during the era of the Atlantic slave trade and the plantation system in the Americas. That is not to say that Black women's experiences and identities are in/valid or insignificant; instead, they provide the demonic ground on which to resist and potentially undermine the "world of Man."[9] Haynes asks a key question: "[…] the Westocentric framing of Caribbean feminisms silences the demonic ground from which the Caribbean subaltern could disrupt the episteme. What are the productive possibilities of the Caribbean's location in the West, yet at its margins?"[10] For the purposes of this discussion, I suggest replacing "Caribbean" with "Haiti" specifically, to apply Wynter's theories to "mad marooning" as an aesthetics that might model resistance for the African Diaspora.[11]

A discussion of madness and Haitian women finds one source of grounding in Dédée Bazile or Défilée-la-folle, one of the scarce female figures in accounts of the Revolution and the early years of the Republic. Credited with gathering the scattered remains of Dessalines's massacred body, in October of 1806, placing them in a sack, and then burying them in Trousse-Côtés Cemetery in Port-au-Prince, Défilée is both a ghost in the archive and a powerful, mythic figure in Haitian culture. As Jana Evans Braziel explains, Défilée has been appropriated at various historical moments to serve purposes both political and cultural, while the actual woman behind the myth has largely been ignored, lost to silences not only around the Revolution itself, but those surrounding Haitian women throughout the past two centuries.[12] But if we look more carefully, Défilée-la-folle stands at the core of the African Diaspora, a madwoman who picks up the bloody pieces of a hero of the Revolution whose body has been ripped apart by his former comrades and allies: Haiti, torn to shreds, fragmented, not knowing what its blackness means outside of a binary system imbibed like a poison from "the West," though the country lies west-of-the-West, ahead of or beyond the Western ideologies, at the heart of a new space, potentially in a position to create new geographies. Yet it sinks again and again under the weight of inherited, adopted, internalized dichotomies that make it other, insane, irrational, savage, unlawful, poor, or to use Sylvia Wynter's term "dys-selected."[13]

Défilée provides the connection to the mad tongues creating an aesthetics of resistance in contemporary fiction by Haitian women, such as those in Trouillot's novel who pass on their stories of capture, the Middle Passage, enslavement, and repeated rape, those who further defy the plantation system by refusing to bear babies resulting from rape, and those who turn to more blatant *marronnage*, all in response to the insanity of the system itself, its violence, its destruction, its abuses.[14] The twentieth century brings US invasion and occupation, political upheaval, unending violence, and the rape, torture, and silencing of women who find their voices in madness and speak from the cracks, the *crises/*creases of history, the ongoing trauma, those who are the other side of insanity, the sane madwomen seeking their voices and demanding witnesses. Thus the works of Marie Chauvet, Jan. J. Dominique, Myriam A.J. Chancy, Marie-Célie Agnant, Marie-Andrée Manuel Étienne, and more. In the present moment, we arrive at Roxane Gay, whose novel shocks in its violence and directness, its vivid detailing of a terrorizing captivity that elucidates the contemporary creases in the fabric, the rents and tears that include a father's acquiescence in the rape and abuse of his daughter due to his misguided belief in his own masculine power. That young woman must be her own Défilée at first, leading her own attack and rescue, and then as a contemporary maroon receive witnessing and healing from her (white American) mother-in-law. Their bond may create a new geography, that called for by theorists like Sylvia Wynter, M. NourbeSe Philip, and Katherine McKittrick.[15]

The history of Haiti, indeed the history of the Atlantic world, is one of repeated wounding—the meaning of the Greek word *trauma*. The "crisis of today's Haiti," evidenced in the boat people, for instance, is that of the Caribbean, Wynter argues, which is "the crisis, too, of our present order of knowledge."[16] She continues: "The post-1492 Caribbean, the world system of which its islands were to be the founding units, and the era of modernity, were all three brought into existence by the same dynamic process of cultural discontinuity, and therefore of historical rupture."[17] Such an understanding of Haitian history correlates with theories of trauma and madness, specifically those advanced by Davoine and Gaudillière. They describe madness as "'a research into uninscribed histories'"; "'sometimes a fit of madness tells us more than all the news dispatches about the left-over facts that have no right to existence.'"[18] As Davoine states in an interview with Cathy Caruth, "Madness is always a fight against denial, double language, manipulation, and falsification." She further explains that "when it's madness, the track of the trauma is lost. You have a witness of what you don't know."[19] We can apply this concept of madness to the experiences of Haitian women as illustrated in texts such as Trouillot's excavation of pre-revolutionary trauma, Chauvet's fictionalized depictions of the Duvalier dictatorship, Dominique's memoirs and novel of that same era, and Gay's narrative of extensive trauma in contemporary Port-au-Prince.

Throughout this body of literature, as in the country's history, trauma returns and repeats itself, a legacy of the colonial period. As Gabriele Schwab elucidates, "[C]ollective trauma is passed down [...]. Trauma as a mode of being violently halts the flow of time, fractures the self, and punctures memory and language."[20] We return again to the fissured memory and mad tongues of my title. Referencing the concept of "cryptonymy," developed by Nicolas Abraham and Maria Torok, Schwab explains that the "crypt is a melancholic, funereal architectonic in inner space, built after traumatic loss."[21] Most importantly for a discussion of Haiti, the crypt can be *national* as well as individual or familial: "While the secret is intrapsychic and indicates an internal psychic splitting, it can be collectively deployed and shared by a people or a nation. The collective or communal silencing of violent histories leads to a transgenerational transmission of trauma and the specter of an involuntary repetition of cycles of violence."[22] We witness such a passing on of trauma (like that in Morrison's *Beloved*) in the violence experienced by Haitian women, in the culture of rape and silence, and in the more generalized terror from the colonial period to the aftermath of Duvalierism. As Schwab states (though not specifically in the context of Haiti), "Silencing these violent and shameful histories casts them outside the continuity of psychic life but, unintegrated and unassimilated, they eat away at this continuity from within. [...] the buried ghosts of the past come to haunt language from within, always threatening to destroy its communicative and expressive function."[23] With Chauvet, that madness finds voice, and Haitian women writers following in her steps have continued to break the silence surrounding "violent and shameful histories." Thus, Jan J. Dominique's fictional *Memoir d'une amnésique* documents both the US occupation of Haiti and the Duvalier dictatorship, and her *Mémoire errante* follows her return to writing in the wake of the assassination of her father, Jean Dominique, voice of Radio Haiti. Marie-Célie Agnant writes from Montreal, both nonfiction and novels such as *Le Livre d'Emma*, which reconstructs the life and lineage of a Haitian woman confined to a mental hospital for allegedly murdering her baby daughter. Myriam Chancy writes both scholarly studies and fiction set in Haiti and the *Dyaspora*, for instance *The Scorpion's Claw*, which takes place in Haiti under the Duvaliers. And the list has grown longer in the last decade and a half.

Among contemporary writers addressing Black women in the Diaspora, Myriam Chancy was the first to produce a scholarly volume focused solely on women writers from Haiti. In an article on state terror in Haiti, she writes: "To work on revealing facets of Haitian women's lives, then, is to be confronted, almost immediately, with a thick wall of silence. Silence typifies the Haitian woman's experience, whatever her class, racial makeup, and occupation."[24] Coining the term "*culture-lacune*" in her book *Framing Silence*, Chancy explains: "In their absence from historical and literary documentation, Haitian women represent the ultimate *lacune* in Haitian society. They are the absence that completes the whole. [… Their visions] describe a culture within a culture, one that embraces its own silencing even as it contests it."[25] Chancy and others have written out of such silence since the mid-1990s, producing a growing body of literature that space does not permit me to discuss here.[26] To return for a moment to Schwab: "How does one write from within an absence of memory, from within a loss that is less remembered as a story or an image or a thought than as a mood, an existential void, or a sense of annihilation? Writing is performed in the shadow of a lost object. Writing is the shadow of an absent voice. Writing assembles an ungrounded body's fragmented speech."[27] Black female experience stands at the center of this site of memory, specifically in the barracoons in Africa and then the slave ships, and also at the core of the madness on the plantations in Saint-Domingue in 1750.[28] As branded letters wound captured bodies in Trouillot's novel, rape and silence mark Haitian women from the colonial period onward, perhaps contributing to the near lack of women's writing until Marie Vieux-Chauvet began to publish fiction in the middle of the twentieth century.

Despite the seeming paucity of female figures in that long history, women could call upon the spiritual realm for models and guidance. In her analysis of Erzulie, *loa* of love, Joan Dayan states that this vodun spirit "recalls and replays all the uses, pleasures and violations of women in Haiti, from colonial Saint-Domingue to post-Duvalier Haiti," seeing in her "a dramatization of how black women saw, reacted to, and survived the experience of slavery and the realities of colonialism."[29] Erzulie embodies on a spiritual level what Défilée represents in the historico-mythic archive, each figure a repository of Haitian women's trauma and madness. Dayan also invokes Sor Rose:

> The mother of all Haitians, her claim of generative reproduction depends upon her violation. The cosmology begins with rape, as the Haitian historian Timoléon Brutus retells the story: Haiti has its origin in the flanks of a black woman "brutalement fécondés par un esclave en rut ou par un Blanc en ébriété, bagnard échappé de Cayenne, ou dégénéré d'une noblesse féodale en quête de richesses à travers le continent."[30]

The perpetrator of the rape that gave birth to Haiti morphs in this telling from a slave, to a drunken white man, to an escaped prisoner, to a degenerate nobleman in search of wealth, as if signifying the pervasive violation of Black women from the country's beginnings. Dayan, like many women writing about Haiti today, asserts that "Haitian history has been written by men, whether colonizers who distort or negate the past or the colonized who attempt to reclaim or reimage what has been lost or denied," further stating that "women left no records."[31] A text like *Rosalie L'Infâme* returns us to the origins, if not with Sister Rose, then with those like Ma Augustine, Grann Charlotte, Brigitte, and Lisette's mother, Ayouba, who suffered captivity, rape, abuse, and silencing, yet who speak (through) their wounds in the mad marooning practiced by them and their descendants. Those acts of resistance involve geography, the "demonic grounds" explored by Wynter and by McKittrick. Dayan specifically connects the land to the rape of women: "Women's bodies violated in colonial Saint-Domingue would become the land mistreated and recalcitrant in independent Haiti."[32] Chauvet makes the connection most explicitly in *Colère*, when Rose's body is exchanged for the family land and she suffers a month-long agony of rape that sends her into madness and death.[33]

In the story of Sor Rose, while the possible rapist is given multiple identities and motivations, the woman herself remains mute in the telling, her body ignored by both the historian and the critic. In her path-breaking study of rape, Jean-Charles argues that while the rape of Sor

Rose "stages a primal scene of violence that focuses on rape as a sign whose signification relates to the creation of the nation," the lack of attention to the actual woman and the violation she suffers partakes in "[…] a critical silence that mirrors societal and cultural responses to rape."[34] How can women confront that endemic violence and move from trauma to healing? Mad tongues provide a potential answer. In "Towards a New Feminist Theory of Rape," Carine M. Mardorossian states that vocalization (such as contemporary speak-outs) is crucial for "the voicing of the experience, the act of narrativizing itself. […] Rape is a reality that feels anything but real to the victim, yet this same reality can become the basis of a representation the speaker can manipulate and gain control of, that can command an audience's attention and be made intelligible in other than the available cultural terms."[35] For Jean-Charles, the available narrative, that of Sor Rose, creates a national narrative that is problematic for Haitian women and that silences the reality of rape across historical periods. She turns to Chauvet's fiction, specifically the middle novel of the trilogy, to analyze the prevalence of "rape trauma syndrome" in Haitian culture.

Chauvet's trilogy, *Amour, Colère, Folie* (*Love, Anger, Madness*), scripts the violence of the US occupation (1915–1934) and its aftermath, as well as the terrors of the Duvalier dictatorship starting in 1957, a dangerous literary endeavor that led to her fleeing to New York and to the works' repression in Haiti (as well as risks for her family who remained in the country).[36] In the novel *Colère*, in particular, the madness directed at and then inhabiting women manifests most viscerally as rape and other forms of physical abuse. Chauvet exposes a reality that in fact existed from the ships' arrival in Saint-Domingue and continued to be a stark reality in women's lives in Haiti.[37] Thus, Chauvet broke silence and opened the way for contemporary Haitian women writers to investigate the archives and read between the lines as well as explore the unvoiced experiences of anonymous women who suffered the violence at the heart of Sor Rose's story. Trouillot continues that process of voicing the past, explaining that "modern Haitian writers needed to situate themselves in regard to that history" of the slave ships and the revolution.[38]

II

Evelyne Trouillot's *Rosalie L'Infâme*, also available in a brilliant translation by M.A. Salvodon as *The Infamous Rosalie*, takes place in 1750 during a period of extreme terror surrounding poisonings on plantations in colonial Saint-Domingue. In interviews (as in a postface), Trouillot explains the inspiration for the novel:

> C'est en feuilletant l'ouvrage *La Révolution aux Caraïbes* de Cauna, Abenon et Chaleau que je suis tombée par hazard sur une référence assez brève, très éloquente dans son dépouillement: 'Descourtilz cite le cas d'une sage-femme arada. Au cours de son procès, la femme dévoila un collier de corde qu'elle portait sur elle où chaque noeud représentait un des soixante-dix enfants qu'elle avait supprimés: *"Pour enlever ces jeunes êtres à un honteux esclavage, je plongeais à l'instant de leur naissance une épingle dans leur cerveau par la fontanelle."*'[39]

This historical record of serial infanticide by a midwife and healer, an African woman enslaved in Saint-Domingue, recalls Margaret Garner, the African American woman who inspired Toni Morrison's *Beloved*, a text that unearths a Black woman's killing of her third child and attempt to kill her other three children rather than see them returned to slavery, or the fictional Emma in Marie-Célie Agnant's *Le Livre d'Emma*, incarcerated in an asylum in Canada for allegedly killing her baby girl, as well as scores of real women throughout the Diaspora and their fictional counterparts.[40] I will return to Trouillot's character Brigitte and that woman's great-niece, Lisette, the protagonist of *Rosalie*, to flesh out the concept of mad marooning, noting here the argument made by Pascale de Souza (writing about women's fiction from Martinique and Guadeloupe): "Les crises de folie ou actes d'(auto)mutilation leur [personages feminins] permettent ainsi de devenir marronnes, se mettant en marge d'un système qui cherche à nier leur existence pour mieux le dénoncer".[41] The emerging scholarship on Trouillot's text also focuses on the "invisible lives" given voice and visibility in the narrative, especially the perspectives of enslaved women, both *bossale* (brought from Africa) and *créole* (born in Haiti). Trouillot herself does not highlight "madness," though she does in one instance ask of those suffering in slavery, "Dans quelle démence avaient-ils sombré?"[42] Nor do those commenting on the novel reference "madness," but *Rosalie* teems with insanity of multiple kinds, as well as the ongoing trauma originating in the barracoons in Africa and on the ships involved in the Atlantic slave trade.[43]

Trouillot, in particular, underscores the deep roots of the madness in her vision of life for enslaved women on a plantation in the north, in the midst of unspeakable horrors that multiply and intensify over the course of several months in 1750. The novel opens with the protagonist Lisette hurrying to meet her lover, the Maroon (and French-literate) Vincent: "I weave through the maze of paths between the shacks, taking care to go the back way, avoiding the one window through which I can glimpse the dark, damp rooms inside the house."[44] In her mind, she follows the tracks of the trauma, "the madness of the flames" that have just burned alive a man accused of attempted poisoning, viciously murdered as his young daughters were forced to watch. "I inhabit the final spasms of Paladin, whose face, before it was turned into a mask of horror by the sizzling stake, I'm unable to reconstruct."[45] The repetition of "I inhabit" serves both as Lisette's testimony (to us, the readers) and as a sign that she is consumed by the traumatic event and lost in its traces, "unable to reconstruct" the specific crossing from living human to lifeless mask. In the first pages, we are immersed in a violent, toxic environment, the "maze" through which she runs and the psyches wounded by those toxins. The central poison is the episteme that Wynter dissects, the binary system that turned humans into Man and other.[46]

Lisette's brief interlude with Vincent is saturated by nightmares of accumulated and inherited trauma: "In my sleep I struggle against miasmas and stagnant waters, barracoons and the steerage of ships, the growl of dogs, bodies too hot and damp, the sounds of bludgeons."[47] The text itself, representing Lisette's coming-to-voice, as well as to *marronnage*, breaks silence and speaks resistance, one that recovers a genealogy of Black women from Africa to the Americas. She is well aware of the dangers of maroon life: "Maroons have severed legs and ears, burned genitals, chained feet; they are cast aside to be sold with missing body parts, maimed and half-dead, when they're not devoured by mastiffs."[48] A litany of wounding and fragmentation, this description of Maroons performs the annihilation of the Black body that dares to resist and deny enslavement, a recognition that makes Lisette's eventual choice to join the Maroons equivalent to her great-aunt Brigitte's choices to abort three of her own fetuses and to kill at least 70 newborn infants, all to prevent further enslavement and perpetuation of the plantation system.

While *Rosalie* opens with Lisette's witnessing of the horrific murder of an enslaved man, and the text frequently describes trauma experienced by other male characters, Black female embodiment frames the narrative. Lisette's godmother, Ma Augustine, eventually reveals not only what happened on the boat but what she remembers as the originary shame and terror: the murder of Brigitte's sons for trying to protect the women; the Arada women captured; and that horrific captivity in the barracoons where they were held by traders. Trouillot has explained her disbelief and frustration when searching for the word "barracoon" in French dictionaries, yet another erasure of history, a gap or crease.[49] The barracoons, like the ship and the plantation that follow for the captives, serve as the kind of landmark described by Joan Dayan in her discussion of Erzulie and women of Haiti: "Memories survive [...] when they attach themselves to certain landmarks, to things that remain."[50] She cites Morrison's *Beloved*, when Sethe talks about a burned down house as both "gone" and yet remaining. "Such repossession," Dayan argues, "is never abstract: the return is rigorously concrete and collective. [It is] a continuing process of re-habitation, a repositioning in terms of locale."[51]

A similar process that is in part geographical occurs in Grann Charlotte's re-memory (to use Sethe's word) of the barracoons: "'But for me the barracoons are the wound that will always bleed deep inside me. That was when I knew for sure that a large part of me had been buried.'"[52] Her words to Lisette enact the coming-to-speech of trauma that appears "mad," as observed by Davoine and Gaudillière.[53] Charlotte further relates: "'To me the barracoons represented the beginning of night, the end of liberty. The first captivity was the most ferocious one, the most irrevocable. Not even my body belonged to me. I no longer recognized it in my own mournful flesh. My spirit left me, as if I were elsewhere, watching this spectacle from a distance. I seemed to be lost in the darkness in which I found myself.'"[54] The passage delineates symptoms of trauma, from a total shock to one's being, to a loss of self, to disassociation or splitting, to a gap or abyss in memory. The sequence—this chapter in Grann Charlotte's story—ends with her rejection of "Western" literacy: the letters "*LR*," the ship's initials, branded onto her breast. She tells Lisette, "'[T]he alphabet will always embody the characters of hell.'"[55] Thus, her re-possession, her emergence from madness, takes the form of oral history, testimony, witnessed by her god-daughter.

In *Rosalie*, Lisette has been raped by the son of the plantation owner, an experience she initially represses and then relates with women at the center. That is, rather than focusing on the male character's violent act, the narrative highlights the support Lisette receives in its aftermath, thus replacing the rapist almost entirely by female agents. The memory first surfaces when an older man, Michaud, refers to the master's predilection for Black women with a certain body shape (unlike Lisette's): "Gracieuse's small, round silhouette closing the door to the master's large room weaves into my memory, and I nod my head to tell Michaud I know what he's talking about. This penchant of the master's has kept me out of his discreet hands. Too bad his son didn't share his father's tastes .... My mind turns this page quickly […]."[56] Nor do Grann Charlotte and Ma Augustine give Lisette particulars of the violations they suffered, so that we understand that such trauma for Black women always already existed once the slave trade had begun and once slavery was established on the plantations. When Lisette does recall the rape, she focuses on the aftermath, Ma Augustine's powers for both healing and revenge. Lisette tried "to chase away the imprint of the white hands inside me," and her godmother bathed her: "With leaves and roots whose smell lingered on my skin, she dabbed my body, my thighs and between my thighs, my buttocks, all of my parts."[57] In this way, the women claim what Philip calls "Dis Place The Space Between," the Black woman's hands replacing and erasing the imprint of the white man's attempt at possession.[58] A month later, the rapist (Raoul) suffers from a "terrible itch,"[59] but Lisette still experiences symptoms of trauma, seeing his face and feeling the violation of her body, which causes her rage and hatred. Jean-Charles explains two ways to see the intersection of politics and rape in Haiti, rejecting the view that rape is uniquely specific to periods of political instability, as she argues instead for the theory that "links politics to power relations, sexual dynamics and social institutions at play in both the reality and representation of rape."[60] Thus, she says, we need to "[…] recognize rape as an institutionalized practice."[61] Trouillot vividly illustrates this institutionalization not only in the central characters in *Rosalie* but also through a secondary one like Gracieuse, who seemingly enjoys the master's favoritism. Late in the novel, she dies an excruciating death caused by an abortion—she has been repeatedly raped by the white man and has aborted each of seven fetuses, her resistance to the nexus of power, sexual dynamics, and social institutions embedded in the plantation.

Repeatedly, Trouillot reminds us that the entire story, like the history from which she has drawn it and with which it is entangled, originates in trauma and the concomitant madness. When Lisette is delighted to be given a cast-off gown by the master's daughter, Sarah, Charlotte realizes she must tell her granddaughter about the barracoons. The passage bears quoting at length:

> "This whole story is like a vast wound. Some parts of it bleed more than others. There are more recent marks, not as fatal. Then there are the old

> wounds that have stopped bleeding but have filled the entire body with a smell of rotting flesh. From time to time this stench rises to the surface with a whiff of decaying bodies, masking makeshift lies, baskets woven with happiness bought on credit. The time of the barracoons is a festering wound deep in the bones, a humiliation for all to see. When one has experienced this kind of humiliation, defeat can call your name at any time and undo your memory."[62]

This story of fissured memory and mad tongues thus begins with imprisonment in Africa, before the ships of the Middle Passage, the barracoons laying the foundation of what McKittrick terms "a crucial geographical paradigm, human captivity."[63] Examining the meanings of that geography for Black women, she states: "The classification of black femininity was therefore also a process of *placing* her within the broader system of servitude—as an inhuman racial-sexual worker, as an objectified body, as a site through which sex, violence, and reproduction can be imagined and enacted, and as a captive human."[64] The barracoons haunt the women surrounding Lisette, creating a geography of wounding, of madness, and of resistance. For as McKittrick explains, Black women do not remain passive captives: "The poetics of landscape allow Black women to critique the boundaries of transatlantic slavery, rewrite national narratives, respatialize feminism, and develop new pathways across traditional geographic arrangements."[65] In *Rosalie*, madness and *marronnage* serve as such routes to new spatial arrangements. Ma Augustine tells Lisette, "'So you came to us from death and love, from nights in the ship's hold and from madness. [...] You came to me also with the rebellious eyes of the island on which you were born, with Brigitte's irrepressible will to be proud and free [...].'"[66] Born of that complicated geography—Africa, Atlantic, Saint-Domingue, or barracoon, slave ship, plantation—Lisette is the daughter of a Maroon (her father, Storm), lover of a Maroon (Vincent), and eventually will choose marooning for herself and her unborn child.

The lens of *marronnage* offers a way to interpret Brigitte's refusal to bear children (her three abortions), as well as the 70 infanticides archived by the knots in her cord. Her choices repudiate the institutions formed by the Western episteme guiding the slave trade and the plantation, attitudes acted out in an increasing frenzy of violence and destruction committed by plantation owners throughout the colony. The Maroons not only occupy the terrain at a remove from the plantation; their presence also saturates the colonial geography, resistance permeating the environment, inciting terror, and providing an antidote to the poisonous institutions of enslavement. Discussions of *marronnage* offer complex and sometimes competing assessments of its practice in the African Diaspora, as well as its meanings in diverse geographical and historical contexts. Dmitri Béchacq, for instance, focuses on *marronnage* in Haitian history, distinguishing between *petit marronnage*, or individual mobility, and *grand marronnage*, collective flight beyond the plantation. He claims that the role of the "neg mawon" was erased after 1804, as the leaders of the Revolution became enshrined as cult figures in Haitian culture. He also sees the incarnation of the Maroon in the statue of the *Marron inconnu* (which survived the 2010 earthquake and remains standing in front of the space occupied by the collapsed presidential palace) as having been exploited in more recent times and turned into the representative of each political cause in turn.[67] Both aspects, the small and the large, appear in *Rosalie*, enslaved women at the nexus of those forms of resistance.

Their acts, including suicide, abortion, infanticide, poisoning, and more, exhibit strategies of "mad marooning." In her study of Jamaican fiction, Barbara Lalla describes the Maroon as follows: "[…] marronnage involves a character in a dialectic of escape and rejection and of violent resistance and violent pursuit. […] *marronnage* requires deviation from the norm, imposes dislocation, and proposes an alternative community. Thus it adjusts perspective, switches points of departure, and reevaluates established propositions to reveal additional or alternative truths."[68] Lalla stresses the role of alienation in the practice of *marronnage*, noting that Jamaican fiction features characters who embody aspects of the Maroon, such as "the stranger, the vagrant, the bumpkin, the trickster, the savage, the rebel, the lunatic, the zombie, the reject, and the outcast."[69] In the context of my argument about "mad marooning," what such figures share is an ability to question, defy, and undermine the binary oppositions that undergird the colonial enterprise.[70]

Most discussions of *marronnage* in Haiti and elsewhere focus on male experience (aside from the prominent figure of Jamaican Nanny of the Maroons). Pascale De Souza offers a corrective to definitions of marooning that emphasize violent resistance, arguing that "the 'herstory' of marooning is indeed less one of resistance than of opposition."[71] She cites De Certeau's distinction between resistance as a "stepping outside of the system to jeopardize it," while opposition "applies to acts perpetrated within the system to achieve a similar end."[72] Although such a division allows for more visibility of women's defiant acts, a text like *Rosalie* illustrates that *marronnage* employs a network both intra- and extra-systemic, operating in the plantation's "big house" (*la grande case*), in the living quarters of the enslaved, and across the "demonic grounds" of the colonial geography in its entirety. In her discussion of female *marronnage*, De Souza states: "Poisoning, self-mutilation, infanticide, laziness were all used against the plantocratic society," noting that in Guadeloupe poisoning brought terror in the 1750s (which parallels the time period of Trouillot's novel). "Poisoning also served to limit fertility or induce abortions," she adds.[73] We see fictional depictions of these forms of female *marronnage* throughout *Rosalie*, woven into the crazed fabric of life in Saint-Domingue.

And that resistance operates as a form of madness. That is, mad marooning works to challenge and destabilize the enforced ideologies of Man/other and all its variations (as explicated by Wynter), blurring the boundaries on which colonialism and enslavement depended. Erin Mackie points to the overlap or contiguity between Maroon and plantation: "[…] marronnage operates as a name for resistance and alterity in the African diaspora but only by dint of a historical complicity with slavery and colonialism that complicates the claims of unity and purity marronnage sets against the disabling hybridity those institutions imposed."[74] She adds that the Maroons "[…] straddled the divide between law and outlaw, at least as it was defined from a colonialist perspective."[75] What results, when we look specifically at Black female experience in Haiti, is a version of the "demonic grounds" articulated by both Wynter and McKittrick, as well as Philip's "genealogy of resistance." Évelyne Trouillot herself states, in an interview with Edwidge Danticat, "And of course, there were so many invisible women. I would like to see an equivalent of the '*marron inconnu*' to symbolize the enslaved women who fought against slavery".[76] Lisette becomes that woman gradually over the course of the narrative, carrying the wounds of the women before and around her, marked by the system's insanity, evolving from "house slave," to "go-between," to the pregnant woman who chooses *marronnage* over enslavement.

Resistance informs Black women's thoughts and actions, traced back to the ships and woven into their lives in the Diaspora. Grann Charlotte's repeated stories of before and after "*Rosalie L'Infâme*" include both suicide and survival, the former enacted by a young Hausa woman on the ship: the whites laughed as she and her partner danced, but the Africans knew that "'she was conjuring death.'"[77] Her dancing intensified: "'She was bidding farewell to the land she'd left behind and that she'd never see again. [...] The music was becoming more and more violent, and then the two bodies crashed into each other [...] filled with pain and rage. [...] In the same spirit the man and the woman sprung forward and threw themselves into the sea.'"[78] Lisette's education, received from the women around her, offers instruction in how to resist and rebel, as well as how to seek freedom. Her godmother's wish for her is a dream "'[...] that one day your children's children would confront the barracoons, fly up into the sky, and write your name on the highest stars.'"[79] That form of literacy would replace the ship's name (and novel's title) and the letters branded on women's bodies.

The dream is challenged by reality, as Lisette's pregnancy (by Vincent) falls under the shadow of Gracieuse's death by self-induced abortion and the capture of historic Maroon leader Makandal. About to be burned alive, Makandal initially "struggled, kicked his legs, and shook his head like a madman," and rushes out of the fire.[80] But he is subsequently recaptured and immolated, his death followed soon after by the suicide of Fontilus, Lisettte's friend since childhood. Madness beckons to Lisette, as does self-destruction: "[...] from start to finish my sorrows have taken on the shape of an abyss that makes jumping into it so tempting. [...] In the big house they're all whispering how Fontilus or Gracieuse want to take me with them, how my dead ones are actively seeking me, and how I'm already halfway gone with them."[81] Lisette has been living a limbo of sorts, between plantation and *marronnage*, serving as messenger between the two sites, attempting to negotiate a border existence.[82] The series of traumatic losses both unhinges her and offers her clear vision into her actual position if she remains in the big house. "I am seized by the crushing truth that I am nothing here but an object at the mercy of whites [...]."[83] She now understands the "truth" at the core of the system, that as "other" (to what Wynter would term "Man"), she has no human value. "The thought severs my mind like the blow of a machete to the back of a hand."[84] At this point, she seeks the truth of Brigitte's cord, the story of infanticide that Ma Augustine now reveals to her. Lisette occupies a liminal position, poised to perform her rite of passage: "Suspended between my current status as house slave and Maroon-in-training [...]."[85] She will cross that threshold—her choice of mad marooning parallel to that of the Hausa woman's leap into the sea, Brigitte's turning herself in to spare others, Fontilus's hanging himself, and Ma Augustine's decision to survive in order to nurture Lisette.

Lisette takes a radical step across the threshold: killing the woman prepared to betray her. "Last night my strength helped me to subdue Clarisse, stifle her screams, and drag her body all the way to the back of the storehouse, where I hid it."[86] The shock of this act is muted by the truncated telling and then silencing performed by Lisette's narration. One might set this scene next to the ways that interracial desire performs a madness in Chauvet's *Amour*, as explored in depth by Valerie Kaussen. I would argue that the perceived irrationality of such transgressive desire, in the context of colonial Haiti as elsewhere, threads persistently through Trouillot's novel. Unlike Claire in *Amour*, however, who enacts and embraces that madness in more and more violent ways, Lisette stands outside of and in negative judgment of Clarisse's sexual liaison with the white master. Her murder of Clarisse is almost erased rather than highlighted, buried in Lisette's frantic rush to escape the plantation.

Thus, Lisette's attention moves immediately to her flight and to the fetus inside her. Ma Augustine has told her that the baby will be a girl: "'May this country be hers one day!'" she told her goddaughter, and we last see Lisette heading west, a Maroon, running as she did in the first scene, but now towards the future. She tells her unborn daughter, "May I find the courage to honor my promise: Creole child who still lives in me, you will be born free and rebellious, or you will not be born at all."[87] Those closing words leave room for multiple outcomes, from freedom and birth as a Maroon, to possible capture and murder by the colonists, to suicide/infanticide. Lisette is in transit at the end, embracing *marronnage* and claiming the country for herself and the next (female) generation. Trouillot thus has scripted the counterpart to the "*marron inconnu*," that of the *marronne* occupying the "demonic ground" of Haiti in the names of the women who preceded her. And her daughter is not the product of rape but of her love for a Maroon whom she aims to rejoin, another rewriting of the history that silences and obscures Haitian women. Lisette demonstrates the potential to seize "dis place" and claim it through strategies of resistance and mad marooning.

III

The title of Roxane Gay's novel *An Untamed State* holds multiple meanings, referring to Haiti, to Port-au-Prince, to the gated compound where the protagonist's parents live, to the run-down apartment where she is held captive, and to the madness that consumes her as she suffers thirteen days of imprisonment, rape, abuse, concomitant trauma, and the ongoing aftermath of her ordeal. The text, framed by a fairy-tale opening, "Happily Ever After," is narrated in the first person by Mireille, reflecting back on her captivity as well as her life "before" in chapters that alternate with third-person narration that situates her white American husband Michael's perspective next to hers in parallel moments, from their meeting, to romance, to marriage and the birth of their son Christophe, to their visit to her parents, the kidnapping, and its aftermath. In my analysis, madness and marooning connect Gay's text to the expanding body of women's writing from Haiti and its *Dyaspora*, works that both aestheticize and rupture silences surrounding female experience from Saint-Domingue, to Haiti throughout the twentieth century, to contemporary Port-au-Prince. In *History Beyond Trauma*, Davoine and Gaudillière state:

> For madness can be defined as the state in which there is no other to respond to it. Indeed, what others could there be to preside over foreclosure, denial, betrayal, erasure, and the wearing down of traces and boundaries if not a totalitarian other for whom otherness is reduced to subjugation—in other words, an other without otherness?[88]

Such is Mireille's state of "otherness" from the moment armed men kidnap her from the car in which she, Michael, and Christophe are leaving her father's gated mansion for a day trip to the beach. She will become "other" to her parents, her husband, her captors, and deeply alienated from her self.

The fairy tale begins with the nightmare, an undoing of the mythic narrative that covers over the reality of women's experience: "Once upon a time, in a far-off land, I was kidnapped by a gang of fearless yet terrified men with so much impossible hope beating inside their bodies it burned their very skin and strengthened their will right through their bones. They held me captive for 13 days. They wanted to break me. It was not personal. I was not broken. This is what I tell myself."[89] These opening lines of the novel break expectations, both Mireille's fantasy vision of her own life and incomplete understanding of Haiti, and the reader's assumptions of what the "fairy tale" will reveal. Her father (Sebastien) and his walled fort of a home will also be revealed to have much in common with the kidnappers' leader and the "cage" where he holds and rapes Mireille.

How can we connect the plantation with its horrific violence in *Rosalie L'Infâme* to the urban setting in 2005 Haiti? Katherine

McKittrick's discussion of "a black sense of place" offers a pertinent analysis, stating that she "[...] is positioning the plantation as a very meaningful geographic prototype that not only housed and normalized (vis-à-vis enforced placelessness) racial violence in the Americas but also naturalized a plantation logic that anticipated (but did not twin) the empirical decay and death of a very complex black sense of place."[90] She uses the term "urbicide" to explore a city's "deliberate death," a concept that can apply to Port-au-Prince as depicted in Gay's novel. McKittrick continues: "[...] the annihilation of black geographies in the Americas is deeply connected to an economy of race, and thus capitalism, wherein the process of uneven development calcifies the seemingly natural links between blackness, underdevelopment, poverty, and place within differing global contexts."[91] While she does not directly incorporate Haiti into her argument, these ideas certainly apply to both the country and its capital, geographies of violence that hinge "on a long-standing but unacknowledged plantation past."[92] While the space of captivity, which Mireille comes to refer to as her "cage," might seem the most obvious comparison to enslavement, the fortress-like house where her parents live provides a striking link backwards to the plantation.

In flashbacks, we learn about Mireille's childhood as a daughter of Haitian immigrants in the US, an upbringing that offers telling clues to her father's own experiences both in Haiti and in the US and the ways that they have shaped his self-image, ambitions, and attitudes. As Mireille thinks about Haiti in the present as "a land of mad indifference,"[93] she considers her father's construction company that has made him wealthy and powerful: "He would reshape the country into the home he remembered, the unvarnished one," but his family will pay the price.[94] She explains the core of his philosophy when she recalls that he taught his children not to cry: "[W]e needed to be strong because as Haitians in America we would always be fighting; Americans wouldn't understand we came from a free people. He said they would always see us as slaves so we had to work harder, we had to be better, we had to be strong."[95] Having grown up impoverished in a family of eleven children in Haiti, he made himself impregnable psychologically and emotionally as he learned to negotiate his way to financial success in the US. He took that mindset with him when he and his wife returned to Haiti and settled into the hills above Port-au-Prince. Thus, when his daughter is kidnapped and held for ransom, even when he hears the sounds of her being tortured over the phone and her voice begging him to save her, he refuses to accede to the demands for money, wanting to bargain, to negotiate her value, and then refusing to communicate at all with her abductors. That set of betrayals, which leads to gang rape and worse, intensifies the trauma that she suffers. "I needed to step out of my skin, abandon my body the way my father was abandoning my body."[96] Her self-alienation, dis-association, attempts at self-erasure, and other symptoms of trauma are compounded by her father's desire to assert his "principles" and prove a point from the safe "decadence" of his "castle."[97]

During her captivity, Mireille descends further and further into madness, even as fragments of her self keep floating back to the surface, splintered memories that shore up her body's resistance to death. Early on in the hands of the Commander, she says that "my face felt broken, the various pieces of me loose and coming apart."[98] When many men violently rape her, "the fairy tale ends"[99] and she contemplates the value of her life, realizing that her father has disengaged from any process of saving her. When her first escape attempt fails, the Commander tells her about the poor in Haiti, about his experiences as the son of a man who drove rich people's cars and otherwise struggled to support his family. She refuses to accept blame for her father's enormous wealth, instead telling the Commander that he, too, is complicit in the system. As she contemplates her situation, sitting in the café where he has recaptured her, she breaks into mad laughter. "I was on the edge of something, a quiet blackness. I found comfort there."[100] During the days of her captivity, as she gradually erases herself, she drives herself to forget, but memory refuses to surrender: "The sky darkened when the Commander appeared. I became two women—the one who remembered everything and the one who remembered nothing. This required a delicate balance."[101] When she forces every memory out of her head and again becomes "no one," she enters the space of mad marooning.

Unlike Lisette, Mireille cannot run from a plantation and join the Maroons. Her initial *marronnage* comes in her retreat to an inner space, that of the book's title: "That [feral] is what I was, from the Latin *fera* for wild animal, something menacing, existing in *an untamed state*."[102] She finds a safe space of sorts in her mental state of forgetting and disassociation, a *kumbla* that will continue to encircle her post-captivity.[103] Yet like Lisette she *does* literally run, fleeing the apartment, entering a church in hopes of a sanctuary. At this point, encountering a priest, she cannot remember her name and is completely lost; when Michael and her father arrive, she does not recognize them and repeats that she is "not safe": "I whispered my name several times, tried to find a way to fit myself into that name, tried to hide the truth. I was no one, a woman with no name, no family."[104] She is still in her cage, she tells us, and her father is a stranger to her: "On that fourteenth day, in the dark empty of my salvation, I saw the hands of a weak, stubborn man. I saw the hands of a man who could not love his daughter enough to save her when there was still something of her left to save."[105] Her first steps running from captivity thus do not free her, and she performs a psychological marooning within her father's domain: "[T]he walls were closing in; this new cage was getting smaller and smaller. There was a leash around my neck."[106] Her resistance continues through the process of leaving Haiti, returning with Michael and Christophe to their home in Miami, and then running away from yet another cage.

Her memory fractured and her body wounded in multiple, unspeakable ways, Mireille's marooning takes her west, through Georgia and Tennessee, to Kentucky, and eventually to the farm house in Nebraska where her husband Michael was raised. There she finds a site of safety embodied in his mother, Lorraine, who assures Mireille that she will have time to find herself. Wanting a "witness," Mireille wakes screaming, unable to remember: "That was all my life seemed to be in the after, trying to orient myself and reorient myself in *new geographies*."[107] Though incoherent, her screaming begins a process of testifying that requires a space of resistance. Mireille's mad marooning, in a hiding place under Michael's childhood bed and in the darkness of a shed on the edge of the farm, will accomplish an un-silencing of trauma and a remapping of Black female embodiment. In this sequence, which follows her stuttering steps towards possible healing, we can observe what McKittrick calls a "poetics of landscape [... that] allow black women to critique the boundaries of transatlantic slavery, rewrite national narratives, respatialize feminism, and develop new pathways across traditional geographic arrangements."[108] Applicable to the memories that Charlotte and Augustine pass on to Lisette, starting with the barracoons, continuing through the Middle Passage and to the plantation in Saint Domingue, this vision of landscape also illuminates Mireille's changing conception of space and place. Her journey also moves into the "provision grounds" as opposed to the plantation's big house, similar to the way Lisette traverses paths into the dwellings and garden plots of the enslaved and then into the spaces of the Maroons.[109]

As Mireille feels more and more "crazy," unable to tell if she is in Port-au-Prince or Nebraska, she is convinced that the Commander is chasing her as she runs through cornfields in the night. In an outbuilding on the property's margins, she finds wire cutters to use as defense and hides herself in a wheelbarrow, under a tarpaulin. Waking from a deep sleep, she says, "I wanted to die but I was already dead. I couldn't bear the thought of the Commander taking me to a new cage. A woman was screaming and she sounded peculiar—hoarse and hollow and hopeless. My skin crawled as I realized I was the woman screaming."[110] Her mother-in-law, Lorraine, is the one who finds and supports her in that site of *marronnage* and in the next stages of shifting the geography. McKittrick explains that the new paths through "traditional geographic arrangements" can "[…] also offer several reconceptualizations of space and place, positioning black women as geographic subjects who provide spatial clues as to how more humanly workable geographies might be imagined."[111] When Lorraine meets Mireille in the space of madness and resistance, we observe a potential replacement of the binary Man/other with the inclusive *human* that Wynter theorizes. That is, rather than the "'space of Otherness' principle of nonheterogeneity" that Wynter discusses as the ideology leading to Du Bois's color line and "our present biocentric, descriptive statement of the human," the way that Lorraine joins Mireille in the shed and gradually guides her out of madness demonstrates a new concept of "the human."[112] An earlier scene of the two women making bread illustrates a contemporary "provision ground" that challenges the incarnations of the plantation where Mireille has been traumatized and from which she has fled. Throughout the scenes at the farm, we witness the value of provision ground connection, "the possibility of an alternative narrative for the future."[113] Lorraine steps into the space of otherness, even embraces Mireille's madness, hearing the wounds speak and offering the witness and the safety necessary to initiate both healing and, more broadly, a new geography.

The remainder of *An Untamed State* traces Mireille's struggles to emerge from "the cage," to find herself, to be able to touch her son without feeling that she is contaminating him, and to learn to trust others to help heal her body and psyche. That process necessitates the creation of new geographies from the space of madness and *marronnage*. Clearly exhibiting signs of PTSD, she sees doctors, learns the extent of her wounds, resists help, yet slowly re-members her self. When she says, "'I'm no one, Lorraine. I'm nothing'," her mother-in-law replies, "'Maybe you don't know just yet but you are someone. Stop saying you aren't.'"[114] Mireille spends months at the farm, "a lot of time alone, locked inside myself," a crucial period of the marooning that serves as her resistance and path to wholeness.[115] The narrative skips ahead five years (and several therapists) and Mireille has a baby girl: "Girl children are not safe in a world where there are men. They need to learn to be strong."[116]

Rather than aligning her concept of strength with Sebastien's fortress philosophy, Mireille is similar here to Lisette, whose story concludes with her promise to her unborn daughter as she heads to freedom with the Maroons. Mireille finds freedom first in a return to Haiti post-earthquake in 2012 and a final confrontation with her father, whom she tells not the truth of the damage done to her but the lie that she forgives him. Back in Miami, an unexpected encounter with the Commander, now working as a restaurant busboy, reminds her of how she died the last time he raped her and how she ran from her captivity. "I did not look back. I listened for his footsteps behind me but there was only the sound of my terrified breathing and my bare feet on the ground. I ran faster. I finally dared to hope."[117] The novel ends with that remembered running, that flight into mad marooning that eventually allowed her the possibility of freedom and wholeness. Her flight continues from Lisette's at the end of *Rosalie L'Infâme*, and together the texts script a "genealogy of resistance" for Haitian women.

Notes

1. Édouard Glissant, *Caribbean Discourse: Selected Essays*, trans. J. Michael Dash (Charlottesville: University of Virginia Press, 1992), 11.
2. "The signs, the symptomatic details emphasized by crises of madness, thus point to the disaster areas in which the social fabric creases (*crises*/creases) or tears." See Françoise Davoine and Jean-Max Gaudillière, *History Beyond Trauma: Whereof one cannot speak...thereof one cannot stay silent*, trans. Susan Fairfield (New York: Other Press, 2004), 13.
3. See Kaiama Glover, "'Black' Radicalism in Haiti and the Disorderly Feminine: The Case of Marie Vieux Chauvet," *Small Axe* 16, 3 (November 2012): 199–207, on Haiti's origins in the Revolution and the derisive ways it continues to be depicted, with a specific discussion of the zombie figure. See also Silvia Federici, *Caliban and the Witch: The Body and Primitive Accumulation* (Brooklyn, NY: Autonomedia, 2014), who posits the connections between attitudes towards "witches" in Europe and towards the indigenous and enslaved in the Americas.

While her focus is on capitalism and labor, her argument resonates with the theories of Wynter. Federici discusses "[…] three key aspects of the transition from feudalism to capitalism: the constitution of the proletarian body into a work-machine, the persecution of women as witches, and the creation of 'savages' and 'cannibals' both in Europe and the New World," 115. And on the ways that History silences the past, especially in the context of Haiti, see Michel-Rolph Trouillot, *Silencing the Past: Power and the Production of History* (Boston: Beacon Press, 1995).

4. Régine Michelle Jean-Charles, *Conflict Bodies: The Politics of Rape Representation in the Francophone Imaginary* (Columbus, OH: Ohio State University Press, 2014), 59.
5. See also Beverly Bell, whose *Walking on Fire: Haitian Women's Stories of Survival and Resistance* (Ithaca, NY: Cornell University Press, 2001) gives voice to contemporary Haitian women, whom she calls "[…] the keepers and recounters of history, truth, and wisdom" (xv). See also Carolle Charles, "Gender and Politics in Contemporary Haiti: The Duvalierist State, Transnationalism, and the Emergence of a New Feminism (1980–1990)," *Feminist Studies* 21, 1 (Spring 1995): 135–164, on gender and the legacy of Duvalierism, and Carolle Charles, "Popular Images of Gender and Sexuality: Poor and Working-Class Haitian Women's Discourses on the Use of Their Bodies," in *The Culture of Gender and Sexuality in the Caribbean*, ed. Linden Lewis (Gainesville, FL: University Press of Florida, 2003), 169–189, on contemporary Haitian women, at the intersections of class, gender, and sexuality, who are producing counternarratives.
6. See Tonya Haynes, "The Divine and the Demonic: Sylvia Wynter and Caribbean Feminist Thought Revisited," in *Love and Power: Caribbean Discourses on Gender*, ed. V. Eudine Barriteau (Kingston, Jamaica: University of the West Indies Press, 2012), 55. See also Sylvia Wynter, "Beyond Miranda's Meanings: Un/Silencing the 'Demonic Ground' of Caliban's 'Woman'," in *Out of the Kumbla: Caribbean Women and Literature*, eds. Carole Boyce Davies and Elaine Savory Fido (Trenton, NJ: Africa World Press, 1990), 355–372. On the "demonic grounds," see Katherine McKittrick, *Demonic Grounds: Black Women and the Cartographies of Struggle* (Minneapolis, MN: University of Minnesota Press, 2006), xxv.
7. Haynes, "The Divine and the Demonic," 58.
8. See, for instance, Sylvia Wynter, "Unsettling the Coloniality of Being/Power/Truth/Freedom: Towards the Human, After Man, Its Overrepresentation—An Argument," *CR: The New Centennial Review* 3, 3 (Fall 2003): 289–290, 304–306. See also David Scott, "The Re-Enchantment of Humanism: An Interview with Sylvia Wynter,"

Small Axe 8 (September 2000): 179, 182. Wynter argues that the distinction rational/irrational drawn by colonial powers created a space of otherness, as Denise Ferreira da Silva explains in "Before Man: Sylvia Wynter's Rewriting of the Modern Episteme," in *Sylvia Wynter: On Being Human as Praxis*, ed. Katherine McKittrick (Durham, NC: Duke University Press, 2015): "From then on, the rational/irrational pair would remap the 'space of otherness' and, significantly, be represented by the bodies and territories subjected to colonial power," 94. Ferreira da Silva continues: "What Wynter uncovers is that the conditions of possibility—the context of emergence of the refiguring of the 'discourse of race' Foucault locates in the nineteenth century—in fact resides in the division of the Human into the rational European and its irrational (American, African, Asian, Australian, etc.) Others," 99.

9 Discussing Wynter's essay "Beyond Miranda's Meanings," McKittrick, *Demonic Grounds*, explains that the demonic model Wynter develops locates "cognitions *outside* 'the always non-arbitrary pre-prescribed,' which underscores the ways in which subaltern lives are not marginal/other to regulatory classificatory systems, but instead integral to them. [...] In developing a second, but related, use of the demonic, Wynter describes 'the grounds' as the absented presence of black womanhood," xxv, emphasis in original. What I term "mad marooning" is an example of this kind of cognition on the part of Haitian women in the works I am analyzing.

10. Haynes, "The Divine and the Demonic," 65.

11. See also Myriam J.A. Chancy, *Framing Silence: Revolutionary Novels by Haitian Women* (New Brunswick, NJ: Rutgers University Press, 1997), 18: "[...] it is critical to view literatures of resistance and/or revolution as establishing their own paradigms that refuse, even as they 'write back' to the colonizing powers (be they patriarchal or imperial), to be entirely subsumed by the cultures that have denied their existence."

12. See Jana Evans Braziel, "Re-membering Défilée: Dédée Bazile as Revolutionary *Lieu de Mémoire*," *Small Axe* 18 (September 2005): 57–85. See also Jana Evans Braziel, "Défilée's Diasporic Daughters: Revolutionary Narratives of *Ayiti* (Haiti), *Nanchon* (Nation), and *Dyaspora* (Diaspora) in Edwidge Danticat's *Krik? Krak!*," *Studies in the Literary Imagination* 37, 2 (Fall 2004): 77–96. See also Joan Dayan, *Haiti, History, and the Gods* (Berkeley, CA: University of California Press, 1995), on Défilée, especially 39–48. Dayan explores the "conjunction of hero [Dessalines] and madwoman" in Haitian history: "The trope of long-suffering or mad *négresse* and powerful *noir* became a routine coupling in contemporary Haitian as well as Caribbean texts. The parallels between literary and historical writing raises questions about

the myth of the Haitian nation and the kinds of symbols required to make a 'national' literature. Haitian history has been written by men, whether colonizers who distort or negate the past, or the colonized who reclaim what has been lost or denied," 46. In his acclaimed history of the Haitian Revolution, *Avengers of the New World: The Story of the Haitian Revolution* (Cambridge, MA: The Belknap Press of Harvard University, 2004), Laurent Dubois does not mention Défilée.

13. See Scott, "Interview," 177. See also Wynter, "Unsettling the Coloniality of Being/Power/Truth/Freedom," especially Part IV, 311–331.
14. See also Tanya Shields, *Bodies and Bones: Feminist Rehearsal and Imagining Caribbean Belonging* (Charlottesville, VA: University of Virginia Press, 2014), who also posits Défilée as embodiment of "silenced traumas," 92. Shields references Dayan and in so doing, downplays if not erases the significance of the *madness* as well as rape in this figure's myth/history/narrative. I disagree with that assessment, however, as we need to read Défilée's trauma and madness as an undoing of categories located in dichotomies of race, gender, and other identifications rooted in the Man/other binary.
15. See McKittrick, *Demonic Grounds*. See also Katherine McKittrick, "'Who do you talk to, when a body's in trouble?': M. Nourbese Philip's (un) silencing of black bodies in the diaspora," *Social & Cultural Geography* 1, 2 (2000): 223–236, and Katherine McKittrick, "Yours in the Intellectual Struggle: Sylvia Wynter and the Realization of the Living," in McKittrick, ed., 1–8.
16. Sylvia Wynter, " The Pope Must have Been Drunk, the King of Castile a Madman: Culture as Actuality, and the Caribbean Rethinking Modernity," in *The Reordering of Culture: Latin America, the Caribbean and Canada in the Hood*, eds. Alvina Ruprecht and Cecelia Taiana (Ottawa, ON: Carleton University Press, 1995), 17.
17. Wynter, "The Pope," 26.
18. Cathy Caruth, "Mad Witnesses: A Conversation with Françoise Davoine and Jean-Max Gaudillière," in her *Listening to Trauma: Conversations with Leaders in the Theory and Treatment of Catastrophic Experience. Interviews and Photographs* (Baltimore: Johns Hopkins University Press, 2014), 81.
19. Caruth, 95.
20. Gabriele Schwab, *Haunting Legacies: Violent Histories and Transgenerational Trauma* (New York: Columbia University Press, 2010), 42.
21. Schwab, *Haunting Legacies*, 45.
22. Schwab, *Haunting Legacies*, 46.
23. Schwab, *Haunting Legacies*, 49.

24. Myriam J.A. Chancy, "'No Giraffes in Haiti': Haitian Women and State Terror," in *Écrire en pays assiégié Haïti Writing Under Siege*, eds. Marie-Agnès Sourieau and Kathleen M. Balutansky (Amsterdam and New York: Rodopi, 2004), 305.
25. Chancy, *Framing Silence*, 17.
26. I discuss Agnant, Dominique, and Chancy in "Words to Heal the Wounds: Amnesia, Madness, and Silence as Testimony in Haitian Women's Fiction," a chapter in my book-in-progress on Caribbean women writers.
27. Schwab, *Haunting Legacies*, 60.
28. Renée Larrier, "In[her]itance: Legacies and Lifelines in Evelyne Trouillot's *Rosalie L'Infâme*," *Dalhousie French Studies* 88 (Fall 2009), states: "Worse than the hold of the ship where [Grann Charlotte] spent several brutal months, it [the barracoons] is a space of total dispossession, for it is there that she first suffers the loss of her body and spirit. A microcosm of the plantation (Glissant's *espace clos*), it prefigures its claustrophobic quarters, surveillance, beatings, ankle shackles, bloodhounds, and wails [...]," 140. See also Larrier, 143.
29. Joan Dayan, "Erzulie: A Women's History of Haiti," *Research in African Literatures* 25, 2 (Summer 1994): 16. On Erzulie, see also Dayan, *Haiti, History, and the Gods*, especially 54–65.
30. Dayan, "Erzulie," 12.
31. Dayan, "Erzulie," 17.
32. Dayan, "Erzulie," 19.
33. Names resonate among these texts: Sor Rose as the "mother" of Haiti; Chauvet's Rose who is brutally raped for a month, serving as a "gift" from her father to a man referred to only as "the Gorilla," in exchange for the family's land; the ship "Rosalie," bringing Lisette's mother, aunt, and grandmother to the colony.
34. Jean-Charles, *Conflict Bodies*, 58, 59.
35. Carine M. Mardorossian, "Towards a New Feminist Theory of Rape," *Signs* 27, 3 (Spring 2002): 765.
36. On the history of the book's publication, see Rose-Myriam Réjouis, translator's introduction, Marie Vieux Chauvet, *Love, Anger, Madness* (New York: Modern Library, 2010), xxii–xxiii. On the context for Chauvet's writing, see Dayan, *Haiti, History, and the Gods*, especially 89. See also Glover, "'Black Radicalism'": "Personal, intimate narratives of marginalized feminine existence during the most radical political moment in Haiti's history, Chauvet's novels feature women who dislocate and disorder the borders of subalternity," 20. See also Hellen Lee-Keller, "Madness and the Mulâtre-Aristocrate: Haiti, Decolonization, and Women in Marie Chauvet's *Amour*," *Callaloo* 32, 4 (Fall 2009): "[...] Chauvet employs the trope of madness to criticize covertly Haiti's

political, class, and social instabilities and contradictions in relation to patriarchy and racial elitism originating in French colonialism and worsened by intervention from the United States," 1294. Lee-Keller discusses madness as camouflage, which is parallel to my concept of "mad marooning." Also on *Amour*, see Valerie Kaussen, "Irrational Revolutions: Colonial Intersubjectivity and Dialectics in Marie Chauvet's 'Amour'," in *Tree of Liberty: Cultural Legacies of the Haitian Revolution in the Atlantic World*, ed. Doris L. Garraway (Charlottesville: University of Virginia Press, 2008), who argues that colonial irrationality—e.g., the preoccupation with interracial intimacy—is used in this novel as the basis for revolutionary change, esp. 146–7.

37. On *Colère*, see Jean-Charles, *Conflict Bodies*, especially 70–83. See also Glover, "'Black Radicalism'," on "blackness" in Chauvet's works.
38. Edwidge Danticat, "Evelyne Trouillot" (interview), *Bomb* 90 (Winter 2004–2005): 52. See also Jessica Agiletti, "Entretien avec Évelyne Trouillot," *Francofonia* 52 (Primavera 2007): 106.
39. Evelyne Trouillot, "L'Infamie revisitée," *Africultures* 58 (janvier-mars 2004): 51. Evelyne Trouillot, *The Infamous Rosalie*, trans. M.A. Salvodon (Lincoln, NB: University of Nebraska Press, 2013): "M.E. Descourtiilz cites the case of an Arada midwife who, during her trial, revealed a necklace made of rope that she wore in which each knot represented one of the 70 children she had killed: 'To remove these young creatures from the shameful institution of slavery, I inserted a needle in their brain through the fontanel at the moment of their birth. The result was trismus, so deadly on the island, and whose cause you now know'," 131.
40. On infanticide in *Rosalie*, *Emma*, and *Juletane*, see Antoinette Marie Sol, "Histoire(s) et traumatisme(s): l'infanticide dans le roman féminin antillais," *The French Review* 81, 5 (April 2008): 967–984. She discusses madness briefly as an effect of trauma and the way that writing can give coherence to the irrational: "Leurs récits prennent forme et cohérence de façon proportionnellement inverse à la désintégration de leur comportement irrationnel et antisocial," 978. She continues, saying that this writing allows the female characters to participate in a community of women.
41. Pascale de Souza, "Folie de l'écriture, écriture de la folie dans la littérature féminine des Antilles françaises," *Présence Francophone* 63 (2004): 130. De Souza discusses marooning in another Francophone novel, Myriam Warner-Vieyra's *Juletane*, in terms that resonate for "mad marooning": "Stratégie de survie et de révolte, la folie s'apparente ici à un marronnage psychologique qui permet de fuir des structures sociales aliénantes avant de s'y attaquer," 132. [A strategy of survival and revolt, madness is here related to a psychological marooning that allows for flight from alienating (or maddening) social structures before then attacking them. My translation.]

42. Trouillot, "L'Infâmie revisitée," 51.
43. In the interview with Agiletti, Trouillot does discuss madness, 109–110. On her protagonist Lisette as not only the enslaved woman experiencing a violent reality but also as the embodiment of resistance, see Jason Herbeck, "Entretien avec Evelyne Trouillot," *The French Review* 82, 4 (March 2009), especially 826–827. See also Evelyne Trouillot, "La Mer, Entre Lait et Sang," in *The Caribbean Woman Writer as Scholar: Creating, Imagining, Theorizing*, ed. Keshia M. Abraham (Coconut Creek, FL: Caribbean Studies Press, 2009), which directly explores madness experienced by a woman imprisoned on a ship, who contemplates leaping into the sea. Referred to as "la folle" by those who watch and mock her, she embraces her madness as protection: "Seul mon statut de folle me protège encore de l'hystérie collective. J'ai payé cher le droit d'être singulière," 115. ["Only my status as madwoman still protects me from collective hysteria. I have paid a high price for my right to be unique." My translation].
44. Trouillot, *The Infamous Rosalie*, 1.
45. Trouillot, *The Infamous Rosalie*, 2.
46. Sylvia Wynter, "1492: A New World View," in *Race, Discourse, and the Origin of the Americas: A New World View*, eds. Vera Lawrence Hyatt and Rex Nettleford (Washington, DC: Smithsonian Institution Press, 1995), makes an extended argument about how this dichotomy emerged and how colonizers like Columbus applied it to those they encountered in the "New World." She states: "[…] the new order of the secularizing modern state would map its own role-allocating mechanisms and unifying code of symbolic conspecificity onto a new notion of order. This new notion was to be based on a *by-nature difference* between Europeans, on the one hand, and peoples of indigenous and African descent, on the other," 38, emphasis in original.
47. Trouillot, *The Infamous Rosalie*, 12.
48. Trouillot, *the Infamous Rosalie*, 13.
49. On the absence of the word "*barracoons*" from the dictionary, see Trouillot "L'infâmie revisitée": "L'occultation de ce mot des lexiques symbolise pour moi le silence qui entoure l'esclavage," 54. ["The omission of this word from the lexicons to me symbolizes the silence that surrounds slavery." My translation.]
50. Dayan, "Erzulie," 13.
51. Dayan, "Erzulie," 13.
52. Trouillot, *The Infamous Rosalie*, 78.
53. Caruth, "Mad Witnesses": "[…] the relationships among trauma, madness, and inscription, what we might call the anthropological constant: the movement by which an erased event is already in search of

inscription. As soon as it is erased, even if there is no visible witness, the event by itself is looking for inscription: people themselves become the event," 93. "When it's madness, the track of the trauma is lost. You just have a witness of what you don't know. [...] And so madness happens when the tracks are lost," 95.

54. Trouillot, *The Infamous Rosalie*, 79.
55. Trouillot, *The Infamous Rosalie*, 80.
56. Trouillot, *The Infamous Rosalie*, 17.
57. Trouillot, *The Infamous Rosalie*, 32.
58. See M. NourbeSe Philip, "Dis Place—The Space Between," in her *A Genealogy of Resistance and Other Essays* (Toronto, ON: Mercury Press, 1997). See also Katherine McKittrick, "'Who do you talk to'," who argues that Philip presents "[...] speaking bodies that embrace a contradictory positionality and use this ambiguous place to think about and contend with the multiple locations of black women," 224. McKittrick further comments that the "reading of black women's bodies as chaotic by empowered men and women suggests that the place of black femininity rests outside modern conceptions of rationality, citizenship, and belonging," 224. Both Philip and McKittrick engage directly with the role of violation, including rape, and the breaking of silence by Black women.
59. Trouillot, *The Infamous Rosalie*, 32.
60. Jean-Charles, *Conflict Bodies*, 63.
61. Jean-Charles, *Conflict Bodies*, 70.
62. Trouillot, *The Infamous Rosalie*, 77.
63. McKittrick, *Demonic Grounds*, xvi.
64. McKittrick, *Demonic Grounds*, xvii, emphasis in original.
65. McKittrick, *Demonic Grounds*, xxiii.
66. Trouillot, *The Infamous Rosalie*, 64.
67. Dimitri Béchacq, "Les Parcours du marronnage dans l'histoire Haïtienne: entre instrumentalisation politique et réinterprétation sociale," *Ethnologies* 28, 1 (2006): "Chaque emploi du terme marronnage fait référence à un contexte d'énonciation spécifique. Dans son sens premier, *mawonaj* désigne un faisceau de comportements s'apparentant à des stratégies d'évitement, sorte d'échappatoire à toute emprise extérieure plaçant l'individu dans une situation d'obligations et de contraintes et l'incitant donc à fuir," 232. See also Béchacq, 220, 223ff, 230–231. See also "Roundtable: Writing, History, and Revolution," *Small Axe* 18 (September 2005), especially Dany Laferrière's comments, 196–197, and his description of Dessalines as a "monster" silenced, 199–200.
68. Barbara Lalla, *Defining Jamaican Fiction: Marronage and the Discourse of Survival* (Tuscaloosa: University of Alabama Press, 1996), 3.

69. Lalla, *Defining Jamaican Fiction*, 19.
70. See Wynter, "The Pope." On the maroon in works by Glissant, see also Sylvia Wynter, "Beyond the Word of Man: Glissant and the New Discourse of the Antilles," *World Literature Today* 63, 4 (Autumn 1989): 638, 642–644. She again draws the connection between European distinctions between Christian and secular (the latter as "Ontological Lack" and aligned with the enslaved) and "the oppositional categories of the Sane (rational nature) and the now asylum-interned, the Mad [...], together with the categories of the jobless and the poor, now coclassified with the Mad as the embodiment of irrational sensory nature," 641.
71. Pascale de Souza, "Demystifying female marooning: oppositional strategies and the writing of testimonies in the French Caribbean," *IJFS* 3, 3 (2000): 141.
72. De Souza, "Demystifying," 141.
73. De Souza, "Demystifying," 145.
74. Erin Mackie, "Welcome the Outlaw: Pirates, Maroons, and Caribbean Countercultures," *Cultural Critique* 59 (Spring 2005): 35.
75. Mackie, "Welcome the Outlaw," 42.
76. Danticat, "Interview," 51. On gender and *marronnage*, see also Laurence Clerfeuille, "Marronnage au Féminin dans *Rosalie L'Infâme* d'Evelyne Trouillot," *Contemporary French and Francophone Studies* 16, 1 (January 2012): 33–44.
77. Trouillot, *The Infamous Rosalie*, 26.
78. Trouillot, *The Infamous Rosalie*, 26–27.
79. Trouillot, *The Infamous Rosalie*, 59.
80. Trouillot, *The Infamous Rosalie*, 102.
81. Trouillot, *The Infamous Rosalie*, 107.
82. On Brigitte, Makandal, and Lisette, see Fremin, "*Rosalie L'Infâme d'Evelyne Trouillot,*" especially 229. On Lisette, memory, and silence, see Fremin 233. On Lisette's evolution, see Larrier, "In[her]itance," 141.
83. Trouillot, *The Infamous Rosalie*, 112.
84. Trouillot, *The Infamous Rosalie*, 113.
85. Trouillot, *The Infamous Rosalie*, 124.
86. Trouillot, *The Infamous Rosalie*, 127.
87. Trouillot, *The Infamous Rosalie*, 129.
88. Davoine and Gaudillière, *History Beyond Trauma*, 209.
89. Roxane Gay, *An Untamed State* (New York: Black Cat, 2014), 3.
90. Katherine McKittrick, "On plantations, prisons, and a black sense of place," *Social & Cultural Geography* 12, 8 (December 2011): 951.
91. McKittrick, "On plantations," 951.
92. McKittrick, "On plantations," 953.

93. Gay, *An Untamed State*, 36.
94. Gay, *An Untamed State*, 37.
95. Gay, *An Untamed State*, 155.
96. Gay, *An Untamed State*, 106.
97. Gay, *An Untamed State*, 225.
98. Gay, *An Untamed State*, 37.
99. Gay, *An Untamed State*, 78.
100. Gay, *An Untamed State*, 150.
101. Gay, *An Untamed State*, 171.
102. Gay, *An Untamed State*, 190, my emphasis.
103. The *kumbla* serves as both necessary and temporary space of retreat, a temporary respite that a state of madness can provide, but also a site where prolonged residency can entrap and immobilize the woman practicing resistance.
104. Gay, *An Untamed State*, 215.
105. Gay, *An Untamed State*, 219.
106. Gay, *An Untamed State*, 231.
107. Gay, *An Untamed State*, 277, my emphasis.
108. McKittrick, *Demonic Grounds*, xxiii. See also McKittrick on Philip's "Dis Place—The Space Between," especially 224, 226, 227, and on rape specifically, 229.
109. On the provision grounds, see Elizabeth DeLoughrey, who discusses this space in the context of Sylvia Wynter's one novel (*The Hills of Hebron*), in "Provision Grounds and Cultural Roots: Towards Ontological Sovereignty," in *The Caribbean Woman Writer as Scholar*, ed. Abraham, 205–224. On madness in this novel, see Kelly Baker Josephs, "The Necessity for Madness: Negotiating Nation in Sylvia Wynter's *The Hills of Hebron*," in *The Caribbean Woman Writer as Scholar*, ed. Abraham, 179–204.
110. Gay, *An Untamed State*, 303.
111. McKittrick, *Demonic Grounds*, xxiii.
112. Wynter offers a vision of how to move beyond categories, as Paget Henry comments in "Sylvia Wynter: Poststructuralism and Postcolonial Thought," in his *Caliban's Reason: Introducing Afro-Caribbean Philosophy* (London: Routledge, 2000): "Wynter hopes to introduce a qualitatively new type of *episteme*, one that would give us greater control over the misrepresentations that have undermined horizontal projects of emancipation," 129. He continues: "To achieve such new orders, it is necessary to reject not only specific ideologies but also the founding *episteme* of the colonial project. Without such an epistemic break, the capacity for original and independent thinking will remain severely limited," 134. See also Walter D. Mignolo, "Sylvia Wynter: What Does It

Mean to Be Human?" in *Sylvia Wynter*, ed. McKittrick: "To decline and decolonize means to adumbrate what was hidden and ignored—invent new concepts," 115; "Decolonial thinking and living are not to assimilate but to deny the universal pretense of *humanitas*," 120. He sums up Wynter's key question as "what does it mean to be human?" 122.

113. DeLoughrey, "Provision Grounds," 219–220.
114. Gay, *An Untamed State*, 339.
115. Gay, *An Untamed State*, 342.
116. Gay, *An Untamed State*, 344.
117. Gay, *An Untamed State*, 367.

Bibliography

Works Cited

Abraham, Keshia N., ed. *The Caribbean Woman Writer as Scholar: Creating, Imagining, Theorizing*. Coconut Creek, FL: Caribbean Studies Press, 2009.

Agiletti, Jessica. "Entretien avec Évelyne Trouillot." *Francofonia* 52 (Primavera 2007): 105–114.

Agnant, Marie-Célie. *Le Livre d'Emma*. Montréal, Canada: Éditions du remue-ménage, 2008 (c. 2001).

Béchacq, Dimitri. "Les Parcours du marronnage dans l'histoire Haïtienne: Entre instrumentalisation politique et réinterprétation sociale." *Ethnologies* 28, 1 (2006): 203–240.

Bell, Beverly. *Walking on Fire: Haitian Women's Stories of Survival and Resistance*. Ithaca, NY: Cornell UP, 2001.

Braziel, Jana Evans. "Défilée's Diasporic Daughters: Revolutionary Narratives of *Ayiti* (Haiti), *Nanchon* (Nation), and *Dyaspora* (Diaspora) in Edwidge Danticat's *Krik? Krak!*" *Studies in the Literary Imagination* 37, 2 (Fall 2004): 77–96.

———. "Re-membering Défilée: Dédée Bazile as Revolutionary *Lieu de Mémoire*." *Small Axe* 18 (September 2005): 57–85.

Caruth, Cathy. "Mad Witnesses: A Conversation with Françoise Davoine and Jean-Max Gaudillière." In her *Listening to Trauma: Conversations with Leaders in the Theory and Treatment of Catastrophic Experience*. Interviews and Photographs. Baltimore: Johns Hopkins UP, 2014. 81–109.

Chancy, Myriam. *Framing Silence: Revolutionary Novels by Haitian Women*. New Brunswick: Rutgers UP, 1997.

———. "'No Giraffes in Haiti': Haitian Women and State Terror." In Marie-Agnès Sourieau and Kathleen M. Balutansky, eds. *Écrire en pays assiégié Haïti Writing Under Siege*. Amsterdam and New York: Rodopi, 2004. 303–321.

———. *The Scorpion's Claw*. Leeds, England: Peepal Tree Press, 2005.
Charles, Carolle. "Gender and Politics in Contemporary Haiti: The Duvalierist State, Transnationalism, and the Emergence of a New Feminism (1980–1990)." *Feminist Studies* 21, 1 (Spring 1995): 135–164.
———."Popular Images of Gender and Sexuality: Poor and Working-Class Haitian Women's Discourses on the Use of Their Bodies." In Linden Lewis, ed. *The Culture of Gender and Sexuality in the Caribbean*. Gainesville: UP of Florida, 2003. 169–189.
Chauvet, Marie Vieux. *Love, Anger, Madness*. Trans. Rose-Myriam Réjouis and Val Vinokur. New York: Modern Library, 2010.
Clerfeuille, Laurence. "Marronnage au Féminin dans *Rosalie L'Infâme* d'Evelyne Trouillot." *Contemporary French and Francophone Studies* 16, 1 (January 2012): 33–44.
Danticat, Edwidge. "Evelyne Trouillot" (interview). *Bomb* no. 90 (Winter 2004–2005): 48–53.
Davoine, Françoise, and Jean-Max Gaudillière. *History Beyond Trauma: Whereof one cannot speak…thereof one cannot stay silent*. Susan Fairfield, trans. New York, NY: Other Press, 2004.
Dayan, Joan. "Erzulie: A Women's History of Haiti." *Research in African Literatures* 25, 2 (Summer 1994): 5–31.
———. *Haiti, History, and the Gods*. Berkeley: U California P, 1995.
DeLoughrey, Elizabeth. "Provision Grounds and Cultural Roots: Towards Ontological Sovereignty." In Abraham, ed. 205–224.
De Souza, Pascale. "Demystifying female marooning: oppositional strategies and the writing of testimonios in the French Caribbean." *IJFS* 3, 3 (2000): 141– 150.
———."Folie de l'écriture, écriture de la folie dans la littérature féminine des Antilles françaises." *Présence Francophone* n. 63 (2004): 130–144.
Dubois, Laurent. *Avengers of the New World: The Story of the Haitian Revolution*. Cambridge, MA: The Belknap Press of Harvard UP, 2004.
Federici, Silvia. *Caliban and the Witch: The Body and Primitive Accumulation*. Brooklyn, NY: Autonomedia, 2014.
Ferreira da Silva, Denise. "Before Man: Sylvia Wynter's Rewriting of the Modern Episteme." In McKittrick, ed. 90–105.
Fremin, Marie. "*Rosalie L'Infâme* d'Evelyne Trouillot": Comment inscrire l'esclavage dans la fiction?" *Présences haïtiennes* (2006): 221–234.
Gay, Roxane. *An Untamed State*. New York: Black Cat, 2014.
———. *Ayiti*. Oregon & New York: Artistically Declined Press, 2011.
———. *Bad Feminist: Essays*. New York: Harper Perennial, 2014.
Glissant, Édouard. *Caribbean Discourse: Selected Essays*. Trans. J. Michael Dash. Charlottesville: U P of VA, 1992.
Glover, Kaiama. "'Black' Radicalism in Haiti and the Disorderly Feminine: The Case of Marie Vieux Chauvet." *Small Axe* 40 (March 2013): 7–21.

———. "New Narratives of Haiti: How to Empathize with a Zombie." *Small Axe* 16, 3 (November 2012): 199–207.
Haynes, Tonya. "The Divine and the Demonic: Sylvia Wynter and Caribbean Feminist Thought Revisited." In V. Eudine Barriteau, ed. *Love and Power: Caribbean Discourses on Gender*. Kingston, Jamaica: U of the West Indies P, 2012. 54–71.
Henry, Paget. "Sylvia Wynter: Poststructuralism and Postcolonial Thought." In his *Caliban's Reason: Introducing Afro-Caribbean Philosophy*. London: Routledge, 2000. 117–143.
Herbeck, Jason. "Entretin avec Evelyne Trouillot." *The French Review* 82, 4 (March 2009): 822–829.
Jean-Charles, Régine Michelle. *Conflict Bodies: The Politics of Rape Representation in the Francophone Imaginary*. Columbus, OH: The Ohio State UP, 2014.
Josephs, Kelly Baker. "The Necessity for Madness: Negotiating Nation in Sylvia Wynter's *The Hills of Hebron*." In Abraham, ed. 179–204.
Kaussen, Valerie. "Irrational Revolutions: Colonial Intersubjectivity and Dialectics in Marie Chauvet's 'Amour'." In Doris L. Garraway, ed. *Tree of Liberty: Cultural Legacies of the Haitian Revolution in the Atlantic World*. Charlottesville: U Virginia P, 2008. 134–152.
Lalla, Barbara. *Defining Jamaican Fiction: Marronage and the Discourse of Survival*. Tuscaloosa: U Alabama P, 1996.
Larrier, Renée. "In[her]itance: Legacies and Lifelines in Evelyne Trouillot's *Rosalie L'Infâme*." *Dalhousie French Studies* 88 (Fall 2009): 135–145.
Lee-Keller, Hellen. "Madness and the Mulâtre-Aristocrate: Haiti, Decolonization, and Women in Marie Chauvet's *Amour*." *Callaloo* 32, 4 (Fall 2009): 1293–1311.
Mackie, Erin. "Welcome the Outlaw: Pirates, Maroons, and Caribbean Countercultures." *Cultural Critique* 59 (Spring 2005): 24–62.
Mardorossian, Carine M. "Towards a New Feminist Theory of Rape." *Signs* 27, 3 (Spring 2002): 743–775.
McKittrick, Katherine. *Demonic Grounds: Black Women and the Cartographies of Struggle*. Minneapolis: U Minnesota P, 2006.
———. "On plantations, prisons, and a black sense of place." *Social & Cultural Geography* 12, 8 (December 2011): 947–963.
———. "'Who do you talk to, when a body's in trouble?': M. Nourbese Philip's (un)silencing of black bodies in the diaspora." *Social & Cultural Geography* 1, 2 (2000): 223–236.
McKittrick, Katherine, ed. *Sylvia Wynter: On Being Human as Praxis*. Durham, NC: Duke UP, 2015.
Mignolo, Walter D. "Sylvia Wynter: What Does It Mean to Be Human?" In McKittrick, ed. 107–123.
Philip, M. NourbeSe. *A Genealogy of Resistance and Other Essays*. Toronto: Mercury Press, 1997.

"Roundtable: Writing, History, and Revolution." Dany Laferrière, Louis-Philippe Dalembert, Edwidge Danticat, Évelyne Trouillot. *Small Axe* 18 (September 2005): 189–201.

Schwab, Gabriele. *Haunting Legacies: Violent Histories and Transgenerational Trauma*. New York, NU: Columbia UP, 2010.

Scott, David. "The Re-Enchantment of Humanism: An Interview with Sylvia Wynter." *Small Axe* 8 (September 2000): 119–207.

Shields, Tanya L. *Bodies and Bones: Feminist Rehearsal and Imagining Caribbean Belonging*. Charlottesville, VA: U Virginia P, 2014.

Sol, Antoinette Marie. "Histoire(s) et traumatisme(s): l'infanticide dans le roman féminin antillais." *The French Review* 81, 5 (April 2008): 967–984.

Trouillot, Evelyne. "La Mer, Entre Lait et Sang." In Abraham, ed. 111–121.

———."L'Infâmie revisitée." *Africultures* 58 (janvier-mars 2004): 51–56.

———. *The Infamous Rosalie*. M. A. Salvodon, trans. Lincoln, NE: U Nebraska P, 2013.

———. *Rosalie L'Infâme*. Paris: Éditions Dapper, 2003.

Trouillot, Michel-Rolph. *Silencing the Past: Power and the Production of History*. Boston: Beacon Press, 1995.

Wynter, Sylvia. "1492: A New World View." In Vera Lawrence Hyatt and Rex Nettleford, eds. *Race, Discourse, and the Origin of the Americas: A New World View*. Washington, DC: Smithsonian Institution Press, 1995. 5–57.

———. "Beyond Miranda's Meanings: Un/Silencing the 'Demonic Ground' of Caliban's 'Woman'." In Carole Boyce Davies and Elaine Savory Fido, eds. *Out of the Kumbla: Caribbean Women and Literature*. Trenton: Africa World Press, 1990. 355–372.

———. "Beyond the Word of Man: Glissant and the New Discourse of the Antilles." *World Literature Today* 63, 4 (Autumn 1989): 637–648.

———. "The Pope Must Have Been Drunk, The King of Castile a Madman: Culture as Actuality, and the Caribbean Rethinking Modernity." In Alvina Ruprecht and Cecelia Taiana, eds. *The Reordering of Culture: Latin America, the Caribbean and Canada in the Hood*. Ottawa: Carleton UP, 1995. 17–41.

———. "Rethinking 'Aesthetics': Notes Towards a Deciphering Practice." In Mbye Cham, ed. *Ex-iles: Essays on Caribbean Cinema*. Trenton, NJ: African World Press, 1992. 238–279.

———. "Unsettling the Coloniality of Being/Power/Truth/Freedom: Towards the Human, After Man, Its Overrepresentation—An Argument." *CR: The New Centennial Review* 3, 3 (Fall 2003): 257–337.

"Dark Swoops": Trauma and Madness in *Half of a Yellow Sun*

Seretha D. Williams

The Nigerian-Biafran Civil War remains a touchstone for twenty-first-century Nigeria. For Igbo Nigerians, the failed secession of Biafra is a historical moment that informs the collective consciousness of more than 27 million people. Survivors, historians, and human rights groups describe the massacres of Biafra as genocide. Depending on the historical document, reports of the dead range from 50,000 to 100,000 Igbo men, women, and children. Numerous combatants and noncombatants were killed by violence; still many more were starved to death. *Life Magazine*'s July 12, 1968, cover, "Starving Children of Biafra War," and the iconic photographs of Don McCullin documented the travesty of the civil war, seemingly happening out of the view of the world; the image of starving Nigerian children, over time, serves as the visual metaphor and cultural referent for all of Africa.[1]

While first-generation Nigerian novelists such as Chinua Achebe and Flora Nwapa[2] documented the literal trauma of Biafra, third- and fourth-generation writers like Chimamanda Ngozi Adichie write Biafra as symbol, as a "universalizing" of the meaning of the conflict.[3] Adichie's *Half of a Yellow Sun* is a war novel that confronts the psychological aftermath of mass violence by recording the testimonies of survivors; it is a trauma

S.D. Williams (✉)
Augusta University, Augusta, GA, Georgia

C.A. Brown and J.X.K. Garvey (eds.), *Madness in Black Women's Diasporic Fictions*, Gender and Cultural Studies in Africa and the Diaspora, DOI 10.1007/978-3-319-58127-9_6

text that foregrounds trauma as a gendered event. However, Adichie's suffering bodies and traumatized minds pose an ethical problem for the African writer. Brenda Cooper, for example, suggests *Half of a Yellow Sun* fails to expand non-Nigerian readers' understanding of the complexities of the war or the postcolonial conditions that created the political landscape upon which Biafra occurred. According to Cooper, the novel perpetuates the "trope of Africa's dark heart" despite Adichie's efforts to wrestle the characters from essentialism.[4] Cooper's observations are valid; the specter of Biafra and other social atrocities loom in the imaginations of Adichie's non-Nigerian audience. However, Cooper reads *Half of a Yellow Sun* primarily as a realist text, not as a trauma text; she does not use the term "trauma," nor does she draw from the scholarship of trauma theory in her critique of the novel. Reading the novel as a trauma text mitigates the Western gaze and creates an opportunity to engage with African women's literature beyond the context of realism, the primary lens through which scholars examine Adichie and other African writers. *Half of a Yellow Sun*, with its preoccupation with the routine of the everyday and its raw depictions of class and gender, love and war, is a realist novel; yet the trauma characters experience and describe is not merely a narrative trope. Instead, Adichie intends readers to grapple with the harm done to Nigeria and invokes the imagery of Biafra to make visible truths rendered invisible by the passage of time and an unwillingness to remember.

Adichie was born in 1977, seven years after the end of the war. Her knowledge of Biafra is inherited rather than lived. Yet from the very beginning of her career, Biafra plays an integral role in her writing. Before the publication of *Half of a Yellow Sun*, Adichie's novel set in 1960s Nigeria, Adichie also wrote a play, *For Love of Biafra*, and short stories—"Ghosts" and "A Private Experience[5]"—that focus on the lives of characters affected by the war. In "Story Behind the Book," Adichie's explanation for her preoccupation with Biafra, she asserts:

> I wrote this novel because I wanted to write about love and war, because I grew up in the shadow of Biafra, because I lost both grandfathers in the Nigeria-Biafra war, because I wanted to engage my history in order to make sense of my present, […], because my father has tears in his eyes when he speaks of losing his father, because my mother still cannot speak at length about losing her father in a refugee camp, because the brutal bequests of colonialism make me angry, because the thought of the egos

> and indifference of men leading to the unnecessary deaths of men and women and children enrages me, because I don't ever want to forget.[6]

Biafra, for Adichie and other Igbo writers, is a story to be remembered, a story to be passed down. The stories of the war told to her by her parents affect her. Consequently, she writes of memories that are not exactly her memories; her memories belong to her as a part of a collective consciousness, a cultural "postmemory." Writing about the Holocaust, Marianne Hirsch argues, "Postmemory describes the relationship of the second generation to powerful, often traumatic experiences that… seem to constitute memories in their own right."[7] Postmemory describes the complexities of the relationship between the people who lived a trauma and those who did not but instead inherited the stories and experiences of the generation before. The postgenerations, as Hirsch labels them, grew up with the stories and experiences; they were the listeners of testimony and as such, the memories become their memories and feel like lived experiences. The traumatic events of the past were so powerful that they continue to be felt in the present. Furthermore, postmemory, a process of transgenerational transmission of trauma, is a fragmented or disjointed form of memory and knowledge. The second and subsequent generations collect information—letters, diaries, archival materials, oral narratives—and attempt to piece together a coherent understanding, to fill in the gaps. As such, they contribute imaginatively to the memory, completing the narrative thread of a story inherently incomplete. Adichie, the inheritor of Biafran trauma, returns to this theme repeatedly. Like Margaret Walker, whose novel *Jubilee* imaginatively recounts the slavery experience of Vyry, Walker's grandmother, Adichie is interested in exploring what is missed when we focus singularly on data or historical evidence; both texts consider a larger truth not limited by written historically accepted proof. Similarly, *Half of a Yellow Sun* is a novel that brings together trauma studies and postmodernist discourse through its preoccupation with the politics of remembering and forgetting and its attempt to bridge the psychic distance between the past and the present. Adichie circumvents the linearity of the text by reenacting the act of testimony in the novel; she documents Olanna's act of telling and Ugwu's recording. Ugwu is a mirror of Adichie, who writes the oral testimonies of her family and of Igbo in the broader sense. (This mirroring is not exact because Ugwu is a house servant and conscripted soldier, and Adichie's background is more aligned with the well-educated, financially comfortable Olanna.) Other authors have broached the theme of postmemory.[8] Adichie's characters are first-generation trauma survivors, but her writing of the text as a postgenerational author influences her telling of the story. Authors of traumatic fiction replicate the symptoms of trauma by employing literary strategies such as fragmented plots and textual omissions. By distorting conventional narrative structures, the writers are able to mirror neurosis, to comment on the sociopolitical structures that create the conditions of trauma, and to evaluate the difficulty of constructing an inclusive historical narrative. *Half of a Yellow Sun's* asynchronous plot and ensemble point of view tell a specifically Igbo story of war and oppression that resists forgetting and silencing.

Adichie's novel is not unique for its preoccupation with remembrance and documentation of Biafra; her literary predecessors, too, have recorded the stories and experiences of war in Nigeria. However, *Half of a Yellow Sun* is a seminal text in that it speaks backward to two distinct Nigerian thematic traditions and reclaims a space for women's activism and participation in nation creation. Adichie, through the character Olanna, comments on and criticizes a culture of violence that grows out of the Biafran War, just as Chinua Achebe, to whom scholars compare Adichie, draws upon what Taiwo Adetunji Osinubi describes as "the colonial moment"[9] in *Things Fall Apart* to record memories and to comment on a Nigeria embarking upon independence and struggling to forge a postcolonial identity, Adichie reexamines the Biafran moment to document the testimony of noncombatant Igbos and to address the persistent problems of Nigerian statehood and national identity. Susan Andrade's evaluation of the nationalist implications of Adichie's fiction suggests Adichie intentionally draws upon the post-independence moment, returns to the site of trauma, and, in doing so, calls attention to the state of twenty-first-century Nigeria. Osinubi's analyses of postcolonial writings identify similar patterns in third-generation novels, and he proposes contemporary novels reflect ways in which "national cultures of violence invade the innermost recesses of the lives of individual characters."[10] *Half of a Yellow Sun*, arguably a fourth-generation[11] text, focuses primarily on the effects of conflict on human lives; numerous scholars have written about Adichie's postmodern approach to the war novel genre.[12] However, Adichie's foray into the trauma fiction genre is not new ground. Nwapa's *Never Again*, for example, describes the toll of war on the individual and foregrounds the role of women in the Biafran conflict. Neither is Adichie's portrayal of the madman or madwoman in a colonial or postcolonial society a new trope. Chinua Achebe's short story "The Madman" is but one example of the mad figure representing the condition of Africa (specifically Nigeria in this story). Iniobong

Uko's analysis of "The Madman" suggests, "The insanity manifests itself in the way Nigeria was embroiled … in excessive corruption, nepotism, a thirst for power…"[13] For Uko, Nigeria is a "symbolic state of insanity."[14] Similarly, in Adichie's novel, the Biafran conflict is a physical manifestation of the symbolic insanity caused by decolonization and the growth of regionalism. *Half of a Yellow Sun*, as a neo-war narrative, succeeds because it is hyperconscious of its literary and historical antecedents and its potential for constructing a new, more democratic literature. Adichie's novel is her own creation, but it is also a collaborative text that draws upon the written and oral texts that preceded it.

Adichie writes back to both Achebe and Nwapa. In Achebe's *Things Fall Apart*, the district commissioner reduces Okonkwo's colonial moment (and, by extension, Africa's colonial moment) to a single paragraph; in *Half of a Yellow Sun*, the poor house servant Ugwu writes the story of Biafra. In Nwapa's *Never Again*, the protagonist Kate is a "mad woman" attempting to rescue her family from the paroxysm of war; she tells her story, giving voice to the plight of women and children. However, Nwapa's novel and the real stories of women in Biafra remain relatively obscure. Adichie, through the character Olanna, revisits Nwapa. Olanna, like Nwapa's Kate, is an upper-middle-class woman who needs to tell her story. Olanna does indeed tell her story to Ugwu, the male house servant, who includes the oral narrative in his written text on the Biafran War. Amy Novak[15] legitimately questions Adichie's selection of Ugwu and not Olanna as author.[16] Certainly, the selection of Ugwu as author disrupts the long history of Europe writing (defining) Africa and removes the power of telling stories from the hands of an educated Nigerian elite. Nevertheless, limiting Olanna, a college professor, to testimony problematizes Adichie's attempt to create independent, subversive female characters in the novel and raises numerous questions about gender. Why doesn't Olanna write? Why is she the only central character who succumbs to madness?

Marta Caminero-Santangelo's analysis of madness in the works of Toni Morrison suggests family and community are integral "to Morrison's envisioning of a strategy other than madness for dealing with racial (and gendered) representations within dominant culture."[17] Olanna, like Pecola in Morrison's *The Bluest Eye* and Sula in *Sula*, occupies a tenuous position within her family and her community. I suggest that Olanna succumbs to madness, in part, because she is disconnected from family and community. The sociohistorical moment renders Olanna vulnerable to mental illness. She is a victim of the war, but prior to the war, the early 1960s, she is also a victim of a patriarchy that undervalues women.[18] Olanna's privilege as an educated woman in Nigeria does not preclude her from the social and familial constraints of womanhood. Characters in the novel question Olanna's decisions to delay marriage and motherhood and to focus, instead, on her career at the university. Her seeming rejection of those institutions is beyond eccentricity. Instead, they suggest her choices are a type of madness. When Olanna becomes surrogate mother to Baby—the child of her lover, Odenigbo, whom she eventually marries, and another (servant) woman—she embeds herself within a social system against which she appears to rebel earlier in the narrative. Although Olanna's Dark Swoops, a condition Adichie describes as an amalgamation of physiological and psychological conditions, are triggered by a specific and seemingly unrelated traumatic event, Olanna's breakdown is foreshadowed through her complicated interactions with other characters and, by extension, an evolving Nigerian identity. Despite her socioeconomic privilege, professional accomplishments, and social charms, Olanna is fearful and insecure. She worries about being judged by other women, especially Odenigbo's colleague Miss Adebayo. Adichie emphasizes Olanna's insecurities by contrasting Olanna with her twin sister Kainene: "She wished she was different, the sort of person who did not need to lean on others like Kainene."[19] Initially, Olanna seems only to act out the beautiful woman trope of Negritude literature from the 1930s and 1940s. She is the embodiment of black Africa—beautiful and vulnerable; she is a synecdoche for Nigeria, and her Dark Swoops are external manifestations of a sickness that overwhelms Nigeria. However, by the end of the novel, Olanna changes and becomes less vulnerable and more capable of standing on her own.

Adichie first confronts the insanity of Nigeria in her examination of Olanna's relationship to her father, Chief Ozobia. Her father uses Olanna's beauty as leverage in business deals. Kainene, Olanna's twin, compares their father's parties to markets and quips, "My sister and I are meat."[20] The sisters, especially Olanna, who is regarded as the pretty one, are valued primarily for their ability to seduce men into deals. Olanna resists her father's commodification of her body by selecting her own lovers and by rejecting external pressures to marry. Her "illogical" prettiness[21] and desirability, nevertheless, inform the other characters' discourse about Olanna. Okeoma, another of Odenigbo's friends, quips upon first meeting Olanna, "'I thought Odenigbo's girlfriend was a human being; he didn't say you were a water mermaid.'"[22] The novel implies, early on, something is wrong with Olanna. She is not like other women. She is compared to a siren or mermaid, both manifestations of the water-spirit Mami Wata.[23] The mother of Odenigbo, Olanna's "revolutionary lover" and eventual husband, accuses Olanna of being unnatural and barren—a witch. Mama levies charges of witchcraft against Olanna because, in her village belief system, witchcraft explains Olanna's difference. First, Olanna is a twin, a bad omen in traditional Igbo culture. Second, Olanna is sexually active but produces no offspring; infertility in traditional belief systems is commonly attributed to witchcraft.[24] Odenigbo dismisses his mother's offensive behavior as village superstition, but Olanna, who already questions her ability to bear children, cannot shrug off Mama's attack, just as she cannot move beyond Miss Adebayo's pointed criticism. Both Aunty Ifeka, Olanna's relative in Kano, and Olanna's friend the American Edna recognize Olanna's lack of confidence. Edna challenges Olanna, asking, "'Why isn't what you are enough?'"[25] Edna's question is Adichie's question. Adichie responds by suggesting the constant struggle against patriarchy—an artifact of colonialism—depletes Olanna. The effects of patriarchy are an integral part of the "traumatic legacy of colonialism,"[26] Amy Novak describes. While patriarchy existed in pre-colonial Nigeria, Gloria Chuku argues, colonialism transformed gender relations, fostered social and economic advantages for men, and relegated women, who once worked in agriculture and markets, to the domestic sphere. Igbo women, in particular, had played a complementary role in the traditional system of production; under colonialism, Igbo and other indigenous women "lost their control of the marketplace and even their dominant role in the trade of the region."[27] Similarly, Chima J. Korieh's refutation of the "myth of the invisible woman" supports Chuku's analysis of pre-colonial gender relations. Korieh proposes, "Before colonialism, Igbo men could in fact accept the 'sitting on a man'[28] mode of conflict resolution… because in these communities, women worked in concert with male authorities in the administration of the community."[29] The Women's War of 1929, also known as the Aba Women's Riots, was a response to the colonial government's attempt to tax women's market goods. Women throughout Nigeria resisted colonial practices that infringed upon established rights of women in the market. *Half of a Yellow Sun*, through Olanna, reflects the continued displacement or disenfranchisement of Nigerian women. Olanna understands that her labor outside the domestic sphere is not enough to validate her personal independence in postcolonial Nigeria.[30] Lillian Temu Osaki, examining the trope of madness in black women's writing, asks, "Is the mad woman any less sane than the society that condemns her?"[31]

Odenigbo acts as the public voice of resistance in the novel, and Ugwu, his protégé, records the individual accounts of that resistance. Novak proposes that Olanna and the other female characters are silenced and "fail to fully give voice to female experiences of neocolonial trauma."[32] Olanna and Miss Adebayo, a Yoruba woman and university colleague, are present at the politically charged gatherings hosted at Odenigbo's house. Miss Adebayo participates fully, while Olanna, a newcomer to the group, listens. However, neither acts as a public voice nor as a recorder of events; neither has the agency to influence the discourse of Biafra's rebellion against the federal government. Olanna's lack of agency is exacerbated by the war because Olanna views the Nigerian-Biafran Civil War as masculine.

Despite the novel's initial framing of war as the purview of men like Odenigbo and Colonel Madu, Kainene's friend and a Biafran sympathizer, Adichie introduces the reader to the developing conflict through Olanna, who is unexpectedly caught in the middle of a pogrom in Kano. Under the protection of her former boyfriend Mohammad, a Hausa, she discovers the mutilated bodies of her maternal uncle, Mbezi, Ifeka, his wife, and Arize, their pregnant daughter. Fleeing for her life along with hundreds of other Igbos, Olanna encounters a woman on the train carrying the head of her dead child in a calabash. In survival mode, Olanna goes numb. Her response to the trauma is delayed. Not until she arrives home does her trauma manifest itself. Adichie writes, "Her legs were fine when she climbed down from the train…But at the front door of Odenigbo's house, they failed. So did her bladder."[33] Olanna's initial response to the violence at Kano resembles a psychosomatic disorder: although nothing is physically wrong, she is unable to walk, to speak, or to control her bladder. In the second stage of her traumatic response, she experiences Dark Swoops, which she describes as "[a] thick black descend[ing] from above and press[ing] itself over her face, firmly, while she struggled to breathe."[34] Olanna's description of Dark Swoops is consistent with panic disorder symptoms. Adichie painstakingly details the circumstances of Olanna's Dark Swoops. They are "a thick blanket" preventing her from breathing, and they cause her to hallucinate about "burning owls at the window grinning and beckoning to her with charred feathers."[35] At a rally, "Odenigbo raised his arm as he spoke, and Olanna thought how awkwardly twisted Aunty Ifeka's arm had looked, as she lay on the ground."[36] Her behavior becomes so odd, "Once [Ugwu] saw her walk over to the guava tree and caress its trunk, and he told himself he would go and pull her away, after a minute, before the neighbors said she was going mad."[37] She has a recurring dream that "[s]he forgot about Baby and ran to the bunker and after the bombs had fallen, she tripped on the burnt body of a child with its features so blackened she could not be certain it was Baby."[38] She grows numb to her surroundings; Adichie writes, "She felt nothing. She was floating away from inside herself."[39] Finally, she relives the experience of her trauma in her everyday life; for example, combing Baby's hair, Olanna recalls, "I keep thinking about the hair on that child's head I saw on the train."[40] Her symptoms are persistent and recur. She cannot taste.[41] Her mind freezes.[42] She is "dazed."[43] Olanna asserts, "It was often difficult to visualize anything concrete that was not dulled by memories of Arize and Aunty Ifeka and Uncle Mbaezi, that did not feel like life being lived on suspended time."[44] Her Dark Swoops are the direct result of her trauma exposure in Kano and the indirect product of the culture of violence and oppression that leads to the Biafran conflict.[45] The violence around Olanna makes her more vulnerable. The Dark Swoops are physical manifestations of the pathology of war and Olanna's response to a broken society. War triggers her anxieties and makes her lack of agency readily apparent.

Olanna, after Kano and in the midst of war, is a different person. Odenigbo tells her "the experience had changed her and made her so much more inward."[46] Ugwu also notices a change in Olanna; he describes her as silent and mechanical.[47] Her attacks are easily triggered and often develop in the form of flashbacks. Commonplace or everyday activities become sources of anxiety for Olanna. For example, intimacy and sex with Odenigbo triggers a flashback for Olanna: "when he slid into her, she thought about Arize's pregnant belly, how easily it must have broken, skin stretched that taught."[48] Comments, sirens, raised arms, accidental separations, and listening to others' stories of trauma trigger Dark Swoops and flashbacks. Moving from house to house and town to town to escape the increasing violence weighs heavily on Olanna, who with each move loses more physical possessions and concrete connections to her former life. Innocuous sagging string and nails in walls serve as reminders of her dead relatives and trigger her attacks.[49] Olanna carries the trauma with her, and, in effect, reexperiences Kano with each Dark Swoops episode. She is no longer the effervescent woman she was when she returned home from England.

Furthermore, within the confines of war, Olanna's attempts to live outside of social expectations fail. She resorts to her expected roles as wife and mother. Olanna, in the throes of her madness, the Dark Swoops, marries Odenigbo. She has already agreed to be surrogate mother to Baby, Odenigbo's child with another woman, and her marriage suggests "the old framework that fit her ideals was gone now that Arize and Aunty Ifeka and Uncle Mbaezi would always be frozen faces in her album."[50] Olanna's trauma exposure disrupts her progressive critique and rejection of patriarchy. To cope with her stress, Olanna embraces familiar institutions. Brinda Mehta's commentary on madness in fiction suggests that, at the literal level, madness mirrors the anxieties and the environmental stressors of a society. Literally, Olanna's Dark Swoops are the manifestation of chaos and terror. She, like the other noncombatants, is powerless. Figuratively, Mehta proposes madness serves as "a metaphor for female cultural and intellectual exile, a sign of protest and rejection of conventionally defined female roles and expectations."[51] Adichie's depiction of madness, in this respect, aligns in part with Mehta's observations about figural madness. However, Olanna's process is reversed. Before the Dark Swoops, she resisted marriage, but in the midst of trauma and war, Olanna embodies culturally (and colonial) defined roles for women. While Novak criticizes *Half of a Yellow Sun* for perpetuating a "dichotomous vision of women as victims and men as social agents,"[52] I suggest Adichie's depiction of Olanna is more complicated than Novak's analysis suggests. Although Olanna's agency as an academic and as a progressive woman is limited by the events of the war and by her decision to participate actively in traditional institutions, she does not lose all agency. Olanna's agency changes as she elects to do work as a mother and wife. Adichie thus creates a new cultural framework within which to view Olanna's development as a character and subverts the bifurcated paradigm that pits Olanna (progressive) against Mama (traditional) and the other female characters earlier in the novel.

Clara Escoda Augusti's analysis of madness in the novels of Gayl Jones and Toni Morrison suggests an alternative reading to Mehta and Novak. Augusti argues, "By attempting to deconstruct madness, both Morrison and Jones tell us that the dominant patriarchal order labels as madness and insanity those behaviours which contain the power to destabilize this dominant order, to highlight its constructed nature."[53] Adichie, too, deconstructs madness. Olanna's madness disrupts the patriarchal narrative of the Biafran War. Dark Swoops are simultaneously a sign of Olanna's loss of control and a "political response" to the culture of violence and instability of post-independent Nigeria.[54] Going mad, in some respects, is the only sane response. Adichie's text resists normalizing mass violence. Olanna's Dark Swoops act as reminders that what is happening is beyond the scope of normal. Her Swoops externalize that which is inexpressible.[55]

Admittedly, Adichie's exploration of the theme of madness is not as pronounced as in Tsitsi Dangarembga's *Nervous Conditions*, Bessie Head's *A Question of Power*, Buchi Emecheta's *The Joys of Motherhood*, and Rebeka Njau's *Ripples in the Pool*. Madness in those texts is an integral element of the plot. Nevertheless, Olanna is similar to other African women characters who go mad as the result of patriarchal stressors that limit their agency and autonomy. Adichie, in addition, is like other African women authors who resist the literary tradition of limiting female characters to the role of victim. She does not condemn Olanna to madness; instead, she incrementally restores Olanna and empowers her to act and to speak. Novak's astute reading of Adichie does not account for Adichie's valuation of oral testimony. I propose that Adichie does not privilege the written text over the oral text. Adichie learns about Biafra through the oral tradition. Her memories are inherited from oral stories. Although Ugwu is the author of the written text, Olanna's testimony of the horrors of Biafra is equally valuable. Her oral narrative is valid, not *made* valid by its inclusion in Ugwu's book. Olanna's testimony is an integral component of her, and, by extension, Nigeria's healing. She must work through her trauma, and it makes sense that Adichie positions that working through within the context of the spoken word.

Ronald Granofsky identifies three stages of trauma response in the trauma novel. The first state is a regression to childhood or a childlike state.[56] Olanna's inability to walk, speak, or control her bladder after first witnessing the murdered bodies of her family constitutes a regression. Odenigbo begins to speak to her as an adult speaks to a child. The second stage is fragmentation, in which Granofsky proposes that the structure of the novel itself works to "undermine the stability of the narrative point of view."[57] *Half of a Yellow Sun* is polyvocal and multiperspectival. In his study of the novel, Mikhail Bakhtin argues language is mediated and collaborative; the "I" of the text is a collective "I." Polyvocality, then, suggests a text—spoken or written—is not the product of a single author. Instead, the text is a social document that reflects many voices—intentionally and unintentionally. Similarly, the multiperspectival[58] text is collaborative, drawing upon knowledge from a variety of sources, audiences, and viewpoints. Adichie disrupts the narrative of the novel by making the reader aware of the multiple voices and sources of knowledge that inform her telling of Biafra. Thus, the asynchronous plot and the absence of a definitive protagonist are by-products of the trauma story Adichie wants to tell. Because Biafra is not a single story and does not belong to any individual, the novel must rely on multiple modes of telling (oral and written); the collaboration of Ugwu, the writer, and Olanna, the teller, leads to Granofsky's third stage of reunification or reconciliation.[59] He argues, "The trauma must be worked through and integrated into the individual's world view."[60] Olanna must integrate the traumas multiple times. Writing about Kosinki's *The Painted Bird*, Granofsky notes, "The loss of voice… represents a physiological reaction to trauma and symbolizes a disjunction between the individual and the collective of which the individual is a part."[61] The recovery of voice restores Olanna to the collective. Odenigbo and Kainene[62] initially silence Olanna; they do not want her to tell the details of her horrific experience in Kano. However, Olanna insists and eventually recounts the story for Odenigbo, for her immediate and extended family, and for Ugwu. Contrary to Novak's supposition, Olanna is not silenced completely.

Olanna is summoned to Umunnachi to answer questions about what happened to the family in Kano. She gives the *umunna*, testimony of what happened in Kano[63]: "The heavy weight of four muted funerals weighed on her head, funerals based not on physical bodies but on her words. And she wondered if she was mistaken, if she had perhaps imagined the bodies lying in the dust, so many bodies in the yard that recalling them made salt rush into her mouth." Adichie never clearly diagnoses Olanna's Dark Swoops, but the salty taste in Olanna's mouth is one of the symptoms of migraine headaches. The exact nature of Olanna's condition is not clear, but the salt is a physical indication of a change in her state of mind. Her testimony triggers a Dark Swoop. Olanna becomes motionless and goes into a trance in the car afterward. "Testimony," Jennifer Griffiths purports, "offers a public enactment of memory, and clearly, the cultural context and content work collaboratively to shape testimony."[64] Other testimony theorists such as Dori

Laub and Shoshana Felman propose that testimony can serve as a critique of collective memory or as an examination of national myths that develop from collective memory. In this scene, testimony is a ritual and a duty Olanna must perform; her words form the foundation of her family's collective memory of the event and facilitate the community's collective healing. Adichie writes, "She had given those left behind a right to mourn and wear black and receive visitors who would come in saying 'Ndo nu.'"[65] Olanna's act of telling empowers the community.

When Olanna explains Kano to Odenigbo, however, her description is filmic; she matter-of-factly outlines the *mise-en-scène* of the events. Her testimony physically affects her and she dissociates from the events in her telling. Although Olanna resists the telling and retelling of Kano, she does and, in doing so, speaks not only for herself but also for the silenced voices of her family and other victims. Laub proposes, "The 'not telling' of the story serves as a perpetuation of its tyranny."[66] Therefore, Olanna must narrate her trauma if she and by extension Nigeria are to recover. Odenigbo, who is unable to "feel the bewilderment, injury, confusion, dread, and conflict"[67] that Olanna feels, does not facilitate her mental recovery. He cannot act as what Dominic La Capra describes as the ideal or empathic listener. Odenigbo responds by silencing her, "'Shush, nkem. You'll be fine.'"[68] Words have power and by stopping Olanna from speaking about the massacre, Odenigbo presumes he can assist Olanna in her recovery. Bedridden, Olanna becomes his patient. Olanna notes, "He spoke too softly to her. His voice sounded so silly, So unlike him."[69] Odenigbo's baby talk reifies Olanna's infantilization. Instead of mothering Baby, she, herself, is being mothered. Olanna needs to tell because telling is a type of reexperiencing. By reexperiencing the traumatic event, Olanna can engage with the trauma. However, Odenigbo does not facilitate this reexperiencing. Instead, he speaks for her. Adichie writes, "When her parents and [her twin sister] Kainene visited, she did not say much; it was Odenigbo who told them what she had seen."[70] Olanna desires to narrate her personal trauma and the collective trauma of colonialism and of patriarchy, but she struggles to tell her story. Even as Olanna endeavors to speak, she is silenced by Odenigbo's unwillingness to listen. Olanna's silence disconnects her from the present time, another symptom of her Dark Swoops. As such, she fails to engage in the present and the narration lapses into stasis.

Dominic La Capra's discussion of agency is helpful here. La Capra proposes two strategies of agency: working through and acting out. La

Capra's analysis of agency, albeit filtered through Freudian psychoanalysis, challenges standard readings of victims and victimhood. In *Half of a Yellow Sun*, the traumatized Olanna begins to recover as she "works through" the Dark Swoops. She does this through her testimony. First, she tells her story to Odenigbo as she returns home from Kano. She describes "the vaguely familiar clothes on the headless bodies in the yard, the still-twitchy fingers on Uncle Mbaezi's hand, the rolled-back eys of the child's head in the calabash and the odd skin tone…."[71] However, Odenigbo is a poor listener. He repeatedly silences or, more correctly, he shushes her, unwilling to hear her story. Then visitors silence Olanna. They do not allow her to testify, to bear witness. Stef Craps and Gert Buelens propose, "Indeed, the psychologization of social suffering encourages the idea that recovery from the traumas of colonialism is basically a matter of the individual witness gaining linguistic control over his or her pain."[72] Adichie's rendering of trauma in *Half of a Yellow Sun* suggests the process of recovery is more complicated than mastering one's own language. Olanna must speak, but also she must be heard and listen to others.

Other friends and family, including Kainene, tell Olanna their own stories of trauma.[73] Ultimately, Ugwu serves as the "addressable other" for Olanna, as Dori Laub defines the role. He listens to her and makes his interest in her story clear by asking details of the event. He does not shush her as did Odenigbo. Adichie recounts the telling of this story to Ugwu multiple times. In the book within the book, which we learn later is authored by Ugwu, the narrator describes the author recording the story:

> For the prologue, he recounts the story of the woman with the calabash. She sat on the floor of a train squashed between crying people, shouting people, praying people. She was silent, caressing the covered calabash on her lap in a gentle rhythm until they crossed the Niger, and then she lifted the lid and asked Olanna and others close by to look inside. Olanna tells him this story and he notes the details. She tells him how the bloodstains on the woman's wrapper blended into the fabric to form a rusty mauve. She describes the carved designs on the woman's calabash, slanting lines crisscrossing each other, and she describes the child's head inside: scruffy braids falling across the dark-brown face, eyes completely white, eerily open, a mouth in a small surprised O.[74]

The author then invokes other genocides—Germany and Rwanda—claiming for Biafra its spot in historical massacres.

The book telling of the events at Kano is actually the second telling. The original telling of the story to Ugwu is documented in the last section of the novel. The war had ended, but Kainene was still missing. Olanna, combing and braiding Baby's hair that is falling out from malnourishment, recalls the thick hair on the head of the child in the calabash and remarks, "'It must have been work for her mother to plait it'."[75] Ugwu asks her, "'How was it plaited?'"[76] Ugwu's question encourages Olanna to focus on the details of her memory. Adichie writes, "Olanna was surprised, at first, by the question and then she realized that she clearly remembered how it was plaited and she began to describe the hairstyle, how some of the braids fell across the forehead. Then she described the head itself, the open eyes, the graying skin."[77] Olanna's account restores the dignity of this child whose carefully braided hair shows she was loved. The decapitated head becomes more than an object of horror for Olanna; instead, she sees the head as a child and associates that child with her child, Baby, now called Chiamaka.

Testimony is the impetus for Olanna's recovery, and she works through the trauma by reintegrating herself into the community. She teaches children, works with the community women, and gives goods from her care packages to neighbors. Anne Whitehead's definitive text on trauma fiction examines "the nature of traumatic experience itself, the role and function of testimony, and the relation of trauma and place."[78] Whitehead makes a similar assertion regarding the function of testimony in trauma fiction. Olanna gets better because she actively works to change the environment and the circumstances of her trauma. The defining moment for Olanna occurs when the bombings have increased and become more intense. Realizing she cannot continue to live paralyzed by her fear, she goes to the yard and makes soap: "She would no longer exist limply, waiting to die."[79] The women of the yard teach her this skill, and Olanna's participation in this mundane act symbolizes her evolving sense of sisterhood. Moreover, she is a mother; Olanna's duty to Baby overrules her inclination to remain paralyzed. She must keep Baby, whom she now claims as her child and not the product of deceit, alive. By having Olanna regain her sanity through her work as a mother/community organizer and not through the creative act of writing, Adichie challenges patriarchal notions of women's agency that devalue domestic labor and over-valorize masculinist forms of productivity outside the home. Like Nwapa, Adichie celebrates the bravery of the noncombatant Igbo women who made ways for themselves and their families to survive

Biafra. Furthermore, Adichie complicates the issue of authorship by valuing oral testimony on par with written narrative. In doing so, she disrupts the western purview of the novel by dismantling the hierarchy of oral and written testimony in the text. Although Ugwu is the writer or the documenter of the novel within the novel, Adichie certainly proposes that Olanna's story and the other oral narratives Ugwu records are stories pertinent and essential to any discourse of Biafra.

Majda Atieh and Ghada Mohammad contend that recovery from trauma is never complete. Applying LaCapra's revision of the Freudian concepts of "working through" and "acting out" for historical studies, Atieh and Mohammad argue that recovery is not a prerequisite for traumatized victims to engage in social transformation. They propose, instead, that Olanna works through her Dark Swoops with testimony and service. Olanna and her family return home after years as refugees; however, order is not restored, and no one is healed at the conclusion of the novel. Kainene is gone. Odenigbo's mother and other relatives and friends are dead. What then is the message of *Half of a Yellow Sun*? Why does Adichie, more than 30 years later, revisit the story of Biafra? Like her predecessor Chinua Achebe, Adichie returns to an earlier historical moment as a way of engaging with the current state of Nigeria, a country still struggling to define itself as a cohesive nation. The conditions that triggered Olanna's Dark Swoops persist, and Adichie offers testimony—truth telling and reconciliation—as a means for the nation to work through its trauma and heal.

Notes

1. Don McCullin's haunting photographs for the *Sunday Times* of a starving albino child and a mother nursing her infant on her desiccated breast and Romano Cagnoni's cover and spread on Biafra for *Life* were some of the first images of starvation in Biafra printed in the mainstream press. The photographs raised international awareness about the plight of the Igbo. Simultaneously, I suggest, the images of Biafra as a site of starvation inform subsequent visual representations of Africa—in general—as a site of starvation. Biafra is one source of the mythology of Africa as a site of crisis.
2. Some of the earliest narratives of Biafra include Victor Uzoma Nwankwo's *The Road to Udima* (1969); Chinua Achebe's *Girls at War and Other Stories* (1972); I.N.C. Aniebo's *The Anonymity of Sacrifice* (1974); and Flora Nwapa's *Never Again* (1975).

3. John C. Hawley, "Biafra as Heritage and Symbol: Adichie, Mbachu, and Iweala," *Research in African Literatures* 39.2 (Summer 2008): 23.
4. Brenda Cooper, "An Abnormal Ordinary: Chimamanda Ngozi Adichie's *Half of a Yellow Sun*," *A New Generation of African Writers: Migration, Material Culture and Language* (University of KwaZulu-Natal Press, 2008), 141.
5. Adichie's 2008 short story "A Private Experience" was published in the *Observer* after the publication of the short stories "Half of a Yellow Sun" and "Ghosts." Chika, an educated and wealthy Igbo woman is rescued by a Hausa Muslim woman, a Northerner, who pulls her into the shop during a pogrom in which "Hausa Muslims are hacking down Igbo Christians with machetes" (44). Chika has been separated from her sister Nnedi; the two had come to the market together. Chika witnesses the decapitation of a man by other Muslim men angry because the man, a non-Muslim, had driven over a Quran dropped in the street. Similarly, decapitation is the central violence of Olanna's trauma in *Half of a Yellow Sun*. Like Olanna, Chika is traumatized. Chika, too, will search for her sister unsuccessfully. Nnedi is Chika's only sibling, just as Kainene is Olanna's. Adichie graphically recounts the sights and smells of human carnage. Through Chika, she tells us, "The smell is sickening, of roasted flesh." Chika sees multiple corpses and recoils at the burned bodies. She also sees her own blood "crawling down her leg." The story is relevant because it shows Adichie's intentional study of the effects of trauma. Placed in danger, two women from different ethnic groups find solace and safety in each other's company. Moreover, gender overcomes the obstacles of ethnicity, language, and religion. Women, Adichie suggests, are willing to cross lines in ways men are not.
6. Adichie, Chimamanda Ngozi. "The Story of the Book." http://chimamanda.com/books/half-of-a-yellow-sun/the-story-behind-the-book/.
7. Marianne, Hirsch, " The Generation of Postmemory," *Poetics Today* 29.1 (2008): 103.
8. Denver in *Beloved*, Ursa in *Corregidora*, Anil in *Anil's Ghost*, Dana in *Kindred*, Lizzie in *Stigmata*, Sam in *In Country* to name a few are examples of postgenerational characters.
9. Taiwo Adetunji Osinubi, "Literacies of Violence after *Things Fall Apart*," *Interventions*, 11.2, (2009): 160.
10. Ibid., 160.
11. Scholars disagree about the categorization of Nigerian Writers. However, scholars who agree with Pius Adesanmi and Chris Dutton accept the classification of Nigerian writers into three categories. The first generation consists of writers publishing between the 1950s and 1970. Amos Tutuola, Chinua Achebe, Wole Soyinka, and Flora Nwapa are

first-generation writers. Second generation writers were first published between 1970 and 1984; Buchi Emecheta and Tanure Ojaide qualify as second-generation writers. Third-generation writers were first published in 1985 or later. Osinubi and other scholars propose millennial writers constitute a new phase of Nigerian writers, a fourth generation.

12. Hugh Hodges's "Writing Biafra: Adichie, Emecheta and the Dilemmas of Biafran War Fiction" is an important essay that juxtaposes Adichie and second-generation writer Buchi Emecheta.
13. Iniobong Uko, "Of War & Madness: A Symbolic Transmutation of the Nigeria-Biafra War in Select Stories from *The Insider: Stories of War & Peace from Nigeria*," *War in African Literature Today: A Review*, 26 (2008): 51.
14. Ibid., 51.
15. Brenda Cooper's chapter on *Half of a Yellow Sun* in *A New Generations of African Writers*, John Marx's "Failed State Fiction," and Joke De Mey's dissertation "The Intersection of History, Literature and Trauma in Chimamanda Adichie's *Half of a Yellow Sun*" also critique the role of authorship in the novel.
16. Amy Novak, "Who Speaks? Who Listens?: The Problem of Address in Two Nigerian Trauma Novels," *Studies in the Novel*, 40.1&2 (Spring and Summer 2008): 48.
17. Marta Caminero-Santangelo, *The Madwoman Can't Speak: Or Why Insanity is Not Subversive.* (Ithaca, NY: Cornell University Press 1998), 145.
18. African women authors, including Buchi Emecheta, Tsitsi Dangaremba, Bessie Head, and others write extensively of the overwhelming social pressures and expectations that exacerbate or even cause madness—temporary and permanent—in women.
19. Chimamanda Ngozi Adichie, *Half of a Yellow Sun* (New York: Anchor Books, 2006), 131.
20. *Half of a Yellow Sun* 73.
21. Lara Adebayo, a Yoruba woman and university professor, disparagingly describes Olanna as "illogically pretty" (61). Miss Adebayo's comment unnerves Olanna. The comment is an attack. Miss Adebayo presumes Olanna is too pretty to be smart. Moreover, Miss Adebayo appears to be romantically interested in Odenigbo and her comments may be colored by jealousy.
22. *Half of a Yellow Sun*, 62.
23. Mami Wata is a water spirit associated with traditional West African spiritual traditions. Mami Wata figures are barren but cure other women of their infertility. This characteristic of Mami Wata further supports reading Olanna as a Mami Wata Figure.
24. Ritgak Dinka and Simon Dein write about witchcraft as an element of "cultural construction of infertility."
25. *Half of a Yellow Sun*, 290.

26. In "Who Speaks? Who Listens? The Problem of Address in Two Nigerian Trauma Novels," Amy Novak argues the "traumatic legacy of colonialism is not only evident in the large-scale events of history but also in the daily private lives of citizens" (34). For Novak, the trauma of colonialism is not a singular historical moment from which Nigerians recover and transcend in time; instead, the legacy of colonialism lingers and the psychological damage of occupation recurs.
27. Gloria Chuku, *Igbo Women and Economic Transformation in Southeastern Nigeria, 1900–1960* (New York: Routledge, 2005), 174.
28. The practice of a sitting on a man refers to the intense pressure women would assert on men to get their attention and to lobby for a specific political or judicial outcome.
29. Chima Korieh, "Gender and Peasant Resistance: Recasting the Myth of the Invisible Women in Colonial Eastern Nigeria 1925–1945," *The Foundations of Nigeria: Essays in Honor of Toyin Falola*, eds. Adebayo Oyebade and Toyin Falola (Trenton, NJ: Africa World Press, 2003), 629.
30. Kainene successfully runs their father's business. Her business acumen is valued; the father says she is like a son in this regard. Nevertheless, he offers Kainene, too, as sexual bait for potential business ventures. Interestingly, Kainene is described as the less attractive twin and valued for her masculine qualities.
31. Lillian Temu Osaki, "Madness in Black Women's Writing, Reflections from Four Texts: *A Question of Power*, *The Joys of Motherhood*, *Anowa* and *Possessing the Secret of Joy*," *The Ahfad Journal*, 19. 1 (June 2002): 5.
32. *Half of a Yellow Sun*, 48.
33. Ibid., 196.
34. Ibid., 196.
35. Ibid., 196.
36. Ibid., 205.
37. Ibid., 243.
38. Ibid., 329.
39. Ibid., 351.
40. Ibid., 512.
41. Ibid., 202.
42. Ibid., 203.
43. Ibid., 224.
44. Ibid., 231.
45. Shannon Young's study of Bessie Head's novel *A Question of Power* identifies similar patterns in the character Elizabeth. Referencing Jacqueline Rose and Helen Kapstein, Young proposes women become "repositor[ies] of an unspoken and unspeakable history" and madness allows women "to escape social forms that are too confining" (230,

232). Just as "Elizabeth is a receptacle of collective experience relating to repressed suffering" (Young 229), so too is Olanna.

46. *Half of a Yellow Sun*, 233.
47. Ibid., 243.
48. Ibid., 201.
49. Ibid., 409.
50. Ibid., 234.
51. Brinda Mehta, *Rituals of Memory in Contemporary Arab Women's Writing* (Syracuse, NY: Syracuse University Press, 2007), 139.
52. Novak, 48.
53. Clara Escoda Augusti. "Strategies of Subversion: The Deconstruction of Madness in *Eva's Man*, *Corregidora*, and *Beloved*," *Atlantis* 27.1 (June 2005): 37.
54. Ibid., 37.
55. Buchi Emecheta's *Destination Biafra* similarly challenges the normalcy of violence. Oxford-educated Debbie Ogedembe, the protagonist, joins the army to fight, but a group of soldiers rape her. She does not recount the rape until much later, but she regains her agency through telling.
56. Ronald Granofsky, *The Trauma Novel: Contemporary Symbolic Depictions of Collective Disaster*, American University Studies Series 3 Comparative Literature (New York: Peter Lang, 1995), 108.
57. Ibid., 109.
58. I borrowed the term "multiperspectival" from Herbert Gans's 1979 discussion of "multiperspectival journalism." In *Deciding What's News: A Study of CBS Evening News, NBC Nightly News, Newsweek and Time*, Gans argues against monoperspectival news and for multiperspectival news, which he argues is more diverse and accurate. Adichie's "Author's Note" identifies the written and oral texts she used as a foundation for the novel. The texts and sources include novels, histories, stories from her parents, and the memories of families and friends (542–543).
59. Granofsky, 110.
60. Ibid., 110.
61. Ibid., 170.
62. Even before Olanna has sex with Richard, Kainene's British lover, Olanna's interaction with Kainene is distant but civil. Adichie never fully explains the reason the two sisters are not close, but through Kainene we learn Olanna is deemed the more beautiful and good twin. Despite sibling rivalry and betrayal, Olanna and Kainene find solace in their relationship. Olanna's trauma and the traumas of friends and family bring the sisters together and lead the reader to presume reconciliation for the twins. The reconciliation never happens because Kainene never returns from "affia attack," or the crossing of enemy lines to trade. The disappearance of Kainene forces Olanna and the reader to look for what will

happen next in the novel and in Nigeria after the civil war of Biafra and compels us to consider the many citizens lost in in the conflict who will never return and the contributions of the women whose stories will go undocumented in the war orchestrated by men. Perhaps Kainene is the manifestation of an impossibility, an independent Biafran state. Perhaps she represents the impossibility of women getting their power solely through work. Kainene, perhaps, cannot exist in a post-Biafra Nigeria. What does this mean? Is Nigeria without hope? Do the Igbo concede and resolve themselves to their failed state?

63. *Half of a Yellow Sun*, 241.
64. Jennifer L. Griffiths, *Traumatic Possessions, The Body and Memory in African American Women's Writing and Performance* (Charlottesville, VA: University of Virginia Press, 2009), 5.
65. *Half of a Yellow Sun*, 241.
66. Dori Laub, "Bearing Witness of the Vicissitudes of Listening," in *Testimony: Crises of Witnessing in Literature, Psychoanalysis, and History*, eds. Shoshana Felman and Dori Laub (New York: Routledge, 1992), 64.
67. Ibid., 58.
68. *Half of a Yellow Sun*, 197.
69. Ibid., 197.
70. Ibid., 157.
71. Ibid., 196.
72. Stef Craps and Gert Buelens, "Introduction to Trauma Novels," *Studies in the Novel* 40.1 & 2 (Spring & Summer 2008): 4.
73. Not only do the visitors tell Olanna their own stories of trauma and loss but they also judge her for her lack of fortitude: "nor did she like the furtive way that guests glanced at her legs, as though to discover a lump that would explain why she could not walk" (198).
74. *Half of a Yellow Sun*, 103–4.
75. Ibid., 512.
76. Ibid., 512.
77. Ibid., 512.
78. Anne Whitehead, *Trauma Fiction* (Edinburgh: Edinburgh University Press, 2004), 161.
79. *Half of a Yellow Sun*, 351.

Bibliography

Achebe, Chinua. *Girls at War and Other Stories.* New York, NY: Anchor, 1991. Reprint.

Adichie, Chimamanda Ngozi. "A Private Experience." *The Thing Around Your Neck.* New York, NY: Alfred A. Knopf, 2009.

———. *Half of a Yellow Sun.* New York, NY: Anchor Books, 2006.

———. "The Story of the Book." http://chimamanda.com/books/half-of-a-yellow-sun/the-story-behind-the-book/.

Andrade, Susan. "Adichie's Genealogies: National and Feminine Novels." *Research in African Literatures* 42. 2 (Summer 2011): 91–101.

Aniebo, I.N.C. *The Anonymity of Sacrifice*. London: Heinemann, 1974.

Atieh, Majda and Ghada Mohammad. "Post-traumatic Responses in the War Narratives of Hanan al-Shaykh's *The Story of Zahra* and Chimamanda Ngozi Adichie's *Half of a Yellow Sun*." In *The Strangled Cry: The Communication and Experience of Trauma*. Eds. Aparajita Nanda and Peter Bray. Oxfordshire, UK: Inter-Disciplinary Press, 2013. 65–86.

Augusti, Clara Escoda. "Strategies of Subversion: The Deconstruction of Madness in *Eva's Man*, *Corregidora*, and *Beloved*." *Atlantis* 27. 1 (June 2005): 29–38.

Bakhtin, Mikhail. *The Dialogic Imagination: Four Essays*. Ed. Michael Holquist. Trans. Caryl Emerson and Michael Holquist. Austin, TX: University of Texas Press, 1981.

Butler, Octavia. *Kindred*. Boston, MA: Beacon Press, 2004. Reprint.

Caminero-Santangelo, Marta. *The Madwoman Can't Speak: Or Why Insanity is Not Subversive*. Ithaca, NY: Cornell University Press, 1998.

Chuku, Gloria. *Igbo Women and Economic Transformation in Southeastern Nigeria, 1900–1960*. New York: Routledge, 2005.

Cooper, Brenda. "An Abnormal Ordinary: Chimamanda Ngozi Adichie's *Half of a Yellow Sun*." In *A New Generation of African Writers: Migration, Material Culture and Language*. University of KwaZulu-Natal Press, 2008. 133–150.

Craps, Stef, and Gert Buelens. "Introduction to Trauma Novels." *Studies in the Novel* 40, 1 & 2 (Spring & Summer 2008): 1–12.

De Mey, Joke. "The Intersection of History, Literature and Trauma in Chimamanda Adichie's *Half of a Yellow Sun*." MA thesis, Ghent University, Belgium, 2011.

Dinka, Ritgak A., and Simon L. Dein. "The Work of a Woman is to Give Birth to Children: Cutural Construction of Infertility in Nigeria." *African Journal of Reproductive Health* 17.2 (June 2013): 102–117.

Emecheta, Buchi. *Destination Biafra*. London: Allison & Busby, 1982.

Gans, Herbert. *Deciding What's News: A Study of CBS Evening News, NBC Nightly News, Newsweek and Time*. New York: Vintage, 1980.

Granofsky, Ronald. *The Trauma Novel: Contemporary Symbolic Depictions of Collective Disaster*. American University Studies Series 3 Comparative Literature. New York: Peter Lang, 1995.

Griffiths, Jennifer L. *Traumatic Possessions, The Body and Memory in African American Women's Writing and Performance*. Charlottesville, VA: U of Virginia P, 2009.

Hawley, John C. "Biafra as Heritage and Symbol: Adichie, Mbachu, and Iweala." *Research in African Literatures* 39.2 (Summer 2008): 15–26.

Hirsch, Marianne. "The Generation of Postmemory." *Poetics Today*. 29.1 (2008): 103–28.

———. *The Generation of Postmemory: Writing and Visual Culture After the Holocaust*. New York, NY: Columbia University Press. 2012.
Hodges, Hugh. "Writing Biafra: Adichie, Emecheta and the Dilemmas of Biafran War Fiction." *Postcolonial Text* 5.1 (2009): n.p.
Jones, Gayl. *Corregidora*. Boston, MA: Beacon Press, 1975.
Korieh, Chima. "Gender and Peasant Resistance: Recasting the Myth of the Invisible Women in Colonial Eastern Nigeria 1925–1945." *The Foundations of Nigeria: Essays in Honor of Toyin Falola*. Eds. Adebayo Oyebade and Toyin Falola. Trenton, NJ: Africa World Press, 2003.
LaCapra, Dominic. *Writing History, Writing Trauma*. Baltimore, MD: Johns Hopkins University Press, 2001.
Laub, Dori. "Bearing Witness of the Vicissitudes of Listening." *Testimony: Crises of Witnessing in Literature, Psychoanalysis, and History*. Eds. Shoshana Felman and Dori Laub. New York: Routledge, 1992. 57–74.
Marx, John. "Failed State Fiction." *Contemporary Literature* 49.4 (Winter 2008): 597–633.
Mason, Bobbie Ann. *In Country*. New York, NY: Harper Perennial, 2005.
Mehta, Brinda. *Rituals of Memory in Contemporary Arab Women's Writing*. Syracuse, NY: Syracuse University Press, 2007.
Morrison, Toni. *The Bluest Eye*. New York: Vintage, 1970.
———. *Sula*. New York: Plume, 1982. Reprint.
———. *Beloved*. New York: Knopf Doubleday, 2007. Reprint.
Novak, Amy. "Who Speaks? Who Listens?: The Problem of Address in Two Nigerian Trauma Novels." *Studies in the Novel* 40, 1&2 (Spring and Summer 2008): 31–51.
Nwankwo, Victor Uzoma. *The Road to Udima*. Enugu: Fourth Dimension Publishers, 1985.
Nwapa, Flora. *Never Again*. Trenton, NJ: Africa World Press, 1992.
Ondaatje, Michael. *Anil's Ghost*. New York: Knopf Doubleday, 2001.
Osaki, Lillian Temu. "Madness in Black Women's Writing, Reflections from Four Texts: *A Question of Power*, *The Joys of Motherhood*, *Anowa* and *Possessing the Secret of Joy*." *The Ahfad Journal*. 19, 1 (June 2002): 4–20.
Osinubi, Taiwo Adetunji. "Literacies of Violence after *Things Fall Apart*." *Interventions* 11.2 (2009): 157–160.
Perry, Phyllis Alesia. *Stigmata*. New York: Knopf Doubleday, 1999.
Uko, Iniobong. "Of War & Madness: A Symbolic Transmutation of the Nigeria-Biafra War in Select Stories from *The Insider: Stories of War & Peace from Nigeria*." *War in African Literature Today: A Review* 26 (2008): 49–59.
Spiegelman, Artie. *Maus*. New York: Pantheon, 1997.
Whitehead, Anne. *Trauma Fiction*. Edinburgh: Edinburgh UP, 2004.
Young, Shannon. "Therapeutic Insanity: The Transformative Vision of Bessie Head's *A Question of Power*." *Research in African Literatures* 41. 4 (Winter 2010): 227–41.

"We Know People by Their Stories": Madness, Babies, and Dolls in Edwidge Danticat's *Krik? Krak!*

Raquel D. Kennon

The book itself, the story, the telling, is meant as a path towards healing. The pain goes into the telling of the story, just as we discussed before. The pain goes into the telling, both for me and for her. The rituals don't exist. No markers. We have to recreate them. Our words are the markers.[1]
Edwidge Danticat

I. Mad Writing

Of the rich imagery that suffuses Edwidge Danticat's *Krik? Krak!* (1995), none is more arresting than the ambiguity between the living human baby and the inanimate baby doll. The perceptual illusion that allows a mother to see a living and breathing infant when faced with a discarded baby's corpse on the side of the road in Port-au-Prince suggests, on the one hand, what psychologists might consider a break with reality, evidence of madness, and on the other hand, a stubborn willfulness to survive devastating sociopolitical conditions. Cast in the image of an infant or small child, a wooden, plastic or cloth figure embodies the nexus between the living and the dead, imagination and reality, and tests

R.D. Kennon (✉)
California State University, Northridge, USA

C.A. Brown and J.X.K. Garvey (eds.), *Madness in Black Women's Diasporic Fictions*, Gender and Cultural Studies in Africa and the Diaspora, DOI 10.1007/978-3-319-58127-9_7

the limits of creativity and make-believe in this interconnected series of nine vignettes. The narrative draws a distinction between the living baby and its mimetic doll, with the stark image of the dead baby existing somewhere in between.

Employing complex layers of representation, *Krik? Krak!* reimagines key events in Haitian history as its primarily women narrators and protagonists seek healing in the telling of their stories. In fact, I would argue that the startling image of a dead baby foregrounds the first Black Republic's constellation of struggles and triumphs. Set across a sweeping historical landscape that includes the story of the heroic Boukman and the successful Haitian Revolution (1791–1804); U.S. occupation (1915–1934); Dominican Republic dictator Rafael Trujillo's reign of terror in 1937; the insidious reprisals of the *tonton macoutes* working symbiotically with the Duvalier dictatorships (1957–1986); brutal gang violence; and waves of immigration to the United States, the short story collection works through the pain to recreate history and erect words as markers of remembrance. As Martin Munro suggests, Danticat's fiction challenges "the culture of violence that has rendered Haiti an uninhabitable place for many of its people," and in so doing "places much emphasis on silenced, abused women, the invisible, unheard victims of largely male violence, and of the ideologies of race and color that perpetuate cycles of social and personal decline in Haiti."[2] Chantal Kalisa's work on political violence echoes this sentiment when she asserts that Danticat's "fictionalized study of gendered violence in Haiti [...] covers these stories from the perspective of a female generation that, like Danticat, barely lived these events first-hand."[3] Indeed, many of these female characters are living in exile. Whether at home or abroad, the healing comes through the telling of the communal tragedy.

Perhaps the most unspeakable of tragedies is the death of an infant or child. In the first instance, the representation of the dead baby in Danticat's work conveys a tremendous sense of loss of promising innocent life before it has begun.[4] That this is one of the recurring motifs in the text speaks to the reality of infant and maternal mortality rates in Haiti, lack of access to prenatal care and medical resources, and the dangers of labor and childbirth outside the hospital setting; and, in the case of discarded babies, perhaps lack of access to birth control and the financial means to support the child.[5] The recurring motif of the baby/doll/dead baby continuum registers the critical necessity of imagination while living in impoverished conditions that would drive many women mad. Far from trivializing or poeticizing infant mortality rates, I suggest that these women narrators demonstrate a remarkable strength and resilience in their ability to continue to speak and tell their stories—despite enduring rape, unjust imprisonment, miscarriage and infant mortality, immigration, exile, and the resultant family trauma. It is the same spirit of resilience one finds in Danticat's carefully crafted poetic prose, which renders the abject with beauty and graceful lyricism.

The representation of the dead baby is closely linked with the representation of the baby doll in these interconnected vignettes that exemplify "mad writing." Even in the tragedy of losing a child, these women characters often use their imagination to construct a story of survival through the pain and suffering of collective national crises. As Judith Herman argues in her classic *Trauma and Recovery*, the dialectic between banishing the memory of atrocities and telling the truth about them emblematizes psychological trauma. Foreshadowing Danticat's proclamation quoted in the epigraph that "[t]he book itself, the story, the telling, is meant as a path towards healing," Herman notes that social order is achieved and victims healed only after remembering and telling the truth about unspeakable events.[6] Gay Wilentz elucidates the powerful way women writers not only remember and tell, but also "cure" cultural dis-ease through the writing of "wellness narratives."[7] In doing so, these women writers reclaim a tradition of women as cultural healers.

Yet survivors often recount narratives of tragic events characterized by "helplessness and terror" in ways that are "highly emotional, contradictory, and fragmented."[8] The kaleidoscopic fragmentation of the survivor's testimonies strategically performs madness. As Caroline Brown posits, "mad" or "lunatic writing" is not only a "recurring trope" in transnational Black women's novels, but also one that—following Cameroonian writer and cultural critic Calixthe Beyala—evidences a heightened rather than impaired consciousness and perception. Beyala reverses the psychopathological interpretation of madness as mental illness or disorder, such that "lunatic writing" represents:

> [...] an excess of intelligence, a story of intellectual and spiritual superiority. When no one else understands what's happening in the world, when no one analyzes what's going on, the person who does understand goes mad. So, I'm not talking about the furious and angry madness that one encounters in a psychiatric hospital. I'm talking about a very special madness that results from the intelligence of people who have *a clear vision of*

things in a world where everyone closes their eyes. Lunatic writing reflects this clarity of vision (emphasis added).[9]

Beyala's notion of the "clarity of vision" and "intellectual and spiritual superiority" inherent in "mad writing"—in which the socially conscious and alert woman goes mad—reemerges in Valérie Orlando's conceptualization of madness for Francophone women writers of Africa and the Caribbean. Orlando, too, establishes a causal relationship between madness and "exile, isolation, and marginalization—either forced by the masculine-centric power or self-imposed—as women seek to challenge age-old traditions in their respective indigenous societies." Eschewing the designation of "hysteria" as a behavioral dysfunction, she declares it "a positive catalyst toward a truer knowledge of the self, a force that empowers and allows her to overcome debilitating obstacles." Thus, madness, and particularly hysteria, signals a "truer knowledge," an illumination, a "clear vision of things."[10]

In *Insanity: The Idea and Its Consequences,* Thomas Szasz provocatively frames mental illness as metaphor; in it, we find echoes of Beyala's formulation of "mad writing" as intellectual superiority and empowerment. Evelyn O'Callaghan makes a similar point in the specific context of Caribbean women writers when she reads "the madwoman in the West Indian novel as social metaphor" that functions to unveil gender, class, language, intergenerational and (post)colonial dynamics.[11] While O'Callaghan relies on R. D. Laing's *The Divided Self*—particularly, the concepts of "ontological insecurity" and disintegration of mind and body—to interpret specific examples of literary madness marked by a fragmented subjectivity, Szasz recalls more generally the oft-cited relationship between art and what he calls *divine madness*:

> As anyone familiar with the history of ideas knows, ancient thinkers entertained quite a different view of the relationship between art and insanity. This is largely because the philosophers of antiquity—for example, Plato and Aristotle—use the word *madness* to mean not an illness but an *illumination*: Madness enhances rather than diminishes a person's dignity and stature as a human being. This is why Plato and Aristotle assert (perhaps take for granted would be more accurate) that poets are mad—that they must be mad in order to write good poetry.[12]

Here, Szasz underscores an important distinction. It is an illumination or "clear vision of things," to use Beyala's phrase, that drives the genius of the artist and justifies his higher status as a human being. However, this also dangerously establishes a gendered and false dichotomy between the artist and madwoman, imbuing the former (male, rational) with a surfeit of intentionality, and by extension, humanity. In modern psychiatric and legal understandings of insanity, then, the actions of a madwoman (female, irrational) utterly lack intentionality, and she is, therefore, considered less than human. Brown echoes this notion when she states, "to be deemed mad is to be placed in a position of penultimate alterity, slipping from the category of human to subhuman, from the locus of reason to that of the irrational."[13]

The dehumanization of a madwoman comes to bear unmistakably in the second vignette of Danticat's collection, "Nineteen Thirty-Seven," for example, in which the unnamed protagonist's mother is imprisoned following accusations of witchcraft. Her presumed madness relegates her to the status of nonhuman, a worker of occult magic, relegated to the carceral space. As Kaiama L. Glover claims about Danticat's literary predecessor, Marie Vieux Chauvet, women characters often occupy the space of the "disorderly feminine,"[14] and their actions, rather than interpreted as evidence of superior illumination or artistic genius, are instead misconstrued as the ravings of madwomen who need to be controlled, punished, and incarcerated. While Szasz rejects the argument that the insane lack intentionality, he also describes a socially constructed third category—*mad artists*—who possess "a combination of these conflicting characteristics."[15] Following Szasz's critique of mental illness and Beyala's explication of "lunatic writing," the women narrators in *Krik? Krak!* enact a strategic intentionality in their actions, even when seemingly performing mad behavior. I argue that through their enhanced, unfettered perception, these women offer, in distinct ways, not a mad vision of a sane world but a lucid vision of a depraved world. Or, in Cameroonian writer Werewere Liking's trenchant declaration, "a lunatic language must be born to allow lunatics to express themselves in the face of an age of lunacy."[16]

Paradoxically, it is this "clear vision" of the happenings in the world, a characteristic of "an excess of intelligence" in Beyala's formulation of lunatic writing, which in fact drives the women mad. By rejecting the cognitive deficiency model often implied in the psychopathological diagnostic label of mental illness, Beyala complicates Sartre's pronouncement of the "nervous" postcolonial or post-occupation condition[17] by associating madness with a denial of past and present tenses, and a lexical insistence on the future:

> Life in the bidonville *denies the present because one lives on hope.* Everyone thinks that they're in transit to a better tomorrow. They think that life in the bidonville is transitory—never fixed, never definitive. No one stays there out of sheer pleasure. So, you conjugate verbs in the future tense. And it's in that space between the present and the future that lunatic writing develops (my emphasis).[18]

The lunacy in this writing resides in an obstinate repudiation of the quotidian indignities, violence, and oppression the women face in favor of the creation of imaginative narratives of hope and prosperity always glancing toward the future. At times, the insistence on the future becomes a willful, intentional denial. As can be perceived with Marie, the protagonist in "Between the Pool and the Gardenias," this insistence on the future causes her to sink into a delusional world. Taken together, Herman's conception of healing, vis-à-vis remembering the unspeakable traumatic acts, and Beyala's formulation of "mad writing," as discourse conjugated in the future tense, jointly encompass how mad writing reinscribes the women protagonists in Danticat's *Krik? Krak!*

In fact, I would argue then that "mad writing" validates memories and empowers the woman who tells her story, thereby making her quite literally, as Herman terms it, "the author and arbiter of her own recovery."[19] These women protagonists often activate their madness—or, perhaps their madness activates them—as an adaptive coping strategy, to resist, to revise, to reimagine, to reenact, and ultimately, to heal. Hellen Lee-Keller, in her analysis of Marie Chauvet's *Amour*, incisively suggests the "trope of madness" is a "strategic move" that covertly illustrates the author's navigation of the "political, class, and social conditions" which produce a "culture of fear, submission, and alienation for the peoples of Haiti."[20] Similarly, we can read the trope of madness in *Krik? Krak!* as a strategic move, a "textual strategy," but also an act of transgression. However, I believe that a straightforward reading of the trope of madness as a discursive strategy could be too limiting. As Suzanne Dow indicates, the relationship between madness, women, and writing, and specifically, "the subversive value of writing on madness" is an ambivalent one. Thus, the project of writing about literary madwomen becomes "fruitful, albeit constantly ambiguous."[21] Located in this ambiguity is the impossibility of wholly reading "mad writing" as "feminist protest," as Shoshana Felman, Elaine Showalter and other critics point out.[22] Even Beyala concedes in her notion of the superior intellect of "mad writing" that she does not refer to "furious and angry madness that one encounters in a psychiatric hospital."[23] Thus, there are limits to the use of "mad writing" as "a rich source of metaphoricity," and therefore a reaffirmation of the existence of "clinical madness" which one cannot deny.[24] In this essay, I want to show how the relationship between "mad writing" and women continues to express itself in ways that are at once fragmented, contradictory, and ambiguous, interrogating the meaning both to the individual story and in relation to Danticat's larger oeuvre.

"Everything Makes Me Mad": Danticat's Tropes of Madness

To play with a doll—sometimes a miniature representation of self or wished for child—exercises the imagination and offers a window into another world of fantasy. To imagine is to hope, to move beyond mere "survival," as Danticat notes in the epigraph, and engage in the aspirational conjugation in the future tense, to quote Beyala, by which the trauma of the past is reconstituted through strategic "mad writing." Madness performs a shifting constellation of strategic functions in the text that enable the women narrators and protagonist-storytellers to survive, resist the bloodshed and sexual violations in their environment, and move toward healing. In the "mad writing" practices evidenced both within and without the short stories, the baby/doll/dead baby rivets as one of the most startling topoi, emblematic of Françoise Lionnet's theory of the "geography of pain." As Lionnet notes, "women writers are often especially aware of their task as producers of images that both participate in the dominant representations of their culture and simultaneously undermine and subvert those images by offering a re-vision of familiar scripts."[25] Danticat, through her narrators and protagonists, constructs migratory "geographies of pain" that seem to deliberately cohere around the chasm between the living, the dead, and inanimate baby.

The graphic and prolonged descriptions of dead babies, imprisoned, or absent mothers in *Krik? Krak!* represent, then, "geographies of pain," that is, the terrifying consequences of poverty and the accompanying infant mortality rates and the ghastly nature of gang and government-sponsored violence. Within these harrowing scenes of traumatic violence, displacement, loss, and dispossession, sometimes the lines become so blurred that one cannot distinguish a baby doll or dead baby from a living, breathing human infant. Whereas this inability or refusal to distinguish might suggest a psychological impairment, an intentional replacement of separated child with a doll, it also signals a coping strategy for families living between two countries. Much of the reason for the surrogate babies and mothers (and fathers) is due to the repressive socioeconomic and political situation that separates families through immigration and exile.[26] Separations, abandonments, and reunions become commonplace as Haitian families seek political asylum or economic opportunity in the United States.[27] Through the separations, the representational valences of motherhood register on multiple levels.

While there has been substantial critical commentary on the abundant symbolism in Danticat's *oeuvre*, less has been devoted to the interconnected stories in *Krik? Krak!* Few interpretations focus specifically on the semiotics of the baby/doll/dead baby motif. Rocio G. Davis, for example, identifies "three recurring images" in the short story cycle—"the butterfly, the wished for flight, and the death of infants"—that she argues illustrate "the painful realities of the immigrant situation."[28] Yet this analysis does not directly center on the ambiguity between dead babies and dolls. Jana Evans Braziel reads *Krik? Krak!* as a "migratory text" that "annihilate[s] definitive national belonging," compelling the reader to "rethink national boundaries, specifically Haiti's borders of *nanchon* (nation) and *dyaspora* (diaspora)."[29] Braziel further argues that Danticat presents a "transnational feminist politics to address the struggles of women in Haiti and its dyaspora," suggesting transnational connections between them. Directly addressing the "images of births, stillbirths, rape, infanticide, and abortions" in Danticat's texts, Braziel theorizes:

> These images do *not* transcend the traumas of female embodiment and historical acts of maternal refusal; *rather*, they re-write Haiti's history both through diasporic distance and through the traumas of female embodiment, insisting that it is only by passing through Haiti's maternal bodies that the country will be reborn, that she will survive and necessarily confront the future.[30]

Whereas Braziel's postulation links the national maternal body to the embodied experiences of Haitian women, in what follows I explore how the baby/doll/dead baby motif transfigures notions of mothering and the embodied maternal body through "mad writing" practices. As a useful literary comparison, in Wendy Knepper's reading of Danticat's *Brother, I'm Dying* (2007), she employs the term "necro-natality" as an essential element in "Danticat's maternal discourse [that] bridges the divide between life and death, bringing a memoir for her dead father together with the hopeful story of her own pregnancy." Knepper reads life writing and specifically, the "life/death potentiality of the womb/tomb" through an interrogation of "Haitian precarity" in a biopolitical framework for justice.[31] The discourse of necro-natality proves useful to my exploration of this theme in *Krik? Krak!*, in which the baby/doll/dead baby motif emerges through polyvocal, intergenerational storytelling practices of "women-centered extended kin networks," to employ Patricia Hill Collins's phrase.[32]

The motif of the baby doll and the related imagery of living and dead babies embody the preoccupation with the transition between the living and the dead in Danticat's fiction. The rag doll, then, becomes a symbol that opens up to the larger themes of how one survives during the consecutive reigns of terror, from US occupation (1915–1934) to the 1937 massacre, from the torture sanctioned during the Duvalier regimes to the poverty of twentieth-century Haiti. Grounded in these major sociopolitical, cultural, and historical events, the baby doll—as a metonym for and intermediary between both the living and the dead infant—codes an often oppositional range of responses: madness, maternal fears and hope for future generations, women's imagination and creativity of the dispossessed, and healing. As Valérie Orlando argues, "Even if there seems to be no exit, women are able to re-create visions of their own selves despite the violence, brutality, and madness around them."[33] In earlier work, Orlando posits that Francophone women writers of Africa and the Caribbean develop these self-visions or "herstories" in which they "take flight and step out of sociocultural boundaries to explore identity" through the process of "*deterritorializating* to build new social projects where the historical, the cultural, and the economic all come into play."[34] Hélène Cixous's exhortation in "The Laugh of Medusa" for *l'écriture féminine* ("feminine writing") that "woman must write her self: must write about women and bring women to writing, from which they have been driven away as violently as from their bodies" is instructive for understanding the conflation between a literally productive woman and a madwoman.[35] As a critique of the role of the woman writer in the patriarchal structure of Western discourse, Cixous recalls the "overflow" and "luminous torrents" of creative energy, and the subsequent feelings of "shame" and "fear," believing herself "mad": "who," she ponders, "feeling a funny desire stirring inside her (to sing, to write, to dare to speak, in short, to bring out something new), hasn't thought she was sick?"[36]

In certain narratives, the overt presence of a doll or dead baby slips away, and other allusions to the boundary between life and death emerge. Employing several familiar stylistic and thematic elements of African Diasporic women's writing—orality in narration and dialogue, signifyin' at communal gatherings, and intimate storytelling—*Krik? Krak!* illustrates responses to and modes of working through cultural trauma and mourning. Danticat's cycle of nine interwoven vignettes maps intergenerational, matrilineal strategies for coping with unspeakable tragedies, political upheaval and violence, poverty, and national suffering. The sexual violence enacted on women's bodies insidiously links the horror of rape with the conception of new life, passing down politicized sexual terror through these inscriptions in the womb. Both the health and life of the mother and child are perpetually at risk in these tales. In fact, it is the mother's inability to protect her fetus, infant, or child from harm that gives rise to expressions of madness, both oral and written.

On the Path Toward Healing

Within a narrative structure of matrilineal orality, many of the Haitian women narrators in this short story cycle engage with and construct stories around recurring images of dead or dying babies, dolls, and figurines, both secular and religious.[37] Comparable to Patricia Hill Collins's notion of othermothers, Dorsía Smith Silva argues that the concept of surrogacy is a defining feature of "Caribbean mothering," as it encompasses "surrogate, communal, and extended parenthood in the stories of generations of women that include grandmothers, godmothers, sisters, and aunts."[38] The inanimate doubles offer a form of surrogacy. Danticat's mostly female narrators rely on the healing capacity of storytelling, what Wilentz terms "wellness narratives" as a "sustained response to our dis-eased condition."[39] These wellness narratives are constituted as a series of intimate conversations: mother and child; husband and wife; grandmother and granddaughter; sister and sister; lover and lover; friend and friend. The baby/doll/dead baby motif further reveals the unstable boundary between the living and dead (human and posthuman), pleasure and pain, and reality and fantasy in these tales. The figure of the doll signals imaginative storytelling, one of the key adaptive textual strategies of "mad writing."

The women narrators, often unnamed in the short stories of *Krik? Krak!*, grapple with the specter of Haitian history, their stories evidence of Michel-Rolph Trouillot's notion that "the past does not exist independently of the present."[40] The delay in naming and even the actual refusal to name these women at all, I argue, contributes to a sense that these tales represent a mythical "every-Haitian-woman" or offer a collective Haitian womanhood as the embodiment of the country's cultural mourning.[41]

In particular, the female narrators in "Children of the Sea," "Night Women," and "Between the Pool and the Gardenias," and "New York Day Women" at turns dissociate, channel, cover, refuse, and reimagine the tremendous weight of the historical past in an effort to preserve ancestral memory and create stories (oral, and, in later generations, written). The interconnected narrative structure foregrounds the baby/doll/dead baby motif, a proxy for imaginative storytelling, in each vignette. This imaginative storytelling, an expression of "lunatic writing," is one adaptive response to living in a world of lunacy. Enacting Beyala's "clear vision of things," the female narrators—perceived as madwomen—survive, resist, and ultimately heal themselves and their communities via the creation of "wellness narratives," as Wilentz delineates them. Indeed, the conscious "mad storytelling" and "mad writing" of these women provide a way to cope, survive, and develop their voices, perhaps their only way to continue living. Miraculously these women move beyond mere survival, as the epigraph notes, and engage in these discursive practices to embark on the path toward healing. I argue here that for many of the female protagonists in *Krik? Krak!*, and indeed in much of Danticat's *oeuvre*, the transport away from reality and into storytelling is not a state from which she later recovers. That is, the willful movement toward "mad storytelling" and "mad writing" *is* the process of self-preservation, political resistance, recovery and healing.

Chikwenye Okonjo Ogunyemi highlights the distinction between feminist and womanist writing and identifies madness for the African diasporic woman character as a temporary state: "In spite of the blues, black women occasionally go mad. Unlike negatively presented white madwomen, the black madwoman in novels written by black women knows in her subconscious that she must survive because she has people without other resources depending on her; in a positive about-face she usually recovers through a superhuman effort, or somehow, aids others."[42] Ogunyemi further argues: "After each mental upheaval there is thus a stasis in the womanist novel when the black woman's communion with the rest of the society is established, a consonance that expresses the black way to authenticity and transcendence. Madness becomes a temporary aberration preceding spiritual growth, healing, and integration."[43] While I agree that we find a distinctly womanist approach to the madness, I would counter that for many of the female protagonists in *Krik? Krak!*, the transport away from reality and into storytelling is not a state from which she later recovers; that is, the willful movement toward "mad storytelling" and "mad writing" *is* the process of recovery and healing. This complements Beyala's contention that perceptions of madness, rather than straightforward psychosis, might instantiate "heightened mental acuity" or "clarity of vision."[44]

In the first vignette of the collection, "Children of the Sea," the young female protagonist's "clear vision of things" slowly drives her mad. She finds solace, however, by engaging in "mad writing." In the third paragraph of the vignette, the reader first encounters an unnamed female narrator who, against her father's prohibitions, performs the daring act of writing to her lover, who is crowded on a small boat with "thirty-six other deserting souls" at sea.[45] She does not know if he has managed to flee Haiti or not after his involvement in the youth federation, yet she continues to write to him in her notebook. It is intriguing to consider that the opening voice of this short story collection, firmly rooted in interwoven matrilineal storytelling, in fact begins with a first person male narrator as a seeming voice of authority. The unnamed male narrator describes what he knows to be true in the manner of an oft-repeated folk tale: "They say behind the mountains are more mountains. Now I know it's true. I also know there are timeless waters, endless seas, and lots of people in this world whose names don't matter to anyone but themselves."[46] Yet he quickly destabilizes his position of authority with a statement about the uncertainty of his precarious condition, "I don't know how long we'll be at sea."[47] The narration alternates between these two narrators, male and female, teetering between the oral ("Someone says, Krik? You answer Krak!" storytelling) and the literary (writing in notebooks), the real and the imagined, the known and the unknowable, the sea and the sky.[48] As Nick Nesbitt argues, "the epistolary form of the story marks out the traumatic disjuncture and alienation" of families "torn apart [...] somewhere between Port-au-Prince and Miami.[49]

While the male narrates his experiences in the form of reportage, the female narrator reacts viscerally to the trauma of dislocation and dispossession, boldly expressing her feelings of alienation. She writes, "haiti est comme tu l'as laissé. yes, just the way you left it. bullets day and night. same hole. same everything. i'm tired of the whole mess. i pass the time by chasing roaches around the house. i pound my heel on their heads. *they make me so mad. everything makes me mad*" (my emphasis).[50] In her emotionally charged stream of consciousness, the young narrator repeats the sentiment of things "making her mad," a double-entendre alluding to the anger raging inside her and the larger motif of madness that runs throughout the text. To be sure, the lowercase first person pronoun use might be read as the transliteration of the French *je* (I). However, I would argue that the lack of any capitalization or punctuation and comparatively formal writing conventions of her lover indicate her refusal to abide by the conventions of written composition. Adding to the knottiness of these linguistic entanglements of the text is the fact that her first sentence to him is written in French. The reader can assume, then, that the prose represents an English rendering of letters most likely written in Haitian creole (*kreyól*). The fact that the star-crossed lovers will never receive each other's letters as they attempt to survive during the reign of terror indicates the curative power of the writing process. Everything is making the female narrator mad, and yet she must continue to engage in "mad writing," conjugating her verbs in the future tense.

In the midst of ubiquitous carnage, rape, and psychic trauma, a commitment to "mad writing" sustains the female narrator. After providing a shocking description of her neighbor, Madan Roger, who "came home with her son's head and not much else"[51]—an almost journalistic report indicating the prevalence of horrific events that surrounds her family—the female narrator promises that she "will never go outside again. Not even in the yard to breathe the air."[52] Indeed, the female narrator barely maintains her sanity as her emotions vacillate between frustration, resentment, boredom, and fear. She longs for her lover and constantly rebels against her father—in a sense, a surrogate for the government—although he sacrifices all to protect her. Within this context, she then immediately pledges her commitment to continue writing to her lover whom she does not know is sailing on a boat toward Miami or the Bahamas:

> i keep wondering if it is true. did you really get out? i wish there was some way i could be sure that you really went away. yes, i will. i will keep writing like we promised to do. i hate it, but i will keep writing. you keep writing too, okay? and when we see each other again, it will seem like we lost no time.[53]

Beyala's notion of the audacious insistence on conjugating verbs in the future terms rings true in this quintessential passage of "mad writing." In these desperate promises, the unnamed narrator boldly makes plans to see her love again, disavowing the precarity of their circumstances. Although she recounts atrocity after atrocity, soldiers who force mothers to sleep with their sons and fathers to sleep with their daughters, she then juxtaposes her prose with minor details from her new life in Ville Rose, the location where her family has found refuge. Here, the female narrator's actions characterize Beyala's explication of "lunatic writing": she "denies the present because one lives on hope."[54]

In this ocean-centric narrative, with its symbolic resonances to the Middle Passage where people "go to the bathroom on the boat [...] probably the same way they did on those slave ships years ago,"[55] the female narrator chooses the world of the banyan tree, writing, and avoiding black butterflies which bring bad news.[56] Her willful denial of reality, a form of controlled fabrication more so than madness, I argue, enables her to continue living and to avoid the fate of the pregnant 15-year-old girl with the scarred face, Célianne, whom her lover describes in his section of the narration. Strikingly, it is the male narrator who mediates our understanding of Célianne's long-suffering and final act of maternal nurturing. This narrator recounts the trauma of his surroundings and describes his sorrowful fellow boat passengers with a certain journalistic distance: "There is a pregnant girl on board. She looks like she might be our age. Nineteen or twenty. Her face is covered with scars that look like razor marks. She is short and speaks in a singsong that reminds me of the villagers in the north."[57] More than any other character in *Krik? Krak!*, Célianne—whose body is scarred, violated, tortured, marked internally and externally (her face and her womb) by state-sanctioned violence—physically embodies and outwardly projects the astonishingly agonizing circumstances of many of these women's lives.

It is remarkable, too, that the reader learns Célianne's name, unlike the main protagonists "whose names don't matter to anyone but themselves" as the male narrator suggests in the opening lines of the vignette.[58] The narrator tells us Célianne's name and later reveals the horrific origin of her self-inflicted facial scarring and the paternity of her baby. One evening at home, Célianne was gang raped by "ten or twelve soldiers" and her brother, Lionel, was forced to have sex with his own mother at gunpoint and then arrested for "moral crimes."[59] Upon the male narrator's questioning, Célianne explains that she "cut her face with a razor so that no one would know who she was."[60] The male narrator's revelation of her name and inscription of her identity in his notebook, then, signals a breach of confidentiality for a teenaged victim of sexual assault who only wished for anonymity. She self-mutilates in an attempt at self-erasure, the scars she carved into her face a representation of her internalized shame of sexual violation. The gendered power dynamic implicit in the male narrator's questioning of Célianne, the circulating rumors that she has committed adultery, and the monstrous truth of her rape, expose the many ways Célianne's life has been out of her control. When Célianne labors and delivers her baby on the boat, the male narrator moved outside of view so he would "not have to look *inside* Célianne."[61] While the teen mother's body is constantly overexposed, her interiority remains shielded. The reader never fully looks *inside* Célianne. Even as she clings to her stillborn baby, also silenced at birth, Célianne is not the one to name her child. The people on the boat call the baby Swiss because "the word Swiss was written on the small knife they used to cut her umbilical cord."[62] Not only is the deceased baby named after an inanimate object, but also she is given the name of an "army knife," a European export.[63] Here, Lionnet's theory of "geographies of pain" emerges most strongly. The young lover's letter of this beloved does not immediately reveal that baby's death, but only repeatedly hints at it: "She still hasn't cried."[64] This is the first example of the ambiguous image of the baby, with the reader initially left uncertain if it is dead or alive.

Célianne's "mad writing" adds instructive layers to the epistolary structure of "Children of the Sea," compelling her to write her own conclusion to a life story principally written and dictated by others. A leak in the boat prevents Célianne from grieving for her baby as the people on the boat are instructed "to throw our extra things in the sea."[65] Eyes glance at Célianne with the expectation that she toss her Swiss overboard because the dead infant is now just "a thing" that is weighing down the boat. The "thingification" of Célianne's baby is swift. The narrator initially refers to her as a "she": "Swiss isn't crying. They keep slapping her behind, but she is not crying."[66] The pronoun usage in reference to the baby soon changes from "she" to "it": "Célianne is holding her baby tight against her chest. She just cannot seem to let herself throw it in the ocean."[67] Here the reader witnesses the absolute vulnerability of the female body, to violation; the vulnerability of the fetus inside the impoverished woman's body, who is only hoping to flee to protect her unborn child; and, the disposability of the body of the baby. Ultimately, Célianne chooses death, plunging herself into the ocean after being forced to cast her dead baby—the product of a gang rape—into the sea: "She threw it overboard. I watched her face knot up like a thread, and then she let go. It fell in a splash, floated for a while, and then sank. And quickly after that she jumped in too. And just as the baby's head sank, so did hers. They went together like two bottles beneath a waterfall."[68] Célianne's act of suicide again echoes the Middle Passage, when countless enslaved Africans chose death by sea rather than captivity. The male narrator is aware of this when he concludes the story noting that he must discard his notebook in the sea, ending the letters to his lover. He finds consolation in the thought that "Célianne and her daughter and all those children of the sea…might soon be claiming me."[69] Interestingly, it is through the first short story's male narrator—through which the reader receives Célianne's mediated story—that the stakes of motherhood so central to *Krik? Krak!* are articulated. Similar to the female narrator who rails against her protective father, Danticat underscores in both instances the struggles women endure in a patriarchal society. While cautious not to valorize suicide, I would argue that Célianne's decision to take her life represents a deliberate act of resistance, an agential, intentional action in which she, faced with a life without her stillborn daughter, chooses to die on her own terms. It is not the final act of a madwoman; rather, it is the act of a woman's "mad writing," exercising Beyala's notion of "a clear vision" of a depraved world.

The unnamed, 25-year-old female first person narrator in "Night Women" also elects to engage in a process of "mad writing" of her own design, existing in an imaginary world to avoid the endless suffering of her circumstances. Much like Célianne, she possesses a "clear vision of things," and instead of crumbling before the maddening injustices of the world, chooses fabrication as strategic tactic of protection for herself, and primarily, her young child. To clarify, I associate creative storytelling as a means of protecting a child from pain with Beyala's notion of conjugating in the future tense. Living in a one-room dwelling with her young son, she supports herself through prostitution, with a different man soliciting her services each night while her son sleeps on the other side of the room, separated only by a "lace curtain" as thin as the boundary between the appropriate and inappropriate in this story.[70] While she states, "the night is the time [she] dreads most in [her] life," she manages to escape her reality too through imagination and storytelling. So convincing in fact is her "mad storytelling" that she often envisions her son as a grown man, sexualizing him and positioning him in the role of one of the men who solicit her. She says this of her son sleeping: "In his sleep he squirms and groans as though he's already discovered that there is pleasure in touching himself."[71] In her fantasy world, the nightly visitors become "suitors." The nighttime itself is a time of distortions and shadows, where even her son's veiled visage reminds her of "the ghost of his father, a lover who disappeared with the night's shadows a long time ago."[72] She observes her son as he "slips into bed" and "stretches from a little boy into the broom-size of a man."[73] The first-person narrator employs the apparition of the absent father as the trigger for the storytelling and make-believe.

To expedite her son falling asleep in order for her to receive the men at night with some modicum of privacy, she masks the reality of her sex work by engaging her son's imagination as her "mad writing" takes shape as fanciful storytelling. She recounts:

> I whisper mountain stories in his ear, stories of the ghost women and the stars in their hair. I tell him of the deadly snakes lying at one end of a rainbow and the hat full of gold lying at the other end. I tell him that if I cross a stream of glass-clear hibiscus, I can make myself a goddess. I blow on his long eyelashes to see if he's truly asleep. My fingers coil themselves into visions of birds on his nose. I want him to forget that we live in a place where nothing lasts.[74]

Echoing the opening line of "Children of the Sea,"—"They say behind the mountains are more mountains,"—the mother's active denial of her status as sex worker and retreat into fable serve as protective measures for her son. In so doing, the narrator teeters on the verge of madness, as she too seems to lose grasp of the distinction between fantasy and reality. She believes that the "ghost women" from Ville Rose who "woo strollers and leave the stars on the path for them" accompany her at night.[75] In the dance of shadow and light, the narrator admits she "almost mistake[s] him for the ghost of his father."[76] She not only eroticizes her son, but she positions him as her lover: "The way my son reacts to my lips stroking his cheeks decides for me if he's asleep. Sometimes I see in the folds of his eyes a longing for something that's bigger than myself. We are like two faraway lovers, lying to one another, under different moons."[77] The mother's almost incestuous behavior imposes a premature sexuality onto her young son, perhaps duplicating the narrator's own early sexual exposure, indicating her own vulnerability in front of men, and her son who will one day grow up to become a man who she has only known to use her for economic sustenance.

She remakes herself as a "goddess," rejecting the societal stigma of the mother as sex worker. Through her motherly love for her son, the unnamed narrator, who actually names and thereby exposes several of her "suitors"—never divulges her own name—weaves together these elaborate fairy tales and stories of adventure, sparing her son from the ugly reality of her occupation as a "night woman." "I have prepared my fabrication," she notes, for the moment when her son wakes up while she is with a man. For now, she tells him "a wandering man is a mirage and that naked flesh is a dream. I will tell him that his father has come, that an angel brought him back from Heaven for a while."[78] For now, this storytelling works. When her son wakes up in the morning, he asks her, "Mommy, have I missed the angels again?"[79] Yet the narrator understands she and her son are both "lying to one another," but she cannot shatter the façade because doing so would force her to face the ugly reality of her economic situation and profession as "night woman."[80]

The most emblematic vignette that exposes the maternal imperative to give birth and raise children emerges in "Between the Pool and the Gardenias." This short story is the structural center of *Krik? Krak!* and presents the living baby-doll-dead baby schemata on which this essay focuses. In this story, the protagonist appears to descend into madness. Marie, the first person narrator, who has suffered many miscarriages, finds what we later learn is a discarded dead baby "a few inches away from a sewer as open as a hungry child's yawn."[81] However, the story begins with a description of the dead infant's external beauty, forcing the reader to join her in this fantasy of motherhood. She comments that the baby is "very pretty" with "bright shiny hair and dark brown skin like mahogany cocoa" and "her lips were wide and purple, like those African dolls you see in tourist store windows but could never afford to buy."[82] The purple lips here recall the description of Célianne's "beautiful" baby in "Children of the Sea" when the narrator writes, "I never knew before that dead children looked purple. The lips are the most purple because the baby is so dark. Purple like the sea after the sun has set."[83] This connection to Célianne's stillborn baby relates to the mother's inability to protect her child. Marie's unfaithful husband, who fathers 10 children with 10 different women, finds her body culpable; he even suggests that she is killing their babies on purpose. Marie also blames her body for the miscarriages, as she imagines Rose "look[s] the way that I had imagined all my little girls would look. The ones my body could never hold. The ones that somehow got suffocated inside me and made my husband wonder if I was killing them on purpose."[84] She cares for this baby and tells stories to Rose, commenting that she "had a sudden desire to explain to her my life."[85] She seems to have succumbed to the madness when she says, "I am glad you are not one of those babies that cry all day long." She then continues, "All little children should be like you. I am glad you don't cry and make a lot of noise. You're just a perfect child, aren't you?"[86] With Rose, Marie finds an eager, if silent, listener of her life story and participant in her "talk therapy" as she notes "Rose listened with her eyes closed even though I was telling her things that were much too strong for a child's ears."[87] Although it might be true that Marie has slipped away into a world of self-delusion and perhaps outright "clinical madness" when she initially seems unable to distinguish a living baby from a dead one, she acts with intentionality as she engages in the "mad writing" of her oral narratives with deceased baby Rose.

Clearly, Marie is somewhat aware of her fabrication when she tells the dead baby, "I *pretended* that it was all mine" referring to the house where she works as a domestic servant, "I *pretended* that it belonged to us: him, Rose, and me" (my emphasis).[88] The male figure in her imitation family is the "sweaty Dominican man" who cleaned the pool; they "once made love" but "he never spoke to [her] again."[89] Just as her philandering husband before him, the Dominican man easily discards Marie after using her body for sex. Abandoning this painful reality, she is able to continue this performance of motherhood until biology intervenes and the baby's body begins to decompose and stink. It is evident to the reader in this moment that the baby (person) Marie rescues from the street is in fact a corpse (thing).[90] Her admission that she pretends to create this family indicates that she has retreated into a world of delusion, imagining a new life to aid in her healing. Although Rose never answers her back or moves at all, Marie refuses to acknowledge these signs and literally goes mad. We cannot, then, position this tale in the tradition of Todorov's fantastic, as Marie's pretending illustrates a strategic and conscious disengagement with reality.[91] Perhaps more apropos is a reading of Marie's relationship with Rose following a Haitian cosmography, if such can be said to exist in a unified form. This would allow for the blending of the seemingly fantastic with the imagination as a means of healing from the trauma of both her husband's infidelity (fathering 10 children with 10 different women) and her own miscarriages. Nevertheless, Marie must eventually face the corporeal reality. After constant bathing and perfuming fail to eradicate the odor, she finally decides to bury the cadaver, who she has named Rose because this is the name embroidered on her collar. This naming strategy recalls the naming of Swiss in "Children of the Sea." Both of these dead female babies are first possessed and loved by a marginalized mother and maternal surrogate, and then forcibly cast off by others. Yet when she looks down at the baby, she still "imagined her teething, crawling, crying, fussing, and just misbehaving herself."[92] Incidentally, one of the baby girl names Marie wished to give her baby was Célianne. Deliberate acts of imagination allow Marie to forget the pain and trauma of her past and speak a new life into existence for herself. She continues to give her life story, this oral history, even as the law is coming to arrest her for the accusation by the Dominican groundskeeper that she killed the baby.[93] Again, this Dominican man, her one-time lover, betrays her with the insinuation that she is culpable in the death of the baby, replicating her husband's charge that she was "killing [her babies] on purpose."[94] It is worth noting, too, that the baby's name, Rose, connects to her home village of Ville Rose which weaves through a number of the short stories as an important marker of intergenerational, matrilineal storytelling.[95]

In the penultimate vignette, "New York Day Women," the reader witnesses the divergent expectations and fragile relationship between mother and daughter who are living across the diaspora. Maternal surrogacy and expectations of the immigrant child emerge through the figure of the doll. The initially unnamed protagonist secretly follows her mother as she walks through the streets of Manhattan on her way to her job as a childcare provider. As she traces her mother's steps down the city blocks, she is surprised by her immigrant mother's navigation of the upscale urban space: she window shops and peers through designer store windows, and stops to purchase a soda and a frankfurter from street vendors. Tellingly, when she spies on her mother perusing a rack of African-print dresses, she assumes that her mother is contemplating buying the dress for her. These are some of the facts she knows about her mother: she is 59 years old, has lost six of her seven sisters, wears dentures because so many of her molars have fallen out, makes homemade cinnamon jam, and refuses to give clothes away at the Goodwill because there are so many people back home in Haiti who need them. But, what is her mother's experience as one of 546,000 foreign-born Haitian immigrants living in the United States? Is it possible to truly know her mother who knows how to negotiate both Haiti and New York? It is certainly a shock, then, when her mother arrives at the park to assume her caretaking responsibilities and the blond-haired child "raises his face to look at my mother...as though he is looking at the sky."[96] When her mother surprises the child with the soda, they seem to exchange a conspiratory smile. That her mother enjoys this nurturing relationship with her young charge, indeed serves as an "othermother" to him, seems to arouse some feelings of envy in our as-yet unnamed protagonist, who grapples to decipher the meaning of her mother.

Indeed, the repetition of the "my mother" epithet which begins or is included in nearly every sentence of this vignette, indicates a sense of possession and vision of her mother solely through her kinship and biological relationship to her children. However, the daughter suffers from erasure and alienation, unsure of her status while her mother wanders confidently. During this secret observational jaunt through the city, her mother becomes a completely different person, one she has never known, who experiences life independently of her daughter. Interspersed throughout the protagonist's reflections about her mother's life as a working "Day Woman" are the familiar aphorisms and admonishments her mother frequently recounts which appear in bold type in the text: "In Haiti when you get hit by a car, the owner of the car gets out and kicks you for getting blood on his bumper"[97] and "You are pretty enough to be a stewardess. Only dogs like bones."[98] She recalls these often-humorous words of wisdom as she trails her mother's path through the city and ponders the poignancy of this saying of her mother's: "I cannot just swallow salt. Salt is heavier than a hundred bags of shame."[99] This is the shame that prevented her mother from attending any Parent-Teacher Association meetings when the protagonist was in school. Yet she endures the traumas of a Haitian immigrant living in New York, raising children in a culture that is not her own. On the sisters she has lost, she comments only that there are "many graves to kiss" when she returns to Haiti.[100] The daughter attempts to translate Haitian cultural proverbs to a United States context and struggles to find meaning.

The protagonist must literally and figuratively chase her mother throughout the city in the hopes of gleaning some understanding of who she is beyond the parabolic axioms. "One day," she concedes, "I would chase an old woman down a street by mistake and that old woman would be somebody else's mother, who I would have mistaken for mine."[101] This admission highlights the protagonist's inability to recognize her mother, to know her truly as she blends into the circle of what she calls "Third World" women taking care of "other people's children."[102] Her mother has become a "professional mother"; her livelihood is mothering. It is through the protagonist's mother's expectation that her daughter become a mother that the reader finally learns her name:

> My mother, who stuffs thimbles in her mouth and then blows up her cheeks like Dizzy Gillespie while sewing yet another Raggedy Ann doll that she names Suzette after me.
>
> **
>
> **I will have all these little Suzettes in case you never have any babies, which looks more like it is going to happen.**
>
> **
>
> My mother who had me when she was thirty-three—l'âge de Christ—at the age that Christ died on the cross.
>
> **
>
> That's a blessing, believe you me, even if American doctors say by that time you can make retarded babies.[103]

Here, we learn that our narrator's name is Suzette and begin to understand the depth of her mother's desire for her to become a mother herself. Conversely, we learn the extent to which Suzette finds her own mother's behavior inscrutable. The idea that Suzette's mother sews countless Raggedy Ann dolls, which she names Suzette, returns to this fascinating exchange between the human baby and the doll in Danticat's work and especially in *Krik? Krak!* In an effort to combat the corrupting influence of New York, Suzette's mother attempts to fashion and fabricate her grandchildren through sewing these cloth dolls in case she never has grandchildren. Thus, the potentially maddening experience of living between two cultures manifests itself as the critical desire to *know* each other (mother and daughter) fully that their very existence in-between two worlds complicates. Poignantly, Suzette's mother names each doll after her daugher, transforming them into inanimate "little Suzettes." The proliferation of Suzette dolls and Suzette's uneasiness with them illuminates the pressure faced by the first-generation immigrant child, that is, expectations to meet the cultural standards and practices of both the Old and New World. For Suzette, the anxiety, depression, and alienation stem from the expectation of her future reproductive life and requirement to assume the role of mother even as she loses sole possession of her own mother to the privileged children of her adopted country.

Part IV. Conclusion

Clarisse Zimra insightfully charts the relationship between biological and ideological motherhood in Caribbean literary contexts:

> For the chosen Mother (rather than the inherited genitrix) through whom ancestral wisdom is transmitted, is often the childless woman; or, as Schwarz-Bart calls her, the "nameless one" (Reine sans Nom). If she cares for children, they are not always her biological ones, that she may be the symbolic ideological Mother to a whole people.[104]

The notion of the "symbolic ideological Mother" echoes the myth of Défilée who reconstitutes the Haitian nation.[105] Women serve as the metaphorical and biological mothers ("bloodmothers") of the nation but also engage in intergenerational, transnational mothering networks, part of the "othermothering" tradition.[106]

The diasporic phenomenon of child fostering is one salient example of the concept of "othermothering," which Patricia Hill Collins defines as "sharing mothering responsibilities" within "women-centered extended kin networks, fictive kin, and othermother traditions."[107] Othermothers support and care for children when their bloodmothers cannot. Integral to diasporic, African-derived notions of Black motherhood, othermothering centralizes women-centered linkages as "Grandmothers, sisters, aunts, or cousin act as othermothers by taking on child-care responsibilities for one another's children."[108] Amanda Putnam addresses the tragic circumstances that lead to what she calls "communal mothering," which occurs because "actual mothers have been displaced, usually by untimely death, but also occasionally via other tragic circumstances."[109] Locating mothering practices in a cartographic context, Pierrette Hondagneu-Sotelo and Ernestine Avila name this relationship between mothers and daughters living across the diaspora "transnational motherhood."[110] Through the generations of storytelling, often across national boundaries, there is continuity and connection across the Haitian diaspora in which mothers (biological, surrogate, and ideological) and daughters become authors of mad writing that is at once fragmentary, complicated, and evidence of a "clear vision of things."

With most of the short stories of *Krik? Krak!* set in Haiti, the thematic constant in the extensive narrative is the persistent degradation and daily indignities many women and girls face precisely because of the vulnerability of the female body. Terry Rey explains that the reign of terror of Lieutenant General Raoul Cedras (1991–1994), who had driven President Jean-Bertrand Aristide from office, "committed arguably the greatest crime against womankind in the Caribbean since slavery."[111] This criminal assault on Haitian women's bodies mnemonically repeats the trauma of slavery and threatens to transform the mother-daughter relationship into a horrific nightmare; when the rape results in pregnancy, the childbirth experience and baby could possibly come to embody a constant shameful reminder of the violation. Even when rape is not involved, *Krik? Krak!* reveals the fragility of the status of black women and their children in a patriarchal society that often leaves women's bodies vulnerable to violence in the public and private spheres. In my essay, I have demonstrated that the matrilineal stories considered here register madness not as a disease or pathological impairment of mental functioning for the central female characters in Haiti and the diaspora that populate these narratives but rather as an agential strategy elucidated by Beyala's "clear vision of things" that allows at once for mental distancing from the mayhem in which they are surrounded (i.e., the often horrendous quotidian realities of life) and the continuance of ancestral memory. What staves off madness is the ability to speak it and thus speak back to it. It is perhaps this sentiment that informs the collection's "Epilogue," which concludes with the imperative to tell stories, to write, to remember the names that came before:

> You thought if you didn't tell the stories, the sky would fall on your head. You often thought that without the trees, the sky would fall on your head. You learned in school that you have pencils and paper only because the trees gave themselves in unconditional sacrifice. There have been days when the sky was as close as your hair to falling on your head.[112]

We end with the significance of the matrilineal storytelling and the generations of mothers and daughters who must not be forgotten or silenced and make their mark. Memorizing their names was "testament to the way that these women lived and died and lived again."[113]

Notes

1. Opal Palmer Adisa, "Up Close and Personal: Edwidge Danticat on Haitian Identity and the Writer's Life," *African American Review* 43: 2/3 (Summer/Fall, 2009): 350.
2. Martin Munro, *Exile and Post-1946 Haitian Literature: Alexis, Depestre, Ollivier, Laferrière, Danticat* (Liverpool: Liverpool University Press, 2012), 218.
3. Chantal Kalisa, *Violence in Francophone African & Caribbean Women's Literature* (Lincoln, NE: University of Nebraska Press, 2009), 164–5.
4. Minogue and Palmer provide a Bakhtinian analysis employing notions of the carnivalesque and the "grotesque body" to examine depiction of abortion in novels of the 1930s and 1950s/60s and the resistance in earlier texts to discuss the "stark actuality of dead babies" as opposed to the more acceptable maternal death to enable a child's life (103). Sally Minogue and Andrew Palmer, "Confronting the Abject: Women and Dead Babies in Modern English Literature," *Journal of Modern Literature* 29, no. 3 (Spring, 2006): 103. This article is instructive for theoretical approaches to literary analysis of dead babies in literature. For example, it helps to consider how the short story can only offer a fictional representation of a living baby; thus, the baby doll becomes a metarepresentation of the fictional representation of the baby.
5. UNICEF's "At a glance: Haiti" website cites the infant and maternal mortality rates in Haiti as the worst in the Western Hemisphere. In 2008, Haitian mothers had a 1 in 93 lifetime risk of maternal death, according to the March 2012 statistics report, "Haiti: Maternal, Newborn & Child Survival." There were a number of news reports of

women who were going into labor shortly after the devastating 2010 Haitian earthquake. One such news report declares "Haiti Dangerous for Mothers, Babies" in Dan Childs and Joanna Schaffhausen's article, "Haiti Earthquake: Mother Gives Birth in a Disaster Zone," *ABC News.com*, January 18, 2010.

6. Judith Lewis Herman, *Trauma and Recovery: The Aftermath of Violence—From Domestic Abuse to Political Terror* (New York: Basic Books, 1997), 1–34.
7. Gay Wilentz, *Healing Narratives: Women Writers Curing Cultural Disease* (New Brunswick, NJ: Rutgers University Press, 2000), 7.
8. Caroline Brown, "A Divine Madness: The Secret Language of Trauma in the Novels of Bessie Head and Calixthe Beyala," *Comparative Studies of South Asia, Africa and the Middle East* 28, no. 1 (2008): 94.
9. Bennetta Jules-Rosette, *Black Paris: The African Writers' Landscape* (Urbana, IL: University of Illinois Press, 1998), 204.
10 Valérie Orlando, "Writing New (Her)stories: For Francophone Women of Africa and the Caribbean," *World Literature Today* 75, no. 1 (Winter 2001): 45.
11. Evelyn O'Callaghan, "Interior Schisms Dramatised: The Treatment of the 'Mad' Woman in the Work of Some Female Caribbean Novelists," in *Out of the Kumbla: Caribbean Women and Literature*, eds. Carole Boyce Davies and Elaine Savory Fido (Trenton, NJ: Africa World Press, 1990) 90, 104.
12. Thomas Szasz, *Insanity: The Idea and Its Consequences* (Syracuse, NY: Syracuse University Press, 1997), 220–21.
13. Brown, "A Divine Madness," 94.
14. Kaiama L. Glover, "'Black' Radicalism in Haiti and the Disorderly Feminine: The Case of Marie Vieux Chauvet," *Small Axe* 17, no. 1 (March 2013): 8. Régine Michelle Jean-Charles argues a similar point in *Conflict Bodies: The Politics of Rape Representation in the Francophone Imaginary* when she notes that "we find the same attention to violence and female body often rendered in graphic detail. When we consider Danticat's esteem for *Amour, colère, folie*, the triple incantation of her debut novel, *Breath, Eyes, Memory*, can be read as an interpellation of Vieux-Chauvet" (83).
15. Szasz, *Insanity*, 236. Although Szasz offers a critique of psychiatry in general, and an interrogation of mental illness as a "brain disease," his theories of intentionality and rejection of the idea that the insane lack intentionality are particularly useful for my argument about "mad writing" and its purposes.

16. Quoted in Valérie Orlando, Writing New H(er)stories for Francophone Women of Africa and the Caribbean, *World Literature Today* 75, no. 1 (Winter 2001): 45. Originally cited in Anne Adams, "To W/rite in a New Language: Werewere Liking's Adaptation of Ritual to the Novel," *Callaloo* 16, no. 1 (Winter 1993): 153.
17. See Jean-Paul Sartre's Introduction to Frantz Fanon, *The Wretched of the Earth* (New York: Grove Press, 2004).
18. Bennetta Jules-Rosette, *Black Paris*, 204–5.
19. Herman, *Trauma and Recovery*, 133.
20. Hellen Lee-Keller, "Madness and The Mulâtre-Aristocrate: Haiti, Decolonization, and Women in Marie Chauvet's *Amour*," *Callaloo* 32, no. 4 (Winter 2009): 1294.
21. Suzanne Dow, *Madness in Twentieth-Century French Women's Writing: Leduc, Duras, Beauvoir, Cardinal, Hyvrard*, ed. Peter Collier, *Modern French Identities* 76 (Oxford: Peter Lang, 2009), 20.
22. Ibid., 158–59.
23. Bennetta Jules-Rosette, *Black Paris*, 204.
24. Ibid., 185.
25. Françoise Lionnet, "Geographies of Pain: Captive Bodies and Violent Acts in the Fictions of Myriam Warner-Vieyra, Gayl Jones, and Bessie Head," *Callaloo* 16, no. 1 (1993): 137, quoted in Régine Michelle Jean-Charles, *Conflict Bodies: The Politics of Rape Representation in the Francophone Imaginary* (Columbus, OH: Ohio State University Press, 2014), 148.
26. Strikingly, the theme of the baby doll permeates much of Danticat's fictive world. The mediation between life and death often coheres around the symbol of the doll as a journey to the afterlife. The reader encounters women who choose to create, tell, and pass on their own stories (mostly to their daughters), and the stories of their ancestors, on their own terms. Although we cannot predict how motherhood has changed Danticat's writing, it is apparent that the breadth of the stories she tells and the audience for whom she tells them has expanded. This expansion of her audience is reflected in her children's and young adult literature. For example, the children's book, *Eight Days: A Story of Haiti*, considers the theme of separation from family and concentrates on a young boy's uses of imagination for comfort in post-Earthquake Haiti while trapped under a building for eight days. He imagines himself playing each day and copes with the death of his friend by pretending he is asleep. *Anaconda: Golden Flower, 1490* preceded this effort and presented historical fiction detailing the pre-Columbian poetry. *Behind the Mountains*, another Young Adult novel, likewise presents fiction about

an immigrant's experience and living between two countries for middle school readers.

27. One such moment is the moving scene of departure in the airport when Danticat's mother leaves Haiti for the US when she is four years old and her brother two years old. Leading up to that day, her mother "had been sewing me dresses: long ones with large bows and elaborate collars, short ones in carnation prints and others with pink lace ruffles. By the end of the week I had ten dresses in total, most of them too big for me, so that, I realized now, I could wear them in the future, while she was gone" (56).
28. Rocio G. Davis, "Oral Narrative as Short Story Cycle: Forging Community in Edwidge Danticat's *Krik? Krak!*" *MELUS* 26, no. 2, Identities (Summer 2001): 72. Indeed, interpretations of the themes of flight and butterflies are common in *Krik? Krak!* analyses. See, for example, Wilson C. Chen, "Figures of Flight and Entrapment in Edwidge Danticat's *Krik? Krak!*," *Rocky Mountain Review* 65, vol. 1 (2011); Carolyn Duffey, "In Flight from the Borderlines: Roses, Rivers, and Missing Haitian History in Marie Chauvet's *Colère* and Edwidge Danticat's *Krik? Krak!* and *The Farming of Bones*," *Journal of Caribbean Literatures* 3, no. 1 (Summer 2001); Renee Shea, "Edwidge Danticat," *Belle Lettres* 10, no. 3 (Summer 1995): 12.
29. Jana Evans Braziel, "Défilée's Diasporic Daughters: Revolutionary Narratives of *Ayiti* (Haiti), *Nanchon* (Nation), and *Dyaspora* (Diaspora) in Edwidge Danticat's *Krik? Krak!*," *Studies in the Literary Imagination* 37, no. 2 (Fall 2004): 77.
30. Ibid., 83.
31. Wendy Knepper, "In/justice and necro-natality in Edwidge Danticat's *Brother, I'm Dying*," *The Journal of Commonwealth Literature* 47, no. 2 (2012): 193, 203.
32. Patricia Hill Collins, *Black Feminist Thought* (New York and London: Routledge, 1999), 192, 194.
33. Valérie Orlando, "Writing New H(er)stories for Francophone Women of Africa and the Caribbean," *World Literature Today* 75, no. 1 (Winter 2001): 42.
34. Yanick Lahen, "L'apport de quatre romancières au roman moderne haïtien." *Journal of Haitian Studies* 3/4 (1997–1998): 87–95, quoted in Valérie Orlando, *Of Suffocated Hearts and Tortured Souls: Seeking Subjecthood through Madness in Francophone Women's Writing of African and the Caribbean* (Lanham, MD: Lexington Books, 2003). Orlando limits her insightful study of madness to Francophone Caribbean and African women writers, and in this excerpted passage is interpreting the work of Haitian writer Marie Chauvet.
35. Hélène Cixous, "The Laugh of Medusa," trans. Keith Cohen and Paula Cohen, *Signs* 1, no. 4 (Summer 1976): 875.

36. Ibid., 876.
37. In the vignette, "Nineteen Thirty-Seven," a crying Madonna figurine emerges at the beginning of the story as an important link between the natural and the supernatural worlds as the protagonist's mother is imprisoned for allegedly being a witch: "My Madonna cried. A miniature teardrop traveled down her white porcelain face, like dew on the tip of early morning grass. When I saw the tear I thought, surely, that my mother had died" (33).
38. Dorsía Smith Silva and Simone A. James Alexander, eds. *Feminist and Critical Perspectives on Caribbean Mothering*, (Trenton, NJ: Africa World Press, 2013), viii. The presence of the mother *in absentia* signals once again the strength of maternal bonds, the longing for mother who may have passed away or passed across the sea to seek a more promising life in the United States. This is a theme that "The Missing Peace" in *Krik? Krak!* first introduces with the character of La Mort.
39. Wilentz, *Healing Narratives*, 23.
40. Michel-Rolph Trouillot, *Silencing the Past: Power and the Production of History* (Boston: Beacon Press, 1995), 15.
41. This collective Haitian womanhood harkens back to Dédée Bazile and her mythic representation as Défilée la Folle, one of the original madwomen, and Haitian site of cultural memory.
42. Chikwenye Okonjo Ogunyemi, "Womanism: The Dynamics of the Contemporary Black Female Novel in English," *Signs* 11, no. 1 (Autumn 1985): 74. This black womanist approach to madness contrasts with Sandra M. Gilbert and Susan Gubar's classic 1979 feminist text, *Madwomen in the Attic: The Woman Writer and the Nineteenth Century*, which positions the raging madwoman as the allegorical woman as artist.
43. Ibid., 74.
44. Quoted in Brown, "A Divine Madness," 95.
45. Danticat, *Krik? Krak!* (New York: Vintage Books, 1995), 3.
46. Ibid.
47. Ibid.
48. Ibid., 14.
49. Nick Nesbitt, *Voicing Memory: History and Subjectivity in French Caribbean Literature* (Charlottesville, VA: University of Virginia Press, 2003), 205.
50. Danticat, *Krik? Krak!*, 4.
51. Ibid., 7.
52. Ibid., 8.
53. Ibid.
54. Bennetta Jules-Rosette, *Black Paris*, 204–5.
55. Danticat, *Krik? Krak!*, 15.

56. Comparative references to the transatlantic slave trade and ancestral African identity surface in "Children of the Sea." The male narrator remarks "Yes, I am finally African" (11) after days of his skin darkening from receiving the direct sunlight on the small boat. Later, he comments, "I feel like we are sailing for Africa. Maybe we will go to Guinin, to live with the spirits, to be with everyone who has come and has died before us" (14). There is a sense of continuity with African ancestors, connected by the eternity of the sea. Further, the male narrator laments anti-Haitian sentiment among Bahamians, especially since "we had the same African fathers who probably crossed these same seas together" (14). In this case, it is the trauma of the Middle Passage and shared African heritage that the narrators believe unites Caribbean people across national boundaries.
57. Danticat, *Krik? Krak!*, 5.
58. Ibid., 3.
59. Ibid., 24.
60. Ibid.
61. Ibid., 18.
62. Ibid., 20.
63. The Swiss knife also calls to mind the butcher knife allegedly used by the "runaway" enslaved African American woman, Margaret Garner, to kill her two-year-old daughter to protect her from re-enslavement in 1856.
64. Danticat, *Krik? Krak!*, 20.
65. Ibid.
66. Ibid., 21.
67. Ibid., 23.
68. Ibid., 26.
69. Ibid., 27.
70. Ibid., 83.
71. Ibid., 84.
72. Ibid., 83.
73. Ibid., 83.
74. Ibid., 86.
75. Ibid., 85.
76. Ibid., 84.
77. Ibid., 86.
78. Ibid., 88.
79. Ibid.
80. Ibid., 86.
81. Ibid., 91.
82. Ibid.
83. Ibid., 20, 25.

84. Ibid., 92.
85. Ibid., 96.
86. Ibid., 97.
87. Ibid., 96.
88. Ibid.
89. Ibid.
90. For an interesting discussion on the distinction between the living person and the static thing, see Barbara Johnson, *Persons and Things* (Cambridge, MA: Harvard University Press, 2008).
91. According to Todorov's definition of the fantastic, he notes the ambiguity between the realm of dreams and reality: "In a world which is indeed our world, the one we know, a world without devils, sylphides, or vampires, there occurs an event which cannot be explained by the laws of this same familiar world. The person who experiences the event must opt for one of two possible solutions: either he is the victim of an illusion of the senses, of a product of the imagination—and laws of the world then remain what they are; or else the event has indeed taken place, it is an integral part of reality—but then controlled by laws unknown to us" (25). See Tzvetan Todorov, *The Fantastic: A Structural Approach to a Literary Genre*, trans. Richard Howard (Ithaca, NY: Cornell University Press, 1975), 25.
92. Danticat, *Krik? Krak!*, 100.
93. The embattled history between the two countries that share the small island of Hispaniola emerged most recently with the Dominican Republic's immigration policy, *El Plan Nacional de Regularización de los extranjeros* (*National Plan for the Regularization of Foreigners*), codified as law in 2013 in Dominican President Danilo Medina's decree (Decreto No. 327–13), which retroactively revoked citizenship from Dominicans of Haitian origin (born after 1929) without documentation of legal migration to the country and/or a Dominican birth certificate. The Dominican government offered the option to Dominicans of Haitian descent to register as foreigners or face deportation to Haiti. Dominican-Haitians protested publicly, raising signs that proclaim: "somos dominicanos como tú" ("we are Dominicans like you"). For further study, see Celoso Pérez, "We Are Dominican: Arbitrary Deprivation of Nationality in the Dominican Republic," July 1, 2015, and Kenya Downs's "Haitian's Lynching Renews Protests Against Dominican Citizenship Law," February 14, 2015.
94. Danticat, *Krik? Krak!*, 92.
95. Braziel also offers a reading of Marie's Rose as a descendent of the myth of Sor Rose in Haitian history.
96. Danticat, *Krik? Krak!*, 151.

97. Ibid., 146.
98. Ibid., 150.
99. Ibid.
100. Ibid., 151.
101. Ibid., 152.
102. Ibid.
103. Ibid., 153.
104. Clarisse Zimra, "Righting the Calabash: Writing History in the Female Francophone Narrative," *Out of the Kumbla: Caribbean Women and Literature*, eds. Carole Boyce Davies and Elaine Savory Fido (Trenton, NJ: Africa World Press, 1990) 156–57.
105. The iterations of storytelling ("the tale within the tale, and the retelling of a retelling") relates to Tanya L. Shields's notion of "feminist rehearsals" in *Bodies and Bones: Feminist Rehearsal and Imagining Caribbean Belonging* (Charlottesville, VA, University of Virginia Press, 2014).
106. The intergenerational feature of the storytelling resonates with a larger Francophone Caribbean women writers' tradition. For example, Simone Schwarz-Bart's classic *Pluie et vent sur Télumée Miracle* (1979) presents the "lives of three generations of Black women" in Guadeloupe. See Catherine A. John, *Clear Word and Third Sight: Folk Groundings and Diasporic Consciousness in African Caribbean Writing* (Durham, NC, and London: Duke University Press, 2003) 135.
107. Danticat's *Breath, Eyes, Memory* addresses the theme of diasporic child fostering explicitly, as does the autobiographical *Brother, I'm Dying*, in which child protagonists are left behind with extended family networks in Haiti while parents seek economic opportunities in the United States, specifically New York. See the chapter "Black Women and Motherhood" in Patricia Hill Collins, *Black Feminist Thought*, 192, 194.
108. Collins, *Black Feminist Thought*, 192–3.
109. Amanda Putnam, "Mothering the motherless: portrayals of alternative mothering practices within the Caribbean Diaspora," *Canadian Woman Studies* 23, no. 2 (Winter 2001): 118–123.
110. Quoted in Heather Hewett, "Mothering Across Borders: Narratives of Immigrant Mothers in the United States," *Women's Studies Quarterly* 37, no. 3/4, Mother (Fall – Winter 2009): 122.
111. Terry Rey, "Junta, Rape, and Religion in Haiti, 1993–1994," *Journal of Feminist Studies in Religion* 5, no. 2 (Fall 1999): 74.
112. Danticat, *Krik? Krak!*, 223.
113. Ibid., 224.

Bibliography

Adams, Anne. "To W/rite in a New Language: Werewere Liking's Adaptation of Ritual to the Novel." *Callaloo* 16, no. 1 (Winter 1993): 153–168.

Adisa, Opal Palmer. "Up Close and Personal: Edwidge Danticat on Haitian Identity and the Writer's Life." *African American Review* 43, no. 2/3 (Summer/Fall 2009): 345–355.

Braziel, Jana Evans. "Défilée's Diasporic Daughters: Revolutionary Narratives of *Ayiti* (Haiti), *Nanchon* (Nation), and *Dyaspora* (Diaspora) in Edwidge Danticat's *Krik? Krak!*" *Studies in the Literary Imagination* 37, no. 2 (Fall 2004): 77–96.

Brown, Caroline. "A Divine Madness: The Secret Language of Trauma in the Novels of Bessie Head and Calixthe Beyala." *Comparative Studies of South Asia, Africa and the Middle East* 28, no. 1 (2008): 93–108.

Chen, Wilson C. "Figures of Flight and Entrapment in Edwidge Danticat's *Krik? Krak!*" *Rocky Mountain Review* 65, no. 1 (2011): 36–55.

Childs, Dan and Joanna Schaffhausen. "Haiti Earthquake: Mother Gives Birth in a Disaster Zone." *ABC News.com*, January 18, 2010. http://abcnews.go.com/Health/Wellness/haiti-earthquake-mother-delivers-baby-disaster-zone/story?id=9587264.

Cixous, Hélène. "The Laugh of Medusa," trans. Keith Cohen and Paula Cohen. *Signs* 1, no. 4 (Summer 1976): 875–893.

Collins, Patricia Hill. *Black Feminist Thought*. New York and London: Routledge, 1999.

Danticat, Edwidge. *Breath, Eyes, Memory*. New York: Soho Press, 1994.

———. *Brother, I'm Dying*. New York: Alfred A. Knopf, 2007.

———. *Krik? Krak!* New York: Vintage Books, 1995.

Davies, Carole Boyce, and Elaine Savory Fido, eds. *Out of the Kumbla: Caribbean Women and Literature*. Trenton, N.J.: Africa World Press, 1990.

Davis, Rocio G. "Oral Narrative as Short Story Cycle: Forging Community in Edwidge Danticat's *Krik? Krak!*" *MELUS* 26, no. 2, Identities (Summer 2001): 72.

Dow, Suzanne. *Madness in Twentieth-Century French Women's Writing: Leduc, Duras, Beauvoir, Cardinal, Hyvrard*. Edited by Peter Collier. *Modern French Identities* 76. Oxford: Peter Lang, 2009.

Downs, Kenya. "Haitian's Lynching Renews Protests Against Dominican Citizenship Law." *NPR*, February 14, 2015. http://www.npr.org/sections/codeswitch/2015/02/14/384344141/haitians-lynching-renews-protests-against-dominican-citizenship-law.

Duffey, Carolyn. "In Flight from the Borderlines: Roses, Rivers, and Missing Haitian History in Marie Chauvet's *Colère* and Edwidge Danticat's *Krik? Krak!* and *The Farming of Bones*." *Journal of Caribbean Literatures* 3, no. 1 (Summer 2001): 77–91.

Fanon, Frantz. *The Wretched of the Earth*. New York: Grove Press, 2004.
Gilbert, Sandra M. and Susan Gubar. *Madwomen in the Attic: The Woman Writer and the Nineteenth Century*. New Haven: Yale University Press, 2000.
Glover, Kaiama L. "'Black' Radicalism in Haiti and the Disorderly Feminine: The Case of Marie Vieux Chauvet." *Small Axe* 17, no. 1 (March, 2013): 7–21.
"Haiti: Maternal, Newborn & Child Survival." Statistics and Monitoring Section/Policy and Practice. March 2012. UNICEF. https://data.unicef.org.
Herman, Judith Lewis. *Trauma and Recovery: The aftermath of violence—from domestic abuse to political terror*. New York: Basic Books, 1997.
Hewett, Heather. "Mothering Across Borders: Narratives of Immigrant Mothers in the United States." *Women's Studies Quarterly* 37:3/4, Mother (Fall – Winter 2009): 122.
Jean-Charles, Régine Michelle. *Conflict Bodies: The Politics of Rape Representation in the Francophone Imaginary*. Columbus: The Ohio State University Press, 2014.
John, Catherine A. *Clear Word and Third Sight: Folk Groundings and Diasporic Consciousness in African Caribbean Writing*. Durham and London: Duke University Press, 2003.
Johnson, Barbara. *Persons and Things*. Cambridge: Harvard University Press, 2008.
Jules-Rosette, Bennetta. *Black Paris: The African Writers' Landscape*. Urbana: University of Illinois Press, 1998.
Kalisa, Chantal. *Violence in Francophone African & Caribbean Women's Literature*. Nebraska: Nebraska University Press, 2009.
Knepper, Wendy. "In/justice and necro-natality in Edwidge Danticat's *Brother, I'm Dying*." *The Journal of Commonwealth Literature* 47, no. 2 (2012): 191–205.
Lahen, Yanick. "L'apport de quatre romancières au roman moderne haïtien." *Journal of Haitian Studies* 3/4 (1997–1998): 87-95.
Lee-Keller, Hellen. "Madness and The Mulâtre-Aristocrate: Haiti, Decolonization, and Women in Marie Chauvet's *Amour*." *Callaloo* 32, no. 4 (Winter 2009): 1293–1311.
Lionnet, Françoise. "Geographies of Pain: Captive Bodies and Violent Acts in the Fictions of Myriam Warner-Vieyra, Gayl Jones, and Bessie Head." *Callaloo* 16, no. 1 (1993): 137.
Minogue, Sally and Andrew Palmer. "Confronting the Abject: Women and Dead Babies in Modern English Literature." *Journal of Modern Literature* 29, no. 3 (Spring, 2006): 103–125.
Munro, Martin. *Exile and Post-1946 Haitian Literature: Alexis, Depestre, Ollivier, Laferrière, Danticat*. Liverpool: Liverpool University Press, 2012.
Nesbitt, Nick. *Voicing Memory: History and Subjectivity in French Caribbean Literature*. Charlottesville: University of Virginia Press, 2003.

O'Callaghan, Evelyn. "Interior Schisms Dramatised: The Treatment of the 'Mad' Woman in the Work of Some Female Caribbean Novelists." In *Out of the Kumbla: Caribbean Women and Literature*, 89–109. Edited by Carole Boyce Davies and Elaine Savory Fido. Trenton, New Jersey: Africa World Press, 1990.

Ogunyemi, Chikwenye Okonjo. "Womanism: The Dynamics of the Contemporary Black Female Novel in English." *Signs* 11, no. 1 (Autumn 1985): 63–80.

Orlando, Valérie. *Of Suffocated Hearts and Tortured Souls: Seeking Subjecthood through Madness in Francophone Women's Writing of African and the Caribbean*. Lanham: Lexington Books, 2003.

———. "Writing New H(er)stories for Francophone Women of Africa and the Caribbean." *World Literature Today* 75, no. 1 (Winter 2001): 40–50.

Pérez, Celoso. "We Are Dominican: Arbitrary Deprivation of Nationality in the Dominican Republic." *Human Rights Watch*, July 1, 2015. https://www.hrw.org/report/2015/07/01/we-are-dominican/arbitrary-deprivation-nationality-dominican-republic.

Putnam, Amanda. "Mothering the motherless: portrayals of alternative mothering practices within the Caribbean Diaspora." *Canadian Woman Studies* 23, no. 2 (Winter 2001): 118 123.

Rey, Terry. "Junta, Rape, and Religion in Haiti, 1993–1994." *Journal of Feminist Studies in Religion* 5, no. 2 (Fall 1999): 73-100.

Schwarz-Bart, Simone. *Pluie et vent sur Télumée Miracle./The Bridge of Beyond.* New York: New York Books Classics, 2013.

Shea, Renee. "Edwidge Danticat." *Belle Lettres* 10, no. 3 (Summer 1995): 12–15.

Shields, Tanya L. *Bodies and Bones: Feminist Rehearsal and Imagining Caribbean Belonging*. Charlottesville, University of Virginia Press, 2014.

Silva, Dorsía Smith and Simone A. James Alexander, eds. *Feminist and Critical Perspectives on Caribbean Mothering*. Trenton, New Jersey: Africa World Press, 2013.

Szasz, Thomas. *Insanity: The Idea and Its Consequences*. Syracuse: Syracuse University Press, 1997.

Todorov, Tzvetan. *The Fantastic: A Structural Approach to a Literary Genre*. Translated by Richard Howard. Ithaca: Cornell University Press, 1975.

Trouillot, Michel-Rolph. *Silencing the Past: Power and the Production of History*. Boston: Beacon Press, 1995.

Wilentz, Gay. *Healing Narratives: Women Writers Curing Cultural Dis-ease*. New Brunswick: Rutgers University Press, 2000.

Zimra, Clarisse. "Righting the Calabash: Writing History in the Female Francophone Narrative." In *Out of the Kumbla: Caribbean Women and Literature*. Edited by Carole Boyce Davies and Elaine Savory Fido. Trenton, New Jersey: Africa World Press, 1990.

PART III

Form, Mythic Space: Syncretic Rituals as Healing Balm

Shahrazade's Sisters and the Harem: Reclaiming the Forbidden as a Site of Resistance in Toni Morrison's *Paradise*

Majda R. Atieh

Women as Harem: An Introduction

This essay reads Toni Morrison's *Paradise* (1998) in light of transgressive harem narratives to investigate how Morrison's novel contests the patriarchal ideologies of space through her incorporation of the Co(n)vent as a site of radical feminist resistance. Morrison's *Paradise* situates the Islamic *hijab* (veil) and the *harem*[1] (forbidden space), historically patriarchal facets of female seclusion, within an African American context. In fact, I would argue that *Paradise* strategically relies on madness both to configure patriarchal forms of oppression and to narrativize a female-oriented revolt through the novel's imaginative reproduction of the subversive structure of tales in the classical *Alf Laylah Wa Laylah* (*Arabian Nights*). Morrison's literary text incorporates a cryptic architecture based on Shahrazadian tropes and elliptical framing, simultaneously integrating the closure of the labyrinth with a

"The essay's layout and research objectives have been implemented as pedagogical samples to train my teaching staff and students at Phoenix Private School and orient them with research methodologies."

M.R. Atieh (✉)
Tishreen University, Latakia, Syria

C.A. Brown and J.X.K. Garvey (eds.), *Madness in Black Women's Diasporic Fictions*, Gender and Cultural Studies in Africa and the Diaspora, DOI 10.1007/978-3-319-58127-9_8

temporal open-endedness fundamental to the harem's structure. Ultimately, what results is that Morrison's complex novel cultivates, from the forbidden space of female madness as literary experimentation, a site of resistance based on women's sociopolitical exclusion, solidarity, and ultimate empowerment.

Before discussing *Paradise*, I believe it necessary to map out the contours of my argument through the concept of the Islamic harem. The institution of the harem is based on a gendered insecurity that conceives women as unruly subjects. The harem's sex-segregated space is shaped by privacy that contains Muslim women's identities through *hajb* (veiling) and construes femaleness as both a disorder and threat that should be confined. In Middle Eastern and North African cultures, the Islamic harem has emerged as a phenomenon of gendered space that displays motifs of separation and confinement. Historical studies reveal that the Islamic harem had originally been established as a secure space to protect women from external abuse.[2] However, the historical and social context that shaped the harem's development highlights its foundation in social and political instability.[3] Ultimately, this instability, generated by patriarchal insecurity, targeted the female presence in public spaces.[4] As such, the harem becomes a space that configures femaleness as both a disorder and threat that should be circumscribed[5] in order for the male elite to consolidate and regain its political power. This shift in the harem's signification manifests a masculine ideology that maintains "political power and social control in the shifting location and function of gender boundaries, especially in response to state-building and class formation"[6] during the colonial encounter with Europe in the late nineteenth century.[7] In essence, the Islamic harem has historically functioned as a spatial manifestation of male insecurity that intensifies women's disempowerment.

Harem literature foregrounds the historical depiction of women as dangerously irrational and disruptive agents in the Islamic patriarchal order. One hallmark is the classical harem narrative of *Alf Laylah Wa Laylah*, which revolves around the stories of the wily Shahrazade. This Arabian legend highlights the infidelity of women who, even locked up, can find an outlet and undermine the harem's stability of hierarchies and frontiers that men erect.[8] The perceived defiance of women increases the antipathy that King Shahrayar feels towards them. To maintain his power, he asserts a monolithic discourse that associates women with impropriety and fickleness, and advances a violent version of the archetypal *hijab*. He decides to marry a new wife every night, deliberately asks her to narrate a story, and commands his *siaf* (executioner) to slay the wife after the end of her narration at dawn.[9] As can be perceived in the above incidents, insecurity drives Shahrayar to enforce a spatial harem that features closed narration in order to seclude and annihilate women. I would contend that another work that could be read as a harem narrative is Morrison's *Paradise*.

Paradise engages in a transhistorical and transcultural interrogation of the Islamic *hijab* and harem practices. In examining *Paradise*'s challenge to gender oppression and historical exclusion, scholars have not fully addressed Morrison's incorporation of what could appear to be Islamic or Arabian traditions in generating her politics and aesthetics of resistance.[10] I believe that reading *Paradise* as a harem narrative rectifies gaps in Morrison's scholarship and addresses calls for an investigation of expansive Islamic influence. In fact, my approach urges an inquiry into how Morrison engages and interprets the Islamic harem tradition in her text, a project that pushes beyond what has been done thus far on naming practices and references to enslaved African Muslims.[11] It will reveal how *Paradise* defines masculinist monomania as a form of patriarchal insecurity—both gendered and sexist—that uses nationalism and racial chauvinism to justify itself, intensifying the stigmatization of women.

Architectural Structures and Gendered Containment

The exploration of the narrative's mimicry of harem architecture presents a framework for my discussion of female resistance in *Paradise*. Scholars have considered certain facets of the harem's erratic architecture as conducive to the emancipation of female identity. Such critical readings have been suggested in light of the dual ideologies of the archetypal *hijab* that simultaneously effaces and identifies women.[12] So the duality that shapes the harem's historically changeable structure has been perceived as an arbiter of harem women's adaptation to destabilize the harem's spatial segregation. In this concern, Ruth Yeazell examines Victorian women's travel accounts that communicate a striking presentation of revolutionary domestic arrangements in Turkish harems.[13] For instance, the traveler Lady Mary Wortley reports on how Turkish women resort to the very act of disguise to effectively locate freedom in the supposed loci of circumscription.[14] Accounts of Moroccan harems also illustrate how women elude the harem's gates and frontiers through their orientation with its "labyrinthine space" of private *dahaleez* (hallways) that lead to clandestine alcoves and hidden doors.[15] So, these narratives reveal how Turkish and Moroccan women have repeated the harem's architecture and attempted to uncover its surreptitious fluidity. Women's replication of the harem's structural doubleness is best theorized as a form of mimicry that involves "double articulation," to use Homi Bhabha's definition.[16] According to Bhabha, double articulation is based on a strategic repetition that exposes the effaced "ambivalence produced within the rules of recognition of dominating discourses as they articulate[…] hierarchy, normalization, marginalization and so forth."[17] As the historical contextualization of the harem suggests, ambivalence also surreptitiously shapes the harem's gendered ideology as reflected in the duality of the archetypal *hijab* that projects both obliteration and identification of women. Thus, harem women's mimicry can be defined as a strategic repetition of the ambivalent harem's ideology that shapes its structure. Harem mimicry therefore conflates the revelation of the harem as an ambivalent locus of visibility/invisibility that mediates identity, which is volatile and elusive.

In this concern, several fictional accounts of harem women particularly display mimicry of the harem's architecture via narration. *Alf Laylah Wa Laylah* presents a rebellious domestic rite of storytelling conducted by Shahrazade, wife of the narcissistic and insecure Shahrayar. As Fatima Mernissi suggests, Shahrazade resists "passive submission to her own death" and decides to fight by using "words [that] are the only arms she has to fight [Shahrayar's] violence targeted against her."[18] So, Shahrazade strategically asks permission to narrate a story and Shahrayar, trapped, honors this request. Unanticipated by the sultan, Shahrazade's tales repeat and narrativize the labyrinthine, opaque, and irreverent architecture of Shahrayar's harem to surpass their allotted time (daybreak).[19] Shahrayar's implicit authorization of Shahrazade's endless narration exposes the sultan's current amnesia of his threat of death, which has been interpreted as a main "sign that Scheherazade's goal has been accomplished."[20] Ultimately, Shahrazade's tales destabilize the closure in Shahrayar's imposed model of narration that now relies on the cliffhanger of her stories that feature postponement, polyglossia, open-endedness, and enframed structure. These hallmarks of narration conflate what I identify as Shahrazade's narratological mimicry of the harem structure, which could be proposed as a paradigm for harem women's war against all forms of male containment.

I believe that the uniqueness of narration in Morrison's *Paradise* lies in its integration of the Shahrazadian model to narrativize the madness of a harem constructed on racial insecurity and forms of exclusion. As will be demonstrated, *Paradise* underscores the irrationality of Ruby's symbolic harem, which is created by black nationalists, men who attempt to contain and thus eradicate the perversion of "uncontrollable" and "unnatural" women.[21] In addition, I will argue that women's madness in the novel can be perceived not only as a symptom of their powerlessness but as a form of "liberatory pathology," what I would deem a form of resistance to male domination and institutional abuse. Thus "madness"—including the discursive emancipation of polyglossic discourse—is not only a symptom but a potential cure. To do so, I will return to the construction of space in Morrison's novel.

Of Communal Ovens and Cloistered Tongues: Ruby and the Male Harem

In *Paradise*, the architecture of space defines racial and communal relations. The narrative presents the story of Haven's establishment and later degeneration into a closed community. Haven was first founded by nine strong "8-rock" families[22] who proudly led 100 formerly enslaved blacks from postbellum Louisiana and Mississippi to the Oklahoma territory. However, in 1890, these travelers experienced constant interracial and intraracial hostility and forms of exclusion due to their caste and color, referred to as the "Disallowing, Part One." They were denied entry to Fairly, Oklahoma, by light-skinned blacks. Seeking purification from Fairly's color-based rejection, the dark-skinned travelers develop a racially defensive ideology to protect themselves from the psychic wounds of racial insult. This reactionary defensiveness is translated into the all-black town of Haven, built in 1891 under the guidance of Zechariah Morgan, the founding father of the community. In establishing Haven, Zechariah constructed the town around a community kitchen, the Oven. He intended the Oven to be both a domestic space, being a kitchen, and a public space for communal affairs. Zechariah's Oven becomes the black patriarchs' holistic alternative to the white kitchen, where the rape of black women was "if not a certainty a distinct possibility—neither of which they could bear to contemplate."[23] So, with the presence of the Oven, Zechariah definitely exchanges the "danger" of white kitchens with "relative safety."[24] The community of Haven was thus originally defined by the supposedly healthy merger of private and public spaces and the public affirmation of the black home and kinship bonds.

Again, Haven experiences another "disallowing" that jeopardizes the Ruby patriarchs' sense of power and transforms them into the harem's reactionary sentries. With the decline of Haven in 1949, the community breaks the Oven and heads for the West to found a new settlement. The decision of Haven's travelers to relocate the Oven entails uprooting it from the founding soil of communal value and produces a separation between the public and domestic spaces.[25] During this communal migration, Ruby Morgan, a young matron who is Zechariah's daughter and the sister of Steward and Deacon Morgan, prominent members of the community, falls ill and dies "on the waiting room bench" of the white hospital that refuses to provide medical care because of her race.[26] This incident marks "Disallowing, Part Two," which further erodes the patriarchal power of Ruby's men. After this series of racial "disallowings," perpetuated either by whites or blacks with greater class and color privilege, Ruby men become increasingly antagonistic toward intruders. They perceive "foreign" women as trespassers who destabilize the tranquility and racial purity of their hard-won community—later named Ruby, after Ruby Morgan, in 1952. Yet, the image of Ruby Morgan as a domestic angel and unsullied matron is a convenient fabrication, a lie produced by her brothers to protect their family's reputation and mobilize a demoralized community.[27] This lie becomes the embodiment of a nationalist discourse, dedicated to female purity and the endless reproduction of domesticity and other patriarchal ideals, that eventually threatens to overwhelm the community.

Spatial schism now becomes symptomatic of Ruby's racialized and gendered monomania. The Oven[28] gradually begins to lose its culinary value and degenerates into a gendered shrine; women are segregated away from communal activity and political conversations to a space of domesticity. Central to this is a sense of fear: of women and young people as potentially disruptive, of outsiders as threats to the status quo. So I would suggest that the curtailment of Ruby's women is a symptom of internalized masculine shame and terror displaced and imposed on women, both spatially and discursively. Consequently, the new ideology—manifested in the Oven—obscures and physically confines Ruby's women to multiple harem quarters presented in the narrative as kitchens,[29] private gardens,[30] and bedrooms.[31] As such, Ruby is transformed into a spatial harem based on cultural and gendered exclusivity and insularity. The spatial confinement of Ruby's women develops into narratological patterns of fear and the increased desire for closure. The Rubyites' discursive coercion curtails women's participation in communal and ethical affairs, particularly debates about and in proximity to the Oven.

For instance, Zechariah's motto "Beware the Furrow of His Brow," inscribed on the Oven's walls, has invited variant disputes among Ruby's men.[32] In all debates, women's opinions were suppressed or even manipulated[33] to maintain the patriarchs' power. One of these inscription disputes is the "black and red fist debate."[34] Presented as a defiant fist painted by the young Rubyites on the back wall of the Oven, this debate marks a generational challenge to the older patriarchs' determined beliefs. While Ruby's women try to wash away the fist painting, they cannot remove it.[35] This incident reveals how Ruby's women are not considered valid participants in this generational debate. They are demonized as short-sighted creatures who lack any foundation of logic or clear thinking. Their role is limited and literally confined to futile domestic activities. Ruby's women secretly mediate their suppressed interpretations of the Oven's debate only in the safety of their separate rooms and kitchens. For instance, Soane Morgan can only convey her own adverse standpoints regarding the black and red fist debate while "standing in the kitchen of the biggest house in Ruby, whispering to the darkness outside the window."[36] So the example of the Oven's debate thereby demonstrates how Ruby's patriarchs narrativize their paranoia into monologues that favor the resolution of meaning and reject varied interpretations. The Oven's new function reveals how the patriarchs' reactionary fear is converted into a collective alienation and discursive closure that refracts a profound divide between the spatial and emotional.

A Western Ethos: The Convent as Harem?

The structure of the Convent suggests another peculiar harem variant in *Paradise*. The association between the institutions of the Islamic harem and the Christian convent has been referenced in a variety of ancient literary and historical texts. For instance, Ottaviano Bon's *The Sultan's Seraglio* highlights shared features in both the harem and the convent. Bon observes that the confined and closely guarded inhabitants of the Turkish Seraglio[37] "live just as nuns do in great nunneries."[38] *Viaje de Turquía* is another text that highlights such similarity and refers to Turkish harem women as "monjas encerradas" or locked up nuns and likens the *valide sultan* to an "abadesa" or an abbess.[39] These two references suggest that the European classification of the harem as an ersatz convent was commonplace. Such a familiar analogy is even validated in European travel literature. In their own travel narratives and journals, European visitors described "the harem, with its society of women enclosed in an impenetrable building and isolated from the outside world, in terms of its seemingly closest Christian counterpart—the convent."[40] Considering this historical analogy, the Convent of *Paradise* gradually acquires and even extends many of the defining features of the Islamic harem.

I would argue that although Morrison may not be cognizant of the texts that foreground the harem-convent analogy, her novel develops harem-convent associations as is evident in the Convent's design. The Convent undergoes a structural metamorphosis and gradually exhibits the harem's defining feature of a spatial enclosure that encapsulates a gendered insecurity. The Convent's earlier architecture as a decadent embezzler's folly mansion becomes a site of "masculine excess."[41] Notably, its closed structure evokes the harem's subterranean masculinity and its extreme containment of space. The mansion also projects fear of the outside world, particularly police arrest. Its northern section displays a guarded tip of huddled windows,[42] as in the buffering gatehouse apartments of the harem's guards. The southern exposure of the mansion parallels the harem's sanctuary part where windows are eliminated and light is only allowed through the opening of skylights and dormers on the roof. Likewise, the windows in the mansion's southern section are removed, and "except from the bedrooms [on the upper level] no one in the house could see the sun rise, and there was no vantage point to see it set."[43] The features of the harem also survive in the mansion's refurbished structure as a Catholic boarding school for Arapaho girls. The four nuns who purchase the mansion establish a boarding school whose design manifests the nuns' deepest fears of and insecurity with masculinity and male sexuality. Again, the school retains the motific harem-like features of a "closed-off, protected 'back,'" a "poised and watchful 'tip,'" and a guarded entrance door.[44] Not only do the four Catholic sisters frustrate males' presence and entry into the school by expelling their kitschy art, presented in the prominent testicles, but they rip "the brass male genitalia" from sinks and tubs and pack them away in "a chest of sawdust."[45] Such symbolic castration of the male statues extends a paradoxical feature of the harem, which is usually "ordered around the absence of the phallus" and proclaims male "frustration."[46] The nuns renovate the mansion in an obsessive manner that also symbolically reenacts the harem's extreme veiling of women. They remove all references to female sexuality by chipping away the hanging "female-torso candleholders" and the "curls of hair winding through vines," and hiding the "nipple-tipped doorknobs" and the "several pieces of nude statuary" underneath the cellar stairs.[47] The nuns' cleansing measures recall the Islamic harem practices that advocate the extremely gendered "separation of the profane from the sacred,"[48] where unveiled women are marked with nudity, profanity, and anarchy in the harem order. However, the nuns develop their own type of harem, being a convent, by authorizing a repressive mission to "cleanse from the Arapaho Indian girls' consciousness the indigenous religion and traumatic cultural memories."[49] Though so different from Ruby, the Convent's harem thus mirrors Ruby's erasure of references to sexuality and its mono-maniacal obsession with order, purity, and moral integrity—both iconic and in its linguistic privileging of patriarchal Eurocentric discourses and cultural ideals. Hence, women and non-whites are occluded and subordinated in the Convent and its classrooms.

Later transformed into a sanctuary for runaway women, the Convent continues to maintain its harem-like locus of spatial enclosure that projects insecurities. When the elderly nuns die or depart, a diverse group of women take over the deserted convent. All have been marked by trauma, violence, and abandonment. Consolata Sosa, the nuns' ward, "rescued" from Brazil as a young girl, was sexually abused during her Brazilian childhood and then abandoned at the age of 38 by Deacon Morgan after a passionate affair. Mavis Albright has run away from an abusive alcoholic husband after the accidental deaths of her twin infants. Grace Gibson (Gigi), left stranded when her boyfriend is arrested, is traumatized by the images of violence at the civil rights protests she attended. Seneca is abandoned as a child by her mother, whom she had assumed was her sister and then temporarily hired to provide sexual amusement for a wealthy older woman. Pallas Truelove, a pregnant runaway, is hiding from rapists. These traumatic memories haunt the new residents who seek the Convent as a sanctuary where they grapple with their insecurities that contain their identities and project their madness. Significantly, these women, victimized outcasts, are later demonized and targeted by the male elites of Ruby's harem—an act of animus that verges on hysteria.

Ruby's reactionary racial and gender bias, arising in part from the trauma of the "Disallowing," projects onto the Convent women monolithic categories that are associated with mental and physical disorder. Once the nuns have departed, the male Rubyites no longer know how to "read" the remaining women. The Convent women are therefore labeled as abnormal, mad, and perverted "witches"[50] who "*could*"[51] disrupt Ruby's order. The women are assumed to be racially impure and morally contagious; they could thus corrupt the purity of 8-rock blood and its genealogy informed by divine struggle. These outsider temptresses anarchize Ruby's patriarchal system in multiple ways. They commit adultery and adulteration (as in the affairs of Consolata and Deacon and Gigi and K.D., Deacon's nephew); befriend and "corrupt" Ruby's women (Lone, Soane, and Billie Delia); and, allegedly abort their babies (as in Soane's and Arnette's cases). By threatening to expose Ruby's fears, social fragility, and cultural vulnerability, the Convent erodes the myth of Ruby's unbridgeable borders and lofty status. This threat is especially pertinent to Deacon Morgan, whose affair with Consolata jeopardizes his authority and the community (harem) he has worked so hard to build. So I would assert that the hypothesis of female provocativeness explains why Ruby's men perceive the Convent women's difference as dangerous madness. Like Shahrayar, Ruby's posse of nine men, led by the twins Steward and Deacon Morgan, attempt to maintain their control, now threatened, by authorizing what can only be deemed a mad plot to annihilate the women, planning on using their guns and weapons to hunt and kill them. They set the dawn of a July day as the deadline for the Convent women's lives.[52]

Shahrazade's Sisters: A Liberatory Pathology

Unlike the Rubyites' stoic emotional repression and sociocultural suppression of difference that transforms itself into a misogynistic mania, the Convent women exhibit dysfunctional behavior that becomes nevertheless liberating. Their realized polyglossic narrative, ironically, replicates what I had termed Shahrazade's narratological mimicry. At first, the Convent's residents behave in ways that are dysfunctional and self-defeating. They are emotionally damaged women who have been abused and traumatized. Thus, their behavior becomes increasingly dangerous: Consolata's excessive drinking, Mavis's delusions and hallucinations, Gigi's self-denial and excessive sexuality, Seneca's obsessive scarring, and Pallas's bulimia. Consolata even perceives that the Convent women's insecurity has degenerated into self-destructiveness. She identifies "disorder," "deception," and "drift" as the symptoms of their internal crisis that "paved the road to perdition."[53] She comprehends that their excessive drift is about to become deadly and transform the cellar of the

Convent into "a space tight enough for a coffin."[54] This shocking realization prompts her to do anything "to stop the fights, the raucous empty laughter, the claims. But especially the drift."[55] Recognizing the emotional instability and destructive self-fracturing of the Convent women, Consolata exposes the effaced ambivalence in the closed structure of the Convent that supposedly conveys invisibility and death only.[56] In other words, Consolata unveils the potential of visibility and regeneration in the Convent. So the psychically attuned, emotionally sensitive Consolata integrates Shahrazade's mimicry of the harem structure, which becomes a performance of Consolata's alternative of madness that now leads to therapy and self-transformation. Consolata's therapeutic madness then features Shahrazade's articulation of the harem's labyrinthine and irreverent structure that projects temporal indifference and postponement, polyglossia, and amnesia of death.

Recalling Shahrazade, Consolata mimics the Convent's disregard for time to counteract the women's repressive insecurities. She directs the traumatized residents to follow her time frame, which is shaped by the Convent's irreverence to the outside world: "If you want to be here you do what I say. Sleep when I say [...] stay here and follow me."[57] As a result, the women "came to see that they could not leave the one place they were free to leave."[58] So they follow the Convent's languor that is shaped by its "hiding places"[59] that initiate a time-consuming journey of self-discovery. Thus, the women "gradually[...] los[e] the days."[60] By stimulating irreverence and suspension of external concerns, Consolata then starts the healing process. She asks the women to draw their own templates on the floor of the Convent's basement. These stencils externalize the women's animas that are shaped by insecurities and traumas, often produced by male abuse. Thus, the women initiate "loud dreaming" through which repressed "half-tales and the never-dreamed [stories] escaped from their lips to soar above guttering candles."[61] Through Consolata's direction, the women then narrativize the Convent's structure—along with the secrets symbolized by their engraved templates—into liberatory stories.

Consolata's liberatory narration features a Shahrazadian polyglossia that generates open-endedness to defy the women's dangerous drift. As mentioned before, Shahrazade manages to produce endless stories that secure her safety and survival. She does so by mimicking the harem's labyrinth of *dahaleez* (hallways) that suddenly reveal unexpected clandestine alcoves and hidden doors. Shahrazade narrativizes and transforms these *dahaleez* into voices of various narrators who would always expand the meaning of her stories and maintain their endless and life-giving core. In *Paradise*, the mad Consolata instructs the women to convert their repressive memories into indeterminate stories that are unregulated by a particular ending as "it was never important to know [...] whether [the dream]had meaning."[62] The irresolution of these stories is activated through the absence of any controlling voice, as "it was never important to know who said the dream."[63] The Convent's stories then feature the Shahrazadian inclusion of all voices of the women who surpass their enmity, "step easily into [each] dreamer's tale,"[64] and accept their varied perspectives. They "enter the heat in [Mavis's] Cadillac" and reimagine the twins' tragic death, speak about and reconsider Seneca's scars, ask Gigi to unveil the gift of heart locket from her father, and inquire about the father of Pallas's baby.[65] The Convent women's indefinite and shared stories become therapeutic in the sense that they transcend all insular boundaries of fear. Unlike the insecure Ruby harem that rejects intruders who convey different thoughts, the Convent women locate their security in difference and open-endedness. The women's collective narration of their traumas also unveils their effaced interdependence and solidarity that "drew them like magnets."[66] Thus, the Convent women's madness constructs a narrative of polyglossic euphoria that eliminates their insecurities and reconstructs their fragmented identities.

Consolata's therapeutic madness is extended into a time-gaining rhetoric that destabilizes the urgency of the "Ruby" narrative. Ruby patriarchs project a destructive need for domination of the women in their midst as well as their desire to control the behavior and discursive patterns of the town's inhabitants. The designated "July day" deadline marks the urgency and violent framework of "Ruby," a closed narrative added to the Oven's archive of exclusive debates. However, the narrator of *Paradise* performs Consolata's madness that features Shahrazadian postponement in order to delay the planned attack on the Convent. One manner through which to conceptualize this strategy is to begin with Morrison's "Unspeakable Things Unspoken." In this essay, Morrison focuses on the first books she wrote and reveals some of the ways she "activates language and ways in which that language activates" her.[67] The aesthetic format of Morrison's language and narration is composed of two significant methods: "loaded" introductory sentences and the engagement of the reader through these introductory sentences.[68] Morrison notes that these loaded sentences may either be simple or complex. However, all these sentences are open-ended, as they "would not force the work to genuflect and would complement the outlaw quality in it."[69] In *Paradise*, the "outlaw quality" of narration is re-envisioned as a manifestation of Consolata's madness that displays Shahrazadian indifference to the challenge of death. A reference to an open-ended span of time appears in the first sentences of the "Ruby" narrative: "Hiding places will be plentiful in the Convent, but there is time and the day has just begun."[70]

Following Consolata's mimicry of the Convent's irreverent structure that creates temporal indifference, the narrative's introductory sentences belie any responsive or interrupted narration that is suggestive of fear from urgent attack. The succession of expressions such as "no need to hurry" and "there is time"[71] prompts the readers' sudden contagion with a mood of languor that recalls the harem's metaphysics of undisturbed leisure and "unending reverie."[72] So the "Ruby" narrative is transformed into a rhetorical facet of Consolata's madness that integrates Shahrazade's postponement to defy the Rubyites' adamant execution of death.

The therapeutic aspect of the Convent women's mad narration is also reflected in their empowering amnesia of traumatization. As mentioned before, amnesia is a strategic effect of Shahrazade's adaptation of the irreverent harem narration to secure her survival from death. Shahrazadian amnesia could also be defined as therapeutic, being a sign of Shahrayar's reclaimed security. He abandons his fear of the inherent evil in women and decides to spare Shahrazade.[73] In *Paradise*, the Convent women's narration of their madness features Shahrazadian therapeutic amnesia that transfers them into different realities. Following their therapy in the cellar, the women are ultimately granted access to imagined worlds of "yellow barrettes, red peonies" and "great rivers [...]on their banks and the edges of oceans children thrill to water."[74] These realms suggest tranquility and transcend the earthly fear of death and all endings. Such transcendence foregrounds the women's visibility as reflected in the "remarkably different look in [their] eyes—sociable and connecting when they spoke to you, otherwise they were still and appraising."[75] They even project a calm and "adult manner" that would mute any visitor's initial alarm at the sight of the young women.[76] Even Consolata no longer covers "her awful eyes with dark glasses."[77] She now looks "straight-backed and handsome."[78] In a word, "unlike some people in Ruby, the Convent women were no longer haunted."[79] So, the women's amnesia-oriented narration suspends the women's invisibility that has been enforced by hostile realities, particularly the Ruby men's rejection and planned annihilation of their presence.

The Convent women's amnesia of impending violence and realization of security are extended into both the narrator and the readers who would forget the inevitability of the destructive, masculinist "Ruby" narrative. The narrator's amnesia is reflected in the sudden suspension of any references to danger. In this regard, Morrison has highlighted the significance of the technique of "suspension" in eliciting changes of perspectives in her novels.[80] However, Morrison's strategy of "suspension" is reimagined in *Paradise* as a manifestation of therapeutic madness that generates communal amnesia of trauma. The narrator first refers to the nine men's dangerous intrusion at the end of "Mavis": "On that July morning [Mavis] had been aware for months of the sourness between the Convent and the town and she might have anticipated the truckload of men prowling the mist."[81] This reference implies that the menace of violence is still serious. However, the narrator's subsequent allusion to Mavis's unconscious feelings of peace communicates her unresponsiveness to any danger: "But she was thinking of other things."[82] This peaceful scene contrasts with the enormity of the impending raid of the Ruby men. Later on, the scene of the nine men's intrusion on the Convent is never recalled in "Grace," "Seneca," "Divine," and "Patricia." The absence of any further allusion to the attackers' violent raid challenges its inevitability for the narrator and readers as well. The narrator's suspension of references to imminent attack changes the readers' standpoints about the relevance of death at the end of the novel. The readers of *Paradise* experience similar security and ensuing amnesia of death which communicates a scene of thwarted and unfinished raid.

The "mad" narration of *Paradise* finalizes the discursive liberation of the "Ruby" narrative from its discursive closure that projects death, as conveyed in "They shoot the white girl first."[83] In "Unspeakable Things Unspoken," Morrison observes that her novels' "indeterminate ending […] follows from the untrustworthy beginning."[84] However, I redirect this correlation instead to what I have deemed a liberatory madness that frustrates the only meaning the raid narrative projects: the women's death. The report on the Convent's attack becomes "suspended in the air"[85] as no one in Ruby's community "had decided on the meaning of the ending and, therefore, had not been able to formulate a credible, sermonizable account of it."[86] The raid report even stimulates the narrator's questions and the readers' "emphatic response."[87] So the attack on the Convent now produces a narrative that involves the communal participation of all voices in the continual reconstruction of its meaning. Thus, this reciprocal contribution to suspended meaning frees the "Ruby" narrative from the urgency and closure marked by the "July day" deadline.

Polyglossia and Narrative Open-Endedness as Healing Strategies

The readers of *Paradise* are invited to decipher the narratives' ambiguity and constantly revise their meaning. As explained before, the Convent women's individual narratives become rhetorical enactments of madness that counteract the pathological obsession with closure of Ruby's male elites. The security of indetermination, symptomatic of the Convent women's liberatory madness, is extended into the other narratives in *Paradise*. To perform the women's therapeutic open-endedness, the narrator integrates the Shahrazadian strategy of enframed narration that features a *récit enchâssé* (Chinese box story) or "story-within-a-story" frame.[88] This enframing strategy enables Shahrazade to include her varied narrators who intrude as new characters and present different tales that expand the meaning of previous stories. In *Paradise*, the pattern of narration is also based on characterization that generates enframed stories, as the appearance of each new character means that the meaning of the current narrative remains contingent and unresolved. "Mavis" is the first unfinished narrative that previews potential stories through the enigmatic characters of Consolata and the Mother. The second enframed narrative is "Grace," connected to the other narratives through Gigi's encounter with Connie and Mavis. "Grace" is also enigmatic through the persistent secret of Connie's eyes and the sudden arrival of "a very young girl in too tight clothes tapping on the screen door."[89] In the same way, "Seneca" is linked to the other narratives through Seneca's arrival at the Convent. "Seneca" is also incomplete, for it does not resolve Connie's secret or explain Soane's mysterious abortion at the Convent.[90] "Divine" resists any definite ending because it introduces the unexplained character of Patricia Best. Likewise, "Patricia" and "Consolata" do not completely explain the character of Lone. So, each tale "signifies a new plot"[91] that is open to varied interpretations and complicated meanings. Thus, the Convent women's liberatory madness shapes the novel's enframed narration that celebrates security in ambiguity and irresolution.

This enigmatic rhetoric of madness cultivates a narratological scene of women's public solidarity that undermines the Rubyites' alienating madness. In *Paradise*, the Ruby men's sexual hypocrisy and divisive attitudes affect the relations between Ruby women and the women of the Convent, creating jealousy and tension between the two groups.[92] For instance, Consolata is in love with Deacon, Soane's husband. Both Gigi and Arnette have an affair with K.D. Soane and Dovey seem married to two twin men, Deacon and Steward. As Dovey reflects: "Maybe Soane felt what Dovey did—the weight of having two husbands, not one."[93] I would assert that this is a form of madness, the madness of women's subordination to masculine priorities and male desire. But even more significantly, it becomes the germ of madness, female madness that causes women to wage petty battles and gendered conflicts against each other. However, I believe that the narrator performs Consolata's therapeutic madness projected in her liberatory narration in order to undermine these pathological forms of hostility and competitiveness. Simulating the Convent women who "step easily into [each] dreamer's tale," accept their difference, and convey their solidarity, the narrator's eight stories, apart from "Ruby," embrace new characters who also step in to create interdependence. So each woman's tale is not completely "self-sufficient"[94] but solidly connected to the other tales through an intruding character. The solidarity in these narratives also "collude to hide knowledge from men"[95] as each woman's narrative proposes a mysterious female figure (whether from the town of Ruby or the Convent) and denies any complete revelation of her racial identity or past. This conspiracy of secrecy constructs a narratological "arena for resistance"[96] against Ruby's insecurity that insulates women's narratives and thoughts of freedom. As mentioned before, the desire for change demonstrated by the women of Ruby and the Convent was initially manifested in monologues and separate harems.[97] However, the novel's alternative rhetoric of madness now creates a discursive space of dialogue where women openly bond,[98] communicate previously hidden aspects of their lives, and defiantly break the pathological alienation of Ruby's masculinist monomania.

By structurally reproducing itself according to a new paradigm, the liberated "Ruby" narrative registers a therapeutic discourse oriented to healing. The Convent women's narration of their insecurities has generated their rebirth. The now "altered" women are "to be reminded of the moving bodies they wore, so seductive were the alive ones."[99]

Their narration becomes a recreation of the Shahrazadian model of "progressive structure"[100] that has a "ransom frame"[101] and bestows life. Literally, Shahrazade's narration compels Shahrayar to keep her alive. They later get married and have children together. The birth of Shahrazade's children stands in opposition to Shahrayar's barren harem that has killed women and engendered mortality. In *Paradise*, the narrator improvises the Convent women's madness of renewal to retell Ruby's racial narrative that rejects language's "mid-wifery properties for menace and subjugation."[102] The narrator's succession of stories simulates pregnancy and rebirth, where every narrative springs from another. Also, the total of the narratives, along with the raid story "Ruby," is nine, which signifies birth and life as it refers to the total of months a fetus normally needs to develop in the mother's womb. Thus, these narratives introduce the arrival of Pallas's newborn baby, Divine. The birth of Divine heals the pathology of the "Ruby" harem, which created a contagious "narrative sequence whose inevitable close is torture and death"[103] of women, exemplified by the final scene of a dead Ruby girl's burial. Consequently, the architecture of these tales transforms Ruby's deadly narrative into a life-generating story. In other words, "Ruby," liberated from the town's destructive monomania, is able to accept the balm of the Convent women's discursive emancipation.

Notes

1. Notes In an earlier published essay entitled "The Revelation of the Veiled in Toni Morrison's *Paradise*: the Whirling Dervishes in the Harem of the Convent," I explore the presence of Sufi allusions and rituals in *Paradise*'s harems. However, I do not highlight the architectural aspect of the harems in *Paradise* or read them as pathology.
2. Historical sources reveal that during the first century of Islam, including Prophet Mohammed's period (AD 570–632), Muslim women were more free and active in public life and participated equally with men in the development of Islamic doctrines.
3. Ahmad ibn Muhammad Ibn Hanbal, *Musnad* (Beirut: Al-maktab al-islami lil-tiba'a wa'l-nashr, 1969), vol. 6, 271.
4. Fatima Mernissi, *The Veil and the Male Elite: A Feminist Interpretation of Women's Rights in Islam* (Reading: Addison, 1991), 106.
5. Afterwards, the Islamic harem has come to refer both to the women themselves, who remain inviolable by adopting the veil when they venture outside, and to the part of the dwelling reserved for their use.

See Ruth Bernard Yeazell, *Harems of the Mind: Passages of Western Art and Literature* (New Haven, CT: Yale University Press, 2000), 1.

6. Elizabeth Thompson, "Public and Private in Middle Eastern Women's History," *Journal of Women's History* 15.1 (2003): 53.
7. Thompson is referring to the profound and explosive shift in the discourses and practices that set gender boundaries. Dichotomous conceptions of "public" and "private" that emerged out of the colonial encounter have combined with older repertoires to create historically contingent categories of Muslim women's veils and complex reality for Middle Eastern women today. See Thompson, "Public and Private," 53.
8. *Alf Laylah Wa* Laylah (Dar Al-Hilal, 1958), vol. 1, 15.
9. Ibid., 16.
10. Religious contextualization of female regeneration in *Paradise*'s scholarship does not allude to any Islamic presence in the narrative's transformation rituals. For further explanation, see Majda Atieh, "The Revelation of the Veiled: the Whirling Dervishes in the Harem of the Convent," *MELUS* 36.2 (2011): 89–90.
11. For instance, Nada Elia contends that Morrison's *Song of Solomon* (1977) "does not address the Muslim genealogy" and is "curiously coy" about its borrowing of the names and stories of Belali's descendants and chronicling the central protagonist's search for his [Muslim] African ancestors." See Nada Elia, "'Kum Buba Yali Kum Buba Tambe, Ameen, Ameen, Ameen': Did Some Flying Africans Bow to Allah?" *Callaloo* 26.1 (2003): 189.
12. The archetypal *hijab* had originally been ordained to identify and protect Prophet Muhammad's wives from abuse but was later imposed by the Islamic patriarchal system to cover women and obliterate their individual identities.
13. Yeazell, *Harems of the Mind*, 84.
14. Lady Mary explains that "[…] there is no distinguishing the great Lady from her Slave, and 'tis impossible for the jealous Husband to know his Wife when he meets her[…] This perpetual Masquerade gives them entire Liberty of following their inclinations without danger of Discovery […]." See Robert Halsband, ed., *The Complete Letters of Lady Mary Wortley Montagu* (Oxford: Clarendon, 1965), vol. 1, 328. Lady Mary's report communicates that the harem "apparently poses no bar to the exercise of its inhabitants' 'Curiosity'--its permeable walls allowing for the expansion of a woman's mind as readily as the circulation of her body." See Yeazell, *Harems of the Mind*, 86.
15. Malek Alloula, *The Colonial Harem* (Minneapolis, MN: University of Minnesota Press, 1986), 72.
16. Homi Bhabha, *The Location of Culture* (London: Routledge, 2001), 129.

17. Bhabha, "Signs," in *The Location of Culture*, 158.
18. Fatima Mernissi, *Scheherazade Goes West: Different Cultures, Different Harems* (New York: Washington Square, 2001), 81.
19. Harems are known for their *mashrabiyya*, an elaborate woodwork lattice that secures the windows of women's quarters. This latticed structure bars sunrays and marks the harem's isolation and irresponsiveness to the changes brought by daylight. See Alev Lytle Croutier, *Harem: The World Behind the Veil* (New York: Abbeville, 1989), 41.
20. Mieke Bal, *Narratology: Introduction to the Theory of Narrative* (Toronto, ON: University of Toronto Press, 1997), 51.
21. Toni Morrison, *Paradise* (New York: Knopf, 1998), 63, 279.
22. They are the original and founding families whose deep skin color is comparable to a "deep deep level in the coal mine." They were known as resolute people who worked to maintain their racial purity. See Morrison, *Paradise*, 193.
23. Morrison, *Paradise*, 99.
24. Ibid.
25. Ibid., 112.
26. Ibid., 113.
27. Ruby has an illegitimate son, K. D. Smith. His father, Coffee Smith, is transformed into a "war hero" to protect the family's reputation.
28. Initially, as an alternative black kitchen, the Oven was the first spatial manifestation of Haven patriarchs' traumatic insecurity caused by racial oppression. The Black Oven, as an exclusively black structure, reflects Haven's rendition of enforced insecurity into a normalized "tragic repetition-with-a-difference" of collective alienation that is thought to reflect power. For more information on the trope of tragic repetition, see Cynthia Dobbs, "Diasporic Designs of House, Home, and Haven in Toni Morrison's *Paradise*," *MELUS* 36.2 (2011): 110.
29. Morrison, *Paradise*, 100.
30. Ibid., 89.
31. Ibid., 187.
32. Ibid., 195.
33. Ruby's elites ascribe the inscription's generational interpretation to Esther, a blind five-year-old child! They manipulate what they tag as Miss Esther's "finger memory" to serve their control. Esther's reading raised controversy as young Rubyists "howled at the notion of remembering invisible words you couldn't even read by tracing letters you couldn't pronounce." See Morrison, *Paradise*, 83.
34. Morrison, *Paradise*, 101.
35. Ibid., 102.

36. Ibid., 100.
37. Seraglio refers to the Grand Harem of Topkapi Palace in Istanbul, Turkey. It represents the most highly and extensively developed harem and is considered the paradigm or quintessence of all harems and systems of separating and confining women. Topkapi Palace was home to all the Ottoman sultans for about four centuries, ending with the reign of Abdulmecid I (1839–1860). The Ottoman sultan, Mehmed II, gave the order for the construction of the Topkapi Palace on the Seraglio Point overlooking both Marmara and Bosphorus after the conquest of Constantinople in 1453.
38. Ottaviano Bon, *The Sultan's Seraglio: An Intimate Portrait of Life at the Ottoman Court*, ed. Godfrey Goodwin (London: Saqi, 1996), 47.
39. Fernando García Salinero, ed., *Viaje de Turquía* (Madrid: Catedra, 1980), 440–41.
40. Cory A. Reed, "Harems and Eunuchs: Ottoman-Islamic Motifs of Captivity in *El celoso extremeno*," *BHS* lxxvi (1999): 205.
41. Dobbs, "Diasporic Designs," 113.
42. Morrison, *Paradise*, 71.
43. Ibid.
44. Ibid.
45. Ibid.
46. Malek Alloula, *The Colonial Harem*, 96.
47. Morrison, *Paradise*, 72.
48. Mernissi, *Veil and Male Elite*, 101.
49. Dobbs, "Diasporic Designs," 113.
50. Morrison, *Paradise*, 276.
51. Ibid., 297.
52. Ibid., 3.
53. Ibid., 222.
54. Ibid., 221.
55. Ibid., 222.
56. Critics have identified Consolata as the chief healer and "architect of the final transformation of the Convent from house to home." See Dobbs, "Diasporic Designs," 114. I argue that Consolata recalls the harem women who articulate the harem as a locus of doubleness.
57. Morrison, *Paradise*, 262.
58. Ibid., 262.
59. Ibid., 3.
60. Ibid., 262.
61. Ibid., 264.
62. Ibid.
63. Ibid.

64. Ibid.
65. Morrison, *Paradise*, 264–65.
66. Ibid., 264.
67. Morrison, "Unspeakable Things Unspoken: the Afro-American Presence in American Literature," in *Modern Critical Views: Toni Morrison*, ed. Harold Bloom (New York: Chelsea, 1990), 20.
68. Ibid.
69. Ibid., 24.
70. Morrison, *Paradise,* 3.
71. Ibid.
72. Alloula, *The Colonial Harem*, 74.
73. *Alf Laylah*, vol.3, 318.
74. Morrison, *Paradise*, 265, 283.
75. Ibid., 265–66.
76. Ibid., 266.
77. Ibid., 265.
78. Ibid., 266.
79. Ibid.
80. Claudia Tate, *Black Women Writers at Work* (New York: Continuum, 1983), 125.
81. Morrison, *Paradise*, 49.
82. Ibid.
83. Ibid., 3.
84. Morrison, "Unspeakable Things Unspoken: the Afro-American Presence in American Literature," 20.
85. Morrison, *Paradise*, 297.
86. Charles Ruas, *Conversations with American Writers*, ed. Danille Taylor-Guthrie (Jackson, MS: University Press of Mississippi, 1994), 111.
87. Morrison considers the reciprocal relationship between the listeners/readers and the narrator as characteristic and distinctive of African-American writing ("Rootedness," 200) and essential to her requirements for the Black novel. Morrison explains that "the reader as narrator asks the questions the community asks, and both reader and 'voice' stand among the crowd, within it, with privileged intimacy and contact, but without any more privileged information than the crowd has." See Morrison, "Unspeakable Things Unspoken," 29. See also Wendy Harding, "Narration as the Past Remembered," in *The World of Difference: an Inter-cultural Study of Toni Morrison's Novels*, ed. Wendy Harding and Jacky Martin (Westport, CT: Greenwood, 1994), 153.
88. In an earlier published essay entitled "Another Night, Another Story: the Frame Narrative in Toni Morrison's *Paradise* and *Alf Laylah Wa Laylah* (the Arabian Nights)," I read *Paradise* as a frame narrative that

recalls the model of narration in the classical frame narrative of *Arabian Nights*. In that essay, I do not refer to the harem tradition or present the model of framed narration as a liberatory facet of the harem's pathology. As such, this current essay is intended to contextualize the frame within the harem's subversive pathology in order to illumine new tropes and themes that develop Morrison's aesthetics or redirect Morrison's politics of female resistance.

89. Morrison, *Paradise*, 77.
90. Ibid.,102.
91. Tzvetan Todorov, "Narrative Men," in *The Poetics of Prose*, trans. Richard Howard (Ithaca, NY: Cornell University Press, 1977), 76.
92. Several Arabian and European historical and travel accounts of the dynamics of the Islamic harem relate how patriarchy may maintain its insecure authority, within the harem, through developing polygamous relations which provoke female rivalry and jealousy that keep women in check and under surveillance. See Yeazell, *Harems of the Mind*, 117. See also Fanny Davis's *The Ottoman Lady* that describes certain distressing rivalries among nineteenth-century Turkish women. See also Malik-Khanam's *Thirty Years in the Harem; or, the Autobiography of Melek-Hanum*, a first-person narration of jealousy conflicts in the Turkish harem.
93. Morrison, *Paradise*, 90.
94. Todorov, "Narrative Men," 76.
95. Lila Abu-Lughod, "The Romance of Resistance: Tracing Transformation of Power Through Bedouin Women," *American Ethnologist* 17.1 (1990): 43.
96. Abu-Lughod, "The Romance of Resistance," 43.
97. Soane and Dovey Morgan imagine their resistance to "emptiness" and their freedom of flying in separate gardens. See Morrison, *Paradise* 102, 91. Away from Ruby's women, the Convent residents nurture their thoughts of freedom in the insular harem of the Convent, a spatial projection of Ruby harem's insecurity as well.
98. It should be noted, however, that the women on both sides have exhibited clandestine bonding through trading between Ruby and the Convent. This trade, mediated by Lone and Consolata, becomes a "front" (see Morrison, *Paradise*, 11) for their friendship that is still strained by the rivalry precipitated by Ruby's hysteria.
99. Morrison, *Paradise*, 265.
100. Wendy B. Faris, "1001 Words: Fiction Against Death," *The Georgia Review* 36 (1982): 71.
101. Mia I. Gerhardt, *The Art of Storytelling* (Leiden, Netherlands: Brill, 1963), 402.

102. Morrison, "Nobel Lecture," *Nobelprize*, December 7, 1993, accessed June 13, 2015, http://www.nobelprize.org/nobel_prizes/literature/laureates/1993/morrison-lecture.html.
103. Yeazell, *Harems of the Mind*, 174.

Bibliography

Works Cited

Abu-Lughod, Lila. "The Romance of Resistance: Tracing Transformation of Power Through Bedouin Women." *American Ethnologist* 17.1 (1990): 41–55.

Alf Laylah Wa Laylah. N.p.: Dar Al-Hilal, 1958.

Alloula, Malek. *The Colonial Harem*. Minneapolis: University of Minnesota Press, 1986.

Atieh, Majda R. "Another Night, Another Story: The Frame Narrative in Toni Morrison's *Paradise* and *Alf Laylah Wa Laylah* (the Arabian Nights)." In *Contemporary African American Fiction: New Critical Essays*, edited by Dana A. Williams, 119–35. Columbus: The Ohio State University Press, 2009.

———. "The Revelation of the Veiled in Toni Morrison's *Paradise*: The Whirling Dervishes in the Harem of the Convent." *MELUS* 36.2 (2011): 89–107.

Bal, Mieke. *Narratology: Introduction to the Theory of Narrative*. Toronto: University of Toronto Press, 1997.

Bhabha, Homi. *The Location of Culture*. London: Routledge, 2001.

Bon, Ottaviano. *The Sultan's Seraglio: An Intimate Portrait of Life at the Ottoman Court*, edited by Godfrey Goodwin. London: Saqi, 1996.

Croutier, Alev Lytle. *Harem: The World Behind the Veil*. New York: Abbeville, 1989.

Davis, Fanny. *The Ottoman Lady: A Social History from 1718 to 1918*. Westport: Greenwood, 1986.

Dobbs, Cynthia. "Diasporic Designs of House, Home, and Haven in Toni Morrison's *Paradise*." *MELUS* 36.2 (2011): 109–26.

Elia, Nada. "'Kum Buba Yali Kum Buba Tambe, Ameen, Ameen, Ameen': Did Some Flying Africans Bow to Allah?" *Callaloo* 26.1 (2003): 182–202.

Faris, Wendy B. "1001 Words: Fiction Against Death." *The Georgia Review* 36 (1982): 811–30.

Gerhardt, Mia I. *The Art of Storytelling*. Leiden: Brill, 1963.

Halsband, Robert, ed. *The Complete Letters of Lady Mary Wortley Montagu*. Oxford: Clarendon, 1965.

Harding, Wendy. "Narration as the Past Remembered." In *The World of Difference: An Inter-cultural Study of Toni Morrison's Novels*, edited by Wendy Harding and Jacky Martin, 149–70. Westport: Greenwood, 1994.

Ibn Hanbal, Ahmad ibn Muhammad. *Musnad*, vol. 6. Beirut: Al-maktab al-islami lil-tiba 'a wa'l-nashr, 1969.

Malik-Khanam. *Thirty Years in the Harem; or, the Autobiography of Melek-Hanum, Wife of H.H. Kibrizli-Mehemet-Pasha*. London: Chapman, 1872.

Mernissi, Fatima. *Scheherazade Goes West: Different Cultures, Different Harems*. New York: Washington Square, 2001.

———. *The Veil and the Male Elite: A Feminist Interpretation of Women's Rights in Islam*. Reading: Addison, 1991.

Morrison, Toni. "Memory, Creation, and Writing." *Thought* 59 (1984): 385–90.

———. "Nobel Lecture." *Nobelprize*, December 7, 1993. Accessed June 13, 2015. http://www.nobelprize.org/nobel_prizes/literature/laureates/1993/morrison-lecture.html.

———. *Paradise*. New York: Knopf, 1998.

———. "Rootedness: The Ancestor as Foundation." In *African American Literary Criticism, 1773 to 2000*, edited by Hazel Arnett Ervin, 198–202. New York: Twayne, 1999.

———. "Unspeakable Things Unspoken: The Afro-American Presence in American Literature." In *Modern Critical Views: Toni Morrison*, edited by Harold Bloom, 201–30. New York: Chelsea, 1990.

Reed, Cory A. "Harems and Eunuchs: Ottoman-Islamic Motifs of Captivity in *El celoso extremeno*." *BHS* lxxvi (1999): 199–214.

Ruas, Charles. *Conversations with American Writers*, edited by Danille Taylor-Guthrie, 93–118. Jackson: University Press of Mississippi, 1994.

Salinero, Fernando García, ed. *Viaje de Turquía*. Madrid: Catedra, 1980.

Tate, Claudia. *Black Women Writers at Work*. New York: Continuum, 1983.

Thompson, Elizabeth. "Public and Private in Middle Eastern Women's History." *Journal of Women's History* 15.1 (2003): 52–69.

Todorov, Tzvetan. "Narrative Men." In *The Poetics of Prose*. Translated by Richard Howard, 66–79. Ithaca: Cornell University Press, 1977.

Yeazell, Ruth Bernard. *Harems of the Mind: Passages of Western Art and Literature*. New Haven: Yale University Press, 2000.

Magic, Madness, and the Ruses of the Trickster: Healing Rituals and Alternative Spiritualities in Gloria Naylor's *Mama Day*, Erna Brodber's *Jane and Louisa Will Soon Come Home*, and Nalo Hopkinson's *Brown Girl in the Ring*

Caroline A. Brown

> The image of…conjuring up imaginary worlds that "the black people needed" confirms [Houston] Baker's description of conjure as "a revered site of culturally specific interests and values." Baker affirms the "definable African antecedents" of conjuring in an effort to establish its racial specificity. In a parallel gesture, critics writing on *Mama Day*…emphasize the African origins of conjuring…For example, Lindsey Tucker argues that Naylor's novel draws on African "magico-religious" views of the world.…The use of magic in novels such as *Mama Day*.… is motivated by the desire to recover an "African" epistemology and to uncover "the probable realms of impossibility beyond the limits of scientific certainty." As a form of "discredited knowledge," in Toni Morrison's phase, conjuring exposes the limitations of modern rationality and reinstates suprarational ways of knowing suppressed by the Enlightenment legacy.
>
> —Madhu Dubey, *Signs and Cities* (167)

C.A. Brown (✉)
University of Montreal, Montreal, QC, Canada

C.A. Brown and J.X.K. Garvey (eds.), *Madness in Black Women's Diasporic Fictions*, Gender and Cultural Studies in Africa and the Diaspora, DOI 10.1007/978-3-319-58127-9_9

> The black tradition has inscribed within it the very principles by which it can be read. Ours is an extraordinarily self-reflexive tradition, a tradition exceptionally conscious of its history and of the simultaneity of its canonical texts, which tend to be taken as verbal models of the Afro-American social condition, to be revised. Because of the experience of diaspora, the fragments that contain the traces of a coherent system of order must be reassembled. These fragments embody aspects of a theory of critical principles around which the discrete texts of the tradition configure, in the critic's reading of the textual past. To reassemble fragments, of course, is to engage in an act of speculation, to attempt to weave a fiction of origins and subjugation. It is to render the implicit as explicit, and at times to imagine the whole from the part.
>
> —Henry Louis Gates, Jr., *The Signifying Monkey* (xxiii–xxiv).

I

In Gloria Naylor's *Mama Day*,[1] a folksy, he said/she said romance that steeps Shakespeare in pop cultural references, the Northern black hero, an urbanite displaced in the barrier islands of the rural South, is forced to confront his deepest fears within a hen house. In order to break the spell causing his desperately ill wife's malady, he must search the nest of a ferocious setting hen, retrieving whatever he finds as healing balm. In Erna Brodber's hallucinogenic *Jane and Louisa Will Soon Come Home*,[2] an experimental prose/poem mapping its heroine's descent into the looking glass world of her psychosis, a mother hen incubates her eggs in "cold December rain."[3] The fragile eggs, protected by the "dark of her bottom,"[4] become a metonym for the mixed-race Jamaican elites nurtured by yet ultimately alienated from the black culture that surrounds them, a world which "infiltrated our nest only as its weave allowed."[5] In the apocalyptic Toronto of Nalo Hopkinson's *Brown Girl in the Ring*,[6] a white sensé fowl is grabbed from her coop and sacrificed in the Vodou ritual that merges Caribbean folk tradition with the dystopian science fiction of a grim Canadian future.

In the works by the African–American Naylor, the Afro-Jamaican Brodber, and the Jamaican-Canadian Hopkinson, the cultural ethos and social tenets of the African diaspora intersect with Western aesthetics, reimagining the New World tradition each novel embodies. Though each text is so distinctive in form and objective, all rely on the framework of the quest as spiritual journey. Thus, culturally alienated protagonists are thwarted by social circumstances and their own emotional ambivalence;

they are then redirected into psycho-spiritual quests by creolized healer figures who are symbolic tricksters.

Fundamental to this dynamic is the incorporation of a bird or, more precisely in these novels, the chicken. Sacrifice or symbol, the fowl serves as augur, setting the stage for the ritual process—here symbolized by the principle of Sankofa—around which each novel coheres and that all, ultimately, become an enactment of. A word from the Twi language of Ghana, Sankofa translates to "reaching back into the past in order to advance into the future."[7] Represented in the image of a bird either looking over its shoulder or whose head twists behind it to lift an egg from its back, Sankofa emphasizes the need for cultural renewal through recovery. Thus, a product of hybridization at once wild and domestic, it is no coincidence that, as developed in these texts, the fowl signals to the presence of the trickster, whose sleights of hand not only rupture the protective bubble in which each protagonist is enmeshed but have the potential to blaze a path both to emotional awareness and spiritual rebirth—or what Gay Wilentz, the literary scholar, deems "cultural healing," the ritualized integration of a marginalized culture's sacred knowledge into an individual's consciousness.[8]

The trickster inhabits a privileged position in the literature of the black diaspora. Embodying the duality/duplicity at the heart of marginalized populations, the trickster symbolizes the extremes of its relation both to its own culture and to cultures of domination—which becomes especially emblematic in black, New World societies, built on histories of slavery and socioeconomic dispossession. Thus the flip side of the trickster's laughter is his or her cunning, rage, and guile—which often serve as self-protective mechanisms in hostile environments. However, the trickster also plays a mediating function in that he or she is often able to deftly navigate antagonistic or perplexing social terrain, nimbly moving between radically disjunctive cultural and geographical spaces. Or, as theorized by Jean Rosier Smith: "In one figure, the trickster unites the sacred and profane. Because western thought tends to separate honesty and goodness from deception and evil, tricksters, who comically unite opposites and upend categories and conventions, seem shocking, sensational, and morally bankrupt. However, a glance at trickster traditions [in] nonwestern cultures reveals quite a different picture. Despite their apparent marginality and irreverence, tricksters are central, sacred, and communal figures in most nonwestern traditions."[9] Furthermore, trickster tales, despite often being "bawdy and even anarchic...teach through comic example and define culture by transgressing its boundaries. It may only be a western aversion to paradox and disorder, then, that so distorts the trickster's image in the popular imagination."[10]

Significantly, I begin this process by reflecting on this essay's internal tension, embodied in its title, competing epigraphs, and the very concepts delineated in this introduction. Magic and madness are the dual strands around which this essay coheres. Specifically, madness as an aestheticized rite and threshold state through which the discredited knowledge identified by Morrison as rooted in the sacred might be processed and thus received; magic as that sacred knowledge, reconfigured and textually reinscribed. However, in juxtaposing the words of Madhu Dubey and Henry Lewis Gates, Jr., I am not only referencing the black diasporic "magico-religious" traditions that are nominally, at least, the focus of this essay, but—through the trickster—also the black epistemological systems that inform its framework. In fact, under contestation in both Dubey and Gates is knowledge itself; I want to use their opposing, yet complementary, perspectives to enter into a discussion of the ruses through which that knowledge is rehearsed in these three novels and its implications both for their particular characters and larger readerships.

As chronicled in Gates's seminal *The Signifying Monkey*, the trickster informs the ethos of black Atlantic culture. From the Yoruba deities that transmogrify into the anthropomorphic animals of African-American folklore, the trickster, scrappy and mutable, is the manifestation of the cultural capacity not only to survive but to literally thrive in the face of tumult and adversity. For Gates, his theory of signification/signifyin' is based on improvisation: from an original call, an appropriate response is crafted anew. He demonstrates that black creativity—from the dozens, the verbal jousts of black male street life, to the literary reinscription manifested in the talking book—can be perceived as an extension of the trickster's playful and inventive energy. While these formal and vernacular exchanges are based on innovation, the tradition itself informs the grammar of the black aesthetic.

Yet, as argued by Dubey in her *Signs and Cities: Black Literary Postmodernism*,[11] some of the assumptions undergirding the construction of this tradition need to be interrogated and problematized. In her provocative chapter on Toni Morrison's *Song of Solomon* and Gloria Naylor's *Mama Day*, "Reading as Listening: The Southern Folk Aesthetic," Dubey challenges both orality as a privileged site of black literary expression and the hegemony of the trickster energy as manifested in the conjurer, whom John Roberts identifies as a "trickster possessed with spiritual power."[12] For Dubey, conjure becomes a site of tension due to the fact that, though supposedly a dynamic exchange, it requires an investment in a static, culturally flattened homeland in the rural, African–American South—whose primary purpose is to affirm an idealized, reconstituted blackness untainted by modernity and Western scientific rationalist discourses. What thus results is "a 'nostalgia for the literal,' which essentially amounts to nostalgia for crisis-free literary representation, for 'a time when an artist could be genuinely representative of the tribe and in it.'"[13] Reading the movement of the protagonists of *Song of Solomon* and *Mama Day* from the urban North to the rural South, Dubey contends that this literary project can be perceived as a form of revivalism that reverses a century of migration and cultural shift. She proposes that, while twentieth-century modernity "couched in urban terms…required aesthetic distance from the 'plantation traditions' of the rural South,"[14] the postmodern era has come to represent disillusionment with modernism's earlier promise. Specifically, because "integration of African–Americans into national public life remains incomplete and unevenly realized,"[15] blacks have turned to the South as not only the site of an ancestral homeland and historical memory but of current literary retreat. I would go further and say that, in this formula, the rural South, with its "organic forms of racial community"[16] and cultural coherence, becomes a metonym for ancestral Africa, embodied in the mystical "flight" of each Morrison's Solomon and Naylor's Sapphira into the unknown.

I am impressed by Dubey's innovative deconstruction of the mechanisms mobilized by Morrison and Naylor to privilege oral modes of expression at the expense of the printed medium in which they appear. Moreover, I agree with her assertion that there are dimensions of their complementary novels that are paradoxically quite culturally conservative, including their privileging of rural culture at the expense of the urban. Nevertheless, I would argue that rather than simply a nostalgic and reactionary reinscription of an idealized past, their novels very powerfully exemplify its opposite. Their works engage in the push to re-envision that past and to make from this re-seeing/re-assessment a more immediate and dynamic engagement with the black aesthetic, which becomes a form of Sankofa. Key to this process is their incorporation of the black epistemological tradition itself.

And this is where I would like to segue from Dubey back to Gates's *The Signifying Monkey*, particularly his assertion of the self-reflexivity and self-awareness of the black tradition. As he points out in the epigraph cited above, the black aesthetic contains within itself the means to its own decoding. While a romanticized potential, it is also informed by pragmatism in that the experience of diaspora—fragmented, unstable, variable—allows for, in fact forces, the constant renegotiation of the tradition and its praxis. Consequently, while Gates specifically addresses the work of the literary critic when he writes that, in "the experience of diaspora, the fragments that contain the traces of a coherent system of order must be reassembled,"[17] he is simultaneously addressing the project of the creative writer (and other cultural producers) as exemplified within the tradition of the black aesthetic and its antiphonal and improvisational ethos. These texts, whether fiction or nonfiction, creative or scholarly, "reassemble fragments"[18] as a manifestation of literary historiography, which is both the search for that often lost diasporic history and the act of reflecting on its production.

Mama Day, *Jane and Louisa Will Soon Come Home*, and *Brown Girl in the Ring*—acts of "speculation" that "imagine the whole from the part"[19]—reassemble these diverse cultural fragments and, in so doing, rewrite our understanding of the black diaspora. In fact, these novels, rather than merely representing "'culturally specific interests and values'"[20] that affirm amorphous black longings for a redeemed and reconstituted past, can be perceived as often volatile spaces of conflict and contestation. This essay examines these sites of contestation as an enactment of the black aesthetic. In each of these novels, a protagonist must undertake a symbolic quest, a spiritual rite of passage into the realm of the occult—what should perhaps be more appropriately referenced as the alternative spiritualities of the New World. Or, to rephrase, each must return to the tradition to improvise and thus reformulate new responses to seemingly novel and insurmountable personal obstacles—often configured in uniquely gendered terms. While these challenges appear almost exclusively mystical and idiosyncratic, they, in fact, have deeper roots in black diasporic experience and generations of political struggle. As significantly, however, the reader, thrown into the increasingly disordered chronicle of each novel—unwinding as mystery, myth, and magic—must partake of that existential thread, both actively deciphering these fragmented forms of knowledge and reassembling the black tradition with the book's protagonist. But strategic to this process is the incorporation of madness. Both ritual process and aesthetic device, madness becomes the trickster's ultimate ruse, potentially transforming discredited knowledge into sites of cultural healing.

II

Healing is at the core of the black diasporic religious tradition. Referencing the Afro-Caribbean, Karen McCarthy Brown maintains that healing is synonymous with spirituality. In effect, fundamental to the tradition is the ability of the healer to address a variety of maladies and ailments, both physical and metaphysical. Within this template, selfhood then is fundamentally relational; the individual is defined by a web of relationships that includes "not only the extended family but also the ancestors and spirits or saints."[21] For McCarthy Brown, healing occurs through ritual adjustments in these relational webs, a process that allows the achievement of a state of equilibrium between the self, society, and the metaphysical entities to which one is bound. Or as she articulates: "[H]ealing involves adjusting or reactivating the reciprocal gift-giving that characterizes all relationships in the Afro-Caribbean, whether they are relationships with the living, the dead, or the divine."[22] This gift-giving is central to Claudine Michel's interpretation of Haitian Vodou, which she calls an "ancestral cult" dedicated to "serving the spirits" (*sévi lwa yo*). Michel emphasizes that Vodou involves "withdrawing the self and serving others," a process in which spiritual connections between "living human beings, their ancestors and their Gods" are nurtured.[23] Beverly Robinson, referencing the African–American folk context, configures this process in a complementary vein: "[I]n addition to a Supreme being there are intermediaries—divinities and ancestors (...the 'living dead'). Their powers are derived from God, and they can serve as mediums between those praying and the Supreme Being."[24] She identifies two categories of healers. The first consists of "spiritual healers or advisers, folk doctors, grannies, and midwives"; the second, the more "fearsome" of the two, includes "root workers, hoodoo, juju, and voodoo doctors, hainsters, and conjurers."[25] As with McCarthy Brown, Robinson points out that "[b]ecause African American healing defines its roots in religion, a common bond of belief and shared religion enhances the power of the folk healer...[who] approaches problems and cures relative to the physical, social, economic, and emotional stresses placed on the individual by the cultural milieu..."[26] Significantly, however, as posited by McCarthy Brown, "…all of these traditions are involved in one stage or another of negotiation with Great Atlantic culture, that is, with the Western world."[27] As she further explains, these are systems that are not only culturally hybrid but pragmatic and adaptable: "Scientific medicine, capitalism, individualism, and modern technology all present challenges to customary attitudes and practices in the area of health…. Yet no area in the Caribbean has been without some contact with the trappings of modern life. African-based systems of spiritual healing characteristically accommodate elements of modernity in their worldview rather than react to them competitively or with hostility."[28] Finally, in all of the above instances, the syncretic religious traditions and the spirituality/healing technologies that inform them are constructed in terms larger than of individual faith or institutional systems of belief. Rather, both are enmeshed in dynamic "relational" webs—whether interpersonal or intrapersonal, social or metaphysical—and the delicate psychosocial balance they maintain. When these webs are disturbed, friction and discord erupt.

The three novels examined are all works that are initiated by disruptions in these relational webs. Characters suffering from some level of psychosocial alienation must tackle their own cultural ambivalence and emotional drift when they encounter healer/trickster figures who embody some form of "discredited" knowledge. This knowledge symbolizes an ancestral claim—which each protagonist has earlier either literally or symbolically rejected. The healer/trickster propels each on a quest to fulfill a cultural gambit and thereby gain access to the gift of greater spiritual insight—which will potentially restore balance within this relational web.

As Dubey argues, there is a conservative dimension in this project that could be perceived as relying on extremes of magic versus science, a limiting paradigm too often based on the West versus the rest. However, what is much more compelling than this binary formulation is the dynamic use of madness in these varied works. Not only does it function as a metaphor for cultural alienation but, perhaps even more crucially, it serves as the ritual state in which the protagonist (and, by extension, the reader) becomes immersed. Hence, each protagonist experiences some form of psychological or spiritual impasse: frantic and despairing (George in *Mama Day*); depressed and seemingly almost catatonic (Nellie in *Jane and Louisa*); or, haunted by incomprehensible visions and increasingly anxious and pathologically fearful (Ti-Jeanne in *Brown Girl in the Ring*). Ironically, however, it is within the context of their encounter with the healer/trickster that they are forced to read and comprehend the seemingly incomprehensible, to reconnect ostensibly disparate cultural fragments in the manner suggested by the Gates epigraph that introduces this essay.

Concurrently, all three protagonists are presented with the trickster's gambit. This becomes the challenge that exacerbates their sense of dislocation, their dissociation from their lived reality, and which reads specifically as "madness." Or as Gates asserts of Esu-Elegbara, the Yoruban trickster: "…Esu….interprets the will of the gods to man […and] carries the desires of man to the gods….Esu [connects] truth with understanding, the sacred with the profane, text with interpretation, the word (as a form of the verb to be) that links a subject with its predicate. He connects the grammar of divination with its rhetorical structures."[29] Confused, alienated, and fearful, confronted with the specter of his or her own madness, each protagonist is forced to read these signs and fragments and interpret the cultural or spiritual resonance for himself or herself. Inevitably, this is initiated by an imbalance in and the misinterpretation of love.

III

Gloria Naylor's *Mama Day* is in part a meditation on healing as a manifestation of love. Love as interpersonal exchange—romantic, platonic, familial, spiritual. But also, love as an entity that binds together not only individuals but the collective, here, African Americans from radically different regions, temperaments, and cultural backgrounds. This crystallizes in the image of the hand—and the potential embodied in George Andrews's hands. As Mama Day expresses, contemplating her great-niece's obstinate husband:

> And now there is that boy. Miranda looks down at her hands again. In all her years she could count on half of her fingers folks she'd met with a will like his. He believes in himself—deep within himself—'cause he ain't never had a choice. And he keeps it protected down in his center, but she needs that belief buried in George. Of his own accord he has to hand it over to her. She needs his hand in hers—his very hand—so she can connect it up with all the believing that had gone before. A single moment was all she asked, even a fingertip to touch hers here at the other place. So together they could be the bridge for Baby Girl to walk over. Yes, in his very hands he already held the missing piece she'd come looking for.[30]

For Mama Day, her touching hands with George would permit them to function in unison, a union that bridges the present to the past and the future. However, it also demands the recognition of the beauty and the vulnerability of the black body, bodies rooted in histories of slavery and dispossession. For Mama Day, love is a form of healing as a shared claim to a collective identity, an identity bound less to an interlinked racial past than to the redefinition and assertion of community. Love is an act of faith—not in oneself and one's individual fortitude but in the values that managed to sustain the people of Willow Springs, her local community, despite slavery and racism, political invisibility, and economic dispossession.

Mama Day is nominally about the whirlwind romance and doomed marriage of George Andrews and Ophelia Day, diametric opposites, who symbolically mediate the fissures in twentieth-century African–American identity and whose ongoing conversation, despite George's death, structures the greatest portion of the novel. George, a foundling raised in a New York orphanage, has no family or traditions to ground him; what he does possess is his empiricism, which becomes the faith that guides him, providing him a confidence in his intelligence and integrity in the face of adversity and change. Ophelia, or Cocoa, has deep roots in the fictional Willow Springs, a largely unmapped island off the coast of Georgia and South Carolina, which belongs to neither state. Rather, a scion of the Day family, virtual royalty in tiny, autonomous, Gullah-inspired Willow Springs, the wise-cracking Cocoa can take her heritage for granted, so embedded is her family in region and local lore. Yearning for change, she becomes an unemployed New York transplant, where she meets and falls in love with the meticulous George, an engineer. The two challenge each other's values and assumptions, including their mutual chauvinism and forms of implicit bias; what results is a meditation on shifting notions of the role of race and place on African–American—and American—identity. Nevertheless, the fact that the novel's title bears the eponymous trace of Mama Day—and not George or Cocoa—suggests a central tension in the construction of Naylor's text. Thus, when Cocoa, visiting Willow Springs with George, is poisoned by Ruby, a neighbor and conjure woman who is jealous of her youth and irrationally paranoid that Cocoa will steal Junior Lee, her philandering husband, Mama Day enters the fray.

The central dilemma of *Mama Day* is who will cure Cocoa and how. George wants to cure Cocoa by doing what he knows how to do: he will remove his wife from the primitive Willow Springs with its lack of advanced health care and reliable forms of medical diagnosis or treatment.

George wants to patch a boat or help rebuild the bridge that will allow him to gain access to the US mainland and its sophisticated technology, spiriting Cocoa away from the remote, hurricane-damaged island. However, Mama Day—a traditional healer, conjure woman, and midwife—contends that the cure to save Cocoa is not material but spiritual. For Mama Day, this cure is bound to belief and what the science-minded George quite literally perceives as discredited—and not sacred—knowledge. As she asserts: "I can do more things with these hands than most folks dream of—no less believe—but this time they ain't no good alone. I had to stay in this place and reach back to the beginning for us to find the chains to pull her out of this here trouble. Now, I got all that in this hand but it ain't gonna be complete unless I can reach out with the other hand and take yours. You see, she done bound more than her flesh up with you. And since she's suffering from something more than the flesh, I can't do a thing without you."[31] Miranda provides him her father's staff and the family slave ledger, requesting that he go into the chicken coop and bring her whatever he finds. His response is to snatch his hands from hers and exclaim: "You're a crazy old woman!," an opinion with which she concurs.[32]

Madness performs a central function in *Mama Day*, informing many of the novel's subplots. Ruby's jealousy of and possessiveness toward her much younger husband—seduced from a rival whom she, in turn, has driven mad—becomes an irrational passion that drives Ruby herself insane. Bernice, Cocoa's childhood friend, suffers from a "baby lust" so intense that it drives her to the precipice of madness—until Mama Day helps her conceive the child she will eventually lose to a premature death. However, madness can also be perceived as the family curse that haunts the female Days. Ophelia, Mama Day's mother, is driven mad when Peace, her youngest daughter, drowns in the family's well; she will spend the rest of her truncated life searching in vain for peace and then drown herself, like Shakespeare's doomed heroine.[33] As Mama Day broods: "There was so little that was ever sane coming from her mouth to hold on to."[34] Cocoa's own mother, Grace, dies embittered and depressed when she is deserted by her husband; she curses her sickly newborn daughter with the name of Ophelia, Mama Day's afflicted mother, before her own untimely passing shortly after her daughter's birth. Ironically, however, though Sapphira, the unnamed and mysterious ancestress who founded the island community—a conjure woman herself—is judged "half prime, inflicted with sullenness and...a bilious nature," it is

Bascombe Wade, her white, sometime master/lover, who is driven insane when she escapes or otherwise disappears from his life. While madness is caused by love as obsession or monomania, what it most fundamentally suggests is a lack of proportion—or an imbalance in the relational web. As a result, while Sapphira is a mystery, Ophelia, Grace, Bernice, and certainly Ruby, are examples of love gone awry—or a lack of proportion resulting from the surfeit of emotion.

As mentioned by McCarthy Brown and Robinson, the black diasporic healing tradition is based on a hybridized cosmology that often integrates modern medical practices into syncretic religious systems, allowing for the creation of forms of cultural reciprocity and balance. I would suggest that in *Mama Day*, though Cocoa is bewitched by Ruby (and thus subjected to the ancestral madness of the Day women as she slowly loses her mind), it is actually George whose life is lacking balance. Though a man of decency and emotional warmth, as an orphan raised within institutional environments, he believes that "only the present has potential." He thus literally fetishizes modernity's ontology: structure, convention, rationality, transparency, and empiricism. Although George adores Cocoa and tells her he wants to move to Willow Springs—which Cocoa resists—he appreciates Willow Springs primarily as local color; he thus accepts it strictly on his own terms, as charmingly idiosyncratic, rather than truly acknowledging its complexity or attempting to comprehend its deeper history or local culture.

While Mama Day tells a desperate George that by believing her and joining his hand to hers (if only for a moment), their hands and faith will build the bridge that will cure Cocoa, I would argue that Mama Day is also attempting to address the enormity of George's cultural alienation and psychological burdens. In her appeal, Mama Day contextualizes George's relationship with Cocoa in terms of community; this consists not only of those alive who also love Cocoa—but of the ancestors themselves, the spirits of the dead whose memory and experiences affirm and reinforce their living community. George, an orphaned black man, was not only raised in an emotionally unresponsive bureaucracy but also culturally deracinated. He has created a vibrant and responsive community for himself both with Cocoa and before having met her. For him, New York is a dynamic urban metropolis consisting of smaller villages and diverse cultures that he then introduces to the skeptical Cocoa, who learns to broaden her outlook and cultural vocabulary. However, he is enmeshed in an individualistic value system marked by conservative political values, the Protestant work ethic, and an almost exclusive commitment to the nuclear family. When Mama Day offers him the opportunity to believe in something larger than himself and his love for Cocoa, it is also an appeal to believe in a more expansive vision of love, intimacy, and community outside of individual worth and scrupulously maintained emotional borders. While George at first refuses, calling Mama Day a "crazy old woman," when he comprehends Cocoa's physical and psychological distress—her nearness to death—he relents. In fact, he wills himself to meet his deepest fears, manifested in the symbol of the hen house. Or as George reads in a fortune cookie he receives shortly after meeting Cocoa: "All chickens come home to roost."[35]

It is no coincidence that Mama Day is so closely tied to the barnyard bird. She spends a lot of time in her hen house, where she speaks to and nurtures her chickens, which are both stock animals and domesticated pets. Throughout the novel, she collects the eggs, using them to bake cakes with her sister, Abigail, in honor of Cocoa's return, or distributing them to various members of the community, including those in economic need. In fact, Mama Day treats Bernice's infertility through her egg ceremony, which is as much about Bernice's willingness to believe in her body's potential to bear a child as the healing symbolized in Mama's Day's touch and medical intervention. (And prior to this, she had worked with and respected the parameters set by Bernice's physician.) Finally, Cicero, the rooster, is Mama Day's familiar—her totemic animal to whom she is emotionally and spiritually connected. With this in mind then, Dr. Buzzard, or Rainbow Simpson, the former vaudevillian turned con man, is not only her professional nemesis—according to Dr. Buzzard they share a "professional rivalry," a pronouncement which is galling to Mama Day—but her human familiar. Like the scavenger whose name he adopts, Dr. Buzzard is a crafty survivor whose rooster feathers stream from his tattered hat.[36] Nevertheless, he and Mama Day share a deep affection for one another, as manifested in his plea to George to participate in the ritual of Cocoa's healing. While his is the more obvious face of the trickster, he, like Mama Day, embodies the trickster's contradictions.

Although Mama Day's sending George to the hen house seems odd and even needlessly cruel, it is also where he is in a sanctuary of nonhuman femaleness, and where he is forced out of his comfort zone, a running theme in a novel in which George attempts to understand women through diagrams and scientific manuals. In confronting the chickens, he confronts his deeper fears: of femininity, of domesticity, of wildness, and the divinity of the egg—which represents the cycles of birth, life, and death. Mama Day's instructions—that he bring her whatever he finds in the coop—is both painfully simple and overwhelming in its enormity. It is to let go of the need to know, the expectation of control. The space of radical otherness—dark, suffocating, female, and mystical—can allow him to join in the matrifocal Day clan and the vibrant, quirkily syncretic community of which they are a part.

However, though he tries, George simply cannot believe. In his panic that he cannot find what Mama Day requests—and that he cannot understand her request—he gives in to the madness that imprisons the ailing Cocoa, ironically sacrificing himself through his internalization of her torment. Rather than confronting his fear—of the hens, of potentially losing Cocoa, of the unknown—he lashes out and destroys that which threatens him. As he ponders: "But there was nothing to bring her. *Bring me straight back whatever you find.* Could it be that she wanted nothing but my hands? Another blur of red feathers…."[37] Significantly, only after he has deciphered Mama Day's riddle as instruction does he break down emotionally, first striking out at the ferocious maternal hen, then destroying everything in his path. In his confusion and rage, George lashes out in a frenzy, ransacking the coop, killing Mama Day's birds, smashing their eggs, breaking her father's hand-carved cane, and tearing the pages of the ledger as he gives in to his fear and despondency. That red hen thus becomes the embodiment not only of his fear but of Mama Day. When he perceives the failure of his mission, George begins to laugh helplessly. Or as he tells Cocoa: "[T]here was nothing that old woman could do with a pair of empty hands…All of this wasted effort when those were my hands, and there was no way I was going to let you go."[38]

Although George refuses to let Cocoa "go," returning to her sick bed to hold her one last time, there is no room in his affection for a broader vision of family, community, or emotional intimacy beyond the immediacy of their bond. That he dies embracing Cocoa is a testament of his loyalty to and love for her. However, this is a privatized love. Mama Day's offer to hold hands would fundamentally make that love more expansive and inclusive. As Monica Coleman writes, describing the importance of hands in the novel: "Hands play an important role in Yoruba art and the storyworld of *Mama Day.* In Yoruba art, hands represent ancestors. The left hand is the mother-hand, and the right hand is the father-hand. Working together, they are described as 'the hand-which-keeps and the hand-which-acts.' These beliefs emphasize the active, creative power of hands, as well as their role in connecting individuals to others and to their own pasts."[39] In a sense, George not only holds hands with Cocoa but, through Mama Day's intervention, he clasps hands with Mama Day and Dr. Buzzard, who become the metaphorical mother/father who connect George, in turn, to living and metaphysical communities—a more expansive relational web. However, this potential is rejected. Rather, even as George symbolically accepts Cocoa's madness as his own, he also wills himself to die in her place. Though George's love is vital and abiding—the book is their conversation once George has died, passing over to the "other place" with the breaking of his congenitally weak heart—it is also a love that is unable to negotiate the trickster's gambit.

And this is the darker, more ominous side of the trickster's ruse: there is no guarantee of success. George could not mediate the trickster's riddle and, from these cultural scraps, reframe the knowledge to let himself into that world and create a space for himself—not only with Cocoa but with her kin. Although he "saves" Cocoa through his love and the sacrifice of his life for hers, he cannot fit himself within the relational web as spun by Miranda Day, who is both conjure woman/healer and trickster. He simply cannot look to the past in order to remake his future with Cocoa in a newer, more vibrant paradigm—the promise of Sankofa.

Once again, though this reading is invested in the mystical or magical, as defined by Madhu Dubey, I would reframe it in terms of the relational web and the possession of both psychological and spiritual balance. After all, Mama Day, as a healer, works both with and outside of Western, scientific epistemologies. She is not hostile to Western medicine: it complements her own healing arts. However, as a trickster, her investment is in permitting the continuation of the Day family line; George's sacrifice allows that to happen.[40]

George's fate, "All chickens come home to roost,"[41] as written in the fortune cookie he receives at the dinner where he suggests a business associate hire Cocoa for a job, becomes especially resonant and multifaceted. Naylor thus subtly shades the original intent of the idiom from "when chickens come home to roost," which metaphorically underscores that harmful words or acts can return and backfire against their perpetrator, to a quite literal meaning, suggesting the return to a site of origins or a symbolic home. This reading implies an embrace of the principle of Sankofa—as well as offering a caveat of the limits of the concept. In shifting the emphasis, the expression can function as a simple statement, a site of potential, or a warning. Here: George will enter a hen house. However, his behavior will differ depending on the contingencies of his emotional response. In encountering Miranda Day and touching her hands—then holding her father's staff and the family ledger—the world is at his fingertips. He tragically fails the trickster's gambit: he is defeated by his mounting panic. He thus cannot use his madness as a site of epiphany and eventual trust. Nevertheless, despite the enormity of his loss, he allows both the continuation of the Day family line and the metaphysical survival of the love he shares with Cocoa, who remarries and bears children for her second husband. The book is a part of their ongoing conversation after his death, a conversation that permits the transfiguration of their earthly love into its divine elements.

IV

Nothing could seem further from a meditation on love, romantic or otherwise, than Erna Brodber's *Jane and Louisa Will Soon Come Home*, particularly when Nellie Richmond comprehends that Baba, her childhood friend, is quite literally taking her for a poppy-show, or mocking her. Over a series of seven political meetings, Baba whittles a doll from discarded pear (avocado) seeds. During the first week's meeting, he fashions the head; the second, the neck and arms; the third, the hip; the fourth, a sexless pair of legs. He is absent from the fifth and sixth meetings. On the seventh, he returns and places the burnished effigy hanging from a stick in Nellie's lap, where the brittle puppet promptly crumbles to dust. Offering a parodic re-enactment of the biblical "Genesis," the shamanistic Baba finally earns his rest on the seventh day; in doing so, he slyly suggests to Nellie his diagnosis of her current state as, as she phrases it, a "cracked up doll."[42] Nellie had earlier compared Baba to a character in a film, "a handsome Haitian man" who "pursued a couple relentlessly with no more weapons than a smile and a doll. I saw once more that couple plunge from a precipice while that man and his smile remained constant." As she adds as a wry afterthought, "The power of the self-assured."[43] Later, the beneficiary of Baba's insulting sleight of hand, she fumes to herself: "How unnecessary, how unoriginal and rude!"[44]

Baba's behavior, in fact, can be perceived as problematic. He makes himself comfortable at the group's political meetings, where he refuses to engage in their performative exchanges, instead fashioning the wretched puppet. When he finishes it, he gives it to Nellie, one of the few women present, ignoring the many men. His behavior could be interpreted as sexist and inappropriate. And, in a sense, it is: Baba is a trickster. Or, as Jean Rosier Smith writes: "As liminal beings, tricksters dwell at crossroads and thresholds and are endlessly multifaceted and ambiguous. Tricksters are uninhibited by social constraints, free to dissolve boundaries and break taboos. Perpetual wanderers, tricksters can escape virtually any situation, and they possess a boundless ability to survive...."[45] Baba's behavior captures the ambivalence that informs the trickster's duality, teetering between laughter and rage. As Nellie admits, "We had seen it coming and we had been powerless to act, to let him know that he was a boor who did not understand the rules of our game. Who made him God? Who told him that he could touch parts of us that we elected to leave untouched! A challenge had been given to me and a challenge I would take."[46] While Baba's act is a declaration of his distaste for the group's pretentiousness and condescension—Nellie acknowledges that they simplified their conversation so that he would not be intimidated by their intelligence and wit—it is also a dare to Nellie, who comprehends the gendered implication behind Baba's insinuation: Nellie is a sell-out. His gesture serves as both caveat and invitation—a dare Nellie accepts, which forces her out of her comfort zone and into Baba's space of interstitial uncertainties.

Jane and Louisa maps the psychological breakdown and subsequent road to recovery of Nellie Richmond following the untimely death of her boyfriend, Robin, her fellow insurgent. Nellie, a young physician of mixed racial ancestry, indoctrinated into Eurocentric psychosocial and discursive systems, is alienated both from Afro-Jamaican culture and herself. Relying on the metaphor of the kumbla, a cocoon spun by a caterpillar, as that which both protects and imprisons her, the novel becomes a study in releasing oneself from the dangerous safety of the kumbla through the spiritual purification that allows racial and cultural reconciliation. Fundamental to this process is the presence of the trickster, who both allows the reader to laugh at Nellie's often absurd and contradictory attitudes and behavior and comprehend, thereby empathizing with, the tragedy of her cultural and gender ambivalence.

Using the eponymous British children's song that becomes a West Indian ring game as a point of reference, the novel is divided in four parts: "My Dear Will You Allow Me," "To Waltz with You," "Into this

Beautiful Garden," and finally "Jane and Louisa Will Soon Come Home." This essay will most thoroughly examine, "To Waltz with You," the novel's second section, which focuses on Nellie's interpersonal exchange with Baba, her childhood friend and adolescent boyfriend, who is the novel's trickster/healer. What the reader slowly learns through decontextualized thought fragments is the nature of Nellie's alienation: raised by her snobbish Aunt Rebecca Richmond Pinnock to assimilate to British colonial cultural ideals, Nellie is taught to reject those parts of herself bound to local Afro-Caribbean culture and repress her budding sexuality as a site of shame and moral weakness. Aunt Becca—or Aunt Khaki, as she is called behind her back, in dubious honor of her complexion—is herself a study in racial and cultural ambivalence. She has lived in the kumbla of her lighter skin tone and middle-class privilege, earlier rejecting a lover and aborting their unborn child whose skin she feared would be too dark. The book, through its ruptured and often confusing trajectory, traces this self-denial and cultural effacement back to Tia Maria, the original ancestress, Becca's grandmother and Nellie's great-grandmother, who married a white man and used his skin color and social status as a kumbla—to enhance the social position of her mixed-race children and reject her own black identity. Although Nellie becomes a political activist when she returns to Kingston, disillusioned, from her medical training in the United States—joining a Marxist organization to work with and empower the urban poor—she is, in fact, like generations of female family members before her, alienated from herself. Therefore, when her equally alienated lover dies in unexpected and "humiliating" circumstances, spontaneously combusting, Nellie cannot sustain the mirage of her mission: her identity is built on an illusion and the unexamined superiority allowed by education, accent, and family background is revealed a sham.

This confusing process is manifested in the disorder of Nellie's madness, which is, in turn, refracted in the chaos of Brodber's literary text. A distraught Nellie thus weeps: "Robin had reached our highest phase of evolution: he had become a dried up bird and could only crumble into dust. I saw that it was us who had killed Cock Robin."[47] As Robin—tied to both Cock Robin of the English children's ballad and Baba's brittle, avocado-seed effigy—is revealed as a "dried up bird," Nellie is too, which signals to the trickster's ultimate entrance. Accordingly, she recounts her increasingly neurotic behavior: "I scratched and walked. Walking fast and scratching, I know I looked like a fowl in an ants' nest but I didn't mind; there were secondary gains in playing to the gallery.

I think I had a right to their pity. After all, how many women's men burn to ash?"[48] Or as she further admits, abandoning herself to her own narcissistic histrionics:

> That night I broke one of the informal rules or perhaps I should use the passive: one of the informal rules was broken by me. I wandered purely by chance into the gambling den. No one recognized me and I knew no one. This is not surprising. There is very little mixing between them and us. This act of mine shamed me and I wept copiously. Not because I stepped out of caste or anything like that but because this act was a subconscious/unconscious one and I feared that this meant that I was losing my grip on myself. As does not surprise you, I'm sure, this awareness made me lose my grip even further. As I worried about it, I wept and wept because I shouldn't weep...and so on. I just wept.[49]

Nellie, needless to say, is enmeshed in her self-pity and despair. A third of the way into the text, the reader is not quite certain of how to respond to the melodrama of Nellie's anguish. A convoluted, encumbered chronicle of mourning, yearning, disjointed memories, and almost haphazard references, the first section of the novel is as peculiar as Nellie's difficult to fathom emotional terrain: tragic and clichéd, bathetic and bitingly funny. Thus, the portrayal of Nellie's fraught emotions is actively undermined by the almost burlesque references to her boyfriend's remains as beef fat cooked in a Dutch oven and her own self-referentiality and intellectually dissociative obsession with grammatical precision in the midst of such trauma. In short, the text is invested in its own risible deconstruction of Nellie's operatic grief. Even as she loses herself in her fitful weeping, she admits the social segregation to which she and her fellow activists choose to adhere. Notwithstanding her commitment to the uplift of "the folk," the Afro-Caribbean proletariat who share her urban housing project, the fact is that they remain an abstraction to her. She neither knows nor interacts with them, and shows no interest in or regard for their individual lives or personalities. They are not her social equals and thus invisible to her. Therefore, as she bawls in public, "*a dried-up bird*" (italics mine), the voice that rips through her self-absorption becomes a voice of insight and instruction: "Blasted idiot," it informs her, "dry your eyes."[50] It is the voice of the trickster.

In *Jane and Louisa*, there are several tricksters: Brer Anancy, the mythic spider; Aunt Alice, Nellie's deceased great-aunt who serves as a spirit guide; and, Baba, or Harris Ruddock, her childhood friend turned Rastafarian/folk healer, who inaugurates Nellie's journey on the initial leg of her passage to health. All are anarchic, polyvalent, and sly, infusing the narrative with the music of polyphony: Caribbean folk tales and English nursery rhymes, Queen's English and Jamaican patwah,[51] the drum and the aria. However, the voice that first challenges Nellie's commitment to her despair is presented as anonymous, unsympathetic, and wry. Even as it insults her, it plants an impersonal kiss on her afro from behind her head—which, though aggravating, makes it "possible to carry on."[52] This voice, the baritone of a man whose aroma carries the hint of sweet lime, tart and purifying, belongs to Baba and—affiliated with the folk, rural life, spiritual healing, and Nellie's past—manages to cut through her defenses. And in calling her an idiot and ordering her to buck up, Baba precipitates Nellie's journey away from the dangerous protection of her kumbla. Or as the novel describes the kumbla:

> A kumbla is like a beach ball. It bounces with the sea but never goes down. It is indomitable....It bounces anywhere....blows as the wind blows it, if the wind has strength to move it: it moves if it is kicked, if it is thrown, if it is nudged...if anyone has that much strength, that much energy or that much interest...But the kumbla is not just a beach ball....It is the egg of the August worm. It does not crack if it is hit...as pliable as sail cloth....It is a round seamless calabash that protects you without caring....Safe, protective time capsule....They usually come in white.[53]

Nellie's kumbla is the indoctrination she has received into middle-class status and cultural values, embodied not only in her rejection of her African heritage and rural roots but her prescriptive, almost reactionary embrace of radical Marxist chic. Ironically, this is gift-wrapped in the acquiescence of her gendered subordination. Although she consciously identifies with "the folk," hers is a purely academic exercise that is removed from passionate engagement, community spirit, intellectual curiosity, or genuine respect. Though nominally an activist committed to political change, she politely takes minutes at the meetings where men's voices drone on. While remaining safe and emotionally untouched within her kumbla, she fixates on her grammar and weeps. Baba, presented as a trickster figure, is associated with Anancy, the transgressive spider.

Baba is a trickster who forces the readjustment of Nellie's relational web. He actively dismantles Nellie's kumbla by chipping at the façade of the group's hypocrisy and lofty self-regard when he creates the Vodou doll from the dried avocado seeds. In addition, when he refuses her emotional manipulation as she recuperates in his small, monastic room, she is confronted with her own contradictory values. Despite her progressive politics, Nellie's identity as a woman is affirmed through the presence of "her" man. With Robin's loss, she attempts to recapture Baba's affection, though she had rejected him years earlier due to pressure from her Aunt Becca. As Nellie confesses: "No sooner would I wax into the tear jerking story of our lives, of whose fault it was that we had been kept apart, of what might have happened if we hadn't been kept apart, than he would say: 'I have heard it all before.'"[54] Instead, he reiterates: "I only want to meet you."[55] Finally, he rejects her sexual advances: "'Sweetheart'—he tenderly, so tenderly said, 'I know you want to give yourself but I fear that you offer yourself because you don't want you. That's no gift love, even if we did need gifts. That's something you throw on a scrap-heap. We won't forage for a thing in a scrap-heap. We need a walking-talking human being—.'"[56] This droll—if potentially sexist—reinscription of a barnyard bird rises, not coincidentally, from Nellie's integration of Sankofa as distorted and self-serving cultural reclamation.

When Baba rejects her, Nellie is thrust out of the protection of her kumbla based on gendered subordination and social pretense. As a result, she is flabbergasted; she erupts into an abusive patois, insulting his arrogance and impudence: "You understand this petti-fogging man who is to look at me and tell me after all these weeks of building up, of taking me from a life I knew, who is to look at me now and tell me I have no worth. You understand this damned shameless rasta-man who is to tell me that he wants to watch me grow. You understand this r...-c...t of a hungry man from nowhere who is to watch and observe me. What the hell he think he is."[57] Hers is the wound of the sexual insult. If, as she claims, Baba denies her worth, it is because her self-concept, her value, is bound to what she believes to be Baba's perception of her erotic appeal. Baba's refusal to validate her feminine wiles or concede to her emotional neediness brings a stinging attack: her rebuke is constructed in the stark language of class privilege. Nevertheless, she suddenly breaks off: "I had been talking aloud. Is that me? with such expressions. Am I a fishwife?"[58] He replies: "Yes, it is you. You have found your language, Ma'am." His own voice is filled "with a new kind of calm...."[59] Baba has forced her to break through the kumbla of her learned helplessness and feminized propriety. And trickster-like, as suddenly as he appears in the text, he departs, as Nellie's narrative suggests: "With that I must have dozed for I felt the light on my pupils and woke to find Baba disappearing into the glow of the electric bulb, a fleeting glimpse of Nancy's transfiguration.... Morning had broken. I was no longer alone. Baba had settled me in with my people."[60] A new ritual process begins with her Aunt Alice Whiting, her father's deceased aunt, over the novel's final two sequences. In these segments, she eventually meets her ancestors and is able to better comprehend their legacy to her of their collective kumbla based on color-stratification and internalized colonial ideals.

Like Anancy, the spider, Baba is a spinner of tales, a charmer who brings Nellie's attention to keen focus. But he not only captures her within the web of his charismatic energy, he allows her to find her own voice and eventually tell her own tales apart from those imposed on her by the rigidly hierarchical social system she ascribes to. As with the androgynous Anancy, gendered male but falling outside of strict sexual categories, Baba does not have to adhere to the dictates of their gendered social codes. As Nellie narrates when she first beholds him after their initial anonymous interaction: "Baba was waiting for me. Straight and tall in a long white gown. He was the bride. His hair neatly plaited... and his beard obviously brushed....What a beauty! His hands, as I knew from memory were soft as a surgeon's hands....[H]e held them shepherd-like out to me."[61] Like a surgeon or a Christ-like Good Shepherd, he treats Nellie with tenderness and care, allowing her fractured consciousness to reorient itself and mend.

Moreover, Baba encourages Nellie's self-assertion away from the gracious subservience of an ever-receptive femininity or the neutered lingo of a stunted and reductive political philosophy. Nellie is not miraculously healed or cured. She is freed to meet him—and by extension herself—as an equal without compunction or guilt. His intervention—which takes place in his simple room, with no mention of time or designated social space—prepares her to embark on her own spiritual quest in search of her ancestral heritage and its ambiguous legacy of the kumbla, which whitens and protects even as it cloisters, diminishes, and removes from emotional authenticity. In trapping a hysterical Nellie in the tangle of his sticky relational web, Baba forces her to de-code for herself the elusive meanings of her individual experience and psychological wounds. This act of love as empathy grants her the ultimate gift: of the self-definition that might eventually produce the conditions providing her a deeper sense of peace and cultural integrity. As Baba tells Nellie after her outburst, "Your dermis is beginning to show and it is beautiful."[62] When she eventually falls, exhausted, into a deep sleep, she enters a dreamscape in which she will eventually open her soul to the ancestral encounters and reciprocity suggested by Claudine Michel's paradigm of serving the spirits or by Sankofa, both of which allude to Nellie's need to return to the past to reformulate her future. Significantly, however, like Nellie's journey into and out of madness, that future remains a mystery.

V

Ti-Jeanne, the heroine of Nalo Hopkinson's speculative novel, *Brown Girl in the Ring*—like George Andrews and Nellie Richmond—struggles with the dangerous ambiguity that is the legacy of her lack of either spiritual faith or cultural grounding. An inhabitant of a metropolitan Toronto that is a sprawling slum severed from its more prosperous suburban neighbors, the Caribbean-Canadian Ti-Jeanne epitomizes the human flotsam—abandoned by the government and preyed upon by violent underworld cartels—of the postmodern urban landscape. Working part-time for her grandmother, Mami Gros-Jeanne, a healer/obeah practioner, and estranged from Tony, the drug-dependent father of her newborn son, the economically disenfranchised Ti-Jeanne comprehends her particular vulnerability: her sexualized body is perceived as a commodity to be exploited in forms of black market labor or by the thugs who proposition her on street corners. While the economic base of Toronto has collapsed—sending its corporations, manufacturers, and more affluent citizens fleeing to contiguous suburbs—the city provides strategic resources, particularly the illicit sex, drugs, and stolen human body parts, surgically excised, on which those adjacent regions rely. As she navigates the streets of "Muddy York," the historical appellation bestowed on the city, she not only feels hunted by unsavory humans but is haunted by Technicolor visions—premonitions of the violent deaths of strangers and acquaintances—and apparitions, ghouls who pursue her in her increasingly macabre hallucinations: "Ti-Jeanne could see with more than sight. Sometimes she saw how people were going to die....this one's body jerking in a spray of gunfire and blood, that one writhing as cramps turned her bowels to liquid."[63] Terrified of what she fears is her incipient madness, the fate of her mother who disappeared from her life when she was a girl, Ti-Jeanne feels equally distressed by her grandmother's obeah, which could provide her the *konesans*, or spiritual knowledge and emotional insight, she so desperately needs. *Brown Girl in the Ring*, a novel fusing science fiction with Afro-Caribbean spirituality, folklore with the fairy tale, becomes the hybridized rite of passage through which Ti-Jeanne, a feminist reinscription of the folk hero Ti-Jean, not only masters but actively reinvents her grandmother's *konesans*, becoming the "seer woman" Mami Gros-Jeanne portends. By learning to trust her perception outside of the often faulty logic of the purely visual, Ti-Jeanne gains access to the second sight she needs to claim her own heroic potential. Fundamental to this process is her initiation into the dynamic of the relational web, particularly as she moves away from her emotional dependence on the feckless Tony to a deeper and more complex understanding of and commitment to serving the spirits, and its role in the continuance of community. An essential component in this process is not only Mami's teachings as a healer but the intervention of the trickster.

As with *Jane and Louisa Will Soon Come Home* and *Mama Day*, *Brown Girl in the Ring* is structured around the concept of Sankofa—critically engaging the past to better reclaim the future, exemplified in the quest that begins as an initiation. For Ti-Jeanne, her rite of passage leads her into the world of her grandmother's healing practices, what Ti-Jeanne calls obeah and Gros-Jeanne refers to as "serving the spirits"—or as the latter informs her, assertively correcting what she senses is her granddaughter's dismissal of her belief system: "I don't work the dead, I serve the spirits and heal the living."[64] While Ti-Jeanne defends her grandmother's spiritual practices against Tony's outright derision, she shares his ambivalence: "There was the drumming that went on in the crematorium chapel, late into the night. The wails and screams that came from the worshippers. The clotted blood on the crematorium floor in the mornings, mixed with cornmeal."[65] The elements of death and the supernatural, the unknown and irrational, unnerve Ti-Jeanne, who expresses an oversized faith in the reliability of book knowledge. As a result, she does not "understand why Mami insisted on trying to teach her all that old-time nonsense. If Mami didn't know how to cure something, she could look it up in one of the growing piles of medical books lining the walls of the cottage."[66] She thus only half listens to Mami's pedagogy, which she hears as "mutterings." Instead, she "fretted silently about Tony."[67]

For Ti-Jeanne, Mami's spirituality, whether called obeah or serving the spirits, is unrelated to the everyday business of her life, whose ethos, like George Andrews's, is based on empiricism and the security of conventional interpersonal transactions. Significantly, in the face of life's stressors—when her mind threatens madness in the form of what she interprets as hallucinations or when she wants to offer Tony her assistance—she turns to Mami for answers and strategic support. However, for Mami, serving the spirits is a core component of her life, intertwined within its textures, rhythms, and ethics. Therefore, when Ti-Jeanne informs Mami: "I don't want to know nothing 'bout obeah, oui," her grandmother responds: "Is a gift from God Father. Is a good thing, not a evil thing. But child, if you don't learn how to use it, it will use you, just like it take you mother."[68] Mi-Jeanne, Ti-Jeanne's mother, had rejected her second sight and fallen victim to the madness that she feared. Moreover, not only does she warn her granddaughter away from the narcissistic Tony but she cautions: "…[I]s not just me being selfish, trying to keep you with me. If you don't learn to use the gift, things going to go hard with you. You want to come like the crazy people it have wandering the streets? Eh? Not knowing if you have clothes on your back or what day it is, just walking, walking and seeing all kind thing that ain't there, not knowing what real and what is vision."[69] She offers Ti-Jeanne practical guidance and assurance in the face of her granddaughter's fear and emotional resistance, including her pan-African/pan-Caribbean cultural context to better appreciate the tradition:

> The African powers, child. The spirits. The loas. The orishas. The oldest ancestors. You will hear people from Haiti and Cuba and Brazil and so call them different names. You will even hear some names I ain't tell you, but we all mean the same thing. Them is the ones who does carry we prayers to God Father, for he too busy to listen to every single one of we on earth talking at he all the time. Each of we have a special one who is we father or mother, and no matter what we call it, whether Shango or Santeria or Voudou or what, we all doing the same thing. Serving the spirits.[70]

With this, she teaches her grandchild the names of those spirits: Shango, Ogun, Osain, Shakpana, Emanjah, Oshun, Oya, and Eshu, explaining that Eshu (also known as Legbara), Ti-Jeanne's father spirit, is a guardian of the crossroads.

In this manner, Gros-Jeanne is attempting to impart spiritual knowledge to Ti-Jeanne that nurtures her granddaughter's diasporic consciousness, moral vision, and intuitive reasoning as an extension of her developing *konesans*. A significant challenge for Ti-Jeanne is learning to embrace her capacity for *konesans*, what Karen McCarthy Brown deems "intuitive knowledge,"[71] or as the anthropologist writes of the term in the context of Haitian Voudou:

> Priestly power is said to reside in *konesans*. This knowledge could be called psychic power, the gift of eyes, empathy, or intuition. It is any and all of these things. Above all, it is knowledge about people.... *Konesans* is the ability to read people, with or without cards; to diagnose and name their suffering, suffering that Haitians know comes not from God and usually not from chance but from others—the living, the dead, and the spirits. Finally, *konesans* is the ability to heal.[72]

Significantly, the etymology of *konesans* is rooted not in the French *savoir*, which is to know a fact, language, skill or abstract concept, but *connaître*, to know or to be acquainted with—or to have an awareness of—a person, place, or thing, which implies intimacy and intuition. For Ti-Jeanne then, *konesans* suggests her learning to look beneath the surface in order to see with a depth of perception that is more penetrating than that which can be perceived by the eyes alone. Correlated with this growth into consciousness is her need to step outside of the conventions of her own patterns of thought and into new emotional frequencies.

This challenge of integrating *konesans* into her consciousness takes on a particular urgency when Tony arrives on their doorstep in a panic, fleeing the posse. Rather than listen to the voice of reason, Ti-Jeanne follows her heart—and erotic desire. She consequently insists that Mami help him, despite the older woman's misgivings. As Gros-Jeanne curtly informs Tony: "Playing big man, saying you running with posse, selling dope. You know how many patients I get because of people like you? You know how many of them draw them last breath in my hands? Is best the posse kill you, yes; one less murderer on the streets."[73] When Ti-Jeanne wins what she perceives as a moral victory against her high-handed grandmother, who is forced to back down from her officiousness and threats, the novel appears to be structured around a clear narrative arc of the family romance. Ti-Jeanne, determined to save Tony from the machinations of the posse—which is attempting to coerce him into committing murder in order to acquire a human heart for transplant—rushes headlong to his rescue. Her trajectory seems set: she will save Tony by intrepidly leading him away from the blighted Toronto and into a neighboring suburb, where he will be free of the posse and can instead seek gainful employment, tackle his buff addiction, and perhaps eventually be in a position to be joined by Ti-Jeanne and their son; in doing so, she will be able to free herself from her grandmother's demands—and the insidious pull of obeah. She thus acts on her strong physical attraction to him and the power of her desire, once again becoming romantically involved despite her grandmother's counsel. With his gift to her of a white rose, a symbol of innocence, spiritual purity, and sympathy in Western culture,[74] she appears to enter into the role of the female hero, who—through her wit and courage—will reverse convention and save the beleaguered Tony, both reinscribing and reinforcing the traditional love plot. She convinces Mami to cast a spell rendering both of the younger people invisible, and she attempts to lead Tony to safety with his white rose attached to her body for protection. However, they are caught by the posse—whose boss, Rudy Baines, a shadow catcher, relies on violence and the supernatural to ensure his power over his corrupt empire. Not only does the mission fail but Mami's predictions come dreadfully true when Tony, who stole the posse's drugs to feed his own addiction, murders her to pay off his debt to them. A stunned Ti-Jeanne watches as her grandmother's disfigured corpse is carted off and her heart prepped for transplant. Not only has Tony killed her grandmother, he shoots Crazy Betty, a mentally ill homeless woman who is revealed to be a spiritually dissociated Mi-Jeanne, Ti-Jeanne's mother.

As in *Mama Day*, madness threatens the women of Jeanne Hunter's family, here because of their neglected spiritual gifts. Mi-Jeanne as Crazy Betty, the dazed vagrant, frequently harasses Ti-Jeanne, who—like Gros-Jeanne—previously had no idea Crazy Betty was Mi-Jeanne. Years earlier, when Mi-Jeanne, herself a resentful single mother of a dependent child, began having visions and premonitions, she refused to take advice from Gros-Jeanne, whom she resented and was rebelling against. Instead, she "spat out all of Mami's potions and screamed at her to stop her prayers,"[75] preferring to believe the lies and flattery of her father, Rudy Baines, a sociopathic drug addict who had abused Gros-Jeanne, blaming his wife for his misfortunes and manipulating her into teaching him how to communicate with the spirits. The ruthless and brutal Rudy then used those skills to catch spirits, most particularly Mi-Jeanne's, and increase his worldly power. Rather than nurture her own *konesans*, Mi-Jeanne gouged out her eyes and offered them to Rudy so that he would have the ability to see into the world of the living and the dead, of the concrete and metaphysical. She willingly, if naively, then becomes a soucouyant, who, ensorcelled, does harm to his enemies. He preserves her soul in a calabash and feeds it human blood to keep her angry, increasingly ravenous spirit appeased. When Rudy releases her from the calabash to kill Ti-Jeanne then Tony, who has been ordered to slaughter the entire family, Mi-Jeanne rejoins her abandoned body, in the form of Crazy Betty. With a new lucidity, Mi-Jeanne informs Ti-Jeanne of Rudy's plans. As a horrified Ti-Jeanne watches, her mother is shot by Tony.

With the loss first of Gros-Jeanne and then Mi-Jeanne, Ti-Jeanne is bereft. She not only feels guilty for causing her grandmother's death through her blind faith in Tony but has also lost her spiritual mentor. Despite the challenging circumstances, Ti-Jeanne does not give in to grief or rage, and she does not have the luxury of allowing herself to become unmoored either by helplessness or her visions, which push her to the brink of madness. Instead, chased by her mother, a soucouyant, invoked by the vindictive Rudy Baines, her grandfather, a man she does not know, she fights for her life and relies on her *konesans* to save herself. Implicit in this process is *konesans* as knowledge that is fluid, adaptable, nuanced, and contextual—the knowledge of a trickster. Thus, not only does Ti-Jeanne learn from the trickster but she must also learn to become a trickster in order to survive. This process is demonstrated in Ti-Jeanne's relationship with Legbara or Eshu/Prince of Cemeteries, the trickster god who is her spirit guide. In fact, Ti-Jeanne's ultimate defeat of Rudy Baines is largely due to her shifting relationship with the mercurial deity and the *konesans* he provides her. Fundamental to this dynamic is the transformation of her perception from modalities of sight—with its enmeshment in the earthly and the temporal—to those of (in)sight, with its allusions to the sacred and metaphysical.

Ti-Jeanne's developing insight, specifically her relationship with what she had considered discredited knowledge, can be mapped in the evolution of her interactions with Eshu as the Jab-Jab. When Ti-Jeanne first sees the Jab-Jab, her response is of repulsion and alarm: "*Man-like, man-tall, on long wobbly legs look as if they hitch on backward. Red, red all over: red eyes, red hair, nasty, pointy red tail jooking up into the air. Face like a grinning African mask…*"[76] She has fallen into a trance-like state, paralyzed by what she perceives as a demon. When she regains consciousness, she is terrified and hysterical. This impression remains when he later challenges the soucouyant, a goat-footed witch disguised as an elderly woman, who arrives in a ball of flame to steal Ti-Jeanne's baby and feast on his blood. The "Diab'-diab'" teases and harasses the witch, ultimately throwing grains of rice at her, which distracts her from her mission of death.[77] When the sunlight arrives, he yells, "*Ti-Jeanne! Draw back the curtain!*" and the soucouyant dissolves into a pile of ash.[78] The two disturb her as much as the "tall, tall woman in a old-fashioned dress…she with teeth pointy like shark teeth."[79] Later, Ti-Jeanne has a vision of a man whose grinning face is a skull and who playfully tips his top hat at her; Tony does not register his presence. All of these phantasms remain undifferentiated and evil to Ti-Jeanne, frightening her equally. When she sees them, she assumes herself insane—not clairvoyant.

Mami's intervention offers her a more measured perspective, first when she interprets her modified Caribbean Carnival tarot cards for Ti-Jeanne and most powerfully when she invokes the spirits in what will be Ti-Jeanne's first experience of the possession-performance—an event Mami obliges both Ti-Jeanne and Tony to participate in since it is Tony who requests her assistance for his own benefit. Ordering the craven Tony to fetch her chicken, a white sensé fowl with elaborately curled feathers, from its coop, she ritually apologizes for its sacrifice. "Sorry, bird," she murmurs, soothing it, "but we need strong."[80] Becoming an element of a ritualized act of Sankofa, the sacred bird's blood summons Eshu, the guardian of the crossroads—which McCarthy Brown explains is "a point of historic confluence between Christianity and the religions of West Africa"[81]—who will then communicate with the other deities on their behalf. Drumming a rhythm, which becomes its own language of supplication, Gros-Jeanne has distributed the other offerings around a center pole where she places a cement head of Eshu. These items furnish her altar, where she includes cornmeal scattered in intricate designs, a bowl of candy, food and herbs, a cigar, candles, and rum as libation. She then intones: "Eshu, we ask you to open the doors for we, let down the gates. Let the spirits come and talk to we. Look, we bring food for you, rum and sweet candy."[82] When Eshu arrives, Ti-Jeanne has no awareness of his presence. She is his unknowing horse, whom he ritually mounts, and through whom he communicates with Gros-Jeanne and Tony during the possession-performance.[83] His first direct message to her: "Well…. old lady, tell Ti-Jeanne…my horse to open she eyes and see the whole thing; death…and life."[84] It is Mami who must translate the experience for Ti-Jeanne, particularly when Ti-Jeanne then listens to the words of Osain, the healer, who is Mami's alienated spirit guide, so resentful is he that she allowed Rudy to gain access to Mami's sacred knowledge. In fact, what Ti-Jeanne comes to understand is that she must destroy the calabash in which Rudy keeps Mi-Jeanne as the duppy who provides him his supernatural power. This act will begin Ti-Jeanne's journey, her quest to right the spiritual balance of their interlocking worlds that Rudy has violated and plundered for personal gain.

However, underscoring Eshu's message on the complementary nature of life and death is Ti-Jeanne's need to embrace the duality that they represent, particularly the complexity of the world around her and of life itself. As McCarthy Brown states in relation to the intersection of life and death in the figure of Eshu—who is also called, in Haitian Voudou cosmology, the Gede: "….a close look into the face of death (Is there any larger affront to the living?) can actually raise our life energy. This point of view helps to explain why the spirit of death is such a randy character and why the one who lives with corpses also dotes on small children."[85] The tricky Eshu, embodied in death, the demonic, and erotic mischief, has been delivering messages to her that she has been unwilling and unable to receive. Rather, so fearful has Ti-Jeanne been of the seeming irrationality of the experience, and her own possible madness, that she shuns the spirituality incarnated in the trickster's playful messages. Unable to read the signs, she suffers the weight of the threat of madness—which becomes, like with Mi-Jeanne, a form of madness, the madness of avoidance and denial. Ti-Jeanne's learned helplessness causes her to reject both Mami's obeah and the messages of her spirit guide that Mami could then interpret for her through her use of obeah.

However, with Mami's death, she is forced to engage more directly with Eshu, still as the Jab-Jab, as her intermediary. Now, her sight transforms into (in)sight. Or as Robert Farris Thompson writes of Eshu in the context of Yoruba cosmology:

> Because of his provocative nature, Eshu has been characterized by missionaries and Western-minded Yoruba alike as "the Devil." Outwardly mischievous but inwardly full of overflowing creative grace, Eshu-Elegbara eludes the coarse nets of characterization. Even his names compound his mystery. Some call him Eshu, "the childless wanderer, alone, moving only as a spirit." Others call him Elegbara (or Elegba), "owner-of-the-power"….a royal child, a prince, a monarch. He is, of course, all these beings and more—the ultimate master of potentiality. Eshu becomes the imperative companion messenger of each deity, the imperative messenger-companion of the devotee…. [86]

Because the Jab-Jab's ghoulish appearance obscures Eshu's "overflowing creative grace," Ti-Jeanne was blind to that grace. When Rudy mobilizes his henchmen and Mi-Jeanne, as his soucouyant, to hunt Tony and Ti-Jeanne, who must run with her baby, Ti-Jeanne becomes increasingly receptive to the Jab-Jab; through him, she learns, eventually, to rely on her own wits. From feeling fear and revulsion, she listens to his coded messages delivered to her in her altered state, comprehending that, to challenge Rudy, she will have to use "Cunning, not force."[87]

Only once Ti-Jeanne relies on her *konesans* to redefine the Jab-Jab as simultaneously sacred and profane, is she able to integrate Mami's lessons to invoke Eshu more directly. This process begins when she humbles herself and becomes his acolyte, redefining her relationship to the deity. Bruised and battered by the unequal chase, she has the wherewithal to comprehend that she needs to substitute simpler ritual offerings for Mami's more elaborate ones: a cigarette, rubbing alcohol, an old, lint-filled mint, the blood of a dying adolescent shot by Rudy's men. Bearing the gift of Rudy's blood in her veins, she becomes invisible when she sneaks into his headquarters. She has asked Legba to make Rudy invisible as well to hide them both from his enforcers and thus more effectively challenge him. Though he catches her, attempting to drug her into submission to become his duppy once she destroys Mi-Jeanne's fetid calabash, she is intimidated and despondent but nevertheless resists. This is because, when she is tempted to give in to Rudy's seduction, released from the bother of caring about other people's needs and her own emotional woundings, the Jab-Jab intervenes. When she fumes at the memory of her grandmother's abuse, the Jab-Jab speaks sympathetically of Gros-Jeanne: "Gros-Jeanne woulda tell you that all she doing is serving the spirits. And that anybody who try to live good, who try to help people who need it, who try to have respect for life, and age, and those who go before, them all doing the same thing: serving the spirits...." He adds: "Yes, Gros-Jeanne was a hard woman. Now Rudy, he does try to make the spirits serve *he*."[88] Simply put, Rudy has no respect for the relational web. And the gods disapprove of his self-serving and unethical actions. Through Ti-Jeanne's intervention, they challenge Rudy's primacy.

The Jab-Jab then forces Ti-Jeanne to do what Rudy is incapable of: feel greater empathy for others. He makes her experience others' emotional states: Gros-Jeanne's misery as she received a beating at Rudy's hands; Mi-Jeanne's endless spiritual hunger and lack of will, enslaved to Rudy's blood-lust; Tony's horror as he watched others' die, tortured to death by an unruffled Rudy. When she despairs, asking the Jab-Jab how she can possibly challenge someone so powerful, the Jab-Jab's final words are elusive: "Rudy is a Bull Bucker…so you have to be a Duppy Conqueror."[89] As suddenly, he disappears; Ti-Jeanne is left to her own devices. She then returns to Mami and their shared past to improvise a solution in the spirit of Sankofa. Her grandmother's words thereby provide a metaphorical crossroads that unite healer with trickster, the embodied world with the realm of the metaphysical: "*The centre pole is the bridge between the worlds.*"[90] Ti-Jeanne is in the CN Tower in Downtown Toronto, Rudy's command center—"the tallest centre pole in the world."[91] Ti-Jeanne's realization highlights her internalization of the trickster ethos and her ultimate transformation: "Her duppy body almost laughed a silent *kya-kya*, a jokey Jab-Jab laugh. For like the spirit tree that the centre pole symbolized, the CN Tower dug roots deep into the ground where the dead lived and pushed high into the heavens where the oldest ancestors lived. The tower was their ladder into this world. A Jab-Jab type of joke, oui."[92] Like the center pole at Gros-Jeanne's altar that allowed the spirits to enter the realm of the possession-performance, like her insight reminding her to exploit Rudy's blood in her veins, she has everything she needs to challenge and defeat the brutal shadow catcher. What she comes to understand is that, in her altered state, she can converse directly with the spirits.

As a result of Ti-Jeanne's cognitive transformation, she is able to interpret perceptions that previously felt like the experience of madness as forms of heightened awareness. Furthermore, she becomes increasingly comfortable improvising—or returning to the tradition to create appropriate new options. Reciting the eight spirit names her grandmother taught her, she further innovates, calling out to "everyone Rudy kill to feed he duppy bowl—come and let we stop he from making another one!…Mami! And Mi-Jeanne! Is Ti-Jeanne calling you! Come up, come up and help your daughter!…Climb the pole, allyou, climb the pole!"[93] She assembles a spirit army consisting both of the dead, particularly Rudy's collective murder victims, and the divine. United in an ethos of righteousness, they ultimately defeat him. His perpetually youthful body withers and dies, as he is dragged down to Guinea Land, the realm of the ancestors. As Farris Thompson explains of *àshe*, an untranslatable concept denoting a vital force or brightness of the spirit,[94] *àshe* "is a privilege of righteous living, not a right, and it can be seriously diminished when someone has slighted a deity or an important person. This means that one must cultivate the art of recognizing significant communications, knowing what is truth and what is falsehood, or else the lessons of the crossroads—the point where doors open or close, where persons have to make decisions that may forever after affect their lives—will be lost."[95] Rudy, a victim to his own hubris, slights the gods and loses *àshe*. However, Ti-Jeanne, though helping to defeat him, is herself vulnerable and must be careful to avoid this fate.

Significantly, this potential hubris is manifested in her own altered state of heightened consciousness. Although Ti-Jeanne has been communicating directly with all eight of the deities, it appears that "[s]he was speaking to thin air. She hadn't slept for two nights."[96] She has entered a realm of the mystical, a trance state—or internalized possession-performance—that could easily appear as a form of psychosis. Here, however, it is depicted as a sacred space, a site of grace in which she has learned to commune with the divine. Nevertheless, it represents a site of danger as well in which she could suffer the consequences of vanity and overreaching. This danger occurs because, in the possession-performance, the possessed submits to the *loa*—or *lwa* (deity or spirit). As explained by McCarthy Brown, the individual's *gwo bonanj* (the big guardian angel) departs and others interpret the words of the *loa* as the horse (the individual possessed by the deity) is ridden; the individual possessed by the spirit of the *loa* has no direct access to or memory of the experience. It has to be retold to the horse, whose memory has been wiped clean.[97] As Eshu informs her, impressed by her valor and skill as a "duppy conqueror": "Well, is you call all my duppy to come do your bidding…[Y]ou do a thing I never see nobody do before. For a few minutes there, you hold eight of the Oldest Ones in your head one time." All the same, he advises: "Don't try it again, eh? It could burn your brain out."[98] In other words, she must respect her limits. Nevertheless, what is so noteworthy here is that Ti-Jeanne uses the lessons of the past to invent possibilities and defeat Rudy. In addition, she learns to define herself away from her constant state of reliance on others, whether Tony or Mami herself. As she confesses to the Jab-Jab when she is held captive by Rudy: "I can't keep giving my will into other people hands no more, ain't? I have to decide what I want to do for myself."[99] When she finally decides that it "was time to go home"[100] from Rudy's destroyed headquarters, and does so, she also comprehends that she must recreate her life—without Mami, and without Tony. While she releases herself from the burden of her anger against Tony, who apologizes for his betrayal, she also releases herself from her obsessive longing for him—simultaneously comprehending that she is not yet ready to forgive him.

Ti-Jeanne, however, is at a crossroads and a new phase of her life commences. This new stage begins with her honoring not only the otherworldly spirits but her own earthly community. Now, returned to the community, she holds a send-off party, a feast paying hommage to Mami's spirit, in which she feeds the community and hosts the sacred rites as Mami taught her to—yet which she had always ignored or avoided. With Mi-Jeanne, who survived Tony's gunshot, and Ti-Jeanne's infant son, in whose body has been (unknowingly) reincarnated Mami's tender lover, the man Mi-Jeanne murdered at Rudy's bidding, she must reconstitute her family according to a new value system. She does this by rejecting love as compulsion and dependence; instead, she embraces it as a field of constantly shifting possibilities. As notably, having returned to the past to innovate future potential in her role of the trickster, she now also accepts the mantle of healer, using the present to redefine her faith with its promise of love as sustenance in community.

VI

Falling as it does outside of the framework of logic and proportion, madness as a purposeful strategy leading to cultural healing could appear both strained and counterintuitive. However, as formulated in *Mama Day*, *Jane and Louisa Will Soon Come Home*, and *Brown Girl in the Ring*, madness, the unreasonable, is a state both perilous and sacred. Madness permits not only the individual protagonist but the larger audience to reframe perspectives on social systems built on the logic of greed, hypocrisy, and dispossession—both historical and contemporary—from the normal and acceptable to the irrational and unjust. The three novels are as much about an individual protagonist's experience of madness as about the reformulation of the concept of contemporary black or African diasporic identity and the nation-state itself. In all three novels, the lack of well-being of a protagonist symbolizes, on some level, the disequilibrium in the nation-state, culture, and/or individual's life. Despite the ability to "get by," to fit in, even to thrive, in often dysfunctional environments, all of the protagonists actually lead existences lacking proportion. To return to McCarthy Brown, they are out of sync with the relational web, symbolized not only by the self in relation to a specific partner or immediate circle of loved ones, but also by the larger community, the ancestors, and god(s) or metaphysical creeds. Their faith is often tentative, circumscribed, and defined in utilitarian ideals. However, the trickster initiates the process through which the diaspora and its traditions—fluid, volatile, fragmented, and often oblique—are reconceptualized and reconfigured: where the protagonist must reassemble those fragments and make sense of the tradition to set right the relational web. This dynamic commences with the protagonist's experience of madness.

Ironically, the only truly "mad" text here is *Jane and Louisa Will Soon Come Home*, whose experimental prose disintegrates into shards of poetry refracting the disordered consciousness of Nellie, the work's protagonist. The novel's entire structure is a trickster's maze that the reader must navigate with caution. While Baba, as trickster, does not cause Nellie's madness, he undermines the logic of her faulty self-esteem. This could eventually allow her to embrace a more expansive vision of herself and her worth away from the mores instilled in her by a colonized Jamaica and her Aunt Becca, who embodies its most troubling contradictions. Rebellion alone cannot accomplish this; healing requires Nellie to acknowledge history, her place in it, and thus reorient her consciousness. Significantly, the novel ends with an increasingly radicalized Nellie renegotiating her role in the discursive reformulation of a post-colonial Jamaica.

Although less overtly avant-garde, both *Mama Day* and *Brown Girl in the Ring* rely on strategic (and sometimes aestheticized) representations of madness to mobilize textual healing. In both novels, generations of women in extended families are haunted by spiritual imbalance. When Cocoa falls victim to Ruby's "magic," George sacrifices himself for her, internalizing her madness, which becomes an extension of his own emotional alienation. His madness—and resistance to an ethos apart from an empirical understanding of the relation of self to knowledge and spirituality—causes his demise. George is deeply enmeshed in mainstream American epistemologies. Because of his lack of faith in non-Western ontological systems, as well as in Mama Day, his spirit guide, he cannot use his experience of psychic disorder and emotional helplessness to gain access to new ways of functioning in a mysterious and often chaotic world.

Like her mother Mi-Jeanne, *Brown Girl's* Ti-Jeanne is a seer. And like her mother, she at first perceives her visions as a form of her own insanity and moral lack. Rejecting her gifts, however, alienates her from her own potential. In committing to her grandmother's spiritual pedagogy, she learns to read for herself the instruction of Eshu, her spirit guide, a trickster who—like Baba and Mama Day—embodies cultural hybridity and teaches her the deeply interconnected nature of life and death. This not only allows her to defeat Rudy Baines but permits her to live in harmony within the relational web: serving the spirits and her community, loving her family and herself, respecting death and embracing life, and maintaining aspects of Caribbean tradition in postmodern Canada.

Madness, as sketched above, is both the cause of these rifts in the relational web—in short, the manifestation of a life out of balance that the protagonists are blind to—and the threshold state in which the protagonists are allowed access to "truth(s)" proffered by the trickster/healer. However, these ambiguous gifts, often adamantly resisted by the protagonists themselves, cannot be forced—they must be received. Each character's response to the trickster's magic—this knowledge at once sacred and discredited—becomes each novel's ultimate test of faith, of cultural healing. For the reader, as with these heroic and ambivalent characters, nothing is assured. This journey into magic and madness—this literary Sankofa—is an act of faith. Nevertheless, through these journeys into cultural literacy and reconstruction, readers, too, gain access to these enchanted gifts as extended by these trickster texts, gifts which they too are free to accept or reject.

Notes

1. Gloria Naylor, *Mama Day* (New York: Ticknor and Fields, 1988).
2. Erna Brodber, *Jane and Louisa Will Soon Come Home* (London and Port of Spain, Trinidad and Tobago: New Beacon Books, 1980).
3. Ibid., 9, 146.
4. Ibid., 9, 146.
5. Ibid., 10.
6. Nalo Hopkinson, *Brown Girl in the Ring* (New York and Boston: Aspect, 1998).
7. Selase W. Williams, "The African Character of the African American Language: Insights from the Creole Connection," in *Africanisms in American Culture*, ed. Joseph E. Holloway (Bloomington and Indianapolis, IN: Indiana University Press, 2005; original copyright, 1990), 424.
8. Gay A. Wilentz, *Healing Narratives: Women Writers Curing Cultural Dis-ease* (Piscataway, NJ: Rutgers University Press, 2000), 1–4.

In *Healing Narratives*, Wilentz borrows the term "discredited knowledge," the alternative healing practices of oppressed cultures, from Toni Morrison. Or as Toni Morrison writes separately: "We are very practical people, very down-to-earth, even shrewd people. But within that practicality we also accepted what I suppose could be called superstition and magic, which is another way of knowing things. But to blend those two worlds together at the same time was enhancing, not limiting. And some of those things were 'discredited knowledge' that Black people had; discredited only because Black people were discredited therefore what they *knew* was 'discredited.' And also because the press toward upward social mobility would mean to get as far away from that kind of knowledge as possible." See Toni Morrison, "Rootedness: the Ancestor as Foundation," *What Moves the Margin: Selected Nonfiction* (Jackson, MS: University Press of Mississippi, 2008), 61. In the epigraph used in this essay, Madhu Dubey specifically references Morrison's use of the term "discredited knowledge."

9. Jean Rosier Smith, *Writing Tricksters: Mythic Gambols in American Ethnic Literature* (Berkeley and Los Angeles, CA: University of California Press, 1997), 8.
10. Ibid., 8.
11. Madhu Dubey, *Signs and Cities: Black Literary Postmodernism* (Chicago and London: University of Chicago Press, 2003).
12. John W. Roberts, *From Trickster to Badman: the Black Folk Hero in Slavery and Freedom* (Philadelphia: University of Pennsylvania Press, 1990), 103.
13. Dubey, 178–179.
14. Ibid., 145.
15. Ibid., 145.
16. Ibid., 144.
17. Henry Louis Gates, Jr., *The Signifying Monkey: A Theory of African-American Literary Criticism* (New York and Oxford: Oxford University Books, 1988), xxiv.
18. Gates, xxiv.
19. Ibid., xxiv.
20. Dubey, 167.
21. Karen McCarthy Brown, "Afro-Caribbean Spirituality: A Haitian Case Study," in *Vodou in Haitian Life and Culture*, eds. Claudine Michel and Patrick Bellegarde-Smith (New York: Palgrave Macmillan, 2006), 2.
22. Ibid.
23. Claudine Michel, "Vodou in Haiti: Way of Life and Mode of Survival," in *Vodou in Haitian Life and Culture*, eds. Claudine Michel and Patrick Bellegarde-Smith (New York: Palgrave Macmillan, 2006), 30.

24. Beverly J. Robinson, "Africanisms and the Study of Folklore," in *Africanisms in American Culture*, ed. Joseph E. Holloway (Bloomington and Indianapolis, IN: Indiana University Press, 2005; original copyright, 1990), 366.
25. Ibid., 365.
26. Ibid., 367.
27. McCarthy Brown, "Afro-Caribbean Spirituality," 3.
28. Ibid.
29. Gates, 6.
30. Naylor, 285.
31. Naylor, 294.
32. Ibid., 296.
33. For more on the development of Shakespearean references in Naylor, see Peter Erikson, "'Shakespeare's Black?': The Role of Shakespeare In Naylor's Novels," *Gloria Naylor: Critical Perspectives Past and Present*, eds. Henry Louis Gates, Jr. and K.A. Appiah (New York: Amistad, 1993), 231–248.
34. Naylor, 279.
35. Naylor, 56.
36. The mostly terrestrial (except when levitating) Dr. Buzzard does bear a striking resemblance to Eshu. See Robert Farris Thompson, *Flash of the Spirit: African and Afro-American Art and Philosophy* (New York: Vintage Books, 1983), 19.
37. Naylor, 300.
38. Ibid., 301.
39. Monica A. Coleman, "'The Work of Your Own Hands': Doing Black Women's Hair as Religious Language in Gloria Naylor's *Mama Day*," *Soundings: An Interdisciplinary Journal* 85.1–2 (Spring/Summer 2002): 128.
40. For a complementary reading, see Karla F.C. Holloway, *Moorings and Metaphors: Figures of Culture and Gender in Black Women's Literature* (New Brunswick, NJ: Rutgers University Press, 1992), 139.
41. Naylor, 56.
42. Brodber, 41.
43. Ibid., 59–60.
44. Ibid., 61.
45. Rosier Smith, 7–8.
46. Ibid., 62.
47. Ibid., 53.
48. Ibid., 66.
49. Ibid., 53.
50. Ibid., 54.

51. "Patwah" is the Jamaican Creole/nation language variant of "patois."
52. Ibid., 54.
53. Ibid., 123.
54. Ibid., 68.
55. Ibid., 69.
56. Ibid., 71.
57. Ibid., 71.
58. Ibid., 71.
59. Ibid., 71.
60. Ibid., 76–77.
61. Ibid., 63.
62. Ibid., 72.
63. Hopkinson 9.
64. Ibid., 59.
65. Ibid., 36.
66. Ibid., 37.
67. Ibid., 37.
68. Ibid., 47.
69. Ibid., 59.
70. Ibid., 126.
71. Karen McCarthy Brown, *Mama Lola: A Vodou Priestess in Brooklyn* (Berkeley and Los Angeles: University of California Press, 2001; original copyright 1991), 349.
72. Ibid., 356.
73. Ibid., 57.
74. It should be noted that in Sub-Saharan Africa, white is often related with death and mourning.
75. Hopkinson, 48.
76. Ibid., 18.
77. See Giselle Liza Anatol, "A Feminist Reading of Soucouyants in Nalo Hopkinson's *Brown Girl in the Ring* and *Skin Folk*" for a critique of the misogyny in the representation of demonic women. *Mosaic: An Interdisciplinary Critical Journal* 37:3 (September 2004), 33–50. [see http://www.jstor.org/stable/44030045?seq=1#page_scan_tab_contents]
78. Hopkinson, 44–46.
79. Ibid., 48.
80. Ibid., 91.
81. McCarthy Brown, *Mama Lola*, 343.
82. Hopkinson, 91.
83. See page 257 (including endnotes 96 and 97) of this essay for a description of the possession-performance.

84. Hopkinson, 94–96.
85. McCarthy Brown, *Mama Lola*, 343.
86. Farris Thompson, 19.
87. Hopkinson, 94.
88. Ibid., 219.
89. Ibid., 220.
90. Ibid., 220.
91. Ibid., 221.
92. Ibid., 221.
93. Ibid., 221.
94. Farris Thompson, 9.
95. Farris Thompson, 19. For an alternative reading, see Henry Louis Gates, Jr, on *ase* in *The Signifying Monkey*: "in Esu's calabash given him by Olorun, god of gods, is the power which propagates itself" (8). "[C]ontrolled and represented by Esu" *ase* "…mobilizes each and every element in the system….the force of coherence of process itself, that which makes a system a system"(8). Gates also calls it "the light that crosses through the tray of the earth, the firmament from one side to the other, forward and backward" (8).
96. Hopkinson, 229.
97. McCarthy Brown, "Afro-Caribbean Spirituality," 8.
98. Hopkinson, 229.
99. Ibid., 220.
100. Ibid., 229.

Bibliography

Anatol, Giselle Liza. "A Feminist Reading of Soucouyants in Nalo Hopkinson's Brown Girl in the Ring and Skin Folk." *Mosaic: A Journal for the Interdisciplinary Study of Literature* 37.3 (September 2004): 33–50.

Brodber, Erna. *Jane and Louisa Will Soon Come Home*. London and Port of Spain: New Beacon Books, 1980.

Brown, Karen McCarthy. "Afro-Caribbean Spirituality: A Haitian Case Study." In *Vodou in Haitian Life and Culture*, eds. Claudine Michel and Patrick Bellegarde-Smith. New York: Palgrave Macmillan, 2006. 1–26.

———. *Mama Lola: A Vodou Priestess in Brooklyn*. Berkeley and Los Angeles: University of California Press, 2001. Original copyright in 1991.

Coleman, Monica A. "Serving the Spirits: The Pan-Caribbean African-Derived Religion in Nalo Hopkinson's Brown Girl in the Ring." *Journal of Caribbean Literatures* 6.1 (Spring 2009): 1–13.

———. "'The Work of Your Own Hands': Doing Black Women's Hair as Religious Language in Gloria Naylor's Mama Day." *Soundings: An Interdisciplinary Journal* 85.1–2 (Spring/Summer 2002). 121–139.
Collier, Gordon. "Spaceship Creole: Nalo Hopkinson, Canadian-Caribbean Fabulist Fiction, and Linguistic/Cultural Syncretism." In *A Pepper-Pot of Cultures: Aspects of Creolization in the Caribbean*, eds. Gordon Collier and Ulrich Fleischmann. Amsterdam and New York: Rodopi, 2003.
Dubey, Madhu. *Signs and Cities: Black Literary Postmodernism*. Chicago and London: University of Chicago Press, 2003.
Erickson, Peter. "'Shakespeare's Black?': The Role of Shakespeare In Naylor's Novels." In *Gloria Naylor: Critical Perspectives Past and Present*, eds. Henry Louis Gates, Jr. and K. A. Appiah. New York: Amistad, 1993. 231–248.
Gates, Henry Louis Jr. *The Signifying Monkey: A Theory of African-American Literary Criticism*. New York and Oxford: Oxford University Books, 1988.
Holloway, Karla FC. *Moorings and Metaphors: Figures of Culture and Gender in Black Women's Literature*. New Brunswick, NJ: Rutgers University Press, 1992.
Hopkinson, Nalo. *Brown Girl in the Ring*. New York and Boston: Aspect, 1998.
Michel, Claudine and Patrick Bellegarde-Smith, Patrick, eds. *Vodou in Haitian Life and Culture: Invisible Powers*. New York: Palgrave Macmillan, 2006.
———. "Vodou in Haiti: Way of Life and Mode of Survival." In *Vodou in Haitian Life and Culture: Invisible Powers*, eds. Claudine Michel and Patrick Bellegarde-Smith. New York: Palgrave Macmillan, 2006. 27–37.
Naylor, Gloria. *Mama Day*. New York: Ticknor and Fields, 1988.
Roberts, John. *From Trickster to Badman: The Black Folk Hero in Slavery and Freedom*. Philadelphia: University of Pennsylvania Press, 1990.
Robinson, Beverly J. "Africanisms and the Study of Folklore." In *Africanisms in American Culture*, ed. Joseph E. Holloway. Bloomington and Indianapolis: Indiana University Press, 2005. Original copyright, 1990. 356–371.
Smith, Jean Rosier. *Writing Tricksters: Mythic Gambols in American Ethnic Literature*. Berkeley and Los Angeles: University of California Press, 1997.
Thompson, Robert Farris. *Flash of the Spirit: African and Afro-American Art and Philosophy*. New York: Vintage Books, 1983.
Wilentz, Gay Alden. *Healing Narratives: Women Writers Curing Cultural Disease*. Piscataway: Rutgers University Press, 2000.
Williams, Selase W. "The African Character of the African American Language: Insights from the Creole Connection." In *Africanisms in American Culture*, ed. Joseph E. Holloway. Bloomington and Indianapolis: Indiana University Press, 2005. Original copyright, 1990. 397–426.

"Recordless Company": Precarious Postmemory in Helen Oyeyemi's *The Icarus Girl*

E. Kim Stone

To narrate the struggles African girls face forming a livable identity in the twenty-first century, many third-generation African novelists have returned to a traditional European genre, the *Bildungsroman*.[1] However, many of these novelists have revised the *Bildungsroman's* conventions because they cannot adequately represent female protagonists who are struggling to develop a livable subjectivity within the turbulent confines of their post-independence nations. What is most striking about these reconfigured coming-of-age narratives is how often mental instability plagues their young girls, suggesting that madness has become an ineluctable endpoint for girls in the contemporary African *Bildungsroman*. For example, in Tsitsi Dangarembga's *The Book of Not*,[2] teenage Tambu experiences mental deterioration that devolves into self-abnegation as she encounters the violent racism of colonial Rhodesia's final days. *Coconut*,[3] Kopano Matlwa's debut novel, laments the fate of Ofilwe, whose soulless affect derives from her over-identification with racist white ideology in post-apartheid South Africa. Chimamande Adichie's *Purple Hibiscus*[4] depicts the chronic mental paralysis suffered by a 15-year-old Nigerian

E. Kim Stone (✉)
English Department, SUNY Cortland, Cortland, NY, USA

C.A. Brown and J.X.K. Garvey (eds.), *Madness in Black Women's Diasporic Fictions*, Gender and Cultural Studies in Africa and the Diaspora, DOI 10.1007/978-3-319-58127-9_10

girl, Kambili, at the hands of her tyrannical father. The unfinished business of African decolonization is not limited to the continent; it also travels with diasporic Africans to their new homelands. When Black British novelists such as Diana Evans and Bernardine Evaristo adapt the genre for their female protagonists, they also identify mental disorder as an inescapable aspect of diasporic African subjectivity.[5] In the conventional European *Bildungsroman*, the young protagonist seeks out and depends upon reliable mentors—exemplary adults whose sense of community models a static, acquiescent role within the national imaginary. However, in the contemporary African *Bildungsroman*, helpful mentors and viable national identities are noticeably absent; indeed, many are set in unlivable communities peopled with adults who exploit these young girls for their own selfish goals.

At first glance, Helen Oyeyemi's *The Icarus Girl* seems to have an anomalous relationship to third-generation African *Bildungsromane* because the protagonist is surrounded by a multitude of loving adults who are eager to serve as role models for her. The novel narrates the troubling eighth year in the life of Jessamy Harrison, a girl with an English father and a Nigerian mother who have loving but contradictory expectations for her. Adult expectations for Jess are further complicated on a trip to Nigeria, where her doting grandfather clashes with her aunts and uncles about how to incorporate Jess into the Yoruba national imaginary that structures the family compound in Ibadan. Her low spirits rise, however, when she meets Titiola, a girl whose fearless playfulness fills her with joy and wonder. In the ensuing plot Jess and Titiola form an intense bond through a series of games they play in Nigeria and England, games that begin as friendly fun but become darker, more conflicted, as the story proceeds. The adult mentors become convinced that Jess's turbulent relationship with the mysterious Titiola propels her descent into madness. In the climactic final moments of *The Icarus Girl*, Jess and Titiola commune in the Bush, a Yoruba ancestral realm, and play a final maddening game of possession that results in a new diasporic identity for our young female protagonist. In contrast to her mentors, I read Jess's madness as a form of resistance to the oppositional versions of communal happiness these adults disseminate, for they can only offer amnesiac neocolonial national identities to Jess, forms of postcolonial subjectivity that don't fit her biracial sense of self. Conventional Western interpretations of the Icarus myth tend to locate responsibility for his death with him. His father, Daedalus, has invented two sets of wings so they may escape from the Minotaur's labyrinth, where they have been imprisoned by King Minos. Overcome by the sublimity of flight, Icarus fails to heed his father's warnings and circles too close to the sun. The wax holding his wings together melts, and he plummets to his death in the sea. Typical interpretations suggest that Icarus had to be punished because he disobeyed his father's orders. However, if we switch this intergenerational conflict to the son's point of view, it is not just Icarus's desires that kill him; it is this coupled with the flawed flight machinery his father has built for him. Icarus's departure from the Minotaur's maze is doomed by the inadequate technologies of escape Daedalus has created to circumvent the intransigent politics he is embroiled in. In Oyeyemi's postcolonial appropriation of this Western myth, the mentors function as Daedalus figures who blame Jess for her troubles rather than face the unlivable aspects of their own neocolonial identities. [6]

The classic European *Bildungsroman* consists of conflicting narratives of identity development. The young protagonist pursues a seemingly endless individuating project until the mentors cut this short with a coercive nationalist narrative that insists on a fixed ideal of adult subjectivity as the endpoint of these novels of development. In his study of the modernist British *Bildungsroman*, Jed Esty argues that this conflictual narrative style was radically revised as a "soul-nation allegory," that often produced youths whose development is frozen in time.[7] Esty contends that colonialism in this era of high imperialism crucially disrupts the soul-nation allegory because the "relatively stable temporal frames of national destiny gave way to a more conspicuously global, and therefore more uncertain, frame of social reference."[8] As colonies gained independence from England in the twentieth century, their national imaginaries were formed by combining residual imperial ideologies with indigenous cultural and political ideals. Such twentieth-century postcolonial novelists as Salman Rushdie and Tsitsi Dangarembga emphasize the fraught neocolonial aspects of these new soul-nation allegories by narrating the physical and mental breakdowns that protagonists must suffer in order to form a livable postcolonial identity.[9] In the twenty-first century, the mad affect afflicting female protagonists of African and diasporic *Bildungsromane* signals a tipping point in postindependence narratives of national progress, suggesting that the fraught gender dynamics of many contemporary African nations create unlivable spaces for girls within their national communities.

Like the mentors in *The Icarus Girl*, critics of the novel definitively conclude that Jess lapses into madness as a result of the games she and

Titiola play, suggesting that Oyeyemi's diasporic novel follows the same narrative trajectory as other twenty-first century African *Bildungsromane*. This makes sense given that Oyeyemi cannily deploys several discourses of madness in her depiction of the girls' games. Initially overlaying the games the girls play in Nigeria with British gothic aesthetics, Oyeyemi then employs Eurocentric psychoanalytic discourses in her representations of the girls' games in England. When Jess returns to Nigeria, Oyeyemi sets these European discourses of madness on a direct collision course with Yoruba animist paradigms. Postcolonial critics of *The Icarus Girl* have done important work analyzing how the African discourses of madness Oyeyemi deploys function as crucial counternarratives to European representations of Jess's mental instability. In these interpretations, British gothic aesthetics and Western psychoanalytic diagnoses proffer inadequate explanations for Jess's diasporic turmoil, and it is only when Oyeyemi offsets these Western narratives with Yoruba animist discourses of *ibeji* and *abiku* that a more integrated explanation for Jess's behavior becomes possible.[10] However, critics differ in their interpretations of the cultural dynamics of this madness. For example, Madelaine Hron uses research from British psychiatric journals to suggest that Jess suffers from "psychotic episodes"[11] in England and depicts Titiola as "successively [a] sad ghost, dangerous doppelganger, and *abiku*,"[12] intent on taking over Jess's body and life. Jane Bryce notes that Jess's encounters with Titiola have "increasingly destabilizing results,"[13] and that Titiola is both an *abiku* and Jess's dead twin sister, Fern, who is freed when the grandfather brings an *ibeji* statue to Jess's hospital room. One reason the critical reception of the novel views Jess's madness as a foregone conclusion is that they tend to interpret this clash Oyeyemi sets up between Western and non-Western discourses of madness as the only intractable opposition at the heart of Jess's stalled development. The critics also empathize with Jess as the beleaguered protagonist and overlook Titiola's plight, suggesting that, like Toni Morrison's Beloved, hers is not a story to pass on. While I find these critical interpretations of Oyeyemi's European and African binaries quite compelling, I don't necessarily conclude, as they do, that Titiola is a sinister antagonal force who catalyzes Jess's increasingly aberrant behavior into an eventual psychological breakdown. This interpretive focus on the diasporic child's biographical narrative does not consider the other narrative that characterizes the *Bildungsroman*—the mentors' conflicting national allegories that offer Jess no livable identity to inhabit. The critics align themselves with the adults in the novel by interpreting Jess's developmental problems as individual psychosis rather than as resistance to the neocolonial aspects of the mentors' competing communal identities. In contrast to these critical readings, I suggest that Oyeyemi's purposeful entanglement of these proliferating discourses of Western and non-Western madness paradoxically uncouples insanity from Jess's diasporic individuating project and, instead, connects this cacophony of madness to the normativizing national allegories the adults perform. The epigraph that opens *The Icarus Girl* is the first three lines of an Emily Dickinson poem: "Alone I cannot be–/For Hosts—do visit me–/Recordless Company" (1).[14] I suggest that Titiola, the young girl Jess befriends, functions as "Recordless Company," a forgotten figure of the traumatic past who steps out from under the fog of adult amnesia and demands to be re-membered as part of contemporary diasporic identity. In her representations of Titiola, Oyeyemi calls into question the maddening models of English, Nigerian, and diasporic communal identities on offer in the novel because they all, to variant degrees, put under erasure a crucial moment in global history—the Trans-Atlantic slave trade.

In recent years, postcolonial scholars have turned to trauma studies to understand how and why the ordeal of the Trans-Atlantic slave trade continues to resonate in today's world.[15] One influential critic, Holocaust scholar Marianne Hirsch, uses the term "postmemory" to identify "the relationship that later generations or distant contemporary witnesses bear to the personal, collective, and cultural trauma of others."[16] The experience of trauma is not limited to the life of the individual enduring an historical event like genocide or slavery; subsequent generations can develop a visceral and emotional connection—a postmemory—that revivifies the embodied affect of first-generation trauma.[17] Hirsch contends that postmemory can be transmitted in two ways—intergenerationally, from parent to child, or shared as a more affiliative dissemination among children of the same generation.[18] In addition, dominant familial and political tropes circulating in a culture mediate the construction of postmemory. Hirsch emphasizes the reparative ethical potential of postmemory, suggesting that it functions as a "lens through which to recognize forgotten or disposable lives and stories, and also to acknowledge injury and injustice and their afterlives for subsequent generations."[19] In explicating postmemory, we should certainly attend to its anodyne capacity to alleviate the pain of traumatic experience. However, if we consider that the perpetrators of that historical trauma have also produced terrifying familial and political tropes, and that these grim ideologies can still circulate in a culture long after this enemy has been vanquished, then we must also attend to postmemory's capacity to perpetuate rather than simply alleviate traumatic harm. I suggest that Oyeyemi's *The Icarus Girl* interrogates both aspects of postmemory by first critiquing the problematic aspects of intergenerational postmemory that her mentors offer Jess and then articulating the unsung potency of affiliative postmemory that Titiola so painfully inhabits. In my reading, Titiola is not a crazed specter who drives Jess into mental illness; instead, she is an affiliative postmemory, a playmate whose games dismantle the neocolonial amnesia overlaying the mentors' intergenerational postmemories. In my interpretation, a new understanding of the roots of black women's madness emerges; the discourses of madness in the novel are narrative by-products of the repressive national allegories the adults unhappily inhabit. Unlike other third-generation African novelists who locate madness in their protagonists, Oyeyemi's competing discourses of madness are attached to the various national allegories the adults model for Jess, which implicates both Nigerian and English culture as impediments to Jess's diasporic identity formation. I argue that Jess learns to work with her volatile playmate, Titiola, to create a precarious postmemory of the trauma of slavery that has been erased from the mentors' amnesiac national imaginaries. This is a fraught, painful journey, for—as twin protagonal forces—Jess and Tilly both experience paroxysms of becoming precipitated by this unfinished business of decolonization. In the girls' games, the history that had been passed over by the previous generation is passed on instead. *The Icarus Girl* does not offer only an affiliative counternarrative to the mentors' ineffable amnesiac affect; this postmemorial work reactivates a more ethical afterlife for the African slave trade within diasporic identity through its depiction of two girls playing.

The Mentors' Amnesiac National Allegories

In the opening scenes of *The Icarus Girl*, Oyeyemi establishes the fraught dynamics of Jess's family by subtly connecting them to neocolonial signifiers of British colonization in Africa. When the story begins in the spring of 1993, Jess is hiding from her mother in a linen cupboard located in the stair landing of her English home. The first word of this *Bildungsroman*—Sarah's simple interrogative, "Jess?"[20]—opens this project of identity formation with uncertainty, for it suggests that the protagonist's mother, arguably her closest mentor, is unable to locate her daughter, either in space or in identity. Jess has retreated to the sterile confines of the cupboard instead of playing outside because she feels the world beyond her house is "a place where everything moved too fast."[21] Jess tries to alleviate the speedy, chaotic homelessness that characterizes English exterior space by burrowing deeply into the antiseptic heart of her biracial home. Although she finds comfort sitting among the newly washed bedding and towels, this static hygienic location sequesters Jess in a "whitewashed" sense of racial identity.[22] Sarah worries that Jess is not acting like other Nigerian children who play outside and "were always getting themselves into mischief,"[23] but her father, Daniel, believes that "sitting inside reading and staring into space" is "more or less normal behavior"[24] for English girls. Her parents' competing memories of playing set up an active-passive binary around *what* constitutes proper childhood activities and an outside-inside binary around *where* this playing should occur. Unable to meet her mother's expectations of appropriate behavior, Jess then embodies her father's idea of the "normal" English girl by writing poetry in her bedroom; however, she finds herself "fighting with words and punctuation,"[25] and her finished verses make her feel "as if she were being punched very hard,"[26] and cause her to fall ill. The English words that flow from Jess's active imagination end up damaging her young biracial body. Oyeyemi's opening montage of family life in the Harrison household makes clear that neither parent is attending to Jess's nascent hybrid feelings because their oppositional views on both the active-passive binaries of what constitutes childhood play and their inside-outside dichotomies mark all play spaces with unhappy affect. Paradoxically, the Harrisons base the happiness of their family on Jess's ability to cultivate good feelings, even though they cannot see how their own oppositional ideas make it impossible for Jess to settle into any one space or affect. Sara Ahmed argues: "[T]he family sustains its place as a 'happy object' by identifying those who do not reproduce its line as the cause of unhappiness."[27] Jess becomes the source of the Harrison family's misery because both Sarah and Daniel lapse into political amnesia that leaves their own postcolonial conflicts unresolved. Ahmed calls family members like Jess "affect aliens"[28]—people located as familial outsiders because they thwart family happiness. Jess is an "affect alien" in the Harrison household because she cannot reconcile herself to the competing concepts of childhood that her parents proffer as gifts of love.

Precarious national narratives connect to more neocolonial signifiers when Jess and her parents travel to visit her mother's Nigerian family. On the plane to Lagos, Jess lapses into an uncontrollable tantrum when her mother demands that she take anti-malaria medication. In the nineteenth century, malaria killed so many British colonials in West Africa that the region became known in England as "The White Man's Grave."[29] Medical expeditions to the area sponsored by both the Royal Society and the Liverpool School of Tropical Medicine led to scientific breakthroughs in the prophylactic treatment of malaria in the early twentieth century.[30] This form of medical colonialism made it possible for greater numbers of British soldiers, missionaries, and administrators to thrive in West Africa. Oyeyemi casts Jess's rejection of the "two white pills and the leering idea of her mother's country"[31] as a repudiation of this colonial legacy, but Sarah reads it as hysteria and, worried that Jess is disturbing others on the plane, "slapped her hard"[32] across the face. In a taxi from the Lagos airport to the family compound in Ibadan, the Yoruba driver suggests that Jess and her father are *oyinbo*, "which means somebody who has come from so far away that they are a stranger."[33] Jess waits for her mother to defend them with a "unifying smile,"[34] but she turns her back on them and reminisces with the Yoruba taxi driver instead. In this scene, Sarah supplants her familial relation by forming an alliance with a fellow citizen of her Yoruba homeland. In these two brief episodes Jess's postmemorial work begins with an affective but as yet unconscious connection to the contemporary afterlife of African colonization. Oyeyemi makes clear that Sarah's vision of familial and national relationality fiercely rejects any link to this colonial past. Sarah not only reads Jess's behavior as mentally disturbing; she also aligns it with Daniel's estranging Englishness.

When the Harrisons arrive in Ibadan, Oyeyemi quickly subsumes Sarah and Daniel's oppositional family dynamics within the Yoruba patriarch's amnesiac national allegory. Sarah's father, Gbenga Oyegbebi, lives with three of his children and seven of his grandchildren in an old-style gated compound containing "groups of buildings that housed related relatives of male lineage."[35] The three-story main house "in which her grandfather reigned"[36] was the largest structure at the center of the compound, while the rest of the family lived in small bungalows surrounding it. As the Harrisons join everyone in front of the main house, Oyeyemi begins her depiction of Jess's grandfather by aligning his "stillness"[37] and "mock consternation"[38] with the "stone-walled corridor"[39] they gather in, implying a reciprocal relationship between the family patriarch and the built logic of his homeland. In addition, she suggests friction between the generations by contrasting the grandfather with the "constant movement"[40] and "barely controlled excitement"[41] of the aunts and uncles. When her grandfather greets her with one loud, declarative word, "Wuraola," all eyes turn to Jess, who "froze, not knowing what to say or do."[42] By welcoming Jess as Wuraola, a Yoruba word meaning precious gold, Gbenga initiates Jess into his national allegory but also erases all other aspects of her diasporic identity as the price of membership. Jess recognizes Wuraola as the Yoruba name her grandfather has mandated in a letter to Sarah, but she wonders: "Should she answer to this name, and by doing so steal the identity of someone who belonged here?"[43] Like her mother's "Jess?" that opens the novel, the grandfather's renaming sets Jess at odds with yet another national narrative of belonging.

Later that evening, as her grandfather's "warming, infectious smile"[44] makes Jess feel more at ease, Oyeyemi juxtaposes this happy affect with Jess's intuitive distaste for the Western material signifiers that taint Gbenga's Yoruba familial ideal with troubling neocolonial affect. When Gbenga dismisses the rest of his family from the parlor, Sarah obediently disappears to catch up with her sister, and Daniel retreats to the roof balcony to talk presidential politics with Uncle Kunle, leaving Jess alone with her grandfather. At first, Jess feels "on the edge of a screaming fit" when she stares at "the crisp lines of his white shirt almost moulding him, fixing him still in her sight."[45] But when he smiles warmly at her, Jess "felt as if the room had been lit up," so she runs into his arms and "buried her face in his shirt, her nose wrinkling up as the scent of his cologne mixed with the nutty, sourish smell of camphor that filled the room."[46] Jess continues to focus on the "starched white before her eyes" as she and her grandfather bond over the realization that they both are "unaccustomed to being seen."[47] The starched crisp whiteness of the European shirt that "moulds" Gbenga aligns him with the hygienic linen cupboard in the Harrison home, giving his body a neocolonial veneer. Cologne, another European cosmetic product, masks her grandfather's bodily essence, just as camphor, a European insect repellant, cloaks the parlor. Colonial botanists developed insect repellents from the camphor tree, an evergreen indigenous to Indonesia, and then exported it to other colonies.[48] Jess is not fully conscious of the import of these seemingly negligible tactile and olfactory indicators of neocolonial affect; she does, however, recognize the anxiety of invisibility that undercuts her grandfather's patriarchal power. Achille Mbembe has argued that African culture displays an anxious amnesia about the slave trade because many Africans have yet to come to terms with the active roles they or their ancestors played in the "murder of brother by brother."[49] Mbembe contends that this amnesia allows continental Africans to 'forget' their connections to slave traders by aligning themselves instead with the misery and suffering experienced by Africans sold to the Americas as slaves. In postindependence African countries, slave trader amnesia is incorporated into their nascent national allegories.[50] The neocolonial signifiers that mask Gbenga's body and home not only mark him as a beneficiary of British colonialism but also mark his national allegory as complicitous with indigenous African slave traders. The transfer of invisibility from grandfather to grandchild makes clear that the national allegory Gbenga's generation has created only perpetuates slavery as a trauma without any reparative effect. Like his daughter and son-in-law, Gbenga wants to be a loving mentor for Jess, but he cannot model a livable subject identity for this diasporic child to inhabit.

Hovering in the background of Gbenga's mentoring of Jess, however, is the "constant movement"[51] of her aunts and uncles away from their "stone-walled"[52] father, which enacts their resentful feelings about the national allegory he so powerfully maintains within the family. Although Oyeyemi narrates their oppositional actions as seemingly innocuous asides, she also connects their powerless resentment to actual political events in Nigeria in the summer of 1993. Jess's father, Daniel, fans himself with a Nigerian newspaper in the taxi from Lagos to cool off after a defensive altercation with Nigerian Muslims who descended on him "as if they wished to swallow him up."[53] As Daniel and Uncle Kunle passively retreat to the roof balcony in response to Gbenga's demand for privacy, Jess hears her uncle declare, "'No, no, it's quite clear to me and to everyone that the reason why they don't want Abiola for president is because he's a Yoruba man!'"[54] Jess's visit with her mother's family takes place in the summer of 1993, the same time period that Moshood Abiola, a politician and an elite member of the Yoruba Egba clan, ran for president of Nigeria. Although many Yoruba believed that he had enough votes to win the elections held on June 12, the current president, Ibrahim Babangida, annulled the election results and subsequently banned Abiola from ever running again.[55] Abiola also led the OAU group that convened the First Pan-African Conference on Reparations in Abuja in April 1993.[56] At the end of the conference, the OAU group adopted the Abuja Declaration, which declared, in part, that the devastation wrought by slavery "is not a thing of the past, but is painfully manifest in the damaged lives of contemporary Africans."[57] Oyeyemi's brief historical reference connects Gbenga's fraught political imaginary with Babangida's attempts to erase Abiola's prescient postmemory. Both her father Daniel's and her Uncle Kunle's potential as mentors for Jess is quickly dismissed as well, for the men's lament for the grim state of the Nigerian national allegory quickly fades away as they move upstairs.[58]

When Jess meets her Aunty Funke, the servile actions she grudgingly performs subtly expose Jess to the sexist parameters of Gbenga's intergenerational postmemory. For example, Jess notes the officious way that Gbenga "moved a hand to beckon at Aunty Funke to open a bottle" when she brings drinks into the parlor.[59] At the end of a meal Aunty Funke begins to clear away the dishes but her father demands that she hold a bowl of water while he "unhurriedly paddled the water and dribbled it over his fingers" and then shook water all over the rug.[60] Aunty Funke then brings Gbenga a toothpick, which he breaks up into little pieces and tosses onto a table after using it. Jess notices that Aunty Funke silently and sullenly "swept up the toothpick shards."[61] Just as she does with her grandfather, Jess associates Funke with a colonial commodity, for she thinks that her aunt smells like "Sunlight soap,"[62] a household cleaning product.[63] In "Sunlight Soap has Changed My Life," postcolonial scholar Timothy Burke argues that British advertisers used discourses from "colonial hygienic training" to construct African blackness as a form of dirt that Western commodities could scrub clean.[64] First developed by the Lever Brothers in the late nineteenth century, Sunlight soap was vigorously marketed to consumers living in British colonies in Africa. When Sarah jumps up to help Aunty Funke serve Gbenga, Jess thinks that her mother, who was an accomplished novelist in England, "looked like the household help."[65] The two women most likely to mentor Jess are thus reduced to the role of cleansing any reference to precolonial African blackness out of the family's national imaginary. The two women's servile actions model the family's ongoing erasure of any connections to the African past, which prevents Jess from relating to this forgotten history herself.

However, Aunty Funke does provide Jess with a spatial connection to the forgotten past when she connects her resentment at being treated like a servant to the Boys' Quarters, an old, empty building on the family compound. When Jess first notices the Boys' Quarters, her aunt dismisses it as an abandoned space, left over from when her great-grandfather had the compound built in the 1870s to house himself and his three wives.[66] The family compound architectural style was common to British missionaries who first moved near Ibadan in the 1830s, when the Oyo Empire was collapsing.[67] The Boys' Quarters, built to house the local African slaves of British missionaries, was located far away from the main house of the family compound because, until science established the *anopheles* mosquito as the source of malaria in the 1880s, Europeans believed that Africans themselves carried the parasites that produced this disease. Burke suggests that "[s]ocial segregation, especially the segregation of urban space, was frequently justified in colonial society by an appeal to images of disease, dirt, and pollution, making particular use of the evolving professional doctrines of tropical medicine," which tended to link tropical diseases, no matter what their source, with the bodies of tropical people.[68] When Nigeria was still a British colony, only elite Yoruba slaveholders from the collapsing Oyo Empire would have been rich enough to construct a family compound in this British colonial architectural style, a spatial configuration that suggests Jess's great-grandfather's wealth may have been complicit with African slaveholding and pre-colonial British Christianity. Oyeyemi further connects Jess's grandfather, Gbenga, to this ignominious past as well when he enlists all of the family members in the work of hosting his Baptist Bible group. Dismayed by her inability to relate to her Nigerian family members, Jess decides to explore the Boys' Quarters after she sees a light burning in a window of this abandoned space.

The Nigerian Games

Jess plays her first game with Titiola in the Boys' Quarters, when she enters the building one day, curious to meet the person whose lighted window she has observed at night. Inside the dark, decaying structure, Jess sees an "old-fashioned writing desk with an inkwell set in the corner" whose "surface was covered with the film of dust that obscured everything."[69] Oyeyemi's description of the Boys' Quarters draws on conventionally foreboding Gothic tropes, but surprisingly, timid little Jess feels curious rather than fearful and tiptoes deeper into the mysterious space. However, when she passes by the desk again while searching for the stairs, "her eye caught on something and she backed up, all thoughts of staircases and balconies and upstairs rooms completely forgotten."[70] On the surface of the desk, "someone had disturbed the dust," and "scrawled in the centre in lopsided lettering were the words '*HEllO Jessy.*'"[71] Paralyzed momentarily by fear, Jess then bolts from the Boys' Quarters back to her grandfather's house. She wants to tell someone what she has just experienced, that "[s]omeone was living in a place where no one lived ...and knew her name," but she didn't know whom to trust.[72] Later she collapses, hysterical and sobbing, in the parlor with her father and her grandfather because "this was the second time that someone had called her something that she had never been called ...First Wuraola, now Jessy. She'd always been Jess or Jessamy, never a halfway thing like Jessy."[73] Oyeyemi suggests in this episode that although Jess is inquisitive about the Boys' Quarters, she is clearly not prepared for her first encounter with this space of forgotten trauma. Nor is she willing to be interpellated by the scrawled greeting as a half and half child. However, Jessamy's fear and panic begin to abate when she meets Titiola in person.

Jessamy and Titiola play another naming game when they first meet in an in-between space, the bottom of a stairway that bisects Gbenga's house. Oyeyemi overlays Titiola's body with slave signifiers, for she first appears to Jess as an unkempt scrawny girl with "dirty white string" tying puffs of her hair, bare feet "whitened with gravel scratches and sand," a worn, oversized dress made of "brown and white, checked cloth" and "knees and elbows ...ashen and grayish in patches."[74] Titiola's neglected young body signifies that she has no adults caring for her, and the pattern of her dress fabric resembles gingham—a fabric commonly used for slave clothing by British colonial administrators and missionaries in Africa because it was very inexpensively produced by cloth mills in Manchester, England, a major slaving port in the nineteenth century.[75] Jess is not afraid when she looks at Titiola; she "felt a smile coming," and when Titiola repeats the dust-scrawled phrase, "'Hello Jessy,'" Jess now "[l]aughed aloud with surprise."[76] Jess asks Titiola for her name, but realizes she cannot properly pronounce "Titiola," so she shortens it to TillyTilly. Titiola, a Yoruba name, joins together two Yoruba words—'titi'–never-ending or eternal, and 'ola'—fulfilling life, so together Titiola represents eternally fulfilling life. However, Tilly, is an English diminutive for Mathilda, an Old German name derived from words meaning mighty warrior. This nickname recasts the Yoruba meaning of Titiola by eliding the enriching aspects of "ola" so that TillyTilly repetitively signifies unending war. Jess is eager for Tilly to like her so she launches into a long explanation for the nickname, but Tilly just starts laughing. The episode ends with Jess feeling "glad that she had been so eager to be friends" for once, thinking that "[i]t was [like] peering through good and pretty coloured glass, this gladness, this feeling that someone had been around the compound, knowing who she was and wanting to talk to her."[77] Although Jess's first encounter with Tilly has helped alleviate some of her fear, her unconscious act of colonial re-naming duplicates for Tilly the very neocolonial gestures that Jess has found so disturbing. Oyeyemi associates Tilly with slavery by locating her home in the Boys' Quarters, which domesticates her within this forgotten history of slavery. Tilly reanimates this forgotten space as an archive of pre-colonial Yoruba history when she shows Jess the shrine she has created with the charcoal drawing of a serene long-armed *ibeji* woman.

The girls continue to play in and around Ibadan in other forgotten spaces that resonate with neocolonial affect—spaces like thresholds and stairwells that signify in-betweenness; the grandfather's locked study, which is full of English literary texts that have been used in colonial reeducation projects; and a closed, run-down amusement park that serves as a critique of both the state in its mockery of NEPA, the government-controlled electrical company, and the dilapidated state of contemporary Nigerian concepts of pleasure. However, the games the girls play in these in-between Nigerian spaces cement a bond between Tilly's connection to the forgotten past of slavery and Jess's burgeoning diasporic identity. Each game ends with Tilly disappearing, leaving Jess longing for more contact with her. Jess is devastated at the thought of losing her new-found friend when she must leave Nigeria, but Tilly reassures her that she will "see you later."[78] The Nigerian games not only represent the collective history of slavery as a playful nurturing child that the adults in Jess's life are so actively forgetting, but they also produce an affiliative pleasure at departing from the neocolonial aspects of Nigerian space, an affect that Jess incorporates as a survival technique.

The English Games

In England, Jess and Tilly encounter more improbable mentors whose diasporic identities can't accommodate Tilly as a precarious postmemory. In the games they play in England, Tilly becomes more aggressive in her quest to revivify her slave history, but this accretioning violence cannot produce a livable subjectivity for Jess. Back in England without

Tilly, Jess reverts to screaming fits in school and revising English coming-of-age tales at home, demonstrating that although she is developing an intuitive anti-colonial affect out of her re-memory of collective history, she is still so fearful and unconscious of her past—without Tilly there to remind her—that she cannot evolve beyond these helpless manic gestures. Jess is once again overjoyed when Tilly shows up in England and suggests a series of *getting* games. In these games, Tilly teaches Jess how to stand up to the children and adults who scare her, but Tilly also suggests that they should *get* each of these people—punish them for treating Jess badly. Tilly's need for retribution begins to code their games with violence and anger as the *getting* games proceed. At first Jess reads Tilly's games reparatively, but then she cannot read beyond Tilly's aggressions in order to understand the losses that inform them. Although Jess is a willing participant in several of these *getting* games—from fighting Colleen McLain, the girl who bullies her, to yelling at her teacher, Miss Patel, to scaring the babysitter because she's from Madeira—she becomes angry and self-destructive when she herself begins to emulate Tilly's games of retribution.

When confronted with Jess's request for the forgotten history of her dead twin, Fern, Sarah's mother reacts by fiercely rejecting Jess as a threat to her national identity. Tilly discloses to Jess that "'there were two of you born, just like there were two of me. The other one of you died.'"[79] Tilly then tells Jess that her twin's name was Fern, but she never got a "'proper name... a Yoruba name, because she was born already dead, just after you were born.'"[80] In traditional Yoruba families it was common to request that an *ibeji* statue be made for a twin who dies young in order to give her soul a body to inhabit.[81] However, Jess's family has not had a statue built for Fern because she and Jess were born in England, not Nigeria. When Jess confronts her mother by asking, "'Was there two of me?'"[82] Sarah is so disturbed that Jess knows this dark family secret that she first decides that Jess is a "witch," and then concludes that Jess is an "*abiku*" spirit.[83] The standard Yoruba translation of "*abiku*" is "one who is born, dies," and traditional priests of the Ifa Yoruba religion believed that an *abiku* is a spirit sent from heaven to steal earthly riches and is embodied in a child who dies young.[84] Douglas McCabe argues that these priests' definition of *abiku* is "replete with the terminology and imagery of slave-raiding,"[85] and is highly politicized as a figure that threatens the powerful Oyo empire, which broadened its power and wealth by "selling domestic slaves and captives of war to buyers on the coast."[86] Sarah's fearful configuring of Jess as an *abiku* suggests that her daughter is an itinerant threat to her national identity. Rather than take responsibility for not telling Jess about her dead twin, Sarah resorts to signifiers of Yoruba madness to account for Jess's knowledge of their forgotten family history.

Tilly says that she, too, is a twin whose other half had died: "'I have been just like you for such a long time,'"[87] and suggests they comfort one another for their mutual losses. To accomplish this Tilly suggests a twins' game that will help Jess be more like Tilly, and Jess "giggled at the idea" and then was "overtaken by a wave of mirth". Tilly then "*hop, skip, jumped inside*" Jess's body and jolts Jess's spirit out of it, which left Jess feeling like she was "being flung, scattered in steady handfuls, literally thrown into things."[88] In Jess's body, Tilly begins to scream because she "was having trouble controlling Jess's face," and her "head and legs bobbed alarmingly in every direction, as if she were some squalling rag doll."[89] Embodied slave history toddles on stick thin legs, unable to negotiate its way in the material world Jess inhabits. Sarah is so frightened by "Tilly-who-was-Jess" that she locks her in the basement and declares to her husband, "'I can't mother this girl. I try, but …I'm scared of her.'"[90] When Jess finally dis-embodies Tilly, she "suddenly knelt down and prayed: (*Dear God, take my skin, take my feet, and my lips, because she's been in them and spoiled them and made them not work*)."[91]

In her representation of this *getting* game, Oyeyemi carefully blends European *doppelganger* mythologies with Yoruba *abiku*. Both of these discourses construct "Tilly-who-was-Jess" as a spiritual invader from another realm, an outsider who challenges the collective amnesiac imaginary. Oyeyemi's realist, reliable tone and mundane descriptions of these fantastical games blur the boundaries between the material and immaterial worlds Jess and Tilly traverse, however; when the giggles and laughter of the two girls melt into this horrifying chaotic re-membering, the pain both Jess and Tilly feel implicates Gothic tropes and Yoruba beliefs in the girls' struggles to know themselves. Jess's parents cannot figure out who Tilly is because although Jess talks about her, they have never met her. They still cannot connect Jess's problems to history, and in particular to the history of the slave trade, because they are so deeply invested in their own amnesiac national allegories that they repetitively encourage her to forget about Tilly. Because Jess has no access to this forgotten past through this older generation, she cannot develop like the protagonist of a conventional English *Bildungsroman* should.

In addition, she has no mentors to protect her from the painful ravages of Tilly's precarious postmemorial desire to be re-membered. In a climactic moment, Tilly tries to put into words the suffering she has experienced as a slave, a tumult of phrases that spills over into uncontrollable rage:

> "Land chopped in little pieces, and—ideas! ...It's all been lost. Ashes. Nothing ...And then our blood ...spilt like water ...like water for the drinking, for the washing ...our blood ...and I am a WITNESS. Twins should know what each other suffer! ...There is no homeland—there is nowhere where there are people who will not *get* you."[92]

When Jess looks up in terror at Tilly she sees the face of a lynched slave with "enormous swollen lips" that were "encrusted with dead, dry skin" and within her mouth a "small mauve stump; the remains of a *tongue*."[93] When Tilly finally declares, "'Stop looking to belong, half-and-half child. Stop. There is nothing; there is only me, and I have caught you,'" Jess begins to scream uncontrollably because this lynched face "engulfed her, baptizing her in its madness."[94] The terrible, forgotten suffering that Tilly is finally able to express threatens to overwhelm Jess with painful despair. As a precarious postmemory, Tilly threatens to destroy Jess rather than repair her connections to her forgotten pasts.

Shortly after Jess's dreadful incorporation into Tilly's anguish, Jess's mother takes her to a psychiatrist, Dr. MacKenzie, who seeks to refute Sarah's traditional spiritual logic with Western psychiatric discourse that locates Tilly within Jess's overactive mind as an imaginary friend. When Jess refuses this understanding of Tilly, Dr. McKenzie decides that Jess is mentally unstable. Psychiatric discourse can only locate Jess's experiences as a form of madness. How best to incorporate Tilly is what both Jess and the readers of *The Icarus Girl* are trying to decide. To accept Tilly as a postmemory is precarious because one runs the risk of being consumed in the flames of Tilly's retributive affect. Jess does not yet have all the tools she needs to reembody this postmemory as a livable aspect of her diasporic imaginary. Stylistically, Oyeyemi implicates the progressive, allegorical logic of the European *Bildungsroman* in her depiction of Jess's mentors. Her mother tries to help Jess by giving her a book with a picture of an *ibeji* statue and telling her about the Yoruba belief that twins live in three worlds—this world, the spirit world, and the Bush, a kind of "'wilderness of the mind.'"[95] Tilly continues to create increasingly vengeful, violent games that make Jess more and more worn out and ill.

The games that Jess and Tilly have played in England opened Jess's eyes to the harrowing sources of Tilly's anger, but neither child has figured out how to create a livable diasporic identity out of their shared anguish. Exasperated with Western psychiatric explanations for her daughter's mental traumas, Sarah decides to bring Jess back to Nigeria.

The Games in the Nigerian Bush

Two kinds of madness guide the girls' final games in Nigeria—Jess's so-called insanity and Tilly's burgeoning anger. When Jess returns to Ibadan, Tilly declares that she has waited long enough and tries to permanently re-possess Jess's body on her ninth birthday. Jess's embodied strangeness causes her grandfather and father to argue over how to deal with it, so her mother takes Jess away from the clash of these patriarchs, and they end up in a car crash. In this climactic moment, the clash of all the amnesiac mentors severely injures Jess, whose body lies in a coma in the hospital. In the Bush, Jess, her dead twin Fern, and Tilly all engage in one final frenetic identity game. Fern serves as a guide for Jess, carrying her on her back through the bewildering terrain. In gratitude, Jess offers to share her Yoruba name, Wuraola, with Fern, a naming game that appeases this restless spirit, allowing her to depart, "taken away into the sky in a stream of light," going "[u]pwards," "spiraling into clear blue light."[96] Fern's upward flight not only resembles the flying Africans of African-American folklore but also revises Icarus's tragic ending by leaving this Icarus girl forever rising up to the sky toward the Yoruba afterlife. This positive reincorporation of her lost personal history gives Jess the strength to face her final challenge—incorporating the precarious postmemory of slavery that Tilly so painfully represents into her burgeoning diasporic identity—so that she, too, can become an Icarus girl.

The end game for the girls occurs when Jess bravely decides to play her own *getting* game with Tilly. Gaining newfound strength from helping Fern, Jess "*hopped, skipped, jumped*" out of the Bush and "into Tilly's unyielding flesh …and back into herself."[97] The girls' final incorporation of Tilly's slave history with Jess's diasporic identity reads like a game in these playful actions, but the excruciating aspects become apparent when Oyeyemi declares that this hybrid embodiment "*hurt them both burningly*."[98] The last line of the narrative then declares: "Jessamy Harrison woke up and up and up and up."[99] Oyeyemi's ending repetition, "up and up and up and up," paradoxically immobilizes this newly forged diasporic identity in becoming, suspending the

Jess-who-is-now-Jess-and-Tilly in that same sublime state of becoming that Icarus experienced in his flight toward the sun, before his father's flight machinery failed him. Oyeyemi foreshortens the Icarus myth to relocate her Icarus girls in an endless process of becoming, thus returning that sense of continuous evolution to the protagonal journey in this postcolonial *Bildungsroman*. Unlike the ending of the conventional *Bildungsroman*, which signals that the child has secured a static adult role in the national imaginary, the end of *The Icarus Girl* moves Jess beyond the stultifying unlivable identities on offer from her neocolonial mentors. By ending Jessamy Harrison's narrative in this fraught form of hybrid becoming, Oyeyemi implicates the mentors' intergenerational postmemorial amnesia as an inadequate technology of escape from the trauma of the slave trade. The games Jess and Tilly play in the Bush are meant to distance them from the unsatisfactory neocolonial amnesia they see around them in England and Nigeria. It is only through this distancing that they find a hybrid identity that is inhabitable for both of them, an identity that embodies the fraught colonial past by marking the future of diasporic identity as evolving. Connecting to the past, no matter how painful that past has been, is necessary to moving beyond the helpless madness so many young female protagonists of third-generation African novels remain mired in.

Oyeyemi ends *The Icarus Girl* with another postmemorial creation, an *oriki* called "Praise of the Leopard." An *oriki* is a panegyric, a Yoruba form of praise poetry composed by clan elders to celebrate the bravery and perseverance of a person, and to catalyze the audience of the poem to emulate the subject's glorious deeds.[100] Oyeyemi's "Praise for the Leopard" revises a Yoruba folktale about "The Leopard Man," who dons a leopard skin to kill for sustenance but can never live with his human beloved for fear he will one day kill her. Leopards are common tropes of animal *orikis*, because the Yoruba admired their hunting skills, natural strength, and tenacity. The Leopard in Oyeyemi's *oriki* is a paradox, a "Gentle hunter," "Beautiful death," and "Playful killer."[101] If we read the leopard in Oyeyemi's *oriki* as Jess, then it celebrates the journey she has taken from fear to anger to bravery in her quest to form a livable diasporic identity. However, we must also read the Leopard as Tilly, for it celebrates the postmemory of the forgotten history of slavery that Tilly represents. As readers of the trauma and the so-called madness of these two young girls struggling to find their place in the contemporary world, we come to understand *The Icarus Girl* as a postmemory that repairs the madness of amnesiac affect in its vulnerable depiction of two girls playing.

Notes

1. Susan Fraiman, *Unbecoming Women* (New York: Columbia University Press, 1994). Developing in the eighteenth century as a literary correlative to the emerging European nation-state, the *Bildungsroman* chronicles a child's quest to develop an individual identity that aligns with accepted concepts of national citizenship. In response to both national and global upheavals in the nineteenth and twentieth centuries, novelists began to revise the conventions of this coming-of-age narrative. For example, when Charlotte Brontë and Jane Austen employ the *Bildungsroman* to plot the development of female citizens in nineteenth-century England, Susan Fraiman notes that their girl protagonists resist and subvert the generic conventions of national citizenry and that their journey to livable subjectivity is hardly guaranteed.
2. Tsitsi Dangarembga, *The Book of Not: a Sequel to Nervous Conditions* (New York: Lynne Reiner Publishers, 2006).
3. Kopano Matlwa, *Coconut* (Johannesburg: Jacana Media, 2008).
4. Chimamanda Ngozi Adichie, *Purple Hibiscus* (New York: Anchor Books, 2004).
5. Diana Evans, *26a* (New York: Harper Perennial, 2006). Bernardine Evaristo, *The Emperor's Babe* (New York: Viking Adult, 2002).
6. Michael Sperber, *Dostoyevsky's Stalker and Other Essays on Psychopathology and the Arts* (Lanham, MD: University Press of America, 2010), 166. Modern psychology has coined the term the "Icarus complex" to describe mental disorders that are characterized by highly overactive imaginations.
7. Ibid., 3.
8. Jed Esty, *Unseasonable Youth: Modernism, Colonialism, and the Fiction of Development* (New York: Oxford University Press, 2012), 6.
9. Salman Rushdie, *Midnight's Children* (New York: Random House, 25th ed. 2006). Tsitsi Dangarembga, *Nervous Conditions* (New York: McDougal Littell Publishers, 1997). Salman Rushdie's *Midnight's Children* is one of the first postcolonial novels to critique Western concepts of development in his depiction of Saleem Sinai's experiences with nascent Indian nationalism. The title of Tsitsi Dangarembga's 1988 *Bildungsroman*, *Nervous Conditions*, aligns female development in late imperial Rhodesia with Franz Fanon's poignant psychological diagnosis of the colonized African mind.
10. Victoria R. Arana, "Fresh 'Cultural Critiques': The Ethnographic Fabulations of Adichie and Oyeyemi" in *Emerging African Voices: A Study of Contemporary African Literature* (Amherst, NY: Cambria Press, 2010): 269–313. Jane Bryce, "'Half and Half Children':

Third-Generation Women Writers and the New Nigerian Novel," *Research in African Literatures* 39.2 (Summer 2008): 49–67. Diana Adesola Mafe, "Ghostly Girls in the 'Eerie Bush': Helen Oyeyemi's *The Icarus Girl* as Postcolonial Female Gothic Fiction," *Research in African Literatures* 43.3 (Fall 2012): 21–35. Jordan Stouck, "Abjecting Hybridity in Helen Oyeyemi's *The Icarus Girl*," *ARIEL: A Review of International English Literature* 41.2 (2011): 89–112. See Arana and Bryce on *abiku* and *ibeji*. See Mafe on the postcolonial female gothic. Stouck reads Jess through the lens of Kristevan abjection.

11. Madelaine Hron, "*Ora na-azu nwa*: The Figure of the Child in Third-Generation Nigerian Novels," *Research in African Literatures* 39.2 (Summer 2008): 35.
12. Ibid., 35.
13. Bryce, "'Half and Half Children,'" 63.
14. Helen Oyeyemi, *The Icarus Girl* (New York: Anchor Books, 2006).
15. Stephen Craps and Gert Buelens, "Introduction: Postcolonial Trauma Novels," *Studies in the Novel* 40.1&2 (Spring and Summer 2008): 1–12.
16. Marianne Hirsch, "Connective Histories in Vulnerable Times," *PMLA* 129.3 (May 2014): 339.
17. Ibid., 339. See Murphy for an analysis of postmemory in Ayei Kwei Armah's work.
18. Marianne Hirsch, "The Generation of Postmemory," *Poetics Today* 29.1 (Spring 2008): 111–14.
19. Hirsch, "Connective Histories in Vulnerable Times," 335.
20. Oyeyemi, *The Icarus Girl*, 3.
21. Ibid., 4.
22. Timothy, Burke, "'Sunlight Soap Has Changed My Life': Hygiene, Commodification, and the Body in Colonial Zimbabwe," in *Clothing and Difference: Embodied Identities in Colonial and Post-Colonial Africa*, ed. Hildi Hendrickson (Durham, NC: Duke University Press, 1996), 189–212.
23. Oyeyemi, *The Icarus Girl*, 6.
24. Ibid., 6.
25. Ibid., 7.
26. Ibid., 8.
27. Sara Ahmed, "Happy Object," in *The Affect Theory Reader*, eds. Melissa Gregg and Gregory J. Seigworth (Durham, NC: Duke University Press, 2010), 30.
28. Ibid., 30.

29. László Máthé-Shires, "Who Lives Where? British Anti-Malaria Policy in Southern-Nigeria (1899–1912)," *Orvostorteneti kozlemenyek* 46.1–4 (2001): 45.
30. Ibid., 47.
31. Oyeyemi, *The Icarus Girl*, 8.
32. Ibid., 11.
33. Ibid., 18.
34. Ibid., 18.
35. Ibid., 33.
36. Ibid., 33.
37. Ibid., 19.
38. Ibid., 20.
39. Ibid., 21.
40. Ibid., 19.
41. Ibid., 20.
42. Ibid., 20.
43. Ibid., 21.
44. Ibid., 22.
45. Ibid., 22.
46. Ibid., 23.
47. Ibid., 23.
48. Karen Brown, "'Trees, Forests and Communities': Some Historiographical Approaches to Environmental History on Africa," *Area* 35.4 (2003): 343–356. Brown discusses the ecological imperialism informing forestation policy in colonial Africa.
49. Achile Mbembe, "African Modes of Self-Writing," *Public Culture* 14.1 (December 2002): 260.
50. Mbembe, "African Modes of Self-Writing," 261. Mbembe also notes that African-American literature is replete with slave narratives, but continental African novelists rarely write about this time period in their history. Arlene R. Keizer, "Gone Astray in the Flesh: Kara Walker, Black Women Writers, and African-American Postmemory," *PMLA* 123.5 (October 2008): 1649–1672. Keizer analyzes postmemory in contemporary African-American women's art and literature.
51. Oyeyemi, *The Icarus Girl*, 19.
52. Ibid., 20.
53. Ibid., 15.
54. Ibid., 21.
55. Max duPlessis, "Historical Injustice and International Law: An Exploratory Discussion of Reparation for Slavery," *Human Rights Quarterly* 25 (2003): 638.
56. Ibid., 638.

57. Jullyette Ukabiala, "Slave Trade 'A Crime Against Humanity,'" *Africa Recovery* 15.3 (October 2001): 5.
58. Oyeyemi, *The Icarus Girl*, 21.
59. Ibid., 23.
60. Ibid., 27.
61. Ibid., 30.
62. Ibid., 23.
63. Today, the company's website still proudly declares: "Sunlight has been making hygiene and cleanliness available around the world since the 1880s." The site also narrates the history of the brand as a remedy for class conflict in Victorian England, which was "plagued by poverty." http://www.unilever.com/brands-in-action/detail/Sunlight/292058/. Accessed February 28, 2015.
64. Burke, 200.
65. Oyeyemi, *The Icarus Girl*, 27.
66. Ibid., 33.
67. C.O. Osasona and A.D.C. Hyland, *Colonial Architecture in Ile-Ife, Nigeria* (Ibadan, Nigeria: BookBuilders Editions Africa, 2006), 14.
68. Burke, "Sunlight Soap Has Changed My Life," 194.
69. Oyeyemi, *The Icarus Girl*, 42.
70. Ibid., 42.
71. Ibid., 42.
72. Ibid., 43.
73. Ibid., 44.
74. Ibid., 47.
75. Lola Sharon Davidson, "Woven Webs: Trading Textiles Around the Indian Ocean," *PORTAL Journal of Multidisciplinary International Studies*, 9.1 (January 2012): 10.
76. Oyeyemi, *The Icarus Girl*, 48.
77. Ibid., 50.
78. Ibid., 80.
79. Ibid., 175.
80. Ibid., 176.
81. Arana, "Fresh 'Cultural Critiques'," 291.
82. Oyeyemi, *The Icarus Girl*, 179.
83. Ibid., 181.
84. Douglas McCabe, "Histories of Errancy: Oral Yoruba *Abiku* Texts and Soyinka's 'Abiku'," *Research in African Literature* 33.1 (Spring 2002): 47.
85. Ibid., 47.
86. Mccabe, 48.
87. Oyeyemi, *The Icarus Girl*, 176.

88. Ibid., 209.
89. Ibid., 210.
90. Ibid., 211.
91. Ibid., 213.
92. Ibid., 259–60.
93. Ibid., 260–61.
94. Ibid., 261.
95. Ibid., 200.
96. Ibid., 333.
97. Ibid., 334.
98. Ibid., 334.
99. Ibid., 334.
100. McCabe, 53.
101. Oyeyemi, *The Icarus Girl*, 335.

Bibliography

Adichie, Chimamanda Ngozi. *Purple Hibiscus*. New York: Anchor Books, 2004.

Ahmed, Sara. "Happy Object." *The Affect Theory Reader*, 29–51. Edited by Melissa Gregg and Gregory J. Seigworth. Durham: Duke University Press, 2010.

Akinyemi, Akintunde. "Integrating Culture and Second Language Teaching through Yorùbá Personal Names." *The Modern Language Journal* 89.1 (Spring, 2005): 115–126.

Arana, R. Victoria. "Fresh 'Cultural Critiques': The Ethnographic Fabulations of Adichie and Oyeyemi." *Emerging African Voices: A Study of Contemporary African Literature*. Amherst, New York: Cambria Press, 2010. 269–313.

Bastian, Misty L. "'The Demon Superstition': Abominable Twins and Mission Culture In Onitsha History." *Ethnology; An International Journal of Cultural and Social Anthropology* 40.1 (2001): 13–27.

Bastida-Rodriguez, Patricia. "Evil Friends: Childhood Friendship and Diasporic Identities in Meera Syal's *Anita and Me* and Helen Oyeyemi's *The Icarus Girl*." *Philologia* 6 (2008): 163–171.

Bryce, Jane. "'Half and Half Children': Third-Generation Women Writers and the New Nigerian Novel." *Research in African Literatures* 39.2 (Summer 2008): 49–67.

Brown, Karen. "'Trees, Forests and Communities': Some Historiographical Approaches to Environmental History on Africa." *Area* 35.4 (2003): 343–356. Web. 14 February 2015.

Burke, Timothy. "Sunlight Soap has Changed My Life": Hygeine, Commodification, and the Body in Colonial Zimbabwe." In *Clothing and Difference: Embodied Identities in Colonial and Post-Colonial Africa*, 189–212. Edited by Hildi Hendrickson. Durham NC: Duke University Press, 1996.

Caruth, Cathy. "The Claims of the Dead: History, Haunted Property and the Law." *Critical Inquiry* 28 (Winter 2002): 419–441.

_________. "Parting Words: Trauma, Silence and Survival." In *Acts of Narrative*, 47–61. Edited by Carol Jacobs and Henry Sussman. Palo Alto, CA: Stanford University Press, 2003.

Cooper, Brenda. "The Middle Passage of the Gods and the New Diaspora: Helen Oyeyemi's *The Opposite House*." *Research in African Literatures* 40.4 (Winter 2009): 108–121.

Craps, Stephen, and Gert Buelens. "Introduction: Postcolonial Trauma Novels." *Studies in the Novel* 40.1&2 (Sp & Su 2008): 1–12.

Dangarembga, Tsitsi. *Nervous Conditions*. New York: McDougal Littell Publishers, 1997.

———. *The Book of Not: a Sequel to Nervous Conditions*. New York: Lynne Reiner Publishers, 2006.

Davidson, Lola Sharon, "Woven Webs: Trading Textiles Around the Indian Ocean." *PORTAL Journal of Multidisciplinary International Studies* 9.1 (January 2012): 1–21.

Davies, Ioan. "Negotiating African Culture: Toward a Decolonization of the Fetish." In *The Cultures of Globalization*, 125–45. Edited by Frederic Jameson and Masao Miyoshi. Durham, North Carolina: Duke UP, 1999.

duPlessis, Max. "Historical Injustice and International Law: An Exploratory Discussion of Reparation for Slavery." *Human Rights Quarterly* 25 (2003): 624–659.

Esty, Jed. *Unseasonable Youth: Modernism, Colonialism, and the Fiction of Development*. New York: Oxford University Press, 2012.

Evans, Diana. *26A: A Novel*. New York: Harper Perennial, 2006.

Evaristo, Bernardine. *The Emperor's Babe*. New York: Penguin, 2004.

Falola, Toyin. "Slavery and pawnship in the Yoruba economy of the nineteenth century." *Slavery & Abolition* 15.2 (August 1994): 221–245.

Forna, Aminatta. "New Writing and Nigeria: Chimamanda Ngozi Adichie and Helen Oyeyemi in Conversation." *Wasafiri* 21.1 (21 August 2006): 50–57.

Fraiman, Susan. *Unbecoming Women*. New York: Columbia UP, 1994.

Gaylard, Gerald. "The Postcolonial Gothic: Time and Death In Southern African Literature." *Journal of Literary Studies/Tydskrif Vir Literatuurwetenskap* 24.4 (2008): 1–18.

Hirsch, Marianne. "Connective Histories in Vulnerable Times." *PMLA* 129.3 (May 2014): 330–348.

———. "The Generation of Postmemory." *Poetics Today* 29.1 (Spring 2008): 103–128.

Hron, Madelaine. "*Ora na-azu nwa*: The Figure of the Child in Third-Generation Nigerian Novels." *Research in African Literatures* 39.2 (Summer 2008): 27–47.

Keizer, Arlen R. "Gone Astray in the Flesh: Kara Walker, Black Women Writers, and African-American Postmemory." *PMLA* 123.5 (October 2008): 1649–1672.

Mabura, Lily G.N. "Breaking Gods: An African Postcolonial Gothic Reading of Chimamanda Ngozi Adichie's *Purple Hibiscus* and *Half of a Yellow Sun.*" *Research in African Literatures* 39.1 (Winter 2008): 203–222.

Mafe, Diana Adesola. "Ghostly Girls in the 'Eerie Bush': Helen Oyeyemi's *The Icarus Girl* as Postcolonial Female Gothic Fiction." *Research in African Literatures* 43.3 (Fall 2012): 21–35.

Máthé-Shires, László. "Who Lives Where? British Anti-Malaria Policy in Southern-Nigeria (1899–1912)." *Orvostorteneti kozlemenyek* 46.1–4 (2001): 45–55.

Matlwa, Kopano. *Coconut.* Johannesburg: Jacana Media, 2008.

Mbembe, Achille. "African Modes of Self-Writing." *Public Culture* 14.1 (December 2002): 239–273.

McCabe, Douglas. "Histories of Errancy: Oral Yoruba *Abiku* Texts and Soyinka's 'Abiku'." *Research in African Literature* 33.1 (Spring 2002): 46–74.

Morrison, Toni. *Beloved.* New York: Vintage, 2004.

Murphy, Laura. "The Curse of Constant Remembrance: The Belated Trauma of the Slave Trade in Ayi Kwei Armah's *Fragments.*" *Studies in the Novel* 40.1 (Spring 2008): 52–71.

Oruene, Taiwo. "Magical Powers of Twins in the Socio-Religious Beliefs of the Yoruba." *Folklore* Vol. 96, No. 2 (1985): 208–216.

Osasona, C.O. and A.D.C. Hyland. *Colonial Architecture in Ile-Ife, Nigeria.* Ibadan, Nigeria: BookBuilders Editions Africa, 2006.

Oyeyemi, Helen. *The Icarus Girl.* New York: Anchor Books, 2006.

Punter, David. *Postcolonial Imaginings: Fictions of a New World Order.* Edinburgh: Edinburgh UP, 2000.

Renne, Elisha P. "Twinship in an Ekiti Yoruba Town." *Ethnology: An International Journal of Cultural and Social Anthropology* 40.1 (2001): 63–78.

Rushdie, Salman. *Midnight's Children.* New York: Random House, 25th ed. 2006.

Smith, Ali. "Double Trouble." *The Guardian* Friday January 21, 2005.

Sperber, Michael. *Dostoyevsky's Stalker and Other Essays on Psychopathology and the Arts.* Maryland: University Press of America, 2010.

Stamp, Gavin. "Counting the Cost of the Slave Trade." *BBC Online Network.* N.p. 20 March 2007.

Stouck, Jordan. "Abjecting Hybridity in Helen Oyeyemi's *The Icarus Girl.*" *ARIEL: A Review of International English Literature* 41.2 (2011): 89–112.

"Trillions Demanded in Slavery Reparations." *BBC Online Network.* N.p. 20 August 1999. Web. 7 January 2013.

Ukabiala, Jullyette. "Slave Trade 'A Crime Against Humanity'." *Africa Recovery* 15.3 (October 2001): 5.

Wisker, Gina. "Crossing Liminal Spaces: Teaching the Postcolonial Gothic." *Pedagogy: Critical Approaches to Teaching Literature, Language, Composition and Culture* 7.3 (2007): 401–425.

Conclusion: Moving Beyond Psychic Ruptures

Johanna X.K. Garvey

The essays in this volume offer a cartography of the African diaspora, a mapping of the madness at its core and the ways that madness is performed and aestheticized in fiction. The insanity is both toxin and cure, an illness that possesses within it the potential to heal. In Dionne Brand's novel *At the Full and Change of the Moon*, we follow generations born from one inhabitant of the Diaspora, Bola, whose family tree spreads across the sea, through the Caribbean, Latin America, the United States, Canada, and Europe. One of her descendants, also named Bola, whose mother sends her back to the island home from Canada, gradually drifts into memory, loss, and longing. "Now the child has gone mad," observe her two aunts, unable to reach her or help her.[1] Yet this young girl experiences a deep connection not only to her grandmother but through that "Dear Mama" back into the familial past where connections are as real to her as the uncomprehending women who want to lock her away in an asylum. The diaspora born of a mad desire to take possession of people and of places, to colonize and to enslave, paradoxically nurtures an insanity that resists domination and reclaims selfhood.

J.X.K. Garvey (✉)
Fairfield University, Fairfield, CT, USA

C.A. Brown and J.X.K. Garvey (eds.), *Madness in Black Women's Diasporic Fictions*, Gender and Cultural Studies in Africa and the Diaspora, DOI 10.1007/978-3-319-58127-9_11

As Brand writes elsewhere, "To have one's belonging lodged in a metaphor is voluptuous intrigue; to inhabit a trope; to be a kind of fiction. To live in the Black Diaspora is I think to live as a fiction—a creation of empires, and also self-creation."[2] She says of the Door of No Return that it is an "inexplicable space," and yet its frame is all that exists for people of the Diaspora: "an absent presence. […] not only physical departure but psychic renting, of our ancestors."[3] As this volume of essays illustrates, the psychic ruptures, tears, and fissures manifest in myriad ways and places, in Africa itself (as "dark swoops," for instance), in the oceanic spaces crossed by the *Zong* and inhabited by its victims, in Caribbean locations such as violent plantations in Haiti, in a haunted house at 124 Bluestone in Cincinnati, or in Londinium in the Roman era. That geography confounds borders and timelines, as the Diaspora defies uniform definition. The voyages cross paths through the water and beneath the ocean, as well as in the air and on land, and the madness seeps and bleeds through those spaces. Yet, as Brand says, while the "fiction" may have been created by imperial powers, it still inspires "self-creation." As many of the essays in this volume demonstrate, Black women of the Diaspora have found inventive ways to craft madness and/as an aesthetics of resistance.

According to Sylvia Wynter, literature makes "social imaginary significations real, makes them visible. […] fiction allows us to see some of these meanings in which we live enmeshed, embedded, not even aware that they exist. […] Literature helps us to grasp their meanings and to be able to help change and transform these meanings when it is necessary."[4] One way that Black women writers do so is through the incorporation of madness into their narratives, via characters who are positioned as liminal, or who occupy what Wynter terms "society's space of otherness," which has creative potential. We can see madness in that light, as a borderline, a threshold space of not (yet) belonging or an (un)belonging that undoes categories of oppression. These authors take the "other"-ness, the madness outside the colonial and neocolonial center/Man, and create a self and a world counter to that discourse. Madness also functions as marooning and resistance, a refusal of assimilation to the order/sanity/control of a system of oppression.

Sylvia Wynter's ongoing project to unsettle and disrupt the colonial enterprise resonates with the concept of madness as the practice of an aesthetics of resistance. Wynter argues for what texts can *do* as opposed to what they *mean*: a novel is active in a process of knowledge formation. She thus envisions texts as part of a "dynamic living process" and a "disenchantment" or undoing of Western epistemologies rooted in colonization.

Wynter's only novel, *The Hills of Hebron* (1962), centers on versions of madness in Jamaica on the eve of independence. The novel is the story of a group of "New Believers" led by a madman (Moses Barton) who thinks he can fly and who eventually has himself crucified. The New Believers may be outsiders, but Moses uses insider/colonized thinking in his vision of a new community or "black kingdom" in Jamaica. His madness mirrors the colonial ideology of Man/other, while the women's madness is a liminal space *inside* liminality, in the interstices. This madness is exemplified by Kate, an older woman whose words frame the book and who mourns the loss of her young daughter. Kelly Baker Josephs discusses madness in this text: "In both her choice of genre and her intimate portrayal of her characters' mental fragmentation, Wynter locates madness as a positive space from which to imagine new ways of being in postcolonial Caribbean society."[5] To that assessment, I would add new ways of envisioning being in the African Diaspora. Kate begins and closes *The Hills of Hebron* such that her psychological state frames and guides the narrative. The madman Moses is complicit in the rape of women, most significantly the young girl Rose, who is sexually assaulted and impregnated by her white British employer. Moses agrees to keep secret the perpetrator's name in exchange for the land in the hills where he plans to build his community. Though Rose never speaks directly in the novel, her silence is broken by others who tell of the abuses that form one legacy of imperialism. Kate's madness, which manifests in a belief that her dead child still lives, veils her own awareness and resistance: "The part of her mind which was secret and cunning accepted that she would have to pretend to practise rites which the others used to assure a reality from which she had escaped."[6] Through the revelations of secrets in this community, Wynter's story performs the undoing of power structures based in colonial ideologies and Western epistemologies of difference and domination.

I

Of necessity and practicality, this collection of essays offers a beginning point, not a definitive or delimiting set of authors and texts addressing madness in Black women's diasporic fiction. Many of the writers represented here have published other texts that explore the topic of psychological fragmentation, including Brodber, Danticat, Evaristo, Morrison, Naylor, Oyeyemi, and Philip. In *Louisiana*, for instance, Erna Brodber creates Ella, a character loosely based on the Zora Neale Hurston of

Mules and Men and *Tell My Horse*. An academic who travels to Louisiana to capture folk tales before they are lost, Ella engages in conversations with the spirits of two women—Louise and Anna—who were involved with UNIA in the early twentieth century. Then, as a psychic in New Orleans, she listens to the trauma of seamen from the West Indies, recording their stories on mental note cards as she takes in their emotional damage. A conduit or vessel for the multiple psychic wounds of the Diaspora, Ella or Louisiana (a melding of names) performs a merging through relation, bringing the United States and the Caribbean together. She asks the reader to form a diamond shape with her thumbs and index fingers, and says, "That hole, that passage is me. I am the link between the shores washed by the Caribbean sea, a hole, yet I am what joins your left hand to your right. I join the world of the living and the world of the spirits. I join the past with the present."[7] She continues, "I am Louisiana. I give people their history."[8] Ella often seems on the verge of coming apart herself, atomized by the traumas she takes in and seeks to heal. Her resistance is rooted in transformation and connection, starting with her becoming the "horse" or vessel for the voices of Louise and Anna: "I had arrived. Passed through my rite of passage with flying colours. I had broken through that membrane and was in, ready and willing to be and see something else. Transform, change, focus. Transform, change. I was a woman among women."[9] She enacts the creative potential of the liminal that Wynter discusses, using a space of otherness to shape a vision of connection and healing.

Not all of the narratives end with a positive image of healing, however. Toni Morrison depicts the process of mental disintegration and failed attempts at wholeness in her first novel, *The Bluest Eye*. Wynter's concept of a text as *doing* applies to the story of Pecola Breedlove's descent into madness in the face of an endless, unrelenting barrage of messages about her perceived "ugliness." Demonstrating the damage done by standards of beauty linked to institutional and societal racism, Morrison illustrates how Pecola receives lessons from her parents, neighbors, other children, and miscellaneous adults, all of whom have been poisoned by the dominant culture's privileging of "whiteness."

We also see the link between Lorain, Ohio, and the Diaspora through the character Soaphead Church, who "gives" Pecola her new blue eyes. Himself a victim of colonial ideologies, Soaphead has ingested poisonous beliefs inculcated by the British in his West Indian home (never specified, but perhaps Jamaica or Barbados). Of his family, Morrison writes:

"They were industrious, orderly, and energetic, hoping to prove beyond a doubt De Gobineau's hypothesis that 'all civilizations derive from the white race, that none can exist without its help, and that a society is great and brilliant only so far as it preserves the blood of the noble group that created it.'"[10] The son, who becomes known as Soaphead once he migrates to the United States, absorbs that education and twists it further: "For all his exposure to the best minds of the Western world, he allowed only the narrowest interpretation to touch him. [He develops a] hatred of, and fascination with, any hint of disorder or decay."[11] His madness affects Pecola, when the young woman who is pregnant due to rape by her father comes to him for help. Promising her the blue eyes she desperately desires, Soaphead poisons a dog to demonstrate his power to make miracles, and the poor animal's death convinces Pecola that her wish has come true. In a letter to God following this performance, Soaphead writes

> I, I have caused a miracle. I gave her the eyes. I gave her the blue, blue, two blue eyes. Cobalt blue. A streak of it right out of your own blue heaven. No one else will see her blue eyes. But *she* will. And she will live happily ever after. I, I have found it meet and right so to do.[12]

Having imbibed the tenets of the colonizers, Soaphead Church uses them like poison to mimic the power he sees in a white God and to "give" Pecola the "beauty" she thinks will make others love her.

We then witness her complete fissure in a scene before the mirror, a depiction of the disassociation of PTSD, as well as of schizophrenia. In an essay on madness in Caribbean women's fiction, Evelyn O'Callaghan discusses psychiatrist R.D. Laing's theories of schizophrenia, noting "his conception of madness as a kind of liberation from false attitudes and values, leading to a rebirth of the 'true self.'" That is, instead of a "breakdown," schizophrenia can lead to a "breakthrough," she says.[13] Though Laing's theories have been challenged, many of the authors discussed in this volume do point to such a rebirth through madness, but in Pecola's case we see no hope of such an outcome. As Claudia tells us in the final section of the novel, "A little black girl yearns for the blue eyes of a little white girl, and the horror at the heart of her yearning is exceeded only by the evil of fulfillment. [...] The damage done was total."[14] Claudia offers a harsh critique of the behavior of the community that allowed Pecola to suffer and become the pariah, inhabiting liminal spaces on the edge of town. "She, however, stepped over into madness, a madness which protected her from us simply because it bored us in the end."[15] Morrison's novel serves as a necessary corrective to visions of madness as a consistently successful form of resistance to ideologies of Man/other based in colonization.

Edwidge Danticat's *Breath, Eyes, Memory* includes both of these outcomes: a woman so traumatized that she becomes incapacitated by her damaged psyche; her daughter, who inherits that trauma, but does not succumb to it due to a process of testifying and healing. The novel moves through the Black Diaspora, specifically between Haiti and the United States, centered on the trauma and insanity engendered by Duvalier's dictatorship. The mother-daughter relationships, as well as the role of a baby doll, connect this novel to the stories in *Krik? Krak!*, deepening and extending the depiction of mental fragmentation through the story of Martine. Raped and impregnated by a *Tonton Macoute*, escaping to the United States, she is unable to find a path to healing. Though she has her daughter Sophie join her in Brooklyn and attempts to create a stable life for the two of them, Martine is reminded of her attacker when she looks at Sophie. And when she becomes pregnant by her new boyfriend, a Haitian American attorney, she imagines the unborn child with the face of the rapist. Sophie tells her therapist ab0out her concerns for Martine's mental state: "'I am very worried about her state of mind,' I said. 'It was like two people. Someone who was trying to hold things together and someone who was falling apart.'"[16] Sophie continues, "'She feels that she has to stay one step ahead of a mental institution so she has to hold it together at least on the surface.'"[17] Her mother cannot, in fact, continue to hold herself together, eventually committing suicide rather than giving birth. Sophie also struggles with what O'Callaghan terms "ontological insecurity,"[18] but through therapy and a process of testimony and witnessing, she does find a way to heal. At the end of the novel, her grandmother tells her that she will now be able to answer when asked whether she is "*libéré*," "free."

II

Besides the authors discussed in this volume, one can list many others who incorporate madness into their fictions of the Diaspora—from Africa, to the Caribbean, from North America to Britain and Europe. As noted above, one central location, at the heart of the Diaspora, is Haiti.

That country's "rape culture of silence," rooted in the abuse of women that traces back centuries to enslavement, is given voice in many novels by female authors. For example, Marie-Célie Agnant's *The Book of Emma* takes place in a mental hospital in Canada, where Emma Bratte is held for observation after she is accused of killing her baby daughter, Lola. The text is a narrative of the madness that came with the "big boats" or slave ships, embedded stories that Emma tells Flore, another woman from Haiti who is asked to serve as interpreter for the doctor whom Emma refuses to speak to in French. Her self-imposed silence recalls that of Rose in Wynter's novel, women who have suffered abuse and choose not to participate in a discourse that both harms and excludes them as human beings.

The doctor has only managed to catch phrases from Emma's monologues in Creole: "'[I]t's only about blueness: the blue of the sky, the blue of the sea, the blue of black people's skin, and about the madness which is supposed to have come over in the holds of the slave ships.'"[19] Flore watches Emma, and they have a mute exchange as the psychiatrist writes in his notebook. "And it occurs to me [Flore] that Emma's soul is imprisoned in the madness that has taken over her body."[20] Agnant complicates that reading of Emma, however, as the text unfolds the layers of history, both personal and diasporic, that have led to the death of baby Lola. M. NourbeSe Philip's reflections on Black women and silence resonate with Emma's refusal to employ the colonizer's language:

> The text—the silence at the heart of. My text—I writing my own silence… and if you cannot ensure that your words will be taken in the way you want them to be—if you are certain that those you talking to not listening, not understanding your words, or not interested in what you saying and wanting to silence you, then holding onto your silence is more that a state of non-submission. It is resistance.[21]

The silence at the heart of Agnant's novel paradoxically speaks louder than the doctor or the newspapers that condemn Emma with racist stereotypes. Both Emma and Flore jointly write that silence and turn it into a manifesto of resistance.

On one hand, Emma's madness is a consequence of the layers of inherited trauma going back to an ancestor torn from her mother in Africa, enslaved in Haiti, baptized and renamed "Rosa", who "'swallowed her tongue and swore to never ever pronounce a single word in the presence of others, as long as she remained a slave.'"[22] Labeled "raving mad," Kilima set fire to the plantation, attempted to drown her baby girl, and then walked into the ocean, dressed in white. "'She had returned to the route of the big boats.'"[23] To cope with that wound, a history written in blood, Emma had turned to history books with the goal of writing her doctoral thesis on the slave trade. She performed a version of archive fever, which drove her to madness as she absorbed the facts and wrote her book, one that her academic advisors in France rejected. That avenue of expression and truth-telling shut down, the rejection propelled the mental fragmentation that sent Emma to Canada with her lover and then most likely led her to kill Lola (her culpability never confirmed in the narrative), and finally to take her own life in the river outside the hospital.

Mattie had told her a vision, one that connects Emma to Morrison's Sethe as well as other instances of infanticide in Black women's fiction, such as South African author Yvette Christiansë's *Unconfessed*. In relating Kilima's story, Mattie said to Emma, "'"As though in a very ancient dream, you will repeat the deeds of the women of the clan, the efforts they made to shelter their children from the garrotes that choked them in the holds of the slave ships and in the fields of sugar cane."'"[24] While Emma's story ends with her suicide, it continues in Flore's offering to us—The Book of Emma that she creates—and also echoes in fiction by other Haitian women, such as Marie Vieux-Chauvet, Jan J. Dominique, Myriam J.A. Chancy, Yannick Lahens, and Marie-Andrée Manuel Étienne. Agnant perhaps most powerfully deploys the trope of silence as resistance, even as she excavates the archives that lie underneath. What these authors, along with those discussed in this volume and many more, produce is the account described by Philip: "And I am speaking, giving an account," she writes. "An enumeration of a genealogy of the Atlantic: a genealogy of bodies. Of ghosts. Of the silenced. Whose voices can still be heard. If you listen closely enough. Of resistance: a genealogy. I would rather be a free woman in my grave. Than a slave."[25]

III

I return to Sylvia Wynter's formulation of the "demonic" as a way to analyze madness and/as resistance in black women's fiction. As Katherine McKittrick explains, Wynter uses physicists' theories to create a model that "serves to locate what Wynter calls cognition *outside* 'the always non-arbitrary pre-prescribed,' which underscores the ways in which subaltern lives are not marginal/other to regulatory classificatory systems, but instead integral to them."[26] This "demonic model" conceives of a new humanness whose "ground" is that of Caliban's absent woman. "Demonic grounds," McKittrick argues, "then, is a very different geography; one which is genealogically wrapped up in the historical spatial unrepresentability of black femininity, and [...] one thinks about the ways in which black women necessarily contribute to a re-presentation of geography."[27] To trace madness through black women's fiction, to map the Diaspora via explorations of psychic distress and dis-ease, is to create a cartography that displaces the normalizing one imposed by Europeans who explored territories to them unknown and uninhabitable.

Wynter argues that the geographies emerging from European exploration include man's "others." In this colonizing schema,

> [...] the place of black women is deemed unrecognizable because their ontological existence is both denied and deniable as a result of the regimes of colonialism, racism-sexism, transatlantic slavery, European intellectual systems, patriarchy, white femininity, and white feminism. Correlated, their grounds are silent and their place is uninhabitable within the given frameworks of Man's geographies.[28]

What is disallowed or excluded from the "normal" and perceived as disorderly, unruly, insane, becomes in Wynter's thinking a space of creativity and humanness newly conceived: a different way of knowing the world and engaging in relation. In texts by the authors explored in this volume, as well as others such as Marie-Elena John, Tessa McWatt, Gisèle Pineau, and Myriam Warner-Vieyra, psychic fissures reveal the inherent insanity of systems that sanctioned rape, enslavement, torture, murder, and genocide. In her essay "Rethinking 'Aesthetics'," Wynter explains how the Judeo-Christian symbolic system replaced one pariah, the leper, with another, "the interned and excluded figure of the *mad* [...]."[29] She connects this shift to the period of European colonization:

> At the same time, the "internment" of the indigenous peoples of the new World in a semi-serf-relation and of peoples of African descent as slaves on the New World plantation system was also legitimated by the discourse on their Caliban-type irrationality, a discourse which, because it was generated also from the "ground" of the post-feudal "public language" order of knowledge and its classical episteme, elaborated itself within the same terms as the discourse on insanity on whose basis the *mad* had also been interned.

> Taken together, therefore, all these three "captive populations" were now the empirical embodiment of the pre-analytic premise on whose basis the disciplinary discourses of the classical episteme of the pre-industrial order were elaborated, the condition of its "truth."[30]

Applicable to the diasporic fictions discussed in this volume, these observations also help to extend the work begun here to other women writers of the diaspora.

Marie-Elena John's novel *Unburnable* illustrates the process by which Black women became pariahs, ostracized by those with colonized minds, and either rendered insane or executed in order to preserve a set of norms derived from the "classical episteme," as described by Wynter. Like Agnant's Emma, the protagonist of John's novel, Lillian, has inherited the traumas experienced by her female predecessors, in this case her mother and grandmother. Though she builds a "firewall" to protect herself, that structure cracks when the ground shifts, when visions and archives alike reveal the roots of her illness. Ultimately, her attempts to shore it up serve to further incarcerate rather than to liberate her. Both Lillian's mother (Iris) and grandmother (Matilda) are "liminal" in the sense that Wynter uses the term (borrowing from Asmarom Legesse): "[…] in every society there is a category that embodies the deviant Other to the normal identity of the society."[31] The society in question in *Unburnable* is the town of Roseau in Dominica, a community invested in a facsimile of the colonial powers (Britain and France) and its own proximity to bourgeois, "white" norms. Matilda lived in a Black community, Up There or "Noah"—later revealed to be a mistaken pronunciation of its real name, *Noir*—above and removed from Roseau (similar to The Bottom in Morrison's *Sula*, perched above Medallion, Ohio). A vivid example of "demonic ground," *Noir* was formed and sustained by Black women as a maroon colony of people who were "every last one of unadulterated African descent."[32] Matilda served the community as Obeah woman and as judge or *magistrat* for their court cases and lived with Simon, a Carib from the colony on the other side of Dominica. That dual ancestry of the "dys-selected" (to use Wynter's term) marks their daughter, Iris, as the potential site of liminality, the pariah/leper/madwoman. And her daughter Lillian bears even further the weight of that dys-selection.

That inheritance has the creative potential to resist hegemonic ideologies and to use madness to "think *outside* the terms in which we *are*," as Wynter postulates.[33] John leaves the ending ambiguous, however, as Lillian seems on the verge of suicide from the heights of *Noir*. She both accepts and rejects the explanations of her mental state offered by her friend/lover Teddy, who has accompanied her to Dominica to discover the truth of Matilda's hanging.

> Lillian agreed with him, with what he never directly said to her but had said repeatedly to the psychiatrist, that her mind was somehow disabled, but it was not because of any mental illness. She was not crazy, of that she was sure. She herself had done it, had built so many blockades that there was little space left for thinking. The sounds in her head were there because she put them there and unwittingly locked herself out.[34]

She thus does not fully *occupy* the demonic grounds that might offer her a space of resistance. Hearing her ancestors' voices and envisioning death as reconnection with her mother and grandmother, Lillian imagines the community below in Roseau finding her body and labeling her *La Diablesse*, a devil like Matilda, a pariah unto death. John herself has said that she does not know whether Lillian kills herself or whether Teddy arrives in time to prevent that act, or whether Lillian changes her mind on her own. Nevertheless, at the end Lillian appears to look into the abyss and choose that path, similar to Emma's decision to follow the route of the big boats, back to Africa.

Not all narratives of madness end in the protagonist's suicide, of course, as seen in several of the texts discussed in this volume. A brief examination of another recent novel rooted in the Diaspora offers examples of how to think creatively *outside* and beyond prescribed terms, using demonic grounds to do so. Tessa McWatt's *Out of My Skin* follows 30-year-old Daphne, whose Guayanese mother committed suicide in Canada—the consequence, Daphne later learns, of being raped and impregnated by her own father, Gerald. Adopted and raised by a Scottish couple in Toronto, Daphne has left that home and family to make a life of her own in Montreal, but she is compelled to seek the identity of her birth parents in order to understand the face she confronts in the mirror. From her mother's sister, she receives Gerald's diaries, which contain familial secrets lodged in the colonial context of British Guiana in the 1950s. From a different angle than in Agnant's or John's texts, or those incorporated in this volume, we witness the madness that came with British colonization in this part of the Diaspora. Daphne will feel "out of her skin" (as the title tells us), when she reads the diaries and pieces together the story of who she is.

The novel maps the Diaspora through Daphne's body and lineage, creating cracks and confusion in her mind, evidenced when she looks at herself in the mirror:

> Generations of submission and rebellion still battled for possession there. Were hers the eyes of the victors or of the vanquished? The ears of slaves or masters? Her hair was born of a cruel passion that sprang up kinky and horny in the moist heat. And her nose was a sculpture: a monument to the history of bones pounding other bones, mixing up dry marrow to unveil the post-historic shape that was displayed like a museum piece in the centre of her face.[35]

The fissures manifest themselves in Gerald's diaries, most of them written while he was interned in Berbice Hospital, a mental asylum, where he was subjected to electric shock therapy to "cure" him. In late 1959, on the eve of Guyana's independence, he wrote to express his sense of loss at the prospect of no longer belonging to Britain: "*All the men in the common room talk about independence and the expulsion of the monarchy from the jungle, and I indulge them, but tell them that they are behaving like ungrateful sons. The gift of civilization is like the gift of life, and a man does not turn his back on his father after he has learned to copulate.*"[36] Daphne absorbs his words as she excavates this mad archive of a colonized mind, and feels herself splintering, disintegrating. One is reminded of Morrison's Soaphead Church or of the attempts to "civilize" Nellie in Brodber's *Jane and Louisa Will Soon Come Home*. To echo Claudia's words about Pecola, for Gerald the damage done was total.

ECT (electroconvulsive therapy) causes amnesia and can gradually erase the patient's memory, and Gerald's words for its effects give the book one meaning of its title. As Gerald describes his experiences in the asylum, what the psychiatrists wanted was for him to relinquish his belief that he was "white," to give up his claims to whiteness, and to acknowledge that he was "*a coloured man.*"[37] Thus "healed," he was released and the diaries end. From her aunt Sheila, Daphne learns that Gerald disappeared into the interior of the country, after his wife and daughters immigrated to Canada. He died of gangrene after his foot became poisoned and he tried to cut it off himself—a metaphor for the ideas he ingested like mental toxins, which left him insane. Daphne also learns the truth about her parentage, when Sheila confirms that her father raped Daphne's mother when she was sixteen. "Her mother had walked into the water to cleanse shame and had never walked out, but perhaps there she'd found the mercy she'd needed."[38] Daphne craves amnesia and erasure, yet she also practices self-invention from her demonic ground, fashioning a "tattoo" of the word "CHAMELEON," taking the diaries with her on a weekend excursion with co-workers, and burying them in a forest. "A bow to memory. To let the snow and rain work on them until they became a place in which her own body could eventually be laid to rest. To have the paper petrify and fill the cleft between vegetable and rock, the words silent and grinning in the earth."[39] Gerald's diaries resemble Emma's book, silent words that speak from the margins and resist the madness of European ideologies. Daphne finds her way out of the forest and back to Montreal, where she arrives at the huge outdoor market on the mountain, announcing, "'I'm here.'"[40] She lands here and now, in the present, having shed the "skin" created by colonial madness and used her liminal space for self-creation.

IV

Space does not permit a discussion of salient texts from Africa and the United States that would add to those analyzed in this collection. A few would include Tsitsi Dangarembga's *Nervous Conditions*, the novels of Bessie Head, Zoë Wicomb's novel *David's Story*, and the previously mentioned *Unconfessed*, by Yvette Christiansë (all from countries in Africa). And from the United States, texts that contribute to the larger picture extending from this volume would include Toni Cade Bambara's *The Salt Eaters*, Carolivia Herron's *Thereafter Johnnie*, Marci Blackman's *Po Man's Child*, and Ayana Mathis's *The Twelve Tribes of Hattie* (again, just a partial list). Also missing in this collection of essays are novels by those of the Spanish-speaking areas in the African Diaspora as well as diasporic fiction reflecting LGBT experience. Two texts that contribute to that deeper understanding of the aesthetics of resistance are Ana-Maurine Lara's *Erzulie's Skirt* and Dionne Brand's *In Another Place, Not Here*. In the former, two women in the Dominican Republic—one Dominican, one Haitian—fall in love, are sex-trafficked to Puerto Rico, escape from that enslavement using spiritual practices deriving from Africa, and return to the DR where they purchase land and establish their a home and a *colmado*. Their narrative is interwoven with the story of two women captured in Africa and forced through the Middle Passage into slavery in the Americas. The parallels between the two narratives demonstrate the ongoing legacies of the slave trade and colonization, the madness at the core of contemporary enslavement, and spiritual means of liberation from that internment.

In Brand's first novel, two women fall in love in Grenada during the revolution, where one (Verlia) dies fighting the US invasion while the other witnesses her leap from the cliffs. The latter—Elizete—loses her mental stability in Canada, where she seeks traces of her lover, is brutally raped, struggles as an undocumented laborer, and eventually meets Verlia's former lover (Abena), a social worker. We read Verlia's diary written during her time in Grenada, which resembles her own island home that she fled as a teenager. She feels weighed down by the place and by the Caribbean as a whole: "It's not only my family. It's the fact. Fact. Fact. Intangible fact of this place. It's not possible to get rid of that. So much would have to have not happened. It's like a life sentence. Call it what we want—colonialism, imperialism—it's a fucking life sentence."[41] Yet Canada is no better for a black woman on her own, as Abena tells Elizete, warning her to "go home." "Go home, it's not a place for the soul, you'll end up damaged, you'll end up blind, you'll end up not knowing, hell, not liking who you are."[42] Pregnant by the white employer who raped her and "illegal," Elizete has sought help from Abena, but more importantly, the two connect through Verlia, whose leap ends the narrative.

Though this act may recall the suicides in other novels discussed here, it is better understood as both resistance and rebirth. "She's flying out to sea and in the emerald she sees the sea, its eyes transparent, its back solid going to some place there's no memory of it."[43] The novel ends where the title began: "She's in some other place already, less torturous, less fleshy."[44] Verlia's choice to leap in the face of a neocolonial power's invasion of a colonized space struggling to maintain or even to establish its independence illustrates the "demonic" that Wynter proposes as the ground of Black women. McKittrick explains: "The demonic, then, is a non-deterministic schema; it is a process that is hinged on uncertainty and non-linearity because the organizing principle cannot predict the future."[45] In leaping into another space/place, Verlia acts for those who refuse the categories of Man/other, most specifically the place assigned to Black women. Wynter herself cites Fanon as she discusses how to "unsettle" coloniality: "The true leap, Fanon wrote at the end of

Black Skin, White Masks, consists in introducing invention into existence. The buck stops with us."[46]

McKittrick's explication of Wynter's thought resonates not only for Verlia's leap but also for the various forms of madness and/as resistance explored in this volume. The binary of Man/other that Wynter traces to 1492 might be unsettled and dis-placed. "Dominant geographic patterns can often undermine complex interhuman geographies by normalizing spatial hierarchies and enacting strict spatial rules and regulations."[47] That logic is illustrated in John's novel when the community in Roseau normalizes the ideologies of the British and ostracizes both Simon (representative of the indigenous peoples) and Matilda (the New World African), and viciously attacks their daughter Iris, whose body and spirit are potentially the "interhuman" but who is driven mad and destroyed rather than nurtured and treasured.

Verlia and other characters discussed here offer an alternative vision, which correlates with the "true leap": "Placeless and silent black women, if legitimately posited in the world (placed, unsilenced), call into question our present geographic organization. The geographies of black women, as demonic grounds, put forth a geographic grammar that locates the complex position and potentiality of black women's sense of place."[48] McKittrick further asks, "If our expressive demands can demonstrate a new worldview, in what ways can ethical human geographies, or interhuman geographies, be mapped?"[49] Brand's suggestion of "another place, not here" joined with Daphne's "I'm here" might provide that new mapping of the interhuman. Wynter herself provides the following observation: "Human beings are magical. Bios and Logos. Words made flesh, muscle and bone animated by hope and desire, belief materialized in deeds, deeds which crystallize our actualities. [...] And the maps of spring always have to be redrawn again, in undared forms."[50] The authors and texts discussed in this volume invite us to envision the "undared" and to invent new geographies that spring from madness and imagination.

Notes

1. Dionne Brand, *At the Full and Change of the Moon* (New York: Grove Press, 1999), 276.
2. Dionne Brand, *A Map to the Door of No Return: Notes to Belonging* (Toronto, ON: Vintage Canada, 2002), 18.
3. Brand, *Map*, 20, 21.

4. Sylvia Wynter, "Interview with Daryl Dance," in *New World Adams* (Leeds, England: Peepal Tree Press, 1988), 277.
5. Kelly Baker Josephs, "The Necessity for Madness: Negotiating Nation in Sylvia Wynter's *The Hills of Hebron*," in *The Caribbean Woman Writer as Scholar*, ed. Keshia Abraham (Coconut Creek, FL: Caribbean Studies Press, 2009), 180.
6. Sylvia Wynter, *The Hills of Hebron* (Kingston: Jamaica, Ian Randle, 2010; c. Jonathan Cape, 1962), 3.
7. Erna Brodber, *Louisiana* (London & Port of Spain, Trinidad and Tobago: New Beacon Books, 1994), 124.
8. Brodber, *Louisiana*, 125.
9. Brodber, *Louisiana*, 52.
10. Toni Morrison, *The Bluest Eye* (New York: Vintage, 2007), 168.
11. Morrison, *The Bluest Eye*, 169.
12. Morrison, *The Bluest Eye*, 182, emphasis in original.
13. Evelyn O'Callaghan, "Interior Schisms Dramatised: The Treatment of the 'Mad' Woman in the Work of Some Female Caribbean Novelists," in *Out of the Kumbla: Caribbean Women and Literature*, eds. Carole Boyce Davies and Elaine Savory Fido (Trenton, NJ: Africa World Press, 1990), 104.
14. Morrison, *The Bluest Eye*, 204.
15. Morrison, *The Bluest Eye*, 206.
16. Edwidge Danticat, *Breath, Eyes, Memory* (New York: Soho Press, 1994), 218.
17. Danticat, *Breath, Eyes, Memory*, 218.
18. O'Callaghan, "Interior Schisms," 92.
19. Marie-Célie Agnant, *The Book of Emma*, trans. Zilpha Ellis (Toronto, ON: Insomniac Press, 2006), 10.
20. Agnant, *The Book of Emma*, 13.
21. M. NourbeSe Philip, *A Genealogy of Resistance and Other Essays* (Toronto: The Mercury Press, 1997), 99.
22. Agnant, *The Book of Emma*, 165.
23. Agnant, *The Book of Emma*, 189.
24. Agnant, *The Book of Emma*, 169.
25. Philip, *A Genealogy of Resistance*, 23.
26. Katherine McKittrick, *Demonic Grounds: Black Women and the Cartographies of Struggle* (Minneapolis, MN: University of Minnesota Press, 2006), xxv.
27. McKittrick, *Demonic Grounds*, xxv–xxvi.
28. McKittrick, *Demonic Grounds*, 133.
29. Sylvia Wynter, "Rethinking 'Aesthetics': Notes Towards a Deciphering Practice," in *Ex-iles: Essays on Caribbean Cinema*, ed. Mbye B. Cham (Trenton, NJ: Africa World Press, 1992), 256, emphasis in original.

30. Wynter, "Rethinking 'Aesthetics,'" 256–7, emphasis in original. See also her "1492: A New World View," in *Race, Discourse, and the Origins of the Americas: A New World View*," eds. Vera Lawrence Hyatt and Rex Nettleford (Washington, DC: Smithsonian Institution Press, 1995), 5–57.
31. David Scott, "The Re-Enchantment of Humanism: An Interview with Sylvia Wynter," *Small Axe* 8 (September 2000): 149.
32. Marie-Elena John, *Unburnable* (New York: Harper Collins, 2006), 3.
33. Scott, "The Re-Enchantment of Humanism," 206, emphasis in original.
34. John, *Unburnable*, 289–90.
35. Tessa McWatt, *Out of My Skin* (Toronto, ON: Riverbank Press, 1998), 186.
36. McWatt, *Out of My Skin*, 107, italics in original.
37. McWatt, *Out of My Skin*, 154, italics in original.
38. McWatt, *Out of My Skin*, 202.
39. McWatt, *Out of My Skin*, 202.
40. McWatt, *Out of My Skin*, 208.
41. Dionne Brand, *In Another Place, Not Here* (New York: Grove Press, 1996), 215.
42. Brand, *In Another Place, Not Here*, 230.
43. Brand, *In Another Place, Not Here*, 246.
44. Brand, *In Another Place, Not Here*, 247.
45. McKittrick, *Demonic Grounds*, xxiv.
46. Sylvia Wynter, "Unsettling the Coloniality of Being/Power/Truth/Freedom: Towards the Human, After Man," *CR: The New Centennial Review* 3, 3 (Fall 2003): 331.
47. McKittrick, *Demonic Grounds*, 145.
48. McKittrick, *Demonic Grounds*, 133.
49. McKittrick, *Demonic Grounds*, 141.
50. Sylvia Wynter, "The Pope Must Have Been Drunk, The King of Castile a Madman: Culture as Actuality, and the Caribbean Rethinking Modernity," in *The Reordering of Culture: Latin America, The Caribbean and Canada in the Hood*, eds. Alvina Ruprecht and Cecelia Taiana (Ottawa, ON: Carleton University Press, 1995), 35.

Bibliography

Agnant, Marie-Célie. *The Book of Emma*. Trans. Zilpha Ellis. Toronto: Insomniac Press, 2006.

Brand, Dionne. *A Map to the Door of No Return: Notes to Belonging*. Toronto: Vintage Canada, 2002.

———. *At the Full and Change of the Moon*. New York: Grove Press, 1999.

———. *In Another Place, Not Here*. New York: Grove Press, 1996.

Brodber, Erna. *Louisiana*. London & Port of Spain: New Beacon Books, 1994.
Dance, Daryl Cumber. *New World Adams: Conversations with West Indian Authors*. Leeds, UK: Peepal Tree Press, 2008.
Danticat, Edwidge. *Breath, Eyes, Memory*. New York: Soho, 1994.
John, Marie-Elena. *Unburnable*. New York: Harper Collins, 2006.
Josephs, Kelly Baker. "The Necessity for Madness: Negotiating Nation in Sylvia Wynter's *The Hills of Hebron*." In *The Caribbean Woman Writer as Scholar*. Ed. Keshia Abraham. Coconut Creek, FL: Caribbean Studies Press, 2009. 179–204.
Lara, Ana-Maurine. *Erzulie's Skirt*. Wasington, DC: Redbone Press, 2006.
McKittrick, Katherine. *Demonic Grounds: Black Women and the Cartographies of Struggle*. Minneapolis: U Minnesota P, 2006.
McWatt, Tessa. *Out of My Skin*. Toronto: Riverbank Press, 1998.
Morrison, Toni. *The Bluest Eye*. New York: Vintage, 2007 (c. 1970).
O'Callaghan, Evelyn. "Interior Schisms Dramatised: The Treatment of the 'Mad' Woman in the Work of Some Female Caribbean Novelists." In *Out of the Kumbla: Caribbean Women and Literature*. Eds. Carole Boyce Davies and Elaine Savory Fido. Trenton, NJ: Africa World Press, 1990. 89–109.
Philip, M. NourbeSe. *A Genealogy of Resistance and Other Essays*. Toronto: The Mercury Press, 1997.
Pineau, Gisèle. *Devil's Dance*. Trans. C. Dickson. Lincoln: U Nebraska P, 2006.
Scott, David. "The Re-Enchantment of Humanism: An Interview with Sylvia Wynter." *Small Axe* 8 (September 2000): 119–207.
Warner-Vieyra, Myriam. *Juletane*. Trans. Betty Wilson. Oxford, UK: Heinemann 1987. (Original 1982).
Wynter, Sylvia. "1492: A New World View." In *Race, Discourse, and the Origin of the Americas: A New World View*. Eds. Vera Lawrence Hyatt and Rex Nettleford. Washington, DC: Smithsonian Institution Press, 1995. 5–57.
———. *The Hills of Hebron*. Kingston, Jamaica: Ian Randle, 2010. (Original 1962, Jonathan Cape).
———. "Rethinking 'Aesthetics': Notes Towards a Deciphering Practice." In *Ex-iles: Essays on Caribbean Cinema*. Ed. Mbye B. Cham. Trenton, NJ: Africa World Press, 1992. 238–279.
———. "Unsettling the Coloniality of Being/Power/Truth/Freedom: Towards the Human, After Man, Its Overrepresentation—An Argument." *CR: The New Centennial Review* 3, 3 (Fall 2003): 257–337.
———. "The Pope Must Have Been Drunk, The King of Castile a Madman: Culture as Actuality, and the Caribbean Rethinking Modernity." In *The Reordering of Culture: Latin America, The Caribbean and Canada in the Hood*. Eds. Alvina Ruprecht and Cecelia Taiana. Ottawa, Canada: Carleton U P, 1995. 17–41.

Index

C.A. Brown and J.X.K. Garvey (eds.), *Madness in Black Women's Diasporic Fictions*, Gender and Cultural Studies in Africa and the Diaspora, DOI 10.1007/978-3-319-58127-9

C

D

O

P

Q

R

T

Lightning Source UK Ltd.
Milton Keynes UK
UKHW020756210821
389200UK00003B/167

9 783319 581262